READING
the GOSPELS
WISELY

READING
the GOSPELS
WISELY

A Narrative and Theological Introduction

JONATHAN T. PENNINGTON

Baker Academic

a division of Baker Publishing Group
Grand Rapids, Michigan

© 2012 by Jonathan T. Pennington

Published by Baker Academic
a division of Baker Publishing Group
P.O. Box 6287, Grand Rapids, MI 49516-6287
www.bakeracademic.com

Printed in the United States of America

Library of Congress Cataloging-in-Publication Data

Pennington, Jonathan T.
    Reading the Gospels wisely : a narrative and theological introduction / Jonathan T. Pennington.
       p. cm.
    Includes bibliographical references and indexes.
    ISBN 978-0-8010-3937-9 (pbk.)
    1. Bible. N.T. Gospels—Criticism, interpretation, etc. 2. Bible. N.T. Gospels—Theology.
I. Title.
BS2555.52.P455 2012
226′.06—dc23
                                                      2012011956

To Mark Gignilliat and Keith Johnson,
in gratitude for many years of life-giving friendship

Contents

Foreword by Richard Bauckham   ix
Preface   xi

Part 1   Clearing Ground, Digging Deep, and Laying a Good Foundation

1. What Are the Gospels? Defining "Gospel"   3
2. What Are the Gospels? Understanding the "Gospel" Genre   18
3. Why Do We Need the Gospels? (Or Why Saint Paul Is Not Enough)   36
4. The Joy and Angst of Having Four Gospels   50
5. Texts and History: The Testimony of the Fourfold Witness   74
6. Reading Holy Scripture Well: Three Avenues   108
7. Reading Holy Scripture Well: Intent, Meaning, and Posture   122
8. Foundations for Reading the Gospels Well   143

Part 2   Building the House through Wise Reading

9. Reading the Gospels as Stories: The "Whatever Strikes Me" (WSM) Hermeneutic versus Narrative Analysis   169
10. Reading the Gospels as Stories: Circles of Contextual Meaning   183

Part 3   Living in the Gospels House

11. Summing It All Up: Applying and Teaching the Gospels   213
12. The Gospels as the Archway of the Canon   229

Scripture Index   259
Author Index   265

Foreword

So much has been written about the Gospels that no one could ever read more than a fraction of it. But anyone who begins to read what scholars have been writing about the Gospels soon discovers that there are many different sorts of important questions one can ask about the Gospels and that most of them have received many different answers. It can be daunting and confusing.

Not so long ago nearly all Gospels scholars would have said, very confidently, that the Gospels are not biographies of Jesus. Now, however, many would say that is precisely what they are, though with the qualification that they are the sort of biography people wrote at that time. But does that make them reliable history, or are they more like legend or myth or novels or propaganda? A lot of the scholarly literature is engaged in the quest for the historical Jesus, attempting to get back behind the Gospels to what the historical Jesus was really like before the early Christians started the process of interpretation that gave us the Gospels. Refined tools of historical method have been developed for studying the Gospels in this way, but the tools and their use are debatable. Furthermore, the results of the quest are so varied and contradictory as to throw the feasibility of the whole enterprise into doubt.

Does any of this matter for Christian faith or for Christian theology? Those questions too have been debated. How are faith and history related? Some would say that the quest for the historical Jesus is necessary for faith and discipleship today; others would say that it is irrelevant or even dangerous. Should Christian faith and theology buy into the Enlightenment notion of "history," as the quest has generally done, or question it? While much of Gospels scholarship has been concerned with historical questions, theological questions also loom large. Should we not, after all, be reading the Gospels primarily as Scripture, with the whole canon of Scripture as their principal context of meaning? This is how the church has usually read them, and there are those who now advocate strongly that we should return to the traditional ecclesial practices of reading the Gospels from which modern historical preoccupations have distracted us. And then there is hermeneutics, the science of interpreting texts, which has its own large literature, some of it philosophical and very technical. This in turn interacts with other questions about the Gospels and generates its own kinds of enquiries. Daunting and confusing?

But here is a book about these questions that is neither daunting nor confusing. Jonathan Pennington is familiar with all the questions, has read widely, and has thought hard about them. His concern is with helping Christians read the Gospels in a way that is faithful to the sort of texts they are. With this concern to guide him (and his readers) he is able to distill from the scholarly discussions what matters most for this task. He does so with admirable clarity and coherence, and, notably, he achieves clarity and coherence without being reductionist. He does not cast aside most of the Gospel texts in a minimalist search for the historical Jesus, but nor does he leave history aside in favor of canon or theology alone. He invites us to read the four Gospels as history and theology—each as a narrative whole in its own right, as the climax of the great scriptural metanarrative, and as the keystone in the archway of the whole canon of Scripture. What is perhaps most distinctive in his approach is his concern for Christian virtue and discipleship. The sort of literature the Gospels are is not sufficiently defined by saying that they are historical and theological. They are also literature that aims to make a difference to the lives of their readers. They are virtue-forming. They call their readers to following Jesus in a way that is transformative.

I have been impressed by Jonathan Pennington's work since he worked on a PhD under my supervision at St. Andrews. I am very happy to commend this book. Reading the Gospels wisely is one of the most important things Christians can do, and I hope this book will help many to do just that.

Richard Bauckham
Ridley Hall, Cambridge

Preface

Every one then who hears these words of mine and does them will be like a wise man who built his house on the rock. And the rain fell, and the floods came, and the winds blew and beat on that house, but it did not fall, because it had been founded on the rock. And every one who hears these words of mine and does not do them will be like a foolish man who built his house on the sand; and the rain fell, and the floods came, and the winds blew and beat against that house, and it fell; and great was the fall of it.

Matthew 7:24–27

The Gospel of Matthew has always stood at the head of the New Testament canon, and its famous Sermon on the Mount has always been considered paradigmatic for understanding both Jesus's teachings and earliest Christianity. It is fitting for us then to listen closely to the climactic conclusion to the sermon in the words above. In this final, parabolic image, Jesus describes his teaching as a fork in the road that divides his hearers into two distinct groups: the wise and the foolish. There is no middle ground.

The wise are distinguished from the foolish in that they not only *hear* Jesus's teachings but also then *act upon them*; that is, they order their lives according to his ways and wisdom. The content of Jesus's teaching matters, but here at the end of his sermon the emphasis is on responsive hearing. Wise people must *hear correctly* what Jesus teaches, but they must also *respond* to this grace with faith and faithful living.

We would be wise to take our cues from Jesus's teaching here as we approach the fascinating topic of how to read the Gospels. Taking direction both from Jesus's call to respond and his figurative parable, it is appropriate that we pursue our reading of the Gospels with both the goal of being wise and the image of building one's house with wisdom.

Thus this book, which contains theoretical discussion of several topics as well as practical instruction on methodology, is ultimately about how to be *a wise hearer and follower*. This is what it means to approach the Gospels as Holy Scripture and with wisdom. We are not looking for simply an arsenal of good techniques, be they premodern, modern, or postmodern. Nor are we seeking mere knowledge (*scientia*) for knowledge's sake. As Kierkegaard wryly quips in his *Provocations*, "He who can sit with ten open commentaries—well, he is probably writing the eleventh, but he deals with the Scriptures *contra naturam*."[1] Not as wryly, but even more foundationally, Saint Augustine makes clear what our goal in reading must be: "So anyone who thinks that he has understood the divine scriptures or any part of them, but cannot by his understanding build up this double love of God and neighbor, has not yet succeeded in understanding them."[2] Less than this kind of responsive hearing cannot truly be granted the status of "understanding."

Continuing with the metaphor of wise building, this book is a proposed blueprint for building a wise Gospel-reading house and thereby life. We may think of the fourfold Gospels as a four-roomed house. This book will *not* explore each of those rooms in depth, neither their furnishings nor their color palette choices; other introductory Gospels textbooks, in addition to the scores of commentaries and homilies on each individual Gospel account, do this well. Instead, this book seeks to do something more foundational and structural.

In part 1 ("Clearing Ground, Digging Deep, and Laying a Good Foundation"), I provide an expansive foundation that marks out our place of building and forms clear architectural lines. These foundational chapters discuss the nature and literary genre of the Gospels (chaps. 1–2), our need for the Gospels (chap. 3), and the perceived problem of having four different accounts rather than one (chap. 4). I then address groundwork issues underneath the Gospel rooms: the question of the type of historical witness the Gospels provide (chap. 5) and hermeneutical matters concerning what it means to read any part of the Bible as Holy Scripture (chaps. 6–7). Part 1 concludes with a survey of the ground that has been covered and draws implications for what it means to read the Gospels wisely (chap. 8).

Part 2 ("Building the House through Wise Reading") shifts the discussion from the theoretical to the practical, from the foundation to the construction. Chapters 9–10 lay out a narrative analysis method for how to read the Gospels

---

1. *Søren Kierkegaard's Journals and Papers*, ed. and trans. Howard V. Hong and Edna H. Hong (Bloomington: Indiana University Press, 1967), 1:210.
2. Augustine, *On Christian Teaching* 1.36.

as stories. This method consists of a narrative model for interpreting individual stories, followed by guidance on reading a Gospel story within ever-widening circles of context.

The final part of the book, part 3 ("Living in the Gospels House"), consists of two subparts. Chapter 11 drives home the point of the preceding ten chapters by discussing how to apply and teach the Gospels. We may think of this chapter as the drywalling and painting of our Gospels house so that we might begin to move in. Chapter 12, then, is finishing the house and unlocking the front door. It is the open-house invitation to enter into the richness of the fourfold Gospels. Or to use another, related metaphor, chapter 12 argues that the Gospels should be understood as the keystone of the archway into all of Holy Scripture. The Gospels are the entrance into the house of understanding who God is in Christ and thereby the entryway into being a wise hearer and doer of Jesus's words.

This book is written for any reader who is interested in learning how to engage the Gospels more deeply and how to apply them for personal study and/or preaching or teaching. It is meant to be a companion to, not a replacement for, traditional introductory texts,[3] which typically focus on providing an overview and explanation of the contents, themes, and background of each of the four Gospels. The book now in your hands offers both a deeper opening to introductory issues in the Gospels and a specific narrative, pedagogical, and homiletical model.

It remains only for me to acknowledge some of the many people who have helped me in the production of this book. First, I thank my wife and family, who have felt with me the burden of "getting the book done." I am also grateful for the countless students upon whom I have tested most of this material and who have always provided helpful feedback. At a deeper level, several students and friends have read many of the chapters and commented on them at a reading group in our home. These contributors include Chris Borah, Nate Collins, Hans Cook, Jordan Goings, Jay Hand, Jesse Morgan, Michael Spalione, Justin Tubbs, and Brett Vaden. For the production of the indexes and other editorial work, I am thankful to Jess Andrews. Thanks also to Chris Borah for producing several of the graphics. I am indebted to other professorial friends far and near who have taken the time to read all or portions of the manuscript in various forms, including Tom Schreiner, Richard Bauckham, Rob Plummer, Mark Strauss, C. Stephen Evans, Matt Crawford, Mickey Klink, Darian Lockett, Jeff Dryden, and Robert Yarbrough. Finally, the comments and kind guidance of my editor at Baker Academic, James Ernest (and all of Baker's editorial team), have been invaluable.

3. For example, see the excellent book by Mark Strauss, *Four Portraits, One Jesus: An Introduction to Jesus and the Gospels* (Grand Rapids: Zondervan, 2007).

I dedicate this book to two dear friends, Dr. Mark Gignilliat and Dr. Keith Johnson; both are very important to me, though they've never met each other. Both are scholars and churchmen who have provided constant encouragement and iron-sharpening for me over the years as I have developed the ideas of this book. Their impact on me intellectually and spiritually is great and greatly appreciated.

For further resources related to this book, please visit www.readingwisely .com.

PART 1

Clearing Ground, Digging Deep, and Laying a Good Foundation

What Are the Gospels?

Defining "Gospel"

Brainstorming "Gospel"

If we were to engage in a little brainstorming about the word "gospel," many different ideas would emerge. Many readers would immediately think of the "Romans Road" or the "Four Spiritual Laws" or some other basic, evangelical Protestant explanation of the "gospel," that is, "the basic message of salvation." For others an obvious answer would be the four stories about Jesus found in the Bible. The lovers of English philology among us, or at least some fans of 1970s Broadway musicals, may offer that our English word "gospel" comes from the older "God-spell," meaning "good" (OE *gód*) plus "tidings" (OE *spel*).[1] Those with a knowledge of Greek may proffer the etymological analysis of *eu* plus *angelion*, "good news." Some may even go further by noting that around the time of Jesus this Greek word was often used to refer to the announcement of "good tidings," especially that a new emperor had been born or ascended to the throne.[2] Opening our Bibles to the beginning of the New Testament would

---

1. This is the etymology as presented in the *Oxford English Dictionary*, 2nd ed. (1989), s.v. "gospel." Interestingly, the editors note that a common misinterpretation is that this word came instead from a compound of *gŏd* (meaning "God") and *spel* (in the sense of "discourse" or "story"). As they observe, "the mistake was very natural, as the resulting sense was much more obviously appropriate than that of 'good tidings' for a word which was chiefly known as the name of a sacred book or of a portion of the liturgy."

2. A regularly cited example of this is an inscription from around 9 BC regarding the birth of the emperor Augustus, which "marked for the world the beginning of good tidings through

3

remind us that this word "gospel" is used in yet another way: in conjunction with the accompanying phrase "The Gospel according to X" as the heading or title for the first four books of the New Testament. That is, it used to be so; many Bibles and commentaries today no longer use "The Gospel according to" in their titles,[3] despite the fact that from the earliest days of the church, the connection of the Gospels with a known person was very important.[4] Such thoughts and possibly others would arise from our brainstorming reflections on "gospel."

"Gospel" in the Apostolic Witness

Moving beyond these reflections we can examine specifically the ways in which the noun "gospel" (*euangelion*) and its verbal cognate "gospelize" (*euangelizomai*) appear in the New Testament. When we consider the apostolic witness *outside* the Gospels, we find that both forms of this word occur with regularity as an overall description of the apostles' message, or kerygma (proclamation). For example, the noun is found sixty-six times in Paul's letters and the verbal form (often translated "to preach" or "to evangelize") another twenty-one times. Significantly, Paul uses "the gospel of God" as the way to describe his ministry at the opening of his missionary letter to the Romans. He unpacks

his coming." Cited in David Wenham and Steve Walton, *Exploring the New Testament*, vol. 1, *A Guide to the Gospels and Acts* (Downers Grove, IL: InterVarsity, 2001), 48.

3. It is lamentable that Bible readers would begin to think of these four stories as merely "Matthew" or "John" without their ancient and important qualifying superscripts, "The Gospel according to . . ." Modern translations of the Bible are mixed in how they treat the titles for the Gospels. Virtually all older English translations had the full "The Gospel according to . . ." This form has survived in several translations, including the NKJV (1979), the NASB (1977), the NEB (1976), and the NRSV (1989), while others have abbreviated the titles simply as "Mark," "John," etc., as in the HCSB (2004), the Living Bible (1971), and the NIV (1973). When the fuller phrase is retained, it is often minimized by its smaller font size and its appearance only at the very beginning of the book but not in the abbreviation of the book throughout (e.g., ESV). An earlier stage of this truncation was the loss of "Saint" before the evangelists' names; thus "The Gospel According to St. Matthew" became "The Gospel according to Matthew" and now just "Matthew." In the history of printing Bibles the only conceivable stage left of this moniker degradation would be "A Story about Jesus," followed by "Another Story about Jesus," and so on. My unscientific survey of modern commentaries on the Gospels reveals this truncating trend even more dramatically. Older commentaries, even if thoroughly higher critical in approach, retained the full title. See, for instance, Ezra Gould's 1896 ICC volume, titled, "A Critical and Exegetical Commentary on the Gospel according to St. Mark." "Saint" is dropped in Lane's 1974 NICNT and "according to" becomes more generically "of" in France's 2002 NIGTC. But France and Lane appear even old-fashioned compared to most post-1980 commentaries, which, regardless of confessional stance, use only the evangelist's name. Thus, Wessel's 1984 EBC, Guelich's 1989 WBC, Marcus's 2000 Anchor, and A. Y. Collins's 2007 Hermeneia all use simply "Mark."

4. See Richard Bauckham, *Jesus and the Eyewitnesses* (Grand Rapids: Eerdmans, 2008). See also Martin Hengel, *The Four Gospels and the One Gospel of Jesus Christ: An Investigation of the Collection and Origin of the Canonical Gospels*, trans. John Bowden (Harrisburg, PA: Trinity Press International, 2000).

what he means by this gospel *from* or *about* God in the following verses. It is the good news that God promised beforehand in the Holy Scriptures (1:2), namely, the coming of Jesus, descended in the flesh from David (1:3) but shown to be so much more, God's very Son, as demonstrated by the power of the Spirit and Jesus's resurrection from the dead (1:4). This is "good news" because it is grace, and consequently it is a call to all the nations to come and believe in this message of hope (1:5–6). In Paul's opening words to the Galatian churches, he reproves them for potentially abandoning this same good news message about Jesus Christ. This is foolish, he says, because the "different gospel" they are turning to is really no good news at all; it is a hopeless attempt at accepting Jesus plus Torah obedience (Gal. 1:6–7; cf. 2:16). In another early letter, Paul likewise repeatedly refers to the "gospel of God" or "gospel of Christ" or just "our gospel" to describe the message that he had proclaimed and taught among the Thessalonian believers (1 Thess. 1:5; 2:2, 4, 8, 9; 3:2). This wording is a particular favorite of Paul's, but the same usage can also be found elsewhere, for example, in Hebrews (4:6) and 1 Peter (1:12, 25; 4:17).

We will not take the time to examine all the occurrences of this important word in the New Testament, which are readily available in other studies.[5] Instead, we may simply observe that consistently throughout the New Testament Epistles the "gospel" refers to *the oral proclamation about Jesus the Christ* (meaning the anointed Davidic King)—who he was; what he accomplished through his life, death, and resurrection; the promise of his future return to establish God's reign; and the concomitant call to repent and have faith.[6] This is not a message of moralism or a call to greater religious obedience but rather is a proclamation of God's grace and the invitation to hope. This is why it is rightly called "good news."

There is another biblical reason it is called good news, and we will explore this below. But before we move on to the question of how the apostles' use of the word relates to the evangelists' usage, we should note one other important connotation inherent in Paul's choice to call his message "gospel." As mentioned earlier, scholars have observed that the noun and verb forms of *euangelion/euangelizomai* are certainly not unique to the Bible or Christian witness but instead have currency in the Greco-Roman world surrounding nascent Christianity. Namely, "good news" was used in a propagandistic way to announce the birth or ascension of an emperor and as part of the Roman imperial cult or worship of emperors.[7] Thus, it has political and religious

5. For example, see the articles for *euangelizō* and *euangelion* in Horst Balz and Gerhard Schneider's *Exegetical Dictionary of the New Testament*, vol. 2 (Grand Rapids: Eerdmans, 1991).

6. Another obvious "gospel" defining text is 1 Cor. 15:1–11, which also particularly emphasizes the connection of this message with the story of the Old Testament via its refrain of "according to the Scriptures."

7. Cf. William Horbury, "'Gospel' in Herodian Judaea," in *The Written Gospel*, ed. Markus Bockmuehl and Donald Hagner (Cambridge: Cambridge University Press, 2005), 7–30; Graham

implications, ones particularly irksome to both Jews and Christians in the first century who refused to honor the Caesars as deity and who certainly did not consider their rise to be "good news." Undoubtedly Paul and the other early Christian missionaries were well aware that calling their message "gospel" or "good news" was not only something related to Judaism and Christianity but also simultaneously a political, worldview, and eschatological claim. It was the claim used by the savvy Jewish leaders to get Jesus crucified by their Roman oppressors (see John 19:12–15; cf. 18:33–37); it was also a claim that at times would land Jesus's followers in trouble (e.g., under the Neronian and Domitianic persecutions). To preach that Jesus is the true King over all kings, the only true Son of God, and therefore the only one worthy of worship is not merely a personal conviction of individual piety but is necessarily a public, political, and polemical proclamation.

From "Oral Gospel" to "Written Gospel"

We have seen that the New Testament's "gospel" is a highly charged and theologically significant expression used by the apostles to summarize their proclaimed message about Jesus. It is a kerygma or proclamation. We still use the word in this way today, such as when we speaking of "preaching the gospel," though usually with a sense narrower than the apostles. That is, at least in much of Protestantism "the gospel" has come to refer to the doctrinal information about the justification possible through faith in Christ. Especially in evangelical circles, "the gospel" has come to refer specifically to the forgiveness of sins available through Jesus's death and resurrection. Although certainly not wrong, this meaning is notably incomplete and narrower than Paul's own usage, which much more comprehensively refers to Jesus's entire life, death, life after death, and future return; it is the whole proclaimed message, not just the particular (and partially polemical) issue of "justification by faith," which Paul has in mind when he speaks of "the gospel."[8]

We use "gospel" to refer not only to the *oral* proclamation of the good news but also to the *written* documents about the life, death, and resurrection of

---

Stanton, *Jesus and Gospel* (Cambridge: Cambridge University Press, 2004), esp. 25–35. See also J. P. Dickson, "Gospel as New: *euangel-* from Aristophanes to the Apostle Paul," *NTS* 51 (2005): 212–30.

8. The discussion of how the NT defines the "gospel" is current and at times rather heated. For a good, generally balanced exploration of "gospel" in the NT, see Scot McKnight, *The King Jesus Gospel: The Original Good News Revisited* (Grand Rapids: Zondervan, 2011). My understanding and definition of the gospel are not identical to McKnight's, but there is much overlap. See also Darrel Bock, *Recovering the Real Lost Gospel: Reclaiming the Gospel as Good News* (Nashville: Broadman & Holman Academic, 2010), in which he describes forgiveness of sins and justification as the hub, but not the whole of, the gospel wheel. We will return to this issue later.

Jesus. This is not a modern invention; as early as the first quarter of the second century AD, the noun *euangelion* was being used to refer to our written accounts, our "Gospels."[9] This raises an interesting question: If the apostles and the New Testament letters use the word to refer to their oral proclamation only, how and when did it come to be a literary designation? The answer is not an easy one and not without a variety of opinions. It is entangled in another, related debate about the publication and manuscript transmission of the Gospels. I can offer a brief explanation of these important questions and suggest a probable answer.

Our inquiry must start with what is likely our first Greek Gospel, the Gospel according to Mark.[10] Mark begins his account with words that are strikingly recognizable to those familiar with Paul's proclamation: "The beginning of the Gospel of/about Jesus Christ" (*Archē tou euangeliou Iēsou Christou*). It is very reasonable to assume that Mark's choice to open his account with this weighty word "Gospel" stems in large part from its current and well-known usage in earliest Christianity.[11]

A couple of comments can be made on Mark's Greek phrase. First, the ambiguity of the genitive "of/about Jesus Christ" (*Iēsou Christou*) is best left as just that. Commentators disagree on whether this is a subjective or objective genitive. The rich flexibility of the genitive here likely accommodates both the sense of a Gospel *about* Jesus Christ (so a heading over the book) and the gospel *from* or *by* Jesus Christ, that is, the message of the good news about God's kingdom that has come from and through Jesus the Christ, or even that preached by him. The comments of A. Y. Collins are well put: The genitive here is ambiguous because those readers familiar with Paul and the other apostles would understand the phrase to mean "the good news *about* Jesus Christ." But "in light of the following portrait of Jesus as proclaimer [of this gospel in 1:14–15], the phrase also takes on the meaning 'the good news announced *by* Jesus Christ.'"[12]

---

9. "Gospel" was used to refer to a gospel book, as in Justin's *First Apology* 66.3 (ca. AD 150–55), which uses the plural *euangelia* to refer to Gospel books; even earlier the *Didache* uses *to euangelion* (8:2; 11:3; 15:3–4) to refer to a book that is probably Matthew. Graham Stanton, *A Gospel for a New People* (Louisville: Westminster John Knox, 1992), 14.

10. I will not enter into the many arguments for or against various source critical views nor the history of this debate, all of which is accessible in many standard textbooks. I consciously use "first Greek Gospel" in reference to Mark to suggest the possibility of an earlier Aramaic document comparable to the Gospel of Matthew. Even though our Greek Matthew is clearly not a translation from Aramaic, the uniform testimony of the early church to the originality of a Semitic-language Matthew, even if there was some confusion of the Aramaic and Greek versions, cannot be easily discounted. See also James R. Edwards, *The Hebrew Gospel and the Development of the Synoptic Tradition* (Grand Rapids: Eerdmans, 2009).

11. This has been suggested by many scholars including C. H. Dodd, *The Apostolic Preaching and its Development* (London: Hodder & Stoughton, 1936); and Ralph P. Martin, *Mark: Evangelist and Theologian* (Grand Rapids: Zondervan, 1972).

12. A. Y. Collins, *Mark*, Hermeneia (Minneapolis: Fortress, 2007), 16.

Second, we may also note the unexpected anarthrousness (lack of the Greek article) of *archē* at the beginning of the phrase. Apollonius's rule would suggest that the head noun "beginning" (*archē*) and the modifying genitive noun "of the Gospel" (*tou euangeliou*) should both be either articular or anarthrous. However, the lack of the article with *archē* here likely signals that this word and phrase serve as a heading or title as can be found elsewhere.[13]

Stemming from this observation, convincing arguments can be made that Mark's opening phrase does not just refer to the first few events of the story, nor is it a mere comment that the Christian proclamation began here. Rather, this opening phrase serves as a title for the whole message of salvation he is presenting, namely, his *narrative* as a "kerygmatic biography."[14] The rest of Mark's uses, as we will see, still have the primary (and older) sense of the orally proclaimed message, but 1:1 serves as an *incipit*, or the beginning of a book, designating this narrative as an *euangelion*. Loveday Alexander, reflecting on the connection of the oral and the written senses of "gospel/Gospel" observes that "from the earliest recorded stages of church tradition, then, the written gospels had a dynamic, two-sided interface with oral performance. They were seen as the deposit of oral teaching and preaching; and they were used as the basis for ongoing oral instruction in the early church."[15]

Thus, we can see that our word "gospel" is already being stretched in a new but not unreasonable way to refer not just to the oral proclamation about Jesus (as in Paul) but now also to the written accounts of the same. Because Paul's gospel is the same as the evangelists'—all are apostolic witness—it is quite natural that "gospel" came to mean both the oral proclamation and the written witness to it, even as it does in our current parlance. Indeed, one striking passage in both Mark and Matthew (Mark 14:9; Matt. 26:13) makes this equation quite specific. As Denis Farkasfalvy notes, in this account of the anointing of Jesus at Bethany, the evangelists suppose that the proclamation of the "good news" (the gospel as salvific message) goes hand in hand with the narrative accounts. Jesus here guarantees or even commands that any presentation of the gospel message include (at least) this narrative account.[16]

We may push this argument a bit further into the question of the titles or superscriptions for the Gospels. As I have mentioned, the title form "The Gospel according to . . ." will prove to be an important aspect of how we understand their witness to history. Related to the fact that in the early second-century the

13. For example, Hos. 1:2; Prov. 1:1; Eccles. 1:1; Cant. 1:1; Matt. 1:1; Rev. 1:1. Robert Guelich, *Mark*, vol. 1, WBC (Dallas: Word, 1989), xix.

14. Hengel, *Four Gospels*, 90–91.

15. Loveday Alexander, "What Is a Gospel?" in *The Cambridge Companion to the Gospels*, ed. Stephen Barton (Cambridge: Cambridge University Press, 2006), 22.

16. Denis Farkasfalvy, "The Apostolic Gospels in the Early Church: The Concept of Canon and the Formation of the Four-Gospel Canon," in *Canon and Biblical Interpretation*, ed. Craig Bartholomew et al. (Grand Rapids: Zondervan, 2006), 117–18.

Gospels were already called *euangelia*, we can note that also from very early on the Gospels were being titled as codices (books as opposed to scrolls) in this way: "The Gospel according to . . ." (*euangelion kata Matthaion, euangelion kata Markon*, etc.).[17] We know that the New Testament documents were organized and transmitted in fairly standard manuscript packets. That is, we find that the Gospels (or more accurately, the fourfold Gospel)[18] were regularly bound and copied together, with the consistent titling of "The Gospel according to . . ."[19] This was often followed by other sections, also grouped and titled: the book of Acts (*praxeis*), the General Epistles (*epistolai katholikai*), the Epistles of Paul (*epistolai Paulou*), and the Revelation of John (*apokalypsis Iōannou*).[20] This indicates that at least by the time of this kind of editorial activity, the word "gospel" had come to refer to a literary genre and not only its older and more generic meaning of "a proclamation of good news."[21]

How early this occurred we cannot know for certain. Martin Hengel argues most strongly for their originality. That is, Hengel believes that Mark's designation of his work as a "Gospel" became well known and widely accepted.[22]

---

17. Much work has been done recently on this important topic. Two of the most helpful entrances to it are Hengel, *Four Gospels*, and David Trobisch, *The First Edition of the New Testament* (Oxford: Oxford University Press, 2000).

18. Irenaeus (ca. 180), defending against a harmonizing of the Gospels (as in Tatian) or a reduction of them to one preferred Gospel (as with Marcion), wrote in favor of the *euangelion tetramorphon* ("the fourfold Gospel" or "the Gospel in four forms") in his *Adv. Haer.* 3.2.8. This eventually results in the widespread Latin reference to the Gospel book as the Tetraevangelium. Hengel notes that in the early church there was great emphasis on the one Gospel about Jesus Christ, and thus the evangelists' narrative accounts were considered a witness to the "Gospel," coming down or given through the witness of the named evangelists. We have not "Mark's Gospel" alongside "Matthew's Gospel" but the one Gospel that is about Jesus Christ, communicated in the version of Mark, Matthew, etc. Hengel, *Four Gospels*, 48–49.

19. From papyri, Old Latin, Coptic versions, and also from Irenaeus, Clement of Alexandria, and Tertullian, we know that at least from the first half of the third century the title form "the Gospel according to X" was widely used. Cf. Stanton, *Gospel for a New People*, 14. But manuscript evidence points toward an even earlier time. The individual Gospel accounts also certainly circulated widely as individual codices, as manuscript discoveries (especially Egyptian papyri) show.

20. Trobisch, *First Edition*, 38–41, details the use of the titles in the manuscript tradition and what they meant. A good example of this is the important Codex Alexandrinus, which is representative of earlier exemplars. This manuscript begins the NT section with a table of contents titled *hē kainē diathēkē* followed by the section's titles. See fig. 5 in Trobisch, *First Edition*, 42. For details on which manuscripts contain which Gospel titles and whether they occur as *inscriptiones* or *subscriptiones*, see 126n142.

21. Trobisch, *First Edition*, 38, states as much: the *euangelion* "designates the literary genre" as do the other titles.

22. Graham Stanton alternatively argues that not Mark but Matthew originated this genre meaning of the word. He acknowledges that while Mark's development of Paul's use of *euangelion* did pave the way for its later reference to the story of Jesus as *euangelion*, Mark did not take that step himself; this was first done by Matthew. Leaning especially on Matthew's reference to "this gospel of the kingdom" in 24:14 (cf. 26:13), Stanton follows Kingsbury in suggesting

Then, when publishing their subsequent and related works, Matthew, Luke, and John also appeared with the same now-accepted literary designation. The other evangelists did not necessarily title their works "The Gospel according to [me]." In fact, they would have presumably been content with other descriptions such as "the book of the genealogy of Jesus Christ" (Matt. 1:1) or an "orderly narrative" (*akribēs diēgēsis* from Luke 1:1–2). But because of Mark's influence, these later Gospels were always published and disseminated with these superscriptions.[23] In my opinion the strongest argument for the originality of these titles (at the publication level) is that ancient books were rarely anonymous, and the apostolic connection for these narrative accounts was especially important for their use in the church.[24] Another weighty argument for their originality from Hengel is that suddenly in the second century these titles appear consistently and are referred to as authoritative. It is difficult to imagine this happening if the titles were not original.[25] Indeed, ancient books were often identified with a variety of titles, but this is not the case for the Gospels; they are consistently referred to together as "The Gospel according to . . ." This is most easily explained if they were on the autographs or at least very earliest copies made.

Regardless of whether one is convinced by these arguments, it is clear that our word "gospel" very early underwent a transition or, better, expansion to include both an oral and written sense of "good news" related to Jesus Christ. But we have still not examined the four Gospels themselves to see how they define and nuance the word. Pride of canonical place leads us to listen attentively to the evangelists' treatment of "gospel." We will find that there is great consistency in their explanation of "gospel," yet it is not exactly what many of us would expect or offer in our earlier brainstorming activity.

"Gospel" in Mark

After his opening salvo, Mark uses the noun *euangelion* six more times,[26] but the most important occurrences are found in 1:14 and 15: "Now after John

---

that the evangelist assumes that his readers will know what "this gospel" is on the basis of their acquaintance with his written document. Stanton, *Gospel for a New People*, 13–17. He reiterates this view in his later book *Jesus and Gospel*, 12. I do not find this argument convincing because the "this" in Matthew's expression is referring not to his Gospel narrative but to Jesus's proclamation in 4:23 and 9:35. See below on Matthew's usage of "gospel."

23. Hengel, *Four Gospels*, 63, 80.

24. Ibid., 52, 54, 81.

25. Ibid., 54. I surmise that Trobisch's interpretation might be a little different, namely, that the consistent use of the titles is evidence of a very early and widespread "canonical edition" of the NT that appeared and quickly rose to prominence.

26. The seven occurrences of *euangelion* in Mark are 1:1, 14, 15; 8:35; 10:29; 13:10; and 14:9. The textually inferior longer ending of Mark (versified as 16:9–17) also contains the word in

was arrested, Jesus came into Galilee, preaching the gospel of God, and saying, 'The time is fulfilled, and the kingdom of God is at hand; repent, and believe in the gospel'" (1:14–15).

After his opening words in 1:1, in a span of a mere twelve verses Mark introduces us to two men. One is a wild-man prophet who is preaching and baptizing in the wilderness. The other is the Spirit-imbued Son of God about whom John is preaching and who undergoes his own wilderness trial before bursting onto the public scene in Galilee. This second man, Jesus, has as his message the announcement that God's promised reign or kingship[27] has drawn near and consequently the call to repent and believe in this message. Most important for our inquiry, this message is explicitly called "the gospel of God" or simply "the gospel" (Mark 1:14–15). This is the key defining point for Mark's explanation of what "gospel" means. The other four uses of "gospel" in the rest of his narrative are nondescript, assuming the definition and explanation given here. What is this definition? It is that the "gospel" is the message about the promised return of God's reign, now appearing through the person of Jesus from Nazareth.[28]

"Gospel" in Matthew

When we go back a book, to the first Gospel in the New Testament canon, we find confirmation and further explanation of this same use of "gospel." Although Matthew does not use the word as many times as Mark (five times[29] compared to seven), this concept proves to be very important for his explanation of Jesus's ministry. This is evidenced in the greater specificity with which he uses the word and the key places where he employs it. Aside from

---

16:15. Whether it is original or not, it adds nothing to our understanding of *euangelion*, being derivative from 13:10 and 14:9.

27. We must note the variety of ways in which *basileia* can and should be understood in biblical Greek. Most of the time its primary sense is not "kingdom" as a location per se, but instead it refers to the act of reigning or the rule of a king. This is not to say that the locative sense is unfound or unfounded either. "Kingship" is perhaps the best translation in most cases, as it straddles the semantic domains of both "kingdom" and "reign." For fuller discussion of the meaning of this word, especially in reference to God's *basileia* and Matthew's "kingdom of heaven," see my *Heaven and Earth in the Gospel of Matthew* (Grand Rapids: Baker Academic, 2009), 253–330.

28. It is worth noting the parallel between the genitive phrases in 1:1 and 1:14. First, we read "the gospel of Jesus Christ" and then "the gospel of God." *EDNT* argues that in contrast to its usage in the OT and Jewish and secular Greek literature (where it usually means "news of victory"), *euangelion* in the NT "denotes the news that concerns God or comes from God." It is a technical term for the "message about Christ" that is widely understood as "joyful tidings," though sometimes this means judgment, not only grace (e.g. Rom. 2:16; Rev. 14:6f.) (*EDNT*, 2:70).

29. Matthew's uses of the noun *euangelion* are in 4:23; 9:35; 24:14; and 26:13. Matthew also uses the verb form, *euangelizomai*, when quoting LXX Isa. 61:1 in Matt. 11:5.

the verbal form (*euangelizomai*, "to 'gospelize' or proclaim the good news") used in Matthew 11:5, quoting Isaiah 61:1, Matthew always uses the noun *euangelion* in combination with a specifying word or phrase. In three of his four uses, this explanatory addition is "of the kingdom" (*tēs basileias*), and in the final occurrence (26:13) he refers back to this same phrase with the anaphoric shorthand, "this gospel" (*to euangelion touto*).[30] In fact, it is the initial phrase *to euangelion tēs basileias* in 4:23 that most clearly explains Matthew's understanding of the "gospel." He repeats this phrase in 9:35 for a very important purpose; its later use in 24:14 is referring back to these earlier uses, indicated by the demonstrative *touto* ("this gospel of the kingdom"), followed then finally by the shorthand version in 26:13.

The key, then, is to examine these first two instances of *euangelion* in Matthew to discover his point. It is a well-crafted and theologically significant emphasis. Not only does the phrase "the gospel of the kingdom" strike the ear as new and intriguing; a closer look at its recurrence reveals that Matthew carefully crafts its usage so that his readers will grasp its weighty implications. Its occurrences in 4:23 and 9:35 are part of the repetition of the paragraphs in 4:23–25 and 9:35–38. This striking and lengthy repetition of words clearly indicates that chapters 5–9 are to be read as a unit; these repeated paragraphs provide a frame around these five chapters. The events, teachings, and revelations of these chapters are summed up at their beginning and their end by repeated verbiage. These two paragraphs describe both Jesus's ministry as teaching and preaching the gospel of the kingdom and his compassionate healing of diseases and infirmities (cf. 4:23 and 9:35). This is precisely what occurs in the intervening chapters—the famous Sermon on the Mount (chaps. 5–7) and a collection of physical-healing stories in chapters 8–9. The sermon provides Jesus's clearest teachings about the coming kingdom of heaven, and chapters 8–9 provide several examples of Jesus's compassionate healing ministry, interspersed with spiritual healings or callings of disciples. These latter examples are just as much about the kingdom as the sermon is, for healings are pictures of God's restorative kingdom.[31] Thus, Matthew provides for us a full-orbed and unmistakable definition of "the gospel of/about the kingdom"; it is the message and reality that God's kingship or reign has now come in Jesus. Jesus teaches about what this "here and yet to be" kingdom is like regarding both the virtue and the character of its disciples and the kind of healing and

30. This is again why I do not find compelling Kingsbury's or Stanton's arguments for Matthew as the originator of "Gospel" as a narrative reference. These two later uses of *euangelion* in 24:14 and 26:13 both contain *touto* not because they are references to Matthew's written document but because they are anaphorically and intratextually pointing back to his previous uses in 4:23 and 9:35, which provide the definition.

31. To the modern mind they do not seem to be readily connected, but in the biblical witness, the hope of the return of God's reign was very much a hope for healing of all sorts of brokenness, as Isa. 40–66 most clearly depicts. See further below on "Gospel(ize) in Isaiah."

restoration that it brings. The proclamation of both John the Baptist (3:2) and Jesus have been identical (4:17): "the kingdom of heaven is at hand." Now this is unpacked and specified as "the gospel of the kingdom." Thus, as in Mark but with greater explanation, we see once again that the "gospel" according to the evangelists is the message of the return of the restorative reign of God.

"Gospel(ize)" in Luke

Our third stop on the tour of the evangelists' self-understanding of the "gospel" is the fertile land of Luke's narrative. Although Luke does not use the noun form *euangelion*, he emphasizes and explains this same idea, using the LXX verbal form *euangelizomai*, "to proclaim good news."[32] Ten times this word appears, spanning the entirety of the Gospel. Twice in the birth narratives it is used to describe the angel's message, first to Zechariah (1:19) and second to the sleepy shepherds on the night of Jesus's birth (2:10). This latter reference is unpacked for us with the information that this announcement is one of "great joy for all peoples" and is about a "Savior, who is Christ the Lord," born in the city of David. The eschatological, Davidic, salvific, and regal focus of this explanation is not difficult to discern. Nor is this new information for the readers of Luke's Gospel. He has already made clear that it is the expectation by the explicit promise that the angel Gabriel gives Mary concerning her son: "He will be great, and will be called the Son of the Most High; and the Lord God will give to him the throne of his father David, and he will reign over the house of Jacob for ever; and of his kingdom there will be no end" (1:32–33). The kingship focus is the dominant note.

In the rest of the narrative this same verb is used to describe John the Baptist's ministry (3:18) as well as Jesus's (4:43; 7:22; 8:1; 9:6; 16:16; 20:1). It is interesting and important to note that in several of these verses the verb is followed by and explained with reference to the kingdom, providing a striking parallel to Matthew's phraseology, but with the necessary adjustments because of the verb rather than noun form of the *euangel*- root.[33] Luke also parallels Matthew by using *euangelizomai* in the quote from Isaiah 61:1, which Jesus employs to describe to the imprisoned John the Baptist his healing and new creational

32. This verb occurs around seventy-five times in the Greek Bible, including twenty-three times in Rahlfs's edition of the LXX. The noun form also occurs around seventy-five times in the Greek Bible, but only once in the LXX, in 2 Reigns (MT, 2 Sam.) 4:10. Horbury also notes occurrences of the word found in particular manuscript witnesses to the LXX. See Horbury, "'Gospel' in Herodian Judaea," 15–16.

33. In Luke 4:43 Jesus says that it is necessary for him to preach the gospel regarding the kingdom of God (*euangelisasthai me dei tēn basileian tou theou*). This is also the description used in 8:1 (*euangelizomenos tēn basileian tou theou*) and 16:16 (*hē basileia tou theou euangelizetai*). Luke 9:6 and 20:1 do not have this full phrasing, but there is every indication that the reference is the same here, based on all the other uses of *euangelizomai* throughout Luke's Gospel.

ministry (Luke 7:22; cf. Matt. 11:5). This parallel between Matthew and Luke finds another fulfillment in the most significant use of *euangelizomai* in Luke, in 4:18. We have already seen that Matthew carefully defines the gospel as being about God's kingdom (4:23; 9:35; 24:14), particularly with its twofold manifestation in (1) teachings about the virtue of kingdom citizens (the Sermon, chaps. 5–7) and (2) the restoration of the broken (chaps. 8–9). Luke's view is precisely the same, though his presentation is different. To introduce Jesus's public ministry, Luke relates Jesus's post-temptation return to Galilee "in the power of the Spirit" (4:14). Jesus enters the synagogue in his hometown of Nazareth and chooses to read for the hearers Isaiah 61:1. Nothing seems overly unusual until Jesus, rather than expositing this prophetic promise, sits down and informs everyone, "Today this scripture has been fulfilled in your hearing" (4:21). This young, eager man hoping in God's kingdom restoration might be forgiven his overzealous words, but Jesus crosses the line when he claims for himself the mantle of this same prophet and reminds his elders that through prophets God judges his people (4:23–27). The result is wrath and an attempt to extinguish Jesus by casting him over a cliff (4:28–30). The point for us is how Luke has chosen to introduce and frame Jesus's ministry—it is the Spirit-empowered, joy-bringing, burden-lifting, captive-freeing message that "the favorable year of the Lord" has come, that is, the restoration of God's ways and reign on earth. Thus, Luke accords with his Synoptic brethren in emphasizing the "good news" of the gospel and defining this "Gospel" as the message about God's restorative reign.

"Gospel(ize)" in Isaiah

Finally in our effort to see how the Gospels define the "gospel," we may turn not to the Fourth Gospel but to the fifth, as it came to be considered in the early church,[34] the book of Isaiah.[35] Here we find that *euangelizomai* plays

34. For a brief survey of the predominant use of Isaiah in the early church, see John F. A. Sawyer, *The Fifth Gospel: Isaiah in the History of Christianity* (Cambridge: Cambridge University Press, 1996), 1–2, 42–64. See also Brevard Childs, *The Struggle to Understand Isaiah as Christian Scripture* (Grand Rapids: Eerdmans, 2004).

35. This is not to exclude the Gospel of John from our theological construction of what "gospel" means, but only to note that because he does not use any form of the *euangel-* word group, the Fourth Gospel cannot help us in our examination of the function of these words in the NT. While John clearly has his own distinctives, some of which are significant, one would be hard pressed to argue that he has an entirely different view of Jesus's life, death, and resurrection than do the Synoptics; he does not. What he calls the word or message about eternal life, the other evangelists, in tune with Paul, call the "Gospel." Moreover, by its canonical placement the Gospel of John has always been considered just that, another rendering of "the gospel." This is the case even to the extent that the manuscript and interpretive traditions consistently place it in such a way that it breaks up the obvious two-part work of Luke-Acts so that the four "Gospels" are kept together. For us to separate it from the other accounts on the basis of

a crucial role.[36] We have just seen that Luke chooses Isaiah as the avenue through which to describe Jesus's ministry. In this he is not alone among the New Testament writers, nor is Isaiah 61 the only place to which he could have turned. Richard Hays rightly observes that the evangelists are concerned to show that Jesus's teachings, actions, death, and vindication "constituted the continuation and climax of the ancient biblical story" and that the Old Testament was the "*generative milieu* for the gospels, the original environment in which the first Christian traditions were conceived, formed and nurtured."[37] The book of Isaiah, and especially the forward vision of chapters 40–66, ranks as one of the deepest and broadest Old Testament wells from which the New Testament authors draw. Isaiah 40–66 is of the utmost importance for the Gospels' self-understanding and proclamation. Sprinkled throughout all the Gospels, but especially Matthew and Luke, are direct quotations, strong allusions, and subtle echoes from Isaiah. We can say without overstatement that the eschatological vision of Isaiah 40–66 serves as the primary subtext and framing for the Gospels' witness.[38] This is not a new insight, as is witnessed by the centrality of Isaiah in Christian interpretation, in everything from homily and commentary to Handel's famous oratorio *Messiah*, which begins with the tenor aria "Comfort, O Comfort my People" (from Isa. 40:1).

What is this Isaianic eschatological vision? *It is the hope in the restoration of God's reign.* Isaiah describes it with a full artist's palette of vibrant colors. It is comfort and tenderness from God (40:1, 2, 11; 51:5; 52:9; 54:7–8; 55:7; 61:2–3), the presence of God himself (41:10; 43:5; 45:14; 52:12), help for the poor and

---

surface differences would be nothing less than irresponsible. On the tradition of Luke as part of the fourfold canon rather than as part of "Luke-Acts" as in the modern period, see C. Kavin Rowe, "History, Hermeneutics and the Unity of Luke-Acts," *JSNT* 28, no. 2 (2005): 131–57.

36. The *euangel-* word group occurs a few places other than in Isaiah, but only in this prophet does it seem to bear much theological weight. In its other few uses, especially clustered in the story of 2 Sam. 18, it seems to mean simply "report of good news."

37. Richard B. Hays, "The Canonical Matrix of the Gospels," in Barton, *Cambridge Companion to the Gospels*, 53.

38. An early article articulating this is Klyne Snodgrass, "Streams of Tradition Emerging from Isaiah 40.1–5 and Their Adaptation in the New Testament," *JSNT* 8 (1980): 24–45. Since then several significant monographs have been written in this same vein, in addition to countless essays. See inter alia Rikki E. Watts, *Isaiah's New Exodus and Mark*, WUNT vol. 2, no. 88 (Tübingen: Mohr Siebeck, 1997); and David W. Pao, *Acts and the Isaianic New Exodus* (Grand Rapids: Baker Academic, 2000). For works on the Isaiah background to "gospel," one can consult Hays's "Canonical Matrix of the Gospels"; Stanton, *Jesus and Gospel*; and Klyne Snodgrass, "The Gospel of Jesus," in Bockmuehl and Hagner, *Written Gospel*, 31–44. More generally, in his extensive works N. T. Wright has argued for Jesus's self-understanding to be that of fulfilling the story of Israel, the story that clearly has as its beginning (and end) the Exodus, especially as this is refigured in Isaiah. See N. T. Wright, *The New Testament and the People of God* (Minneapolis: Fortress, 1992) and his *Jesus and the Victory of God* (Minneapolis: Fortress, 1996). For the discussion of the Isaianic background to the meaning of "gospel," see Wright's *What Saint Paul Really Said: Was Paul of Tarsus the Real Founder of Christianity?* (Grand Rapids: Eerdmans, 1997), 40–44.

needy (40:29–31; 41:17; 55:1–2), the renewing of all things (42:9–10; 43:18–19; 48:6; 65:17; 66:22), the judgment of God's enemies (42:13–17; 47:1–15; 49:22–26; 66:15–17, 24), the healing of blindness and deafness (42:18; 43:8–10), the forgiving of sins (44:22; 53:4–6, 10–12), and the making of a covenant (41:6; 49:8; 55:3; 59:21). All of this will be accomplished through God's anointed, humble Servant (42:1–4; 45:4; 49:3–5; 52:13–53:12) and witnesses (43:10; 44:8). To read Isaiah 40–66 is to be washed over with a vision of God's power and grace. And this is why this vision is described six times in the LXX as the proclamation of good news, *euangelizomai* (40:9 [2x]; 52:7 [2x]; 60:6; 61:1). It is the good news of salvation (60:6), the restoration of God's people (61:1ff.), God coming with his might (40:9), and most simply and comprehensively, the proclamation that "your God reigns!" (52:7). This beautiful Isaianic mural of hope is evoked continually in the Gospels via the evangelists' reference to it and outlining of Jesus's ministry with its brushstrokes.

Provisional Definition

This extended reflection on the Scriptures' uses of "gospel" allows us to now offer a provisional definition. It must remain provisional until we explore the other part of our definitions discussion, the related question of the Gospels' genre. But for now we can observe that the New Testament authors, building especially on the Isaianic vision, define the "gospel" as Jesus's effecting the long-awaited return of God himself as King, in the power of the Spirit bringing his people back from exile and into the true promised land of a new creation, forgiving their sins,[39] and fulfilling all the promises of God and the hopes of his people. This Isaianic vision is itself based on God's work at the exodus, which the prophets take up and reappropriate to describe God's future work.[40] Because of this vision, described as the proclamation of good news, the apostles call their kerygma "gospel," and it is why the evangelists likewise

---

39. It is very important that we note this essential aspect of what the "Gospel" is for both Isaiah and the evangelists. In the recent rediscovery of the kingdom-centrality of Jesus's message of the "gospel" there has often been a naive and sophomoric pendulum swing away from the essentiality of Jesus's atoning death on behalf of his people. Not only is sacrificial atonement clearly testified to as essential in the apostolic witness (e.g., 1 Cor. 15:3; 1 Pet. 3:18), it is also the obvious endgame of all four Gospels, one of the few ways in which all the witnesses are in total agreement and emphasis. But if this were not enough, one only has to read Isa. 40–66 to see that this theme is at the heart of the "good news" Isaiah is sent to proclaim, as witnessed in 52:13–53:12. As mentioned above, McKnight's *King Jesus Gospel* keeps in balance the important ideas of the gospel as both broad restoration and the individual's need for forgiveness of sins through Jesus's death and resurrection.

40. Although Hengel does not note the importance of the Isaiah influence on the NT "gospel," he clearly sees its deeper roots in the exodus. Hengel, along with many others, sees the essential root of the *euangelion* in the radically new eschatological message that the exodus is to be reinterpreted in light of the dawning of Jesus Christ. Hengel, *Four Gospels*, 161. This

describe the work of Jesus and the narratives about him as *euangelion*. In this there is univocality; Paul and the Gospel writers all understand their message to be one of God's reign coming in the person of Jesus through the power of the Spirit.[41] The "gospel," whether in oral or written form, is the message of God's comprehensively restorative kingdom.

---

comes from Hengel's concluding chapter intriguingly titled "Torah and Gospel as Narratives of Two Different Saving Events."

41. For examples of the kingdom emphasis in Paul's understanding of the gospel, see Rom. 14:17; 1 Cor. 15:24; Col. 1:13; 1 Thess. 2:11; 2 Tim. 4:18. For works on this topic, see Brian Vickers, "The Kingdom of God in Paul's Gospel," *Southern Baptist Journal of Theology* 12, no. 1 (2008): 52–67; David Wenham, *Paul: Follower of Jesus or Founder of Christianity?* (Grand Rapids: Eerdmans, 1995); Ben Witherington III, *Jesus, Paul and the End of the World: A Comparative Study of New Testament Eschatology* (Downers Grove, IL: InterVarsity, 1992); Frances Young, "Paul and the Kingdom of God," in *The Kingdom of God and Human Society*, ed. R. S. Barbour (Edinburgh: T&T Clark, 1993). See also chap. 3 of this volume.

2

What Are the Gospels?

Understanding the "Gospel" Genre

In the previous chapter we discovered that in both the evangelists' understanding and very early in the church, "gospel" refers to an announced story of God's restorative kingdom. In this chapter we will complete this first "definitions" section by focusing on the "story" part of that description. Particularly, we may ask what kind of story these narratives are. To what genre or type of literature do these narratives belong? Are they more like biographies, histories, news reports, documentaries, or virtue stories? Are they comparable to modern biographies or ancient ones, folk tales or novels, closed-circuit television or eyewitness accounts? Or are they a new and unique genre of their own (sui generis)? This question of genre is not merely academic. Rather, it is very relevant to our experience of reading the Gospels and our ability to read them well because understanding the genre of the Gospels will guide us in reading them with the right motivations and expectations and with the proper focus.

The word "gospel," placed as a title for our four stories about Jesus from the earliest days, served to identify for the readers and hearers *what kind of literature* was about to come forth from Mark or Matthew or Luke or John. But we must ask, what would this title "Gospel" prompt them to expect? What would this title communicate?[1] Herein lies a very important point: readers

---

1. In his *Postscript to the Name of the Rose* (San Diego: Harcourt Brace Jovanovich, 1984), 2–3, Umberto Eco reflects on the power of the title of a literary work. Whether it be *War and Peace* or *David Copperfield* a title inevitably provides a key to interpreting the whole, even if it is not immediately apparent to the reader what the title means. For Eco titles are an unfortunate

or hearers in any culture naturally develop a "literary competence" by which they are able to discern what to expect from a communicative event. For the person embedded in his or her own culture, this literary competence may not be something he or she is aware of or able to articulate, but it is influential nonetheless. A foundational element in such literary competence is the ability to discern genre, or what type of literature or communicative event is occurring.

Genre and Literary Competency

We use the word "genre" to describe a recognizable type of writing with a certain style, purpose, and identifiable features. Genres are neither purely prescriptive nor descriptive. That is, there are no concrete, unbreakable rules for a genre, or even a set number of genres that exist (such as in a classical prescriptive view).[2] However, this does not mean genre is a useless term that has as many meanings as there are different works of literature (thus, only descriptive). Rather, a genre is an overall term that we can use to describe a grouping of literary works that share a set of characteristics, allowing flexibility for any particular work to manifest or omit some of these characteristics or to emphasize others. A genre is a matter of culturally understood conventions. The best analogy to describe this is that of a "family resemblance." Even as the various members of a family might share identifiable characteristics, such as height or shape of cheekbone or nose, yet remain distinct people, so too we can note that the members of a family of literary works—or a genre—clearly overlap with one another yet are not identical.[3] Thus, when we speak of a genre we are discussing certain characteristics that are identifiable as overlapping between different pieces of literature. These are conventional and may vary by culture.

In fact, this understanding of "genre" as conventional yet flexible has given it a new application and meaning in our current age, as applied not just to literature but to music. iTunes and internet radio programs such as Pandora consciously use the category of genre to describe families of music, allowing flexibility and variation within identifiable characteristics. This can be quite sophisticated, as in, for example, the description of musical genre that

---

necessity because in his view a novel is "a machine for generating interpretations," and thus a title imposes the author's view too much. Even if one does not fully agree with this understanding of the "openness" of a novel, the point still stands that a work's title strongly influences the reader's expectations and overall interpretation.

2. Cf. Plato's *Republic* and Aristotle's *Poetics*. See Richard A. Burridge, *What Are the Gospels? A Comparison with Graeco-Roman Biography*, 2nd ed. (Grand Rapids: Eerdmans, 2004), 26–27.

3. One might reflect how the exception to the family resemblance analogy is the case of identical twins. Even in this situation, however, experience shows that even DNA-identical twins often have distinguishing marks, not readily observable by the stranger, but clear to those familiar with both.

I get from the Music Genome Project when I create a new Pandora station called "Miles Davis"—music that, according to their description, "features cool jazz qualities, blues influences, a leisurely tempo, trumpet lead, and a sparse trumpet solo." Or it can be as instinctive and unarticulated as when my nine-year-old son, sitting in my office at home, hears Wynton Marsalis playing from my computer and remarks, "Dad, this is the kind of music like we hear in Pink Panther." Of course, I know that Marsalis was not even on the musical scene yet when the classic Pink Panther cartoons were created, nor should Marsalis and Henry Mancini be identified musically. But somehow my son could recognize *something* similar, some family resemblance—some shared genre—between these two musical expressions, even though he could not articulate it.

A large part of literary competency, then, is coming to understand what these conventions are and how they are part of the communication between writers and readers in any particular culture and time, even if the reader (or hearer) does not fully understand these conventions. These conventions create a set of unstated expectations between the writer and the reader. We might compare them to body language or tone of voice as a framing element in communication. (And we have all experienced the frustration of miscommunication via an impersonal medium such as email!) Though unstated, the genre that an author chooses to use is very much part of the communication event.

This discussion significantly overlaps with the previous chapter and the question of the meaning of *euangelion* and the superscriptions to our four Gospels, because the titling of these accounts as "The Gospel according to . . ." inevitably created an expectation for what was about to be heard, read, and experienced. For Mark this is most obvious with his opening words, "The beginning of the gospel about/from Jesus Christ." Matthew's opening words—"the book of the genesis of Jesus Christ . . ."—identify his work as a literary one (and not just a collection of aphorisms or sayings) and especially evoke a strong and obvious connection with the book of Genesis and the genealogical portions of the Old Testament.[4] In Luke's much more technical prologue (1:1–4) he calls his own account an orderly narrative (*diēgēsis*). John's strikingly different opening—"In the beginning was the Word"—stirs up its own set of associations, both with the beginning of Holy Scripture at the creation in Genesis 1:1 as well as the deep and important Greek philosophical tradition regarding the Logos (*logos*). Despite this variety, especially on the part of Matthew, Luke, and John, the fact that all four come to be described and published as *to euangelion* ("the Gospel") affects our understanding of them greatly. This title of "Gospel" becomes the overarching "master word" that

---

4. See Jonathan T. Pennington, "Heaven, Earth, and a New Genesis: Theological Cosmology in Matthew," in *Cosmology and New Testament Theology*, ed. Jonathan T. Pennington and Sean M. McDonough (London: T&T Clark, 2008), 28–44.

creates a rich set of expectations. Increasingly for early Christians the title "Gospel" came to refer to a *narrative* about Jesus. But from the beginning this master word would also connect in their minds with the apostolic proclamation already described as "good news," with the broader Hellenistic use of the word and its political ramifications, and for readers knowledgeable of the Old Testament, with its connection to the Isaianic hope.

Some readers at this point may ask, if genre is truly natural and unstated as argued, why do we need to labor to identify the genre of the Gospels? The answer is that there is an unavoidable gap of time and culture between the original hearers of the Gospels and us as readers. This distance between us and the compositional setting of Scripture can be overdone and abused, and it is in fact eliminated in some crucial ways by the canonization of the Gospels. Nevertheless, when it comes to the question of genre, we need to beware of our own prejudicial expectations when reading and of conventional expectations that may be different from those of the original writer. A couple of crucial questions in this regard will be raised in chapters 5–7—particularly what the genre of the Gospels does for us regarding the question of historical expectations and what our overall goal in reading the Gospels should be. But for now the most important point is that genre creates conventional expectations for readers, and good readers will ignore this only to their peril.

So, for example, at some mysterious point in our intellectual development, we know instinctively what to expect and how to approach a poem as different from a newspaper report or the textbook for our economics class. When we read the headline of the *Weekly World News* "Two-Headed Alien Is Found Hiding at the President's Ranch," we know from the type of tabloid genre not to take this as seriously as the *Wall Street Journal*'s report that the Federal Reserve is raising interest rates. In one sense the difference here is one's expectation of *credibility* of the witness, an issue to which we will return. But underneath this is also the literary competency to know that a tabloid paper has as its goal to produce short, quickly read, sensational, and shocking bits of "news." The *Wall Street Journal* also has a goal and an agenda—no writing or communication lacks these elements—but they are tied more closely to publicly used factual information from reputable sources. The difference here is a change of genre; the competent reader knows to change the mental gears of expectation.

Or to use a biblical example, when we read the proverb "A slack hand causes poverty, but the hand of the diligent makes rich" (Prov. 10:4) or "The LORD does not let the righteous go hungry, but he thwarts the craving of the wicked" (Prov. 10:3), we should know that as proverbs these are generally true principles of wisdom, not promises or assured absolutes. Experience easily proves this out. There are plenty of diligent people in third-world nations, often faithful and pious, who are financially oppressed, and no matter how much they work, they can never make ends meet. There are plenty of truly righteous people, in places such as North Korea or China, who have nothing to eat today. Has God failed in these promises from Proverbs? No. Discerning the genre of proverbial literature enables us to recognize that these are principles of wisdom that by their nature apply variously in various situations. Another biblical example is that of apocalyptic language. When we read, "The sun shall be turned to darkness, and the moon to blood," we should know instinctively that, as the scholar John Barton quips, the next line will not be "the rest of the country will have sunny intervals and scattered showers."[5] Apocalyptic writing is a particular genre that uses its own conventions of symbolic language and images. Because that of which it speaks is wholly other, its language must necessarily be imaginative, even though it is not imaginary.[6] Recognizing this is a key component in interpreting this kind of literature, even as it is for poetry and parable. Even more frequently than with the Proverbs, failure to understand the genre of apocalyptic language results in misapplication. A good and competent reader will recognize that these images are conventions of language and should not be taken "literally" as if somehow this were a virtue.

We already see by these last two examples that misunderstanding genre can have weighty interpretive implications. We will return to this matter below and in subsequent chapters. But for now we must turn to our original question and ask what kind of literature or what type of genre may best describe our fourfold Gospel.

The Gospels as *Bioi*, or Greek Biographies

In the last one hundred years or so, there has been voluminous discussion and debate about the genre to which the Gospels belong. In late nineteenth- and early twentieth-century scholarship, accompanying the rise and dominance of form criticism, the canonical Gospels were considered by many to be sui generis, or their own unique Christian genre that evolved from the preaching or kerygma of the early Christian missionaries. For much of scholarship (especially German higher criticism) this was a somewhat pejorative judgment, seeing the Gospels as *Kleinliteratur*, or "low-brow" writing, that was little more than random, folk anecdotes strung together. The Gospels were evaluated as poor in terms of literary quality and really little more than windows to look *through* onto the history and debates of the (generally uneducated) early church.[7]

---

5. John Barton, *Reading the Old Testament: Method in Biblical Study*, 2nd ed. (Louisville: Westminster John Knox, 1996), 17.

6. Cf. Richard Bauckham and Trevor Hart, *Hope against Hope: Christian Eschatology at the Turn of the Millennium* (Grand Rapids: Eerdmans, 1999).

7. For the following discussion I rely on the analysis of Burridge's *What Are the Gospels?* and especially the shorter but thorough and balanced treatment of Adela Yarbro Collins in her essay on genre in *Mark: A Commentary*, Hermeneia (Minneapolis: Fortress, 2007), 15–43.

In the latter part of the twentieth century, New Testament scholarship began to turn away from this evaluation on every point, with a move toward a more literary reading and greater respect for the theological and narrative nature of the Gospels and the evangelists' skill. Corresponding to this, the question of the nature of the genre arose again, and a variety of scholars began comparing the Gospels to other contemporary Greco-Roman literature, something that had been done earlier in scholarship but that had gone out of fashion. With increasing examples of ancient biographies being analyzed and sophisticated classifications of different types of ancient biographies, several scholars began to turn the tide toward seeing the Gospels not as unique per se nor as unliterary, but as a version or subgenre of the Greco-Roman biography.

Today, these arguments have prompted a trend toward describing the Gospels as *bioi*, or "biographies," acknowledging that these were not the same thing as modern biographies and that they also have much in common with ancient "histories" (*historia*) and other forms of writing. Richard Burridge's book *What Are the Gospels? A Comparison with Graeco-Roman Biography*, now in its second edition, is regularly referenced as the definitive English work on this topic, though it is not without its detractors and problems. It will be worth our while to examine briefly his arguments to see in what ways this genre identification of *bioi* proves helpful and whether we might qualify and expand it in some ways.

Burridge's main argument is that the Gospels do indeed share a family resemblance to a wide variety of Greco-Roman biographies from the Hellenistic period before and after the time of Christ. As he argues, he is aware of the preceding scholarly debate on this topic, and he is especially keen to dispel the notion that the Gospels are somehow a new and unique form of literature. His rejection of this latter point is in reaction to the mistaken path of form criticism and in large part stems from his analysis of the idea of genres overall.

Burridge seeks to critique the sui generis view and to establish his *bios* argument by more carefully laying a theoretical and methodological foundation for understanding genre. He rejects defining genre either too narrowly or too broadly and emphasizes the flexibility and conventional nature of genres, even as I have articulated earlier. Burridge observes that because no communication occurs in a vacuum nor can any literature be created ex nihilo, there can be in reality no such thing as a "unique" genre. By its nature a piece of writing will always share *some* characteristics with other works yet without being identical. Indeed, analysis of a large swath of ancient literature shows that the genres regularly overlap in any given author and even within a literary work. So, while there are generally identifiable characteristics of the *bios*, such works will regularly overlap moral philosophy, encomia (laudatory writing about some great figure), and historical works.[8] Great writers always stretch

---

8. Burridge, *What Are the Gospels?* 61–63. See also the helpful map (fig. 1) on 64.

and extend into new forms what currently exists, but they can only do so by making associations with and resemblances to current forms. Therefore, in Burridge's analysis, sui generis is nonsensical.[9]

Having established this understanding and definition of genre, Burridge prosecutes the rest of his argument through a literarily informed and textually based taxonomic analysis of Greco-Roman *bioi*. He subjects to analysis several ancient biographies that occur before and after the first century in view of a series of common characteristics. These include opening features such as the title and opening words, external features such as the typical length and mode of presentation, and internal characteristics such as the structure, topics addressed, atmosphere, types of literary units employed, use of sources, and purposes. Also very determinative for *bioi* is the focus on a particular person as the subject, in contrast with histories or philosophical treatises. For each of these features, Burridge identifies what is characteristic for the average *bios*.[10] He sums up this detailed analysis by noting that *bioi* "are works with a setting focused upon a person, about whom the writer selects topics from a group of standard motifs" such as the person's ancestry, birth, boyhood and education, great deeds, virtues, and death and its consequences. Their style and level are usually fairly literary, indicating a generally educated social setting yet with popular tendencies, with an atmosphere that is mostly respectful and serious, and with a wide variety of purposes ranging from encomiastic to the exemplary to the informative and the didactic.[11]

With these tools in hand, Burridge turns to the four canonical Gospels. He finds that the Gospels fit nicely into this mode of communication. They clearly focus on one subject, Jesus;[12] they allocate a significant amount of space to his final days and death while also telling us something of his ancestry, great deeds, and virtues; they are of a medium length; they follow a basic chronological sequence, but not slavishly and with topical material inserted; they combine stories, sayings, anecdotes, and speeches to form a narrative; they show Jesus's character not through direct, narrator analysis (or psychoanalysis), but indirectly through his words and deeds; and they have many similarities in purpose, especially exemplary, didactic, polemic, and mnemonic.[13] Thus, Burridge fairly concludes that there is "a sufficient number of shared features"

9. Ibid., 45. It is a curious fact that while many current textbooks quickly quote Burridge as the authoritative evidence that we should consider the Gospels to be *bioi*, they also move seamlessly to talk about the Gospels' sui generis nature, the very thing Burridge is attempting to overthrow.

10. Ibid., 129–47.

11. Ibid., 148. Burridge similarly summarizes post-first-century AD *bioi* on 183.

12. To definitively substantiate this claim, which otherwise is rather obvious for the Gospels, Burridge provides data for the very high frequency of Jesus's appearance as the subject of the verbs in the Gospels, presented to us in the form of the always-delightful pie graph. See 318–21.

13. This summarizes Burridge's analysis for the Synoptics in *What Are the Gospels?* 185–212. He argues similarly for John on 213–32.

and certainly enough family resemblance to identify the Gospels as part of the genre of the Greco-Roman *bios*.[14] For Burridge, the key implications here are that we must no longer speak of the Gospels as a unique genre, but form our expectations for reading the Gospels from the comparable genre of the *bios*.[15] Additionally, the focus of our interpretation of the Gospels must return to the person of Jesus.[16]

Bioi *Plus—Toward a More Comprehensive Understanding of the Gospels*

I find Burridge's argument to be cogent and convincing, though not comprehensive. He has done an admirable job of laying out a methodologically sound and clear argument for our identification of the Gospels as *bioi*. It is a solid framework upon which we can build other important arguments, especially regarding the exemplary and virtue-forming purpose of the Gospels and the nature of their history retelling.

Nevertheless, Burridge's presentation, even in its expanded second edition form, does not range broadly or deeply enough. First, we may note that the conclusions and implications he provides are rather thin and do not explore some of the most pressing questions, including those I have just mentioned—how the Gospels relate to virtue formation and how their genre affects their presentation of history.[17] Even more significantly, in his attempt to make a detailed and tidy argument for the *bios* identification, his case is at times *too* neat and tidy; that is, he does not look beyond the *bios* genre option to consider other, coexisting genre considerations that might temper and balance his argument. He understandably wants to sound the death knell on form criticism's approach, but this narrowing focus does not incline him to consider other overlapping contexts useful for analyzing and describing the Gospels' genre. Although the *bios* connections are strong and clear, they are not the only voices that should have been allowed the microphone at the genre debate club.

Loveday Alexander's excellent essay "What Is a Gospel?" offers an indirect critique of Burridge by exploring the genre issue with greater sensitivity to the realities of oral tradition, folk tales transmission, early Christian witness,

---

14. Ibid., 211.

15. Ibid., 247–48.

16. "It is our contention that this *bios* nature of the gospel genre should also restore the centrality of the person of Jesus." Ibid., 250, italics in original.

17. I am well aware that one cannot do everything in any one book, and indeed, Burridge has now followed up this work with one that explores the imitation of Jesus theme for our understanding of ethics: *Imitating Jesus: An Inclusive Approach to New Testament Ethics* (Grand Rapids: Eerdmans, 2007). Nevertheless, with his opportunity to republish the work in a second edition, in my opinion the most beneficial addition would have been deeper exploration of these two issues that are quite pressing in the current hermeneutical environment.

and especially the Jewish Old Testament narrative context for the Gospels.[18] Alexander observes that while there is much to be said for the biographical connection, the Gospels still stand apart especially in their kerygmatic nature.[19] Moreover, when looking for a narrative model for the Gospels, much closer to hand is the Hebrew Bible, which is "much more deeply prone to 'bio-structuring' than is classical Greek historiography," with its many biographical "story cycles" like those of Samson or Elijah. "It is to the biblical tradition, surely, that we should look for the origins of the 'religious intensity' of the gospel narratives and their rich ideological intertextuality with the biblical themes of covenant, kingdom, prophecy, and promise—all features hard to parallel in Greek biography."[20] Or, as she concludes, in their written form the external shape of the Gospels is "strongly reminiscent of the Greek *bios*," but their "narrative mode and theological framework . . . owe much more to the Bible."[21]

Even more thorough is Adela Yarbro Collins's treatment of the genre debate as part of the introduction to her commentary on the Gospel of Mark. With deftness and clarity Collins summarizes a wide array of scholarly discussion on the matter (especially in German works) and offers her own evaluations and views. In line with Loveday Alexander, Collins critiques Burridge for not giving due credence to the biographical material in the Hebrew Bible.[22] Moving beyond both Burridge and Alexander, Collins also notes the importance for the Gospels of the apocalyptic and eschatological traditions as well as the variety of contemporary historiographic writings, including in the Jewish Scriptures.[23] Collins also carefully elucidates a number of subgenres or types of the ancient *bios* genre. These are encomiastic, scholarly, didactic, ethical, entertaining, and historical. Without falling into the trap of seeing these as separate or unrelated genres, she observes that recognizing these subtypes helps us make comparisons to the Gospels. She finds that the Gospels (or at least Mark) have the most affinity with the didactic and historical. The didactic has as its primary aim instructing "the reader, not only about the life of a particular individual but also about the way of life that he founded,"[24] while the historical type of ancient biography serves to

18. Loveday Alexander, "What Is a Gospel?" in *The Cambridge Companion to the Gospels*, ed. Stephen Barton (Cambridge: Cambridge University Press, 2006), 13–33.

19. Alexander, "What Is a Gospel?" 26. Cf. Martin Hengel's description of the Gospels as kerygmatic narratives in *The Four Gospels and the One Gospel of Jesus Christ: An Investigation of the Collection and Origin of the Canonical Gospels*, trans. John Bowden (Harrisburg, PA: Trinity Press International, 2000), 90–91.

20. Alexander, "What Is a Gospel?" 27–28.

21. Ibid., 29.

22. Collins, *Mark*, 29–30. "Burridge's case for defining the Gospels as *bioi* ('lives') appears strong in large part because he did not seriously consider any alternative" (29).

23. Ibid., 29, 33–40.

24. Ibid., 31.

"give an account of an important series of events and to explain the events in terms of their causes."[25]

In the end, however, Collins understands the Gospel of Mark (and presumably the others as well) as an "eschatological historical monograph."[26] With Mark a new type (or maybe better, subtype) of writing emerged, one stemming from and relating to existing biographical and historical forms. Influenced by both the Jewish heritage of biblical narratives, especially the apocalyptic and eschatological emphasis on the fulfillment of the divine plan, and Hellenistic historiography, Mark created a historical monograph that focused on eschatological fulfillment through the man Jesus Christ, a work that could appropriately be called "good news."[27] This is a very helpful analysis. I would add to it only a greater emphasis on the ethical nature of the Gospels, their kerygmatic function,[28] and a more explicit connection with Isaiah, as discussed above. Additionally, we should explore the ways in which the Gospels stand apart from other contemporary writings.

Particular Aspects of the Gospel Biographies

Burridge is correct, on methodological grounds, to reject the idea of any genre as sui generis because all writing must come from, relate to, and overlap known literary forms. Going beyond Burridge, we have also seen that the Gospels are influenced by literary examples other than just ancient biographies, most notably the Jewish Scriptures, both postexilic narratives and apocalyptic traditions. Yet we may push the analysis one step further and suggest a number of ways in which the Gospels, while perhaps not their own independent genre, *do stand apart in particular and important aspects*. These particularities are worth noting because they will affect our overall reading strategy for the Gospels.

First, we may observe that unlike even the most laudatory ancient biographies or histories, the Gospels do not present Jesus as one great figure alongside others of interest. Rather, the claims made about Jesus in the Gospels are much greater than any claim that would ever be made about Alexander the Great or Socrates. Namely, *all of human history is seen to be consummated in him*. This is intimately related to the evangelists' perspective that Jesus is not merely a great leader or teacher who exists in a vacuum, but he is the epicentric and climactic point of the grand story of what God is doing in the world. As John Nolland remarks, "The story of Jesus is told as a continuation—indeed as some

25. Ibid., 32.
26. Ibid., 42.
27. Ibid., 42–43.
28. Though Hengel does not address the genre question very much, he does remark that the Gospels can be called a new literary genre of a "religious" or "kerygmatic" nature, meaning they are proclamatory of religious realities. Hengel, *Four Gospels*, 49.

kind of culmination—of the long story of God and his people." The Gospels are not freestanding narratives but are stories that "must be set into a larger frame supplied by the history of God's prior dealings with his people."[29] Any doubt that we are meant to understand the Gospels this way can be dispelled by simply reading the first two chapters of the Gospel of Matthew. From a purely aesthetic perspective these opening chapters to the fourfold canon are rather poorly written narrative precisely because they are trying so painfully to make clear that the story of Jesus is the consummation of the story of Israel, going back to its beginning in Genesis 1:1. Each short, almost plotless story in Matthew 1–2 is concluded with a repetitious explanatory comment, "All this took place to fulfill what the Lord had spoken by the prophet. . . ." Few people would enjoy a novel or a film in which the narrator (or the person sitting next to you in the theater) regularly breaks in with an explanatory aside such as, "FYI: this happened so that she would learn that he didn't really love her. . . ." But precisely this excessiveness at the opening of Matthew's Gospel makes it abundantly clear that this story cannot be received as a mere *bios* or history. This emphasis on the uniqueness of Jesus and his role in history sets the tone for the fourfold witness of the Gospels.

Closely related to this point is the important fact that the Gospels are also a particular kind of biography in that they depict Jesus as the inaugurator of God's reign. That is, unlike other ancient *bioi*, the life and death of Jesus are presented as something that changes the course of history from a divine perspective. Writing long before the current genre debate, Alfred Edersheim suggested that the scantiness of human particulars in the Gospels (especially concerning Jesus's family of origin) was intended to prevent interest in such matters from overshadowing the "grand central Fact" that the Gospels are designed "in organic connection with the Old Testament, to tell the history of the long-promised establishment of the Kingdom of God upon earth."[30] On this basis Edersheim argues against the Gospels being understood as biographies. In this he overstates in that, as we have seen, there is much benefit to Burridge's clearer view of what a *bios* was. Nevertheless, this is a helpful reminder of the kingdom centrality of the Gospels that makes them stand apart. Indeed, in this we see the importance of their being titled "Gospel" (*euangelion*) and not just "*Bios*," as was explored in chapter 1.

A third exceptional aspect of the Gospels is that while they share with *bioi* the emphasis on the subject's character, depicted indirectly through his sayings and actions, they go far beyond this to emphasize Jesus's very nature as divine. In the Gospels Jesus's insight, wisdom, virtue, and example are certainly important, but even more so is the evangelists' christological point: who Jesus

29. John Nolland, *The Gospel of Matthew*, NIGTC (Grand Rapids: Eerdmans, 2005), 19.

30. Alfred Edersheim, *The Life and Times of Jesus the Messiah* (McLean, VA: MacDonald, 1883), bk. 2, chap. 4, 145.

is by his nature as the Messiah, the Son of God. In other biographies, whether modern or ancient, the reader naturally cares about the deeds and character of the subject. But one does not generally read a biography considering whether the person might be more than human.[31] But it is precisely the reality of Jesus as God's "only begotten" Son that sets him apart from any other great thinker, leader, prophet, or religious man about which a *bios* would have been written. Bookending Matthew's emphasis on the consummating role of Jesus in salvation history is John's clearly stated purpose in writing, "that you may believe that Jesus is the Christ, the Son of God, and that believing you may have life in his name" (20:31). Again, this claim goes far beyond that of the model of virtue or teacher of universal truths, though it does not exclude those.

On this score it is interesting and important to note how different the Gospels are in comparison to contemporary Jewish documents. The two siblings that are born out of the Second Temple period and especially the aftermath of the destruction of temple-based Judaism in AD 70 are rabbinic Judaism and Christianity. Both produce writings and traditions, and overlap can be found between the teachings of Jesus and Paul and those of various rabbis. But they stand apart in a striking way: the rabbinic tradition never produces a biography, especially four lengthy ones, about any of its leaders or wise men. Several scholars have wrestled with this issue, especially the renowned Jewish scholar Jacob Neusner, who has addressed the question in several books. He notes that while the Talmuds "present stories about sages, neither one contains anything we might call a 'gospel' of a sage or even a chapter of a gospel."[32] The reason for this is strikingly clear and significant. As Neusner remarks, "*Sage-stories turn out not to tell about sages at all; they are stories about the Torah personified*. Sage-stories cannot yield a gospel because they are not about sages anyway. They are about the Torah. . . . The gospel does just the opposite, with its focus on the uniqueness of the hero."[33] Philip Alexander likewise observes that for rabbinic Judaism the center was Torah, but for Christianity the center was clearly the person of Jesus.[34] Thus, for rabbinic Judaism what matters is the teaching of Torah. But for the Gospels and for Christianity, while the teaching of Jesus is certainly very important, what makes him stand apart is his person by nature. Speaking of Matthew but equally applicable to all the Gospels, Dale Allison remarks that "for Matthew, revelation belongs supremely to a life. . . . The substance of Matthew's faith is neither a dogmatic system nor a legal code but a human being whose

---

31. Though it should be noted that Suetonius's *On the Life of the Caesars* (ca. AD 121) makes claims that certainly tend this way!

32. Jacob Neusner, *The Incarnation of God: The Character of Divinity in Formative Judaism* (Philadelphia: Fortress, 1988), 213, quoted in Burridge, *What Are the Gospels?* 302.

33. Jacob Neusner, *Why No Gospels in Talmudic Judaism?* (Atlanta: Scholars Press, 1988), 52–53, italics in original, quoted in Burridge, *What Are the Gospels?* 303.

34. Philip Alexander, "Rabbinic Biography and the Biography of Jesus," *ZNW* 74 (1983): 41.

life is, in outline and detail, uniquely significant and demanding of record."[35] This sentiment is often echoed in the Gospels in the astonished question of those who encountered Jesus, "Who is this man?" (e.g., Mark 4:41). And it appears shockingly in places such as the Sermon on the Mount, where Jesus does not just call people back to Torah obedience like a good prophet would but instead presents his message in contrast to Torah—"You have heard that it was said. . . . But I say to you . . ." (Matt. 5:21–48). One cannot read the New Testament and get the sense that Jesus is being presented as just another great teacher or prophet; the New Testament documents, in contrast to rabbinic Judaism (and also a collection of sayings such as the Gospel of Thomas), are making ontological claims.

Fourth, we may also note the related idea that in the Gospels, unlike other biographies or histories, Jesus is presented not as just a great figure of the past but as "a figure who is still our contemporary."[36] With several weighty promises (e.g., Matt. 10:40; 18:20; 28:20; John 15:4), Jesus emphasizes that he will continually be with his disciples, even after his death. This is intimately connected with his divine nature and is the means through which God himself fulfills his promise to be with his people. It is no accident that Matthew begins in 1:23 by ascribing to Jesus the name Emmanuel—"God is with us"—and then concludes with Jesus promising, "I am with you always, to the close of the age" (28:20). The conviction of the apostles is that Jesus the Christ is no longer dead but is alive again. The expectation of the evangelists is that through their Gospels believers can experience the risen Christ. One can read a memoir of Socrates and learn great things, grow in wisdom, and gain insights into reality, but in no way does an ancient biography present that person as still alive for us and as a living and abiding voice with us.

Finally, interwoven with what we have already said, we must note the soteriological declarations coming forth from the Gospels. These biographies of Jesus not only present him as the culmination of history, as ontologically distinct, and as still alive (as if that were not enough!), but they each also clearly point to the salvific effect of Jesus's life, death, and resurrection. Many ancient biographies concentrate on the hero's last days and even last words; how one dies is often seen as a revelation of one's character. This is no less true for the Gospels, which are each heavily weighted toward the last week of Jesus's life.[37] The Gospels yet again stand apart from other ancient biographies, however, in that they focus on Jesus's death not only to present his

---

35. Dale C. Allison Jr., *Studies in Matthew* (Grand Rapids: Baker Academic, 2005), 144.

36. Nolland, *Gospel of Matthew*, 20.

37. This is not difficult to discern from a cursory reading of the Gospels and is one of the distinct things that the Synoptic tradition shares with John. Burridge's analysis of how much space the Gospels allocate to Jesus's passion and resurrection confirms this. For Matthew: 15.1 percent; Mark: 19.1 percent; Luke: 15.6 percent; John: 15.7 percent. Burridge, *What Are the Gospels?* 191–92, 218.

character and his model of virtue while suffering (though this is *one* of the goals, as can be seen in this kind of reading of the Jesus traditions in 1 Pet. 2:21–3:2), but also to claim that Jesus's death and resurrection make available to us forgiveness of sins and deliverance from coming wrath (e.g., Matt. 1:21; 26:28; Mark 10:45; Luke 24:46–47; John 6:40; 11:25; 20:30–31). This is *good news*, not just a biography![38] Thus, more than any history or biography, the Gospels have a message to preach; they are kerygmatic, not *merely* exemplary. Both the exemplary nature of Jesus's death (typical of *bioi*) and its salvific effect (atypical) are wedded together in the apostolic witness, and what God has joined let no man put asunder. No better example of this is found than in 1 Peter 2:18–24, which exhorts the reader both to follow Jesus's example in not returning insult for insult *and* at the same time to hope in Jesus, who "bore our sins in his body on the tree" (v. 24).

Implications of This Genre Identification

Having explored the ways in which the Gospels are both like ancient biographies and also particularly their own, we are now in a position to ask what implications this genre discussion might have for our reading and interpretation of the Gospels. The original hearers and readers, assuming they had some degree of literary competency, would have shared a set of expectations, even if the Gospels stretched and extended the *bios* genre in new, more theological ways. Ancient readers would have detected such differences precisely because of their understanding of these narratives as some sort of historical biography. For us, as readers whose genre conventions may differ from those of ancient writers and readers, it is beneficial to articulate what those differences may be so that we will read the Gospels "along the grain" of the authors.

There are four main ways in which understanding the Gospels as theological historical biography should affect our reading. First, we should note that calling the Gospels "biographies" should not imply that they are identical to our current genre of a modern biography. This crucial difference between ancient and modern biographies is why we often refer to the Greco-Roman biographies as *bioi*, to help maintain this difference and prevent confusion. What are the differences? Regarding structure, ancient biographies often mix chronological and topical elements in a way that we may not expect. Because the sources were mostly oral and these traditions had existed for some time

---

38. Hengel observes the odd construction of the Gospels' titles relative to other ancient biographies. Rather than having the author's name followed by the title, such as *Philostratou bioi sophistōn* ("the biographies of the wise by Philostratus"), the Gospels are instead presented as being handed down through a particular witness (*euangelion kata. . .*). Hengel remarks that "the unusual titles of the Gospels already indicate that the evangelists are not meant to appear as 'biographical' authors like others but to bear witness in their works to the one saving message of Jesus Christ." Hengel, *Four Gospels*, 48–49, here 49.

before the Gospels were written, flexibility in how each evangelist composed the various stories and sayings of Jesus was inevitable. This is easily borne out by reading a synopsis of the Gospels. Although each follows a basic chronological outline (John the Baptist as forerunner; Jesus's ministry and increasing opposition by the Jewish leaders; final entry into Jerusalem; passion, death, and resurrection), there is considerable variation in where certain stories occur, and there are clear topical collections as well (especially obvious in Matthew's five major discourses). Also, in the pre–tape recorder ancient world, it was expected that the words of characters would often be paraphrases.[39] To accurately present a *bios* of a great character meant to accurately present the *ipsissima vox* ("the exact voice") of the hero, if not always the *ipsissima verba* ("the exact words"). Finally, we may also note that, unlike ancient biographies, modern biographies often focus on both the sensory details of the story and the interior person, his or her feelings and psychological development. As Mark Allan Powell observes, however, the Gospels give little physical description or sensory information. If a Gospel were written today, we would likely read about the "waves lapping at the shore of the Sea of Galilee" and the feel of "course dry sand trod underfoot in the Judean desert."[40] One finds little to nothing of this sort in the Gospels. This is one of the factors that has made modern readers either look down upon the Gospels as undeveloped narrative or rewrite them in more modernly engaging ways.[41] Similarly, action in the Gospels (as in folktales) is always public. That is, there are no narrative breaks to the characters' internal dialogue nor are there descriptions of a character's emotional wrestling or the effect of an event on the person's psyche. Rather, "the action proceeds through a series of encounters between the hero and the groups or individuals with whom he interacts, and it is through these public interactions that his personality is defined."[42]

In reality, however, these differences between ancient biographies and modern ones are often more perceived than real. This is not to say there aren't differences but to observe that even in modern biographies one finds much more chronological and topical arrangement and paraphrasing of speech and situations than the modern, positivist historicist would have us believe. When I consider some of the fine biographies I have read in recent years, such as George Marsden on Jonathan Edwards, Walter Isaacson on Albert Einstein, or John D'Elia on George Eldon Ladd, these works often digress into topical

---

39. Craig Keener, *The Historical Jesus of the Gospels* (Grand Rapids: Eerdmans, 2009), 110.

40. Mark Allan Powell, *What Is Narrative Criticism?* (Minneapolis; Fortress, 1990), 71, quoted in Alexander, "What Is a Gospel?" 18.

41. Although I am certainly not opposed to film or literary retellings of the Gospel accounts, we should observe that they do function quite differently than our canonical Gospels, and the modern reader must be wary of preferring such re-creations over and supplanting the fourfold witness.

42. Alexander, "What Is a Gospel?" 18.

discussions and discuss events backward and forward in time to create a coherent and interpreted narrative.

A second way our genre identification affects our expectations for reading the Gospels is closely related to what we have just discussed, concerning the question of history. We will address this issue fully in a subsequent chapter, but we should note its importance here. In short, ancient historians did not fool themselves as modern ones often have by proclaiming their disinterested objectivity to present things simply "as they really happened" ("*wie es eigentlich gewesen*," in Leopold von Ranke's famous and programmatic expression). Ancient biographers and historians valued interested, involved witnesses[43] and consciously wrote for polemical, apologetic, and hortatory reasons. With that in mind, we should be sensitive to these purposes in reading the Gospels, not viewing them as mere clear-glass windows on the events behind the text, but receiving and listening to them as intentional and personally invested interpretations of the events.[44] In reality, as in the case of biography, modern historians are doing the same even though some strands of modern historiography would present themselves as free from such goals. Again, we shall return to this important topic subsequently.

The third way in which our genre identification benefits our reading is again related to the preceding discussion: ancient biographies, such as the Gospels, very consciously present their character *as one to be emulated*. We have touched on this previously and will return to it in the context of the virtue formation goal of the Gospels. The effect of this insight into our genre expectations for the Gospels is, I hope, clear: If the goal of the evangelists is (at least in part) to present Jesus as a model of God-ward virtue, then we should receive them as such, keeping this goal as an important part of what it means to interpret the Gospels and to read them well. This will prove to be a major difference between earlier Christian readings of Scripture and what developed during the Enlightenment. It is one of the reasons why much modern "historical-critical" or even "grammatical-historical" exegesis, whether done by the most liberal liberal or the most fundamental fundamentalist, can be so flat and off the mark; it misses this foundational aspect of biographies—they are written so that people will desire to follow the model of the main character. Any interpretation of the Gospels that neglects this aspect is missing a major function of the genre. As a side note, it is important to clarify that this modeling and virtue-forming aspect of our biographical Gospels is not to be understood apart from faith in Christ. That is, the Gospels make clear that their mega-purpose is to elicit believing response (especially seen in the

43. Cf. Richard Bauckham, *Jesus and the Eyewitnesses* (Grand Rapids: Eerdmans, 2008). See the fuller discussion of this in chap. 5.

44. As Hengel remarks on Mark (and by extension, on all the Gospels), whether done by fundamentalists or modernists, "any 'historicist' interpretation which seeks to construct it 'as it really was' misses his [Mark's] theological intention." Hengel, *Four Gospels*, 89.

programmatic statement of John 20:31). This is the foundation of following and cannot be neglected. But many readers today understand this aspect without appreciating the disciple-making, virtue-forming emphasis that is a function of the Gospels as *bioi*.

The fourth and final way our expectations for reading should be affected is closely related to the others. Simply, we should come to the Gospel narratives as we do to a sermon; they are to be treated not as mere conveyors of (historical or doctrinal) information but as instruments of transformation. We have already hinted at this by speaking of the Gospels as presenting virtue models to be emulated, but we can now push this even a bit further. Augustine famously claimed that unless our reading results in greater love for God and neighbor we have not truly understood the Scriptures. This certainly applies to the Gospels. Because the stories that the Gospels tell concern someone who is more than human, who is the epicenter of history, who is the harbinger of a new creation, and who is the source of salvation, to read the Gospels well is to submit to their proclamation. As Hengel remarks, a great mistake in scholarship has been to "tear apart and play off each other" the historical narration and the kerygma of the Gospels. "From the beginning the proclamation of Jesus Christ and narratives about him were inseparably associated. One could not 'preach' Jesus as the crucified Messiah and Son of God who had been raised . . . without telling his story."[45] So, contra the reading habits of many, the Gospels are not *supplements* to the message about Christ (found, for example, in Paul); rather they are the kerygma or proclamation itself. The message of salvation is necessarily a historical narrative. Therefore, the Gospels are to be read, at least in part, as proclaimed, exhortational sermons. While they are in genre ancient *bioi*, as a "saving event" they are incomparable. "Ordinary biographies do not contain a message of faith which is decisive for eternal life and the last judgment. That is what is completely new about the 'genre' Gospel."[46] This is certainly right. As discussed above, we must not forget that the Gospels are making a claim and call to faith response. They are a proclamation.

Conclusion

Bringing our discussion of the first two chapters to a close we may ask again, what are the Gospels? After our exploration of the origin and usage of the *euangelion* word group, I proposed that for the New Testament authors the "gospel" is the proclamation of Jesus's fulfillment of the promised return of the reign or kingdom of God. We have seen that this oral apostolic proclamation naturally and understandably is eventually written down, and the result

45. Ibid., 86.
46. Ibid., 266.

is our canonical Gospel, given to us in its fourfold narrative form, or as we say today, the Gospel*s*.

Our investigation of the genre of the Gospels strengthens and extends this definition. We have discovered that this written form of the Gospel is both comparable to ancient biographies and goes beyond them in significant theological ways. Leaning on Burridge but casting our glance to a wider biblical context, we should think of the Gospels as "*bioi* plus" or, more fully, "eschatological kerygmatic biblical historical biographies." This latter mouthful is admittedly more detailed than catchy, so I will allow the reader to make his or her choice of moniker.

Putting all this together, conscious of the intended effect of the Gospels, I may now offer a fuller definition. Our canonical Gospels are the *theological, historical, and aretological (virtue-forming)[47] biographical narratives that retell the story and proclaim the significance of Jesus Christ, who through the power of the Spirit is the Restorer of God's reign.*[48] This definition is admittedly heavy with thick adjectives that beg for further explanation. Each of these adjectives is indeed vitally important for our reading of the Gospels as Holy Scripture. There are many aspects of this definition that yet need to be proven and explored. The subsequent chapters will seek to do just this.

47. It is important to note that I am using this term, which stems from the Greek word *aretas*, to mean simply a type of literature that has an explicit goal of inculcating particular virtues in its hearers. I am not using it in the sense of some scholars in the twentieth century who referred to the Gospels as "aretology," meaning accounts contrived to provide a model for a martyred leader or in connection with other ancient miracle-worker or divine-man (*theios aner*) stories. For an explanation of this blip on the radar of twentieth-century interpretation, one may consult the discussion in E. J. Epp and G. W. MacRae, eds., *The New Testament and Its Modern Interpreters* (Atlanta: Scholars Press, 1989), 253–54.

48. Mark Strauss's introductory textbook describes the Gospels under three headings—historical literature, narrative literature, and theological literature—and sums them up as "historical narrative motivated by theological concerns." This corresponds in many ways to my own definition, though I am particularly emphasizing the virtue-forming aspect and a trinitarian framework; I will also push some elements of this definition in new ways. Mark Strauss, *Four Portraits, One Jesus: An Introduction to Jesus and the Gospels* (Grand Rapids: Zondervan, 2007), 27–29.

3

Why Do We Need the Gospels?

(Or Why Saint Paul Is Not Enough)

A Case of Benign Neglect

I must begin with a confession: I haven't always liked the Gospels. For many years, including during some of my seminary training and while first serving as a pastor, I was not at all interested in the Gospels. I don't think I would have *said* I didn't like them, but my lack of interest in the Gospels was manifested by how little time I really spent teaching or preaching from them. It was a case of benign neglect that revealed my lack of true affection.

I think this was so for several reasons. First, I had never been exposed much to the Gospels. The churches I went to didn't preach much from or talk much about them. We talked and preached about "the gospel," which we defined as the forgiveness of sins available through Jesus's death and resurrection, but curiously "the Gospels" didn't fit much into that; rather, we got it from Paul.

I was also not much interested in the Gospels because the way I was taught to study them during my education was unfortunately rather dry and lifeless. I am sure my memory does not do full justice to my professor's intentions or skills. Nevertheless, not without *some* justification, my impression of what it meant to study the Gospels consisted of detailed notes on how the different Gospel accounts overlapped or differed from one another, discovered through hours dedicated to colored-pencil underlining of my Gospels synopsis. This primarily source critical and redaction critical approach to the Gospels was very erudite but not very exhilarating. It was scientific and helpful in some

36

ways but not very engaging nor clearly theological. As we jumped from one pericope (separate story units) to another, always cross-referencing the accounts, we never got a sense of the beauty and wonder and power with which each evangelist composed and wove the tapestry of his own story. So I left my Gospels class pretty uninterested.

But I think the main reason I was never much interested in the Gospels is because I didn't know what to do with them. For Protestants, especially evangelicals, especially Reformed, doctrine-oriented ones, we love Paul. Give us Romans and thirteen years to preach through it phrase by phrase, and we'll be in heaven! We love chewy, heady doctrine—wrestling with election, justification, sanctification. We know doctrine is important, and we know the Bible makes claims about theology and how we ought to live, so we love Paul. He's a straight shooter; he nails it on the head; he lays out the truth in powerful and straightforward ways. He provides a clear map of the theological landscape and the moral path for our lives.

But the Gospels? Well, certainly it is nice to see Jesus in action, taking down the Pharisees, doing cool water-walking miracles and all, but sometimes his teaching is confusing. We have all these parables, which are open to so many interpretations and are even (gasp!) allegorical at times. Take the parable of the workers in the vineyard (Matt. 20:1–16). What does this mean? Is the doctrinal point that there won't be different levels of reward in heaven? Or is this a parable about salvation history—the different stages of people coming into the kingdom? Or is it a word of assurance that even if you become a Christian at the end of your life, you're still just as good and valued as Hudson Taylor or Dietrich Bonhoeffer? Or does it mean something else? And what about that Sermon on the Mount—you're blessed if you're poor, persecuted, and merciful? How do I even begin to relate that to my experience as a middle-class, unpersecuted American evangelical? How can Jesus say that if we don't forgive others, we won't be forgiven (Matt. 6:14–15)? How does that fit into justification by faith? And what does it mean that our righteousness needs to surpass the righteousness of the Pharisees? Where does that fit into what we teach on Sunday about the gift of righteousness from God?

I thought this Christianity thing was nice and simple as I had read in Romans—we're sinners; we're forgiven and justified by faith in Jesus! Get the abstract concept. End of story. Believe that, and don't engage in premarital sex. Right? That's Christianity, we sometimes think. But in contrast, the Gospels just don't seem easy to interpret and transfer to others.

Another problem is how we are supposed to apply Gospel stories to our lives. Are we supposed to do just what Jesus did? WWJD to the max: What would he drink? Where would he dine? What would (eco-friendly) Jesus drive? Additionally, those with some training in hermeneutics will wave us off the Gospels runway because of the all-important principle that narratives are "descriptive," not "prescriptive." And going even further, for some believers of a particular theological persuasion, the use of the Gospels must especially be curtailed because this is all pre-Pentecost, pre-church, and so really of a different era or dispensation.

Some might respond that the Gospels do at least show us how Jesus was a master teacher, a man of the people who used simple stories to reach the average layman in the (grassy hillside) pew. But what does this mean when we realize that Jesus's purpose in using parables is stated to be quite the opposite? We see in the Gospels that the disciples almost always misunderstood what the parables meant (e.g., Matt. 13:10, 36; 16:5–12), and even more strongly, Jesus himself states that he taught in parables so that many would *not* understand (Matt. 13:10–17)!

"No," we cry, "just give me straight-shooter Paul and tell me what to believe and what to do. Lay out for me what the truth is, what I'm supposed to do and not do, and let me at it; I'll do it seriously and work hard at it."

Admittedly, I am being a bit facetious and hyperbolic. My early attitude toward the Gospels was certainly not all bad, nor is it, I think, for most people in the church. Nonetheless, I suspect that many readers can resonate at least in part with my experience. And I think most readers will admit to being somewhat at a loss in terms of how to handle the Gospels and how they relate to the apparently more straightforward Paul. Most of us may think of the Gospels as beneficial because they give us some nice images about Jesus and his teaching, but when it comes to doctrinal formulation and day-to-day living, most of us probably tend to prefer the letters of Paul and the rest of the New Testament.[1]

So, why do we need the Gospels? If Paul and the other apostles give us both right doctrine and, stemming from this, right moral principles, why mess with the interpretively messy Gospels? Why isn't Saint Paul enough? In many ways, the goal of this whole book is to answer this question. My desire is to ignite a flame of interest in studying and preaching from the Gospels and reading them well as Holy Scripture. But in this chapter in particular, which is part of our cornerstones section, we can articulate a number of ways in which a steady consumption of the Gospels is an essential part of a complete and nutritious spiritual diet. We need Saint Paul, but he's not enough, nor would he want to be.

Nine Reasons We Need the Gospels

First, we need to study the Gospels because *they have been central to the church throughout its history*. Much of the church's prayers, liturgy, and vision

---

1. Eugene Lemcio notes the same. He observes that very few Christian hymns (and we could add, other contemporary Christian music) have any reference to Jesus's life. Additionally, even among "Bible-believing Christians" the Gospels are "dramatically underrepresented or highly censored." Eugene E. Lemcio, "The Gospels within the New Testament Canon," in *Canon and Biblical Interpretation*, ed. Craig Bartholomew et al. (Grand Rapids: Zondervan, 2006), 125.

have come from the Tetraevangelium, the fourfold Gospel book. This is still the case in many branches of Christendom, especially those that include in their services regular lectionary readings and homilies from the Gospels. The problem I have described above is primarily one within conservative Protestantism with its desire for superdoctrine. This is where Paul most usually supplants Jesus and the Gospels. While living in Britain and attending Anglican services, I remember being struck by the weekly confession of the first and second greatest commandments according to Jesus, coming straight from the Gospels (Matt. 22:36–40), a central text that I had never heard regularly in church. Likewise, lectionary readings from the Gospels played a central role, especially in the Scottish liturgy, where they stand apart even from the other readings. It is a somewhat disturbing reflection that these things in a worship service would strike me as odd!

In many ways the loss of emphasis on the Gospels is a function of a reductionism of the Protestant Reformation, especially in some Lutheran versions that run all Scripture through a hypersensitive law versus gospel grid. The result of this paradigmatic grid is a desire for clearer justification doctrine than the narrative Gospels allow. Thus, the Gospels are often downplayed. I don't fully blame this on Luther nor do I claim that this was necessarily the practice of the Reformers themselves or all their subsequent adherents. But movements over time always get dehydrated and reduced down to a bouillon-cube state so that they can be easily transferred and promulgated. The first thing to go is always nuance and balance. Thus, in much of evangelicalism, which at times is quite polemical and which prides itself on being the heir of the Reformation, the Gospels' narrative ambiguity is less than preferred, and the result has been their neglect. But the model and history of the church's practice testifies to a problem with this approach. In the final chapter of this book I will offer a full historical, theological, and canonical argument for the central role of the Gospels in the church's life.

A second reason we need the Gospels is because *Paul and the other New Testament writers presuppose and build on the story and teaching of Jesus.* The story of Jesus and his teachings form the basis for the preaching of the gospel in the early church. We may recall the arguments from chapter 1, in which we saw that the oral gospel proclaimed by the apostles (namely, the restoration of God's reign through Christ) is the same gospel in written form via the evangelists. We may also mention what we know of the early churches' worship experience, namely, the role that the stories about Jesus (what we may call the Jesus traditions) played. By the time of Justin Martyr, our written Gospels already formed the core of the Scripture-reading portion of a Christian gathering: "And on the day called Sunday, all who live in cities or in the country gather together to one place, and the memoirs of the apostles or the writings of the prophets are read, as long as time permits; then, when the reader has ceased, the president verbally instructs, and exhorts to the imitation of these good things" (*First Apology* 67.3).[2]

This must have been the case as well before our four Gospels became widely disseminated. That is, both in oral and written form the stories of what Jesus did and said were certainly widely known and highly regarded. Luke makes as much clear by referring in his prologue to the "many [who] have undertaken to compile a narrative" (1:1). This is in addition to the many oral traditions that obviously existed, going back to the time when Jesus was yet alive on earth; news about Jesus's deeds spread so far and fast that he soon had trouble entering any town.

This very reasonable description of the role of the Jesus traditions in the earliest church and the apostles' kerygma is unfortunately not something that is usually understood or clearly articulated today. Many believers, especially those in the Protestant tradition who avow adherence to the "expository sermon," unknowingly assume that our contemporary experience of the centrality of the Epistles in preaching and worship has always been the case. But much evidence can be produced that in fact the Jesus traditions served as the bread and butter of early Christian proclamation. Second place would go to the Jewish Scriptures, probably especially the prophetic writings that point (and were used to point) to Jesus as the promised Messiah.[3] The latter would likely prove especially important in Jewish dialogue and polemical situations, such as those in which the apostle Paul regularly involved himself. His scrolls and his notebooks (2 Tim. 4:13)[4] were valued because of the kind of synagogue-based evangelism he frequently engaged in (cf. descriptions of his activities in Acts 9:20; 13:5, 14; 14:1; etc.). In due time Paul's own writings would also be read, first in the original congregations to whom they were addressed, but likely soon afterward also in other cities' churches.[5] But to think that these specific, occasional documents soon did (or should) replace the Jesus traditions themselves (now canonized in the Gospels) makes little sense.

Contributing to this confusion is readers' sense that very little of the actual stories about Jesus is found in the Epistles. This can lead one unconsciously (or consciously) to think of the Gospels as merely data about Jesus now to be

2. Roberts-Donaldson translation. On this passage in Justin and how it relates to the use of the Gospels in the early church, see chap. 12 of this volume.

3. Note again Justin's description of the reading of the Gospels and the prophets, here certainly referring to the OT Scriptures. Cf. Stanton, *Jesus and Gospel* (Cambridge: Cambridge University Press, 2004), 99–100.

4. These notebooks were very possibly small codices containing proof texts of "faithful sayings" from OT passages and/or even Jesus traditions. See the fascinating discussion of this development in Graham Stanton, "The Early Reception of Matthew's Gospel: New Evidence from Papyri?" in *The Gospel of Matthew in Current Study: Studies in Memory of William G. Thompson, S.J.*, ed. David Aune (Grand Rapids: Eerdmans, 2001), 53–61.

5. For one explanation of how Paul's writings came to be collected and read widely, see David Trobisch, *Paul's Letter Collection: Tracing the Origins* (Minneapolis: Fortress, 1994).

discarded (in practice, if not in theory) in favor of the authorized theological and moral application of them in the rest of the New Testament. We might be able to think of a few cases where references to Jesus's teachings and his actual life (and not just his death and resurrection) crop up in the Epistles, but the fact that they are few and not more obvious is rather conspicuous. There are really only two ways of explaining why the Jesus traditions don't appear more frequently in the Epistles. One is that the apostles (or at least Paul) rejected them, and we have instead a new, christological, postresurrection, and post-Pentecost Christianity based on propositional theology and/or Paul's mystical experience of the risen Christ. This is the belief of some scholars of the past few generations, namely, that what we see in the New Testament is a disjunction between Jesus and Paul; Jesus came preaching the kingdom, and Paul created the church instead. This kind of approach has been famously promulgated by heavyweight scholar Rudolf Bultmann, who was wont to quote 2 Corinthians 5:16 as evidence of his view: "From now on, therefore, we regard no one from a human point of view; even though we once regarded Christ from a human point of view, we regard him thus no longer." This claim founders on several fronts, including the poor exegesis of this particular verse as well as the obvious fact that the Gospels themselves are no less postresurrection and post-Pentecost than the Epistles!

Nevertheless, while most readers of this book and those who receive the Gospels as Holy Scripture would not adhere to this radical and unorthodox view, its ghost still haunts in a milder version. That is, it lingers in the practice that privileges the Epistles over the Gospels, usually out of habit more than thoughtfulness. This is yet another version of the Jesus-versus-Paul interpretation.

The other interpretation of this lack of Jesus traditions in the Epistles, however, is quite different. Instead of seeing the Epistles as separate from the Jesus traditions, we do better to understand that underneath the Epistles is the assumption of the Jesus traditions on the part of both the writers and the readers. In fact, the tools of intertextuality are now helping us see that the Jesus traditions actually do appear quite regularly in the Epistles, even though they are rarely quoted and are usually found at the more subtle but no less significant level of allusion and echo.[6] Indeed, one important fact that must be remembered when dealing with times and cultures different from our own, and with no living and abiding voice with whom to dialogue, is that the

---

6. Many good resources that are useful for further exploring this topic have appeared over the last few decades, including David Dungan, *The Sayings of Jesus in the Churches of Paul: The Use of the Synoptic Tradition in the Regulation of Early Church Life* (Philadelphia: Fortress, 1971); and David Wenham, *Paul: Follower of Jesus or Founder of Christianity?* (Grand Rapids: Eerdmans, 1995). On the intertextual use of the Jesus traditions in Paul, one good place to start is Michael Thompson, *Clothed with Christ: The Example and Teaching of Jesus in Romans 12:1–15:13* (Sheffield: JSOT Press, 1991).

most assumed and often most important things are *not* stated in discourse between people. That is, the Epistles were originally written into specific, occasional situations requiring particular information and exhortation, and therefore the most agreed upon and mutually understood elements—such as the Jesus traditions—are *not* explicitly discussed. This is not at all to diminish the abiding canonical value of the Epistles, but to observe that there is much more *not* said in the Epistles than there is said, particularly, often, the basic information about what Jesus said and did. His sayings and deeds are *applied* and *explained* in the Epistles more than explicitly stated.

The point, then, is that although it may not be immediately apparent, in reality it is the Jesus traditions, later codified into the Gospels, that are presupposed in all the apostolic kerygma, including the specific, written applications of this in the Epistles. One implication of this, I would suggest, is that we cannot truly understand Paul's or Peter's or James's doctrine or teaching without reading them through the lens of the Gospels. All the later teaching and pronouncements from the apostles assume and build on the Jesus traditions. We shall return to this important idea in our concluding chapter.

Third, another, closely related reason we need a healthy diet of the Gospels is because although the *written* form of the Gospels is subsequent to most of the Epistles, *the traditions behind them* are not; they go back to the time of Jesus himself and the immediately following years, passed down through oral (and eventually written) repetition. This point is related to the previous one but serves a different purpose, specifically, to respond to those who would value the oldest or earliest Christian proclamations (supposedly the Epistles) as if these were somehow necessarily superior to the later-written Gospels. At a general level, this developmental view that the oldest is necessarily better is patently naive, for movements, ideas, and cultures not only progress but often digress and even regress. Moreover, equally naive is the assumption driving much of modern historicism, that proximity to events is somehow better. As has been observed, only with the passage of time can many historical occurrences or ideas be truly understood, as their ramifications unfold.[7] Proximity is no guarantor of perception. We can see this already in the case of Jesus's disciples, who, during their historical proximity to Jesus while he was alive, understood very little of what he was saying and doing, but later, upon reflection and revelation, the significance of his words was clearer.

I do not grant that technically "older" writings such as the Epistles would necessarily be superior to "later" ones such as the Gospels. To those who hold this view, we may respond that in fact it is the Jesus traditions that can claim historical proximity over the Epistles, in many cases by twenty-five years or more. Thus if one is tempted to take a purely chronological view, that person

---

7. This insight, found in Gadamer and others, is argued recently in Peter J. Leithart, *Deep Exegesis: The Mystery of Reading Scripture* (Waco: Baylor University Press, 2009), 40–52.

might want to begin "New Testament theology" with Galatians or 1 Thessalonians. My point, however, is that one cannot understand Galatians or Thessalonians or any of the apostolic witness without recognizing that they come to us in the historical and theological context of the Jesus traditions, which were already disseminated throughout the church. It is the teaching and life of Jesus as recorded in the Gospels that formed the entire mind-set and framework for what the New Testament authors preached and wrote.

A fourth reason we need the Gospels is that *in them we get a more direct sense of the Bible's great story line.* It is essential we realize that the message of the New Testament does not come to us in a vacuum but is the focal point of the great story of the Bible. The apostles understand that their proclamation is not just something new but is the consummation of something old—as old as creation itself. There is, of course, the ancient story of God's dealings with humanity that begins with Adam and Eve and includes important turns with Abraham, Moses, David, and the prophets. This is the "theology" of Israel—it is a narrative that creates their identity. We must understand that this story continues into the New Testament and that the New Testament continues to be a story. The entire Bible's theology is at its core a narrative of God's work in the world from creation to new creation.

Even those who recognize the predominantly narrative nature of the Old Testament often assume—consciously or unconsciously—that story time is over, children, and now "doctrine and truth" have arrived. C. S. Lewis, J. R. R. Tolkien, and countless others have shown us that the supposed "maturation" of moving from childlike stories to abstract thinking is only cutting oneself off from being fully human and alive to the greatest truths and mysteries.[8]

Rather, the scriptural revelation is of a great story—the story of stories—from Genesis to Revelation. This is not to say that every part of Holy Scripture is narrative. There are, thankfully, doctrinal, doxological, poetical, and proverbial parts, riches untold and a full smorgasbord to satisfy the pickiest and hungriest of guests. But there is a discernible overarching metanarrative that spans from the forming of heaven and earth (Gen. 1) to their reuniting (Rev. 21).

More than any other place in Holy Scripture, the Gospels manifest, highlight, and explain this story. The Gospel narratives are the perfect combination of story recapitulating story (telling Jesus's stories in ways that intentionally evoke and complete older stories) and theological and exhortational application in story form. The grand story of Scripture is to be found in the Epistles, but it is not as easy to see and sense there as it is in the Gospels.

8. Some helpful essays that address this topic include Lewis's "Sometimes Fairy Stories May Say Best What's to Be Said" and "On Three Ways of Writing for Children," in *On Stories and Other Essays on Literature*, ed. Walter Hooper (New York: Harcourt Brace Jovanovich, 1982). Also very well known and influential is Tolkien's essay "On Fairy-Stories," which can be found in his book *Tree and Leaf* (London: Allen & Unwin, 1964).

Closely related to the preceding point, the fifth benefit of the Gospels is that *they offer a concentrated exposure to the biblical emphasis on the coming kingdom of God*. The grand story of Scripture can be described as the message of the restoration of God's reign from heaven to earth, spanning from creation to new creation.[9] This is precisely why in Isaiah and the New Testament *euangelion* is such an appropriate description: this is a royal announcement of royally good news.

Yet again, this emphasis on the gospel as the inauguration of the consummation of God's reign ("already but not yet") can be found throughout the New Testament, including in the Epistles. It finds its greatest concentration, however, in the Gospel accounts. In the Gospels like nowhere else in the Bible, we receive a foretaste of the coming kingdom of God. This is stated explicitly and constantly through Jesus's teaching, which he says is a message about the kingdom, as well as implicitly through his ministry of healing. As we observed in our earlier discussion of the meaning of "gospel," Jesus is presented in the Gospels as fulfilling the Isaianic promise of the restoration of all things (see especially Isa. 61 in Luke 4). This is a promise not only of a new covenantal relationship and the forgiveness of sins but also, intimately related, a promise of binding up brokenness, setting the crooked straight, and healing all disease. Jesus performs innumerable acts of such healing and restoration not merely because he is compassionate or to apologetically prove that he really is a special one sent from God, but rather primarily because they are pictures of the promised kingdom that is to come. They are like our mother's secret gift of a piece of turkey breast in the kitchen before the anticipated Thanksgiving feast that is soon coming.

In the Gospels we see a glimpse of the King in action—restoring to health those in need, binding up the brokenhearted, welcoming the suffering, exalting the weak and humble, and giving joyful awe by his very presence. The Gospels beautifully give us not just truths but images of the kingdom of God that is to come. Next to the Gospels, the closest comparable part of the New Testament that does the same is John's Apocalypse, a book that does indeed overlap the Gospels significantly. The book of Revelation functions to provide a glimpse behind the veil into the true nature of things and the future so that we are energized and resourced to live now in light of that reality. So too in the Gospels. They provide a rich and full panoply of narrative images of hope.

Sixth, we need the Gospels because *there are different languages or discourses of truth*. Propositional doctrine, whether it be in the Westminster Confession or a local Baptist church's bylaws, is one crucial and necessary

---

9. Although this description is mine, I am happy to acknowledge the influence on my thinking of Craig Bartholomew and Michael Goheen, *The Drama of Scripture: Finding Our Place in the Biblical Story* (Grand Rapids: Baker Academic, 2004); and Al Wolters, *Creation Regained: Biblical Basics for a Reformational Worldview*, 2nd ed. (Grand Rapids: Eerdmans, 2005).

discourse of truth, but it is not the only one. Story or narrative is another equally valid way of presenting and approaching truth.

Kevin Vanhoozer discusses this and suggests that we think of different ways of speaking truth as different kinds of maps that we use.[10] For example, for Jefferson County, Kentucky, where I live, we could look at a topographical map that shows terrain and elevations or a road map; at a map that records annual rainfall or one that indicates historical landmarks and points of scenic interest; or we could consult a survey that shows where property lines begin and end. These are all different maps, and they would look very different if set beside one another. But of course they don't contradict one another. They are complementary and beneficial. They are different discourses of truth—or different ways of approaching and presenting knowledge.

If this is true for maps of Jefferson County, Kentucky, how much more for theology and Holy Scripture. We need to think of the Bible not as a single map that just gives us doctrinal statements or moral commands, but we must realize that the Bible is like an atlas—a collection of maps/books that shows us the way, the truth, and the life but in a variety of languages or discourses or ways of communicating. To privilege—or worse, to rely exclusively on—only one form is detrimental to apprehending truth; a topographical map helps little when we're seeking the best restaurants. Vanhoozer observes: "Propositional theology . . . risks reading Scripture as if one size fits all, as it were, or rather, as if there were only one kind of fit. Yet the Spirit has not seen fit to inspire one kind of text only. . . . There is more than one way to 'map' reality. The proof: there is no such thing as a universal all-purpose map."[11] God himself has given us different kinds of discourses of truth in Scripture. We have poetry, narrative, and proverbial wisdom, as well as didactic, straightforward propositions. But one should not be promoted to the exclusion of others, which is what we tend to do. Many tend to look to one type of map for "truth"—abstract propositions—and view the other maps (if they are recognized as such at all) as parasitic or merely illustrative of the propositions.

We should be mindful that the Gospels provide us with a very different discourse or map of the truth than do the Epistles, one that needs to be retained in our theological constructions. The different maps or discourses of truth in Scripture need not be pitted against each other; we need them all. The Bible is an atlas of different kinds of maps. As Timothy Wiarda wisely notes, "Theology does not overwhelm story, story does not crowd out theology, and neither operates independently of the other"; story and theology should be "partners in the process of life transformation, not competitors."[12] We must

10. Kevin Vanhoozer, "Lost in Translation?" *Journal of the Evangelical Theological Society* 48, no. 1 (2005): 89–144.

11. Ibid., 103.

12. Timothy Wiarda, *Interpreting Gospel Narratives: Scenes, People, and Theology* (Nashville: Broadman & Holman, 2010), 67, 86.

resist the temptation to use the Gospels' kind of map merely to get elsewhere. "Conceptual points may indeed be abstracted from Gospel narratives—there is no reason to shy away from this—but it does not follow that the stories themselves, with all their concrete and human detail, can therefore be discarded, or that systematic conceptual presentations can replace the Gospels themselves."[13]

The Gospels are a beautiful and different kind of map of the truth than the New Testament letters are. They are a discourse of truth that is narrative. This means we must interpret them differently—as a different kind of genre—and it also means that we need to appreciate and revel in them in their difference from propositional statements we might find elsewhere.

Seventh, pushing this even further, I would suggest that not only are the Gospels a different discourse of truth; *they are in many ways a more comprehensive and paradigmatic type of map*. That is, while acknowledging the helpful role that different types of literature in Scripture have (like different types of maps in an atlas), we can also note that some maps and some types of writing provide a more comprehensive and framing view of the world. This is true for the narrative genre in Scripture, including the Gospels, because they are story, and another reason we need the Gospels is because *story communicates truth most comprehensively and transformatively*. Speaking of "art" in its broadest sense, Dana Gioia observes: "Art addresses us in the fullness of our being—simultaneously speaking to our intellect, emotions, intuition, imagination, memory and physical senses. There are some truths about life that can be expressed only as stories or songs or images."[14]

This is true and well said. The most powerful discourse of truth is not abstract doctrinal propositions but stories and images and art because these engage our whole person, not just our minds.

We are story people. In the very fabric of our being we are spring-loaded for story. Story is how we make sense of the world and our own lives. Story powerfully creates life and hope, the lack of which is depression. Hope is imagination, and imagination is central for human flourishing and life.[15] When we hope, we are using God's image-bearing gift to envision a reality that does not yet exist. Creating story (including the writing of history) is at the height of our abilities as those made in God's image or, to use Tolkien's language, as "subcreators" modeling after the Creator. Story is created by and creates imagination. Abstract reflection and doctrine are necessary and good, but they do not have the same kind of effect and transformative power that a story does.

13. Ibid., 95.

14. Dana Gioia, commencement address at Stanford University, June 17, 2007.

15. See Richard Bauckham and Trevor Hart, *Hope against Hope: Christian Eschatology and the Turn of the Millennium* (Grand Rapids: Eerdmans, 1999). See also Jonathan T. Pennington, "Christian Psychology and the Gospel of Matthew," *Edification: The Journal of the Society of Christian Psychology* 3, no. 2 (2009): 39–48.

Thus, when Jesus tells the story of the two men who go to pray—the Pharisee who stands proudly and thanks God that he is not like the nearby sinner and the other man who knows his sin and won't even lift up his eyes to heaven, but beats his breast and cries, "God, be merciful to me a sinner" (Luke 18:13)—this is the functioning of the imagination, on the part of the speaker and the hearers. And it is intensely more powerful and robust and engaging than simply making the theological proposition that "God likes humble people." Which would you rather have at your cancer bedside? That vision of what God loves or simply the statement "God loves humble people"? Thankfully, we are not forced to have only one or the other. The buffet that Holy Scripture is provides appetizers, main courses, and desserts. But the main course is story. This is how God has made us, and this is why the vast bulk of the Bible is narrative in form.[16]

One of the many scholars who have reflected on the power of story and its relation to Scripture is Leland Ryken.[17] He observes that one of the many fallacies about the relationship of art and truth is that the usefulness of a work of art consists in its abstract ideas. But, as he observes, "to reduce works of art to their ideational content is to rob them of their power, distort their true nature, and make them finally unnecessary. If the ideas are the important thing in a work of art, we obviously do not need the work itself once we have deduced the ideas."[18]

Along these lines, imagine that a man wants to take his beloved wife on a date to a romantic movie. At the last minute he decides that it would be far cheaper and much more efficient to go to Blockbuster, find the "Romantic Comedy" section, and together read all the synopses on the back of the DVD boxes. Why would that not have the same effect? Why would this be a failed date? Because it is the story—its setting, development, climax, resolution, and the fact that it takes *time* to experience—that is the film's power. The (often deceitful) summary on the back cover may guide one choosing a selection, but it cannot replace the experience of the story because story cannot be reduced to its content. If the narrative did not matter, then we could just have the synopsis and be done with it. We could suck the doctrinal truth out of the Gospels, and then we wouldn't need to waste our time with studying them anymore. We have the "truth"; mission accomplished. But this fails to understand God's revelation or our God-created human nature.

16. Narrative makes up the largest portion of the Hebrew Bible or Old Testament. Speaking specifically of the NT, Hengel notes that almost half of the NT consists of the Gospel narratives. Adding Acts makes it two-thirds and even more with Revelation. Thus, "the earliest churches evidently preferred vivid narrative to abstract letters with their 'pure doctrine' or paranaetical admonition." Martin Hengel, *Four Gospels and the One Gospel of Jesus Christ: An Investigation of the Collection and Origin of the Canonical Gospels*, trans. John Bowden (Harrisburg, PA: Trinity Press International, 2000), 8.

17. Leland Ryken, *The Liberated Imagination: Thinking Christianly about the Arts* (Eugene, OR: Wipf & Stock, 2005). Also Ryken, *Words of Delight: A Literary Introduction to the Bible* (Grand Rapids: Baker, 1987).

18. Ryken, *Liberated Imagination*, 128.

Ryken further notes that the arts (including story) are a road map to essential humanity. They tell us the truth about foundational human experience. They keep calling us back to bedrock humanity by putting us in touch with the universal images of life—both ideal and un-ideal.[19] Story also embodies and incarnates truth in concrete form, not just stating abstract propositions. The artist does not simply theorize abstractly about human experience but rather presents it, thereby giving experiential knowledge or truth. For example, Jesus uses the famous story of the good Samaritan to enable his hearers to experientially and transformatively learn the definition of a "neighbor."[20] Thus story, even more than propositions, communicates the most foundational kind of truth: worldview.

Much more could be said about the power and importance of story. Our simple point here is that we need the Gospels because they provide the foundational worldview for Christianity by presenting to us the "author and perfecter of our faith" in narrative form.

An eighth reason we need the Gospels is because *encountering Jesus in narrative helps us grow in experiential knowledge* and realize that reality does not always fit into neat little boxes of "truth." In the Gospels we encounter the Lord Jesus in the flesh in a way that we cannot in theological summaries of what he did. The followers of Jesus could have simply told us that Jesus is compassionate, that he is caring, that he welcomes children and gentiles. These are all potential and true apostolic statements. But they don't engage us or enable us to know Jesus in the same way we can when those same apostles give us in narrative form Jesus's words and actions. Moreover, what it means to be compassionate and welcoming is much deeper than this summarized statement can convey. Experience alone brings fullness of knowledge, and story (and more broadly, art) enables us to gain life experience vicariously.

As an example of experiential knowledge, we understand that we can be right or correct in our understanding of something yet still be too small in our thinking. This is certainly one of the purposes of the epic poem that is the book of Job. The story of Job shows us that while it is true that God blesses the righteous and punishes the wicked, there is a mystery to all of this, and what we perceive as blessing and punishment may not always be so. A cookie-cutter approach to life that seeks its justification in the blessings and cursings of Deuteronomy and Proverbs is thoroughly critiqued by the narrative poem of Job.

Finally, we need the Gospels because *in the Gospels alone we have a personal, up-front encounter with Jesus Christ.* As much as we love and need the Epistles, they are not enough. There is a reason why the fourfold Gospel witness has always stood at the head of the New Testament canon and why the

19. Ibid., 132.
20. Ibid., 135.

Gospels have always been so beloved. It is because in them we encounter the risen Christ in person. We learn not just about him and what he theologically accomplished for us and what we are supposed to do as a result, but we get to see the sweet Lion and the roaring Lamb in action—loving people, showing compassion, teaching and discipling, rebuking and correcting, suffering and ultimately dying for us. We encounter him in a way unique to the Gospels.

One of my first impulses after discovering a new author or musician is to seek to know more about the person and her or his personal life. We all have a curiosity and desire to know not just the movies and songs and books of a person but also who that person is and how he or she lives, whether it be through preposterous tabloid stories about Brad Pitt or a respectable magazine article about Norah Jones. This can be perverse (and can become perversely obsessive), but there is also something very natural and understandable about the desire to know and relate to famous people by gaining knowledge about who they are. And this is not just a modern phenomenon. The tendency to write biographies in a more inward and psychological way is a modern turn (cf. our discussion in the previous chapter), but the desire to know more is not, something attested to in the ancient world by the numerous productions of other, "noncanonical"[21] stories that give more of such information about famous people like Moses, Enoch, and Daniel.[22] This is certainly so in the case of Jesus, as witnessed by the great number of noncanonical Gospels that give more information about Jesus's birth, boyhood, and other desirable knowledge.

The doctrinal and moral truth that results from Jesus's life, death, and resurrection is not enough. The Gospels are written so that we might experience firsthand the risen Christ, even as the original followers experienced him, through the abiding ministry of the Holy Spirit (John 16:13–14). Thus we should read the Gospels with this goal in mind, seeking not simply to reduce the Gospel stories to their "point" but to enter into the narrative world of the Gospels experientially.

A New Start

I am happy to report that the sin of my opening confession—that I didn't like the Gospels—has been repented of. I have come to love the Gospels for the reasons given above and many more. The ultimate arbiter of the truth of my argument about the power of story and experience, however, must be the reader's own experience of actually reading and coming to love the Gospels.

21. My scare quotes acknowledge that exactly *which* stories were considered canonical varied somewhat given the vast number of Second Temple Jewish documents, many of which have always been considered part of the Septuagint.

22. For example, the books of *Assumption of Moses, 1 Enoch*, and the additions to the Daniel story as found in Bel and the Dragon, Prayer of Azariah, and Susanna.

The Joy and Angst
of Having Four Gospels

Introduction: An Extraterrestrial Thought Experiment

Imagine that you are an alien who lands in the middle of the Bible Belt in the American South. You have been sent to research the religions of Earth, and you are starting with Christianity. You begin to read the Christian holy writings titled the "New Testament" and you find that, not surprisingly, it begins with a life story of Jesus the Christ, the founder of Christianity. You greatly enjoy reading this informative book called "The Gospel according to Matthew." It seems to give a comprehensive understanding of who this Jesus figure was. But imagine your surprise when you turn to the next page, and you see another book with a similar title, this time called "The Gospel according to Mark." You are a little taken aback, but you press forward. You read it with pleasure. You notice that this one is quite a bit shorter than the first and doesn't have as much teaching from the person of Jesus. Also, there are a few different elements, but the basic story line is the same, and you are not overly disturbed. You're not quite sure why there are two accounts of Christianity's founder, but then you almost fall off your (alien green) chair when you finish Mark and turn the page over to find yet a third account—"The Gospel according to Luke"! What is going on? Are these Christians confused about what happened with their own spokesperson? Maybe there are different factions or sects within Christianity, and these are the particular documents of each. Undeterred, you dive in and again you find this Gospel story to be very engaging. You notice some totally new aspects in it, yet there are again many obvious similarities with the others you've read. Moreover, like the previous two accounts the story consistently focuses on the end, on the death and resurrection of the central character, Jesus. Finally, you turn the page once more, and you are almost not surprised anymore to find yet another book with the title "The Gospel according to John." You admire the narrative productivity of these Christians and are beginning to expect that their holy book in its entirety must be full of writings titled "The Gospel according to Fred" and "Tony" and "Paul" and "Jim." This time, however, you don't have to read very far into this Fourth Gospel to see quite a few differences. The narrative style and use of language are different, and there is very little overlap of content (around 8 percent, according to your spaceship supercomputer's calculation). Compared to John, the previous three look a lot alike, despite their differences. Yet again, at least there is consistent focus on the hero's last week of life, his death, and his rising from the grave.

Upon completion of John, you find yet another narrative work, but you soon realize that it is not another story of Jesus but a chronicle of early Christianity. Both disappointed and somewhat relieved, you realize that the Christians' holy book is not *all* biographical stories about Jesus but instead contains just these four. As to why four and not one, you are yet perplexed. You phone home to report that your progress is going well and your research will continue. You are particularly excited that you have been invited to something called a "revival meeting" tonight, complete with a "home-style potluck" to follow.

The point of this imaginary exercise is to help us realize that on the surface, it does seem more than a bit odd that we have *four different yet authoritative* stories of Jesus's life. Especially in this age that believes that eyewitnesses are often fallible and that stories (especially by religious types) are spun to one's advantage, having four different and apparently conflicting accounts seems a detriment rather than a help. For the one who believes in the New Testament as Holy Scripture, it is a fair question to ask whether it wouldn't have been apologetically wiser on the church's part if we had just one ironed-out, comprehensive, jumbo Gospel, one straightforward, definitive account that shows the irrefutable historicity of Jesus's life. And not only for apologetic reasons, but also for the believer, would it not be easier to study and learn from *the* Gospel rather than have to compare and contrast the different accounts and figure out "what really happened"?

The Gospels in the Early Church: To Harmonize or Not to Harmonize?

The reading experience described above is indeed how many aliens—those outside the commonwealth of God—in the first centuries viewed Christianity's fourfold Gospel account, though often less sympathetically than our research-oriented extraterrestrial did.

The predicament of having four diverse accounts rather than one was a problem for many of the earliest Christians. It was already being addressed by Papias (early second century AD) and undoubtedly was considered an issue by the end of the second century, with the production and widespread use of Gospel harmonies.[1] A Gospel harmony is an attempt to produce from the four accounts one unified whole that irons out and inherently explains the differences.[2] Due to the obvious advantage of such a wrinkle-free version, such harmonies have been produced throughout church history and continue to be popular.

The earliest extant and most widely used such harmony, which came to be called the *Diatessaron*,[3] was produced by Tatian, a disciple of Justin Martyr. It is unclear whether Tatian's *Diatessaron* was originally written in Greek or Syriac,[4] but we know for certain that the Syriac version became very influential in the Tigris-Euphrates area. Tatian was not the first person to compose a harmony,[5] and he was probably following in the Greek harmonizing tradition of his teacher, Justin Martyr. However, Tatian is the first to attempt to separate the different units of the gospels and rearrange them into one continuous narrative. The title, *Diatessaron*, comes from Greek musical terminology meaning (perfect) "harmony of four."[6]

Another very important and influential early Christian writer was Eusebius of Caesarea. He is best known for his work as the great church historian, but like others of his contemporaries, he was also very engaged in apologetic defense of Christianity and the Gospels. For example, his *Demonstratio*

---

1. Richard Bauckham, from his lecture "The Johannine Jesus and the Synoptic Jesus," available at http://www.richardbauckham.co.uk.

2. There is another kind of work sometimes called a harmony that does not iron out the differences but instead keeps each Gospel account separate but lines them up in parallel columns and rearranges the stories so that similarities and differences can be seen at a glance. This type of work is now usually called a "synopsis," as in the case of Kurt Aland's *Synopsis of the Four Gospels*, available in English, Greek, or parallel, and in many editions. A. T. Robertson's *Harmony of the Gospels for Students of the Life of Christ* (Nashville: Broadman, 1922) is similarly a "synopsis," despite the potentially confusing title of *Harmony*, which we may more clearly distinguish as a conflated, singular account.

3. A brief discussion of the influence of the *Diatessaron* can be found in Lee Martin McDonald, "The Gospels in Early Christianity: Their Origin, Use, and Authority," in *Reading the Gospels Today*, ed. Stanley E. Porter (Grand Rapids: Eerdmans, 2004), 174–75. A much fuller work is W. L. Petersen, *Tatian's Diatessaron: Its Creation, Dissemination, Significance, and History in Scholarship* (Leiden: Brill, 1994).

4. We do not have any manuscripts of Tatian's work, but only portions of it as recorded in Syriac in Ephraem the Syrian's commentary on the *Diatessaron*. The fact that a commentary was written based on Tatian's jumbo Gospel is a strong bit of evidence for its widespread usage and influence, at least in Syriac-speaking Christianity.

5. Jerome mentions one Theophilus of Antioch, who did so in the late second century. Seán Kealy, *Matthew's Gospel and the History of Biblical Interpretation* (Lewiston, NY: Mellen Biblical Press, 1997), 18.

6. Ibid.

Evangelica (*Proof of the Gospel*)[7] seeks to assure believers of the trustwor-thiness of the Gospels and was likely written in partial response to the critic Porphyry.[8] Also, very significantly, Eusebius produced his "Gospel Canons." As he explains in his accompanying letter addressed to Carpianus, rather than rearranging the Gospel pericopes so that they are out of order, Eusebius had drawn up a system of tables or canons by which one could immediately tell which pericopes occurred in which Gospels.[9] This is a different approach than that of Tatian, one that keeps the fourfold witness of the Gospels intact.

I mention both Tatian and Eusebius to point out that already by the early fourth century, Christian scholars were very aware of the ways in which the Gospel accounts both overlapped and differed from one another, and they were producing sophisticated means of comparing the accounts—some that were harmonizing attempts and some not. The early popularity of Gospel harmonies in particular speaks to the natural desire for both devotional and apologetic reasons to have but one simplified Gospel story.

On the apologetic front, in addition to Irenaeus against Marcion and the Valentinians, Origen against Celsus, and Eusebius against Porphyry, Augustine labored to defend Christianity's historical accuracy as found in the Gospels. Early Christianity had many enemies who used many different weapons— persecution, slander, and arguments about the novelty of Christianity (not a good thing), its inconsistency, and the spurious nature of the apostolic authors. An argument particularly popular among the Manicheans, contemporaries of Augustine, was that the Gospel writers contradicted one another.[10] Refuting this is very much the point of Augustine's well-known *Harmony of the Four Gospels* (produced ca. AD 400), a book that proved to be very influential and remained so for over a millennium after its composition.[11]

7. This work consists of ten books, which is in fact only the latter half of the fuller work, now lost.

8. Porphyry had possibly been a convert before his turn against Christianity, evidenced by his intimate knowledge of the Christian faith. Eusebius wrote another definitive, twenty-five-book rejoinder to Porphyry (*Kata Porphyriou*), but his *Proof of the Gospel* also shows knowledge of and response to Porphyry's work *Contra Christianos*. W. J. Ferrar, *The Proof of the Gospel Being the Demonstratio Evangelica of Eusebius of Caesarea*, 2 vols. (London: SPCK, 1920), 1:xi–xii. Another of Eusebius's works on the reliability of the Gospels, his *Gospel Problems and Solutions*, exists only in portions and spread across a variety of languages and different manuscripts. Very recently for the first time the various pieces have been pulled together and translated in one work. See Roger Pearse, *Eusebius of Caesarea: Gospel Problems and Solutions* (Ipswich: Chieftain, 2011).

9. Eusebius's letter (in Greek) can be found in the supplemental materials of the Nestle-Aland 27th edition of the Greek New Testament, and his system of canons or identification of shared pericopes by Roman numeral, can be found in the margins throughout the Gospels in the NA[27]. An English translation of Eusebius's explanatory letter is available at http://www.tertullian.org /fathers/eusebius_letter_to_carpianus.

10. S. D. F. Salmond in his translator's notes to Augustine's *Harmony* in Schaff, *NPNF[1]* 6:71.

11. M. B. Riddle, in introducing the *Harmony* notes that "All Gospel Harmonies, all Lives of Christ, all discussions of the apparent discrepancies of the Gospels, stand related to it." M. B. Riddle, "Introductory Essay," in Schaff, *NPNF[1]* 6:67.

Very significantly, however, we must note that what Augustine does *not* do is take the Tatian harmonizing route. The jumbo-Gospel approach of the *Diatessaron* was roundly rejected by the church. Despite its popularity in some pockets, it was eventually lost because even though discrepancies between the Gospels would be defended against pagan accusers, *this defense would not be pursued at the expense of losing the fourfold apostolic witness as such*, warts and all. Augustine defends the importance of keeping all four Gospels, all the while working to show that they still offer a unified picture of Jesus. To smooth out all the differences in a kind of harmony that creates just one new Gospel as a result is too high a price to pay; it goes against what was greatly valued in the church, the testimony of the Gospels given through individual eyewitness apostles (Matthew and John) and their close associates (Mark and Luke).[12]

Along these same lines we may also note how the famous preacher of the East, John Chrysostom, deals with the issue of the four Gospels. In the first of his ninety homilies on Matthew, Chrysostom notes a heretical and anti-Christian complaint that the four canonical Gospels vary from one another. Chrysostom responds by turning this argument on its head. As Margaret Mitchell observes, Chrysostom uses the discrepancies as "proof of their veracity, by insisting that the extent to which the four agree with one another is unaccountable proof that they gave true testimony to the same historical events. John allows that there is variability in wording and expression, but insists this does not amount to discord or contradiction."[13] Chrysostom offers by way of contrast a comparison with the "unruly canon" of the Greek philosophical writings which do not accord with one another but are often contradictory. Thus we have yet another example of early opposition to Christianity based on the perceived discrepancies in the Gospels, and the defense given does not iron out all the differences or produce just one new harmonized Gospel.

---

12. Much earlier than Augustine, the foundational church father Irenaeus also argued for the importance of the fourfold Gospel witness. Though we do not have from him anything like a Gospel harmony, his polemical and apologetic work does offer clear arguments for the necessity of having four Gospels, no more or less. He argues that the church has these four pillars (the Gospels), even as the world has four zones and four winds, and as the cherubim have four faces. *Adv. Haer.* 3.11.8. Although these analogies may not strike the modern reader as overly convincing, the broader point is clear: from the earliest days the four Gospels were seen as essential and not to be conflated. Irenaeus accounts for the differences in the evangelists more on theological grounds—John emphasizing Jesus as divine Word, Luke his priestly role, Matthew Jesus as a human, Mark on the importance of prophecy.

13. Margaret Mitchell, "John Chrysostom," in *The Sermon on the Mount through the Centuries*, ed. Jeffrey P. Greenman, Timothy Larsen, and Stephen R. Spencer (Grand Rapids: Brazos, 2007), 28. It should be noted as well that it appears Chrysostom came to limit the Bible's infallibility to matters of faith and practice rather than all the details. See Craig Blomberg, *Historical Reliability* (Downers Grove, IL: InterVarsity, 1987), 4.

Thus, the church's experience in the early centuries forced it to address the potential historical discrepancy problems in the fourfold Gospel book, yet it chose not to harmonize all the accounts into one consistent report.

In our current time we might be tempted to dismiss such a focus on historical issues as merely modernist positivism and the result of corrosive historical criticism. I have been tempted by this view myself. However, coming to recognize that these kinds of historical questions go back to the earliest days of the church and continue to be debated forces us to seek a balanced approach that recognizes a real role for explaining historical discrepancy while also not simplifying everything into an airtight historical case. Again, the church fathers serve as a great model.

We can and should take our cues from this same balanced position: We are certainly justified to explore and try to explain historical discrepancies between the accounts, but we must also allow their witnessing diversity to stand. But now we are getting ahead of ourselves a bit. First, we must slow down and face squarely the angst that understandably comes from having four diverse canonical accounts before we can turn to some solutions. What kind of ammunition did the fourfold Gospel account give to early Christianity's enemies?

The Angst of Having Four Diverse Gospel Accounts

As we have said, the fourfold canonical witness of the Gospels can be seen as a problem, and from the earliest days of the church the question of the historical accuracy of the diverse accounts has arisen. By contrast, in late nineteenth- and early twentieth-century critical scholarship, the discrepancies between the Gospels focused especially on the supposed *theological* differences between the Synoptic tradition and John. The historical incongruity between the Gospels had long been accepted and assumed in critical scholarship, finding its foothold especially in the eighteenth century; most critical scholars simply accepted what seemed to be irrefutable historical inconsistencies. But in earlier periods the problem of the four Gospels was considered not so much theological as more straightforwardly historical, at least in apologetic situations.

First, John is very different from Matthew, Mark, and Luke. The four accounts all have the climax of their story in Jerusalem with the focus on Jesus's death and resurrection, and they share numerous places and people, but in general there is very little narrative overlap between John and the Synoptics.

But even just within the first three Gospels themselves—called the "Synoptics" because they look so much alike—there is significant diversity. For example, regarding the birth of Jesus (an aspect of Greco-Roman biographies that was common and important), we note that Mark lacks this part of the story completely. This may be excused, given the intentional brevity and action-packed nature of his Gospel. But even in the accounts that do give a birth narrative—Matthew and Luke—there is almost no overlap at all. Matthew traces Jesus's lineage through Joseph's Davidic line. Then he gives us a whole raft of little stories concerning Joseph's plans to divorce Mary, the mysterious magi from the East who arrive a couple of years after Jesus's birth, Herod's paranoia and slaughter of children, and the holy family's flight to and return from Egypt. Luke has none of this but traces Jesus's lineage back to Adam. He also includes a rather lengthy cycle of stories about the miraculous birth of Jesus's kinsman John, the visit of angels to Zechariah and Mary, Joseph and Mary's census-forced journey to Bethlehem, an angelic visit to some nondescript shepherds on the night of Jesus's birth, and stories of the infant and boy Jesus's experiences in the temple in Jerusalem. Despite our conflation of all these events at the annual church Christmas pageant, these stories do not in fact overlap at all. If Jesus did not appear as the named figure in both of these accounts, one would never suspect they were stories about the same person. Add to this John's abstract philosophical and theological introduction to Jesus and we have an unexpectedly high degree of diversity right from the beginning of the Gospel accounts.

Going not much further into the Gospels we meet Jesus's prophetic forerunner, John the Baptist. In the four accounts of John's appearance there is much more obvious overlap than in the case of the birth narratives. Nonetheless, many differences do still occur. Looking at a synopsis of the four Gospels here is very enlightening. We note first that once again the evangelist John stands apart. He does not record Jesus being baptized by John at all but rather has John simply identify Jesus publicly with explicitly soteriological language: "Behold, the Lamb of God, who takes away the sin of the world!" (John 1:29). By contrast, the Synoptic accounts each have Jesus being baptized by John, followed by the Spirit descending on him like a dove, and concluding with the voice of God from heaven affirming Jesus's Sonship. In these essential elements Matthew, Mark, and Luke are identical. But the devil is in the details. Matthew alone has John being reluctant to baptize Jesus and Jesus's response that it is fitting "to fulfill all righteousness" (Matt. 3:15); this language is clearly from Matthew's strong "fulfillment" motif, and it is not found in Mark and Luke.[14] Additionally, what exactly did the Spirit's descent on Jesus consist of? Was it an actual dove that alighted on Jesus ("bodily" in Luke 3:22), or is this merely a *symbol* for the Spirit's anointing? If the former, how do we understand the Baptist's words in the Fourth Gospel, "I saw the Spirit descend as a dove from heaven, and it remained on him." No other account of Jesus remarks that his earthly ministry was memorable because of a constant shoulder-perched avian companion. John must be speaking symbolically, not "bodily" as Luke is. And finally, what did the heavenly voice actually say at Jesus's baptism? With Mat-

---

14. In addition to the many places where the language of fulfillment appears in Matthew (especially in the two chapters preceding Jesus's baptism), it has been observed that the overarching theme of Matthew can rightly be described as that of "fulfillment." Cf. R. T. France, *Matthew: Evangelist and Teacher* (Downers Grove, IL: InterVarsity, 1989), 166–205.

thew, was this a public announcement to John and the crowds, "This is my beloved Son, with whom I am well pleased"? Or was this a word of affirmation to Jesus himself, as Mark and Luke have it: "Thou art my beloved Son; with *thee* I am well pleased"? And how does this all relate first to the remarkably similar occurrence at the Mount of Transfiguration (Matt. 17:5; Mark 9:7; Luke 9:35) and to John's comparable but different situation in John 12:28–30?

Sometime later Jesus and his disciples crossed over the storm-tossed Sea of Galilee and upon landing somewhere encountered some kind of demonic possession (Matt. 8:28–34; Mark 5:1–20; Luke 8:26–39). We must describe it with such generalities because the apparent discrepancies between the accounts prevent easy specificity. Namely, we're not sure what to call the place of Jesus's landing. Was it the country of the "Gadarenes" (Matthew, *Gadarēnōn*) or of the "Gerasenes" (Mark and Luke, *Gerasēnōn*)? And what did Jesus encounter there? Was it a demon-possessed man (Mark and Luke) or *two* demoniacs (Matthew)? Jesus's casting out the demons into a herd of swine, which subsequently committed lemminglike suicide, is consistent in the stories, but Matthew's sparseness on every other detail is striking. Luke and especially Mark give us a descriptive picture of this demoniac's previous experience and reputation as well as his postdeliverance request that he become a follower of Jesus. Regarding this remarkable story, John tells us nothing.

One gets a similar sense when comparing the accounts of the story that occurs just following this one. In the sandwiched pericope of the raising of Jairus's daughter and the healing of the woman with a chronic hemorrhage (Matt. 9:18–26; Mark 5:21–43; Luke 8:40–56), we have another good example of apparent differences between the accounts. Again, John does not give us this story at all. The Synoptics are clearly relaying the same, interrelated account, but with notable differences. Matthew is typically sparse in his details; his story is much shorter and tells us almost nothing specific, such as Jairus's name (which we get from the other accounts), the hemorrhaging woman's previous unsuccessful medical experiences, the words Jesus spoke to the dead girl that made her rise, her age, her parents' response, Jesus's instructions afterward that the girl should be given something to eat, and the command to tell no one what had happened. Also missing in Matthew is the dialogue between Jesus and his disciples in which Jesus asks who in the crowd touched him for healing and the woman fearfully confesses that it was she. All of this we tend to mentally import into Matthew's account, but it is noticeably lacking in the text.

But the most obvious difference concerns the time of death of Jairus's daughter. In Matthew this generic "ruler" approaches Jesus and announces that his daughter has just died (9:18). Jesus then rises and begins to follow Jairus back to his house. It is during this journey that he encounters and heals the sick woman. But in Mark's and Luke's accounts, Jairus states that his daughter is dying (Mark 5:23; Luke 8:42). Only later, after the interaction with the hemorrhaging woman, does a man come to Jairus and report that his daughter has now died and that beckoning Jesus is now useless. Jesus encourages Jairus to have no fear but to continue to believe (Mark 5:36; Luke 8:50). Then Jesus arrives at his home, and the three accounts coincide once again.

Another important example of apparent discrepancies in the Gospels is the various retellings of Jesus's Last Supper. The historical questions here are legion and complicated, with differences both within the Synoptic tradition and especially between the Synoptics and John.[15] Probably for this reason, this is one of the passages that Augustine particularly concentrates on in his *Harmony* (the entirety of book 3). When one reads this story, natural questions arise about when the Last Supper took place. Was it at the official Jewish Passover meal or a day earlier, as the differing accounts seem to suggest? And what exactly happened there? How many cups of blessing were there (one or rather two as in Luke)? And what exactly did Jesus say? Why does John alone have the very potent story of Jesus washing the feet of the disciples? Even more perplexing, why does John's upper-room description entirely omit the bread and wine—which was considered in the early church the essence of the Last Supper—while using this kind of scene and the same symbols much earlier in a public setting in John 6?

These last questions recall the puzzling issue mentioned above concerning the overall differences between John and the Synoptics. That is, even if the variations within the Synoptic accounts were all easily explained, one still faces the less appealing task of reconciling John's wording, chronology, and overall depiction with that of the Synoptics. For example, it is notable that John omits all of Jesus's parables as found in the Synoptics, nor do we see Jesus performing any exorcisms or anything like his Sermon on the Mount/Plain or his transfiguration. Related, John presents Jesus teaching in long, dialogical discourses rather than pithy parables and encounters. Also, the Christology of John seems evidently "higher" with much more explicit claims of Jesus's divinity (John 1:1–3; 8:58; 10:30). Additionally, Jesus's message in John is about eternal life, with an emphasis on resurrection. Where is the Synoptic Jesus's constant preaching of the *kingdom of God*? On the more historical side, the chronology of John appears considerably different, with Jesus going in and out of Jerusalem multiple times and cleansing the temple at the beginning of his ministry. This is in contrast to the Synoptics, in which Jesus is never shown in Jerusalem until the end of his life, at which time he cleanses the temple.

These are but a few examples of what can be found on every page of a Gospels synopsis. For the skeptic and the critic they are evidence of historical confusion and illegitimacy. For the believer they can be a source of great angst. Such reactions go back to the earliest days of the church.

---

15. I explore these questions more extensively and provide some solutions in my essay "The Lord's Last Supper in the Fourfold Witness of the Gospels," in *The Lord's Supper*, ed. Tom Schreiner and Matt Crawford (Nashville: Broadman & Holman, 2010), 31–67.

Assorted Solutions

How are we to understand these discrepancies? Are the Gospels merely theological and not concerned about what really happened? Is historical accuracy unimportant to the evangelists and to early Christians? Apparently not. By the Gospel writers' own testimony, they are witnessing to real events because they are true and so that readers may believe that Jesus is the Christ (John 20:30–31; 21:24–25). The rest of the New Testament assumes this approach as well, most pointedly in the arguments of the apostle Paul that if Jesus did not really rise from the dead in history, then our own future history is mere tomfoolery and a vain hope (1 Cor. 15:1–58). Additionally, as we have observed, early Christian leaders regularly defended the reality of these historical events (and their internal consistency) by harmonizing them together as much as possible. If their understanding was that the *theological* idea of Jesus mattered more than the historical reality, then there would be no understandable motivation for either a jumbo-Gospel harmony such at Tatian's or apologetic books dedicated to showing the accuracy of the accounts such as those of Augustine and Eusebius.

As we begin to reflect on responding to such claims, we should note that the sense of discrepancy between the Gospels is artificially heightened by the fact that we have four accounts and by the habit of horizontal reading, that is, reading across all four accounts rather than reading each Gospel as a whole (vertical reading). In other words, the stories by themselves within each Gospel do not generally raise historical problems (unless one begins with a presupposition that no miracles can occur in a closed universe) nor are any of the Gospel writers internally inconsistent in their individual accounts. Thus there is a somewhat self-inflicted and simulated *overemphasis* on the differences in the Gospels precisely because we have four overlapping accounts. Also, *focusing* on the differences gives one a distorted picture, for despite discrepancies such as those highlighted above, overall the picture of all four Gospels is amazingly consistent in terms of Jesus's character, tone, teaching emphases, and the general course of his life and death.

Nonetheless, even though each Gospel would have generally been read/heard on its own ("vertically"), this does not mean that its hearers would have been unaware of existing oral and written traditions to which the reading would be compared.[16] Thus we cannot avoid facing the diversity of the accounts, and again these questions of difference are not new.

---

16. The mention of previous assorted Gospel accounts in Luke's preface is the easiest place to show the truthfulness of this observation. Also, the obvious interdependence of the Gospels reveals that the evangelists (and presumably other readers as well) were aware of one another's work at least in part and/or some other sources that they (and presumably other readers) knew. Additionally, good arguments can be made that the Gospel of John shows and assumes his readers' knowledge of the Markan tradition in some form. See Richard Bauckham, "John for

Beginning then with the position that history matters and that Christians can and should be willing to address these issues, we may explore an assortment of possible solutions and explanations for the various differences among the Gospel accounts.

Maximalist Harmonization

The first approach to note is what I call the maximalist harmonization (MH) view. In this approach, common among many fundamentalists, one assumes (usually quite unreflectively) that everything the Gospels record must have happened in precisely just that way, comparable to a closed-circuit television recording, allowing no flexibility or interpretation. Thus, for example, at the baptism of Jesus the voice from heaven must have said *both* "This is my beloved Son" and "Thou art my beloved Son," and the different evangelists have each chosen to record only part of what happened.[17] Or when the rich young ruler approaches Jesus and the evangelists record his words differently,[18] MH readers would offer a conflated reading. The young man must have *really* said the lengthy and almost stuttering: "Teacher, good teacher, by doing what will I inherit eternal life? I mean, what should I do in order to inherit eternal life?"[19] to which Jesus must have responded, "Why do you call me good? No one is good except God alone. Anyway, why are you asking me about what is good? Like I said, there is only one who is good." Examples like this could be multiplied. The result of this kind of approach is something akin to the Amplified Bible and a truly jumbo-sized Gospel that includes everything that any evangelist records. All of this is done in the name of "historical accuracy" and preserving the Bible.

Not only is the MH approach fundamentally flawed in its understanding of history retelling (see the following chapter on what history is), but it also does not account for most of the apparent discrepancies. For example, in Jesus's temptation, when the order of the devil's offers differs in Matthew and Luke, which is correct? The MH view does not have any kind of mechanism to adjudicate this.

Readers of Mark," in *The Gospels for All Christians: Rethinking the Gospel Audiences*, ed. Richard Bauckham (Grand Rapids: Eerdmans, 1998), 147–71.

17. Interestingly, this kind of reading is not entirely new but can be found on occasion in the ancient world such as in the heretical Gospel of the Ebionites, which has the heavenly voice speak twice, as cited in Epiphanius, *Against Heresies* 30.13.7–8. As Blomberg notes, this harmonization is "both misguided and unnecessary." Blomberg, *Historical Reliability*, 118.

18. Mark 10:17–18 reads: "A man ran up . . . and asked him, 'Good Teacher, what must I do to inherit eternal life?' And Jesus said to him, 'Why do you call me good? No one is good but God alone." Matthew 19:16–17 reads: "One came up to him, saying, 'Teacher, what good deed must I do, to have eternal life?' And he said to him, 'Why do you ask me about what is good? One there is who is good.'"

19. From Kelly Osborne, "Impact of Historical Criticism on Gospel Interpretation: A Test Case," quoted in Grant Osborne, "Historical Criticism and the Evangelical," *Journal of the Evangelical Theological Society* 42, no. 2 (1999): 201.

An even more radical version of this kind of maximal approach can be found in Andreas Osiander (1498–1552), from whom we likely got the terminology of a Gospel harmony. *Any* differences between the accounts, no matter how small, must be evidence, thought Osiander, of different events. Thus there must have been two storm stillings, four blind men healed before and after Jesus's visit to Jericho, and Jesus was anointed three times and drove the traders out of the temple area three times.[20] This is an extreme version of harmonization that most would not follow today, but it does reveal the problem inherent in such a misunderstanding of what historical retelling must comprise. In many ways, Osiander's untenable approach is the logical outworking of a maximalist harmonization approach.

Reasoned Harmonization

Aside from that rather extreme approach, there are several other observations that can be made that help alleviate most of the apparent differences between the Gospels. First, many of the supposed discrepancies can be understood simply as a result of different perspectives entailed in the normal reporting of events. We might call this a reasoned harmonization approach. Multiple reports of the same events, not surprisingly, often differ in details. This is not an indictment of inaccuracy or untrustworthiness but is simply the recognition that different participants have different perspectives on the event. One common analogy is that of different reports of a car accident or a football game. On the physical level one might think of different lines of sight obtained by different viewers of an event. We can analogize this to different authors having different "perspectives" in terms of worldview, experience, and goal. Thus we might rightly think of the Gospels as providing us with different kinds of pictures of Jesus's life and teaching.

Another analogy would be to think of different pictures of the Manhattan skyline, made from different perspectives.[21] If taken from a boat in the harbor, many of these pictures would be similar yet somewhat different from those taken from a different side of the city and from the top of a building. Additionally, some of the pictures could be paintings in different media (watercolor, acrylic, etc.) and in different styles (impressionist, realism, pointillism), while some are photographs (color, and black and white). Some may have been taken in the morning, others at night. And some were taken on September 10, 2001, and some after September 11. In all these various scenarios several of the buildings and landmarks may be visible in all the pictures (e.g., the Empire State Building), while others will not. But none of them will be identical. They all depict the same reality but with inevitable differences of hue and texture and viewpoint.

---

20. Martin Hengel, *The Four Gospels and the One Gospel of Jesus Christ: An Investigation of the Collection and Origin of the Canonical Gospels*, trans. John Bowden (Harrisburg, PA: Trinity Press International, 2000), 23.

21. This analogy was first suggested to me by Carl Mosser.

No one would say that they are contradictory or refer to different places despite these differences, but rather would consider them complementary pictures.

This understanding goes far in explaining many of the differences among the Gospels. So, for example, we can see that the wide differences between Matthew's and Luke's birth narratives don't really contradict each other but are complementary; they can be reasonably harmonized. For whatever reasons Matthew chooses to emphasize the Davidic lineage of Jesus and Luke the Adamic (and possibly Marian) origins. The stories they tell about Jesus's early earthly days entail different perspectives on the events but are not contradictory. Reasoned harmonization also helps us understand the general sparseness of Matthew's stories relative to his canonical brothers; his style is simply different, and his concerns are generally *not* to tell a detailed and plot-driven story but rather a simple and theologically pointed one.

The Itinerant Nature of Jesus's Ministry

Another helpful perspective for addressing the discrepancies in the Gospels is the recognition of the itinerant nature of Jesus's ministry. Many times in the Gospels we have Jesus giving some specific teaching, but the evangelists record the words somewhat differently. This kind of discrepancy can be explained in several ways, one of which is to note that, given Jesus's constant traveling and preaching, he almost certainly said many similar things in a variety of places. Many of us who preach regularly and in different places have experienced this as well. I write out my sermons in manuscript form, and thus when I re-preach a message, the bulk of it will be the same. Nonetheless, in the moment of preaching I always end up saying many things that are not in my manuscript and skipping over parts of my printed message to adjust "on the fly." Additionally, I am sensitive to my audience so that before I preach a message again I always revise and refresh it with appropriate wording and illustrations. This was especially true when I preached in Scotland some sermons that I had previously delivered in the States. Thus when the Gospels have different wording for the same teaching, this may at times be simply because Jesus said it one way in one place and another way somewhere else.

In this regard we may recall again the editorial comments at the end of the Gospel of John: "This is the disciple who is bearing witness to these things, and who has written these things; and we know that his testimony is true. But there are also many other things which Jesus did; were every one of them to be written, I suppose that the world itself could not contain the books that would be written" (John 21:24–25; cf. 20:30–31).

Even as we understand that Jesus said many things that we don't have in the Gospels,[22] so it is reasonable to assume that he also said the same things in

---

22. We know of at least one quoted Jesus tradition that occurs in the NT but not in any of the Gospels: "It is more blessed to give than to receive" in Acts 20:35.

different ways at different times. An example of this is Matthew 7:11, where Jesus says that a loving father will give "good things to those who ask him." Yet in the parallel context, Luke 11:13 says that the Father will give "the Holy Spirit to those who ask him." One simple way to understand this difference is that Jesus could have said both of these things at different times and the evangelists record them differently.

Ipsissima Vox Jesu *and* Ipsissima Verba Jesu

On the other hand, we might want to explain this incongruence between Matthew 7:11 and Luke 11:13 on another important basis, the difference between "his own voice" (*ipsissima vox*) and "his exact words" (*ipsissima verba*). This is simply an acknowledgment that what we often have in the Gospels is not necessarily the "exact words" of Jesus, though we can reasonably trust that they give the gist of his teaching, his "voice." Even conservative scholars such as those who in the 1970s produced the Chicago Statement on Biblical Inerrancy have adopted this important notion. One of the scholars involved with this document was Paul Feinberg. To quote from his well-known article "The Meaning of Inerrancy":

> Inerrancy does not demand that the *Logia Jesu* (the sayings of Jesus) contain the *ipsissima verba* (the exact words of Jesus), only the *ipsissima vox* (the exact voice). . . . When a New Testament writer cites the sayings of Jesus, it need not be the case that Jesus said those exact words. Undoubtedly, the exact words of Jesus are to be found in the New Testament, but they need not be in every instance. For one thing, many of the sayings were spoken by our Lord in Aramaic, and thus had to be translated into Greek. . . . Thus, it is impossible for us to know which are direct quotes, which are indirect discourse, and which are free renderings.[23]

This helpful statement rightly observes that historical accuracy—even "inerrancy"—does not require that we always have from the evangelists direct quotes, despite what misleading "red letter editions" might have us believe. This comes partially from the recognition that we are dealing with translations, so having the exact words of Jesus is impossible. Jesus was probably teaching in Aramaic, and aside from a few places where the original Aramaic occurs (e.g., Mark 5:41; 15:34), what we have in our Greek Gospels is necessarily at best the accurate "voice" of Jesus but not the actual words.

In other words, the idea of *ipsissima vox* and *ipsissima verba* is the recognition that, for various reasons, the evangelists provide us with a paraphrase of Jesus's words. We can be confident that the Gospels, as inspired, canonical documents, accurately reflect Jesus's teaching, but we need not (and cannot)

---

23. Paul Feinberg, "The Meaning of Inerrancy," in *Inerrancy*, ed. N. L. Geisler (Grand Rapids: Zondervan, 1979), 270, italics in original.

insist that they always contain the *exact words* of Jesus (or any other character in the story). This is to demand too much and goes beyond what is required in historical discourse.[24] To paraphrase someone's words—even as you might do if trying to explain my point here to someone else—is entirely acceptable as long as the main thrust and sense accords with the original situation. This important idea enables us to recognize the role of the inspired evangelists themselves in crafting and shaping their accounts, to which we will return later.

Thus the difference between Jesus saying that the Father will give "good things to those who ask him" (Matt. 7:11) and that he will give "the Holy Spirit to those who ask him" (Luke 11:13) can easily be understood as the evangelists' paraphrasing of Jesus's words, all within their own discourse and interpretive point of view. But even more so, when we encounter texts that clearly refer to the same event and are not merely itinerant teachings—such as the raising of Jairus's daughter—we need not be anxious about the differences in wording of any of the characters' speech in the story, including Jesus's.

This principle also applies to our previously mentioned example of the rich young ruler approaching Jesus in Mark 10:17–18 (= Luke 18:18–19) and Matthew 19:16–17. I suppose one might argue that there were two different instances when such a specific person came up and asked Jesus about obtaining eternal life, but this doesn't seem very likely, given the many obvious similarities in these parallel stories. The best solution is to recognize that each of the evangelists, under the inspiration of the Holy Spirit, has skillfully reported paraphrased words of the characters in this story, words that are true to the sense of the event (the *vox*), yet at the same time are paraphrases that reflect their own theological and literary purposes. The same could be said for the different order of the temptations in Matthew 4:1–11 and Luke 4:1–13.

The Interlocking Relationship of John and the Synoptics

We have given above several ways in which we can understand a variety of discrepancies between the Gospels. Previously we mentioned that some of the most difficult differences concern the relationship between John and the Synoptics. On this score we should note that such differences are often overdrawn because of an overly microscopic approach. That is, even though the differences mentioned above are real, the bigger picture of Jesus—as the Jewish Messiah, as a teacher and healer, as the One who ultimately died and rose on behalf of God's people, and who calls us to faith in him—remains amazingly consistent in the fourfold witness of the Gospels. Going beyond this, even the apparent differences in John can be understood as providing an interlocking picture with the Synoptic accounts.

24. See esp. chap. 5 of this volume.

For example, even though the language of Jesus is quite different in John, closer inspection reveals that it is meant to be seen as compatible and overlapping, not contradictory. Thus, as Don Carson observes, John's "eternal life" description of Jesus's teaching falls within the "preacher's prerogative of shaping his message" according to his purpose and audience, specifically, to "present the fewest barriers" to his hearers by using more universally understood language. Additionally, even though "kingdom" language doesn't occur much in John, the theme is still prevalent (e.g., chaps. 18–19).[25] Moreover, we also find clues that John wants his readers to understand that his "eternal life" language is meant to correspond to the more familiar Jesus tradition expression of "kingdom." In John 3 "kingdom of God" is used in close connection with "eternal life." Likewise, in Mark 9:42–10:31 several texts use "kingdom of God" and "life" or "eternal life" in parallel and interchangeably. This is our literary clue that these expressions are to be understood as the same, and this allows John, who can assume knowledge of the Markan tradition, to use "eternal life" the rest of the time.[26]

Similar to this example, the Synoptic tradition and John dovetail when it comes to the famous "I am" sayings so crucial to John's Christology. While it is clear that John has developed the fourteen "I am" sayings into an extended pattern,[27] it is not often recognized that these seem to intentionally stem from and unpack the same notions already present in the Synoptic tradition—the divine "I am" in the parallel in Mark 6:50 (= Matt. 14:27) and the predicated "I am" sayings as they relate to Synoptic parabolic sayings (e.g., Matt. 18:12–13; Mark 4:21; Luke 13:23–24).[28]

We may understand this relationship with the analogy of a flower. "The Synoptic Gospels present in seed form the full flowering of the incarnational understanding that would develop only later; but the seed is there, the entire genetic coding for the growth that later takes place. If John lets us see a little more of the opening flower, it is in part because he indulges in more explanatory asides that unpack for the reader what is really going on."[29]

Finally, and intimately related to these examples, John does seem to intentionally craft a narrative with important historical information that is aware of at least the Markan tradition and intends to fill in gaps and fill out that

25. D. A. Carson, *The Gospel according to John*, PNTC (Grand Rapids: Eerdmans, 1991), 46–47.

26. This insight comes from Richard Bauckham, "Historiographical Characteristics of the Gospel of John," in his *Testimony of the Beloved Disciple: Narrative, History, and Theology in the Gospel of John* (Grand Rapids: Baker Academic, 2007), 35. See also his essay "John for Readers of Mark."

27. Not accidentally, these appear in two sets of seven: seven "I am" sayings with predicates ("I am the bread of life," etc.) and seven absolutes ("I am") which are divine self-declarations. Bauckham, "Johannine Jesus and the Synoptic Jesus."

28. Ibid.

29. Carson, *Gospel according to John*, 57.

widely known story in important ways.[30] Thus one finds in John comments that seem odd until one realizes that they are clues about fitting the following material into the already-known Markan chronology. For example, the statement in John 3:24 about John baptizing, "For John had not yet been put in prison," is so redundant that it makes no sense unless we understand it as John's subtle way of communicating that the material of John 1:19–4:43 fits in the presumed gap between Mark 1:13 and 1:14, showing how the two Gospels dovetail together. Another example of the same is John 11:2, which serves to fill in more information for Mark's readers of the event in Mark 14:3–9 and also clarifies which Mary is being spoken of here. Bauckham suggests that this kind of dovetailing, which occurs in other places in John, enables us to understand that the two Gospels can be read not as incompatible alternatives but as complementary. John's account does not require a knowledge of Mark; it stands alone. However, "it is so written that, for readers/hearers who are also familiar with Mark, it rarely repeats and largely complements Mark's narrative, and in such a way that chronological dovetailing of the two narratives can easily be accomplished."[31]

The Differences between Ancient and Modern History Writing

A final important idea for wrestling with the discrepancies between the Gospels is the recognition that what counted as valid historiography (the writing of history) was somewhat different in the ancient world than it is today. We will return to this important idea more fully in the following chapter, but for now we can explore it briefly as one of the solutions to the supposed discrepancies in the Gospels.

Like it or not, the sense of "historical accuracy" that we apply to modern history is not exactly the same as that of the ancient historians. This is not a matter of right and wrong but simply a difference. Therefore, it would be anachronistic to expect the ancient Gospel writers to portray things in precisely the way we have come to expect since the development of modern principles of historiography.

This point is connected to our earlier discussion of the genre type of the Gospels. The Gospels are similar in many ways to ancient *bioi*, and as such, this genre sets parameters for how they report the events of Jesus's life. We do well to consider the words of the first-century AD biographer Plutarch:

> I am not a writer of histories but of biographies. My readers therefore must excuse me if I do not record all events or describe in detail, but only briefly touch upon, the noblest and most famous. . . . As painters produce a likeness by the representation of the countenance and the expression of the face, in which the

---

30. The following argument comes from Bauckham, "John for Readers of Mark," 150–69.
31. Ibid, 159.

character is revealed, without troubling themselves about the other parts of the body, so I must be allowed to look rather into the signs of a man's character, and by means of these to portray the life of each, leaving to others the description of great events and battles. (*Alexander* 1.1)[32]

Of course, we must not press such analogies too far. As we have seen, the genres of history, biography, encomium, and so on were not hermetically sealed compartments but overlapping and flexible literary conventions. Thus, Plutarch's words do not offer us the kind of hard and fast rules that they might appear to at first. Nevertheless, they do reveal that a biographer (and indeed, a historian as well) understood his or her task not merely as a "just the facts, ma'am" description but as selective, interpretive, and intentional. Ancient writers exercised greater freedom of composition than their modern counterparts when reporting real, historical events, something their readers generally expected. We will see that modern history writing has come to understand this again, but many of us still labor under unrealistic, modernistic notions of what history-telling comprises, as if it were an unbiased, comprehensive, closed-circuit television view.

We can be more specific and identify a couple of ways in which ancient historiography clearly differed from our common modern expectations. First, there is the matter of plagiarism. It is worth noting that in the ancient world adopting and passing on the words of others was not regarded as immoral. Today the blatant use of someone else's words as one's own is considered wrong and a violation of copyright laws and intellectual property rights. Although at times, for reasons of validating authority, an ancient author would cite another author, there was in general a much freer use of others' thoughts, words, and phrases as stories and sayings were passed down over time and across space. It was not considered theft of intellectual property; rather, to use someone else's words and ideas was to honor him. Among other things, recognizing this helps us understand the close literary and oral interrelationship between the Gospel accounts, which obviously overlap extensively, even in exact wording, without citing each other or other sources.

Another characteristic of ancient history writing that differs from our expectations is that ancient historians tended to flesh out narratives to make a cohesive and flowing story. This practice also affected the reporting of speech, an area in which much more flexibility was allowed and expected than today. None of this means, however, that most ancient historians felt free to simply make up events.[33] "History was supposed to be truthful, and historians harshly criticized other historians whom they accused of promoting falsehood."[34]

---

32. Quoted in David Wenham and Steve Walton, *Exploring the New Testament: A Guide to the Gospels and Acts* (Downers Grove, IL: InterVarsity, 2001), 49–50.

33. Craig Keener, *The Historical Jesus of the Gospels* (Grand Rapids: Eerdmans, 2009), 110.

34. Ibid., 96. Succinct, well-documented arguments on this issue can be found in Keener's chap. 7, "Ancient Historiography as History," and chap. 8, "Ancient Historiography as Rhetoric."

Nevertheless, ancient authors had freedom to flesh out stories in a reasonable and accurate way.

Another, even more important difference between ancient and modern historiography is the greater flexibility of the former in presenting chronological and narrative sequence. When comparing the Gospels, we quickly realize that ancient historical narratives do not maintain the chronological sequence of events as strictly as we might desire. In the Gospels narrative sequence or time does not always equal real-time chronology. Grant Osborne describes it well:

> None of the Gospel writers are interested in a strictly chronological narration of the life of Jesus. This is obvious first by comparing the Synoptics with John. In John Jesus makes several trips to Jerusalem during his ministry, and there are three passovers (2:13; 6:4; 11:55 = 12:1), indicating at least a two-year ministry. In the Synoptics Jesus only goes to Jerusalem at the end of his ministry and seems to have a one-year ministry. Moreover, even the Synoptics differ widely at times on the order of events in Jesus' ministry. There is no evidence anywhere of a week-by-week or month-by-month itinerary of Jesus' life. This is hardly a new realization. Augustine himself realized that there was no actual temporal chronicle of Jesus' movements in the Gospels but often a topical organization. However, this does not mean that there is no chronology in the Gospels.[35]

Ancient historians were not under strict constraints to be chronological in that sense and instead often organized the work topically. Osborne goes on to point out that sometimes chronology is assumed, such as when the text explicitly says something like "and the next day" such and such happened. But overall, the Gospels are apparently organized by topic rather than chronology. Matthew's five major teaching discourses provide one of the most obvious examples of this. Indeed, it can be shown that elements in these topically arranged "sermons" collect material from various places and contexts in the Jesus traditions, and Matthew has arranged them as such for didactic and pedagogical purposes. Even Calvin, who was obviously no modern historical critic, held this view. He, along with many in the history of interpretation, recognized this aspect of inspired historiography.[36]

35. Osborne, "Historical Criticism and the Evangelical," 202.

36. Calvin, writing on the Sermon on the Mount (s.v. Matt. 5:1 in his *Commentary on a Harmony of the Evangelists*), says, "Those who think that Christ's sermon, which is here related, is different from the sermon contained in the sixth chapter of Luke's Gospel, rest their opinion on a very light and frivolous argument. . . . It is probable that this discourse was not delivered until Christ had chosen the twelve; but in attending to the order of time, which I saw that the Spirit of God had disregarded, I did not wish to be too precise. Pious and modest readers ought to be satisfied with having a brief summary of the doctrine of Christ placed before our eyes, *collected out of his many and various discourses*" (John Calvin, *Commentary on a Harmony of the Evangelists: Matthew, Mark, and Luke*, trans. William Pringle [Grand Rapids: Baker, 1996], 1:259, emphasis mine).

Moreover, when one begins to think carefully about modern history writing, it becomes apparent that it also often has a more topical rather than strictly chronological element. In reading the recent biography of Albert Einstein by Walter Isaacson,[37] I was struck by how elements of the later part of Einstein's life found their way into the earliest chapters. Isaacson not only foreshadows certain events to come, but he relates and explains these events so that the rest of the story will make sense and have an interpretive guide rail. This is good history writing. Thus, in many ways this practice is an inevitable part of historiography, despite unexamined notions that many of us have concerning the nature of historical narration. And while this topical arrangement may seem odd to us, it was not so for ancient writers or readers. Thus, we need not feel perplexed or defensive that Matthew has the healing of the leper before the healing of Peter's mother-in-law (Matt. 8:1–4, 14), followed by the calming of the storm and the healing of the Gadarene demoniac (8:23–34), while Mark puts these in a different order (1:29–31, 40–45; 4:35–5:20), nor about the irreconcilable difference (from a modern perspective) of the order in which Jesus's temptations occurred (cf. Matt. 4:1–11 and Luke 4:1–13).

Thus, again, it is very important that we recognize these basic differences in the expectations of ancient history writing compared to our own. It is a matter not of truthfulness or accuracy but of genre expectation and convention. Note that we are not talking about *whether* these things really happened—on this the Gospels and the church fathers rightly are univocal, "Yes they did!"—but rather, on how these things are retold. The reporting and retelling of the Gospel events necessarily follow ancient conventions, not our own.

Summary

I have provided several potential approaches to understanding how the fourfold Gospel account can be read as agreeing rather than conflicting. Many other solutions can be offered. Indeed, whole books have been dedicated to these important issues.[38]

There is really nothing new in what I have suggested in this discussion. As we have seen, these kinds of historical questions and challenges to the Gospels are very old, and they have been answered astutely throughout the generations. Much of what I have said has already been articulated by Augustine.[39] None-

---

37. Walter Isaacson, *Einstein: His Life and Universe* (New York: Simon & Schuster, 2008).

38. Very accessible is Craig Blomberg's *Historical Reliability of the Gospels*. Blomberg offers other approaches to resolving historical discrepancies such as theological clarification, representational changes, partial reports of longer sayings, presupposing information available elsewhere, and compressing or telescoping a narrative.

39. Salmond summarizes Augustine's approach as "characterized by simplicity and good sense." For parallel sayings and stories, Augustine often supposes different instances of similar events (my "itinerant nature"), and he considers of little consequence mere differences in verbal variation between the accounts of the same events (my "*vox* versus *verba*"). In other instances

theless, it is important to face such issues squarely, and Christians throughout the ages have sensed the rightness of always being ready to give a defense for their hope (1 Pet. 3:15).

In the following chapter I will offer yet one more solution, the most important and macro-level answer that goes beyond the detailed ones given here. Although these assorted solutions do relieve much of the tension, they do not solve every problem, and some critics will perceive them as mere special pleading and/or naive fideism. To fully address the question of the historical issues of the Gospels, we need to make an important side trip into the development and nature of historical discourse, what we may call "the history of history." But before taking up this issue, let us conclude this chapter by discussing briefly the positive side of this issue, or the joy of having a fourfold account.

The Joy of Having Four Gospels

In light of all the centuries of labor expended and ink employed to defend the fourfold Gospel witness, is it worth it? Is there any corresponding joy? We should recall that having only one Gospel *was* an option, but it was rejected. What good comes from having four Gospels, or to use Irenaeus's language, a "fourfold Gospel"?

In short, there is a richness in the four that one Gospel alone could not provide. We already have hints of this in John's poetic epilogue, where we read that if everything that Jesus did were written down, even the whole world could not contain the books this would produce (John 21:25). If it is indeed true that Jesus was God's Son incarnate, the Creator of the universe, and the consummation of all knowledge and wisdom, then it stands to reason that no one account—or a million—could begin to describe and plumb the depths of his person, teaching, and actions.

To a lesser degree this is true of any person, especially one who has stood out in his or her time as a leader and influencer. For example, we can think about the many sides of the great Winston Churchill. Richard Burridge describes various portraits of Churchill taken at different times and places— some pre–World War II, some during, some after, some public, some private, some joyful, some somber. They are all clearly pictures of the same man, but each reveals a different side and perspective.[40] How much more is this true of any report (or *logos*) of the Divine Logos who briefly tabernacled among us in the flesh (John 1:14)? Our four Gospels are like stained-glass windows, which capture and refract the sun into different shapes and hues and images.

---

he gives rather elaborate and detailed explanations, not all of which are equally convincing. Salmond's translation notes, Schaff, *NPNF*[1] 6:72.

40. Burridge develops this illustration to great effect in his *Four Gospels, One Jesus? A Symbolic Reading*, 2nd ed. (Grand Rapids: Eerdmans, 2005), 1–5.

Even as a mighty cathedral would be unduly darkened and underappreciated if illuminated by only one pinhole window, so too the intricacies and beauty of God's revelation in Jesus the Christ deserve a flood of light from all sides of the building. Our four Gospels all open onto the same inner sanctum and altar, but with different and complementary angles of light. We would be much impoverished without the highly structured, intratextual account of Matthew, the high-speed rush toward the cross and resurrection of Mark, the self-consciously Isaianic-fulfilling Luke, and the unexpectedly subtle profundity of John's simple story.

This imagery is reminiscent of the way that many fathers of the church spoke about the Gospels, particularly Irenaeus and Augustine. As mentioned above, Irenaeus suggests that it is not only good that we have four Gospels, but it is *necessary* on analogy to having four zones of the world and four winds. We have the Gospel in four forms bound together by one Spirit.[41]

Augustine follows this line of thinking and expands upon it. Like Irenaeus before him, and contributing to a strong tradition in sacred art ever since, Augustine also uses the four images of an angel/man, lion, ox, and eagle to picture the four Gospels.[42] This fourfold set comes from Ezekiel and John's Apocalypse and becomes a potent image for exploring the different perspectives and emphases of the four evangelists.[43] Augustine offers precisely such a discussion at the beginning of his *Harmony of the Gospels*, partly to defend having four Gospels but also to help explain how they differ yet are complementary. Augustine observes that the Synoptics reveal Jesus in his *fleshly* ministry as both King and Priest, with Matthew and Mark focusing on the former and Luke the latter.[44] At the same time, John provides us with a loftier view that sets forth Jesus's *divine* nature "in such a way as he believed to be adequate to men's needs and notions."[45] We are indebted to John for giving us understanding of how the Christ is divine and equal with the Father, for John alone is "like one who has drunk in the secret of His divinity more richly and somehow more familiarly than others, as if he drew it from the very bosom of his Lord on which it was his wont to recline when He sat at meat."[46] Comparing the Synoptics and John, Augustine also suggests that in this fourfold richness we are given both of the virtues "proposed to the mind of man," the active and the contemplative. The Synoptic accounts speak of the Lord's temporal doings and sayings, "which were meant to bear chiefly upon the molding of the manners of the present life," that of active virtue. In complementary contrast, John narrates far fewer of Jesus's actions "but

41. Irenaeus, *Against Heresies* 3.11.8.
42. Augustine, *Harmony of the Gospels* 1.7.9.
43. See also the use of this as the rubric in Burridge's *Four Gospels, One Jesus?*
44. Augustine, *Harmony of the Gospels* 1.3.5–6.
45. Ibid., 1.4.7.
46. Ibid.

records with greater carefulness and with larger wealth of detail the words which He spoke, and most especially those discourses which were intended to introduce us to the knowledge of the unity of the Trinity and the blessedness of the life eternal," commending to us the contemplative virtue.[47] There are many other such analogies and reflections that could be offered. The point is clear: there is a richness, beauty, strength, and joy in retaining the unified diversity of the fourfold witness.

Speaking on a more practical level and closely related to Augustine, we may also rejoice in having four Gospels because they enable us to see different theological points. Real insight can be gained here from doing a horizontal reading of the accounts and even redaction critical work, if it is done with constraint. As we have seen, recognizing different emphases in the different evangelists' accounts is not new, but a *focus* on this kind of reading, and particularly, reading horizontally across the Gospels to discern theological differences, is a more recent development. I will not explore the pros and cons of redaction criticism here, which can easily be found in other introductory books. For our purposes the point is simply that by having four diverse accounts we can often gain insight into particular emphases *precisely because they do differ at points.*

For example, a comparison of Matthew's beatitude "Blessed are the poor in spirit" (Matt. 5:3) with Luke's "Blessed are you poor" (Luke 6:20) prompts reflection that these two parallel sayings lean in different directions and evoke diverse reactions. This realization in turn leads us to recognize that indeed Luke speaks regularly about the poor and financial matters, far more often than do the other evangelists. Real insight is then gained into the meaning not only of Luke 6:20 but of many passages throughout the Third Gospel. Similarly, pondering the different order of the devil's offers in the narratives of Jesus's temptation (Matt. 4:1–11 and Luke 4:1–13) can stimulate further reflection on the significance of which temptation is the final and climactic one. Further reading and study may enable one to conclude that Matthew has highlighted Satan's offer of "all the kingdoms of *the world*" because of the contrast it provides to Jesus's preaching of "the kingdom of *heaven*."[48] At the same time, it is entirely appropriate that Luke concludes the temptations with Jesus at the pinnacle of the temple in Jerusalem, arguably the place that serves as the thematic epicenter of both Luke and Acts. Without these differences between the accounts one would be less likely to notice the way in which these particular passages form part of broader literary and theological themes in each respective Gospel. This kind of horizontal analysis is not *necessary* for such good reading, but it certainly provides a welcome "stimulus package" for all of us as we develop our reading skills.

47. Ibid., 1.5.8.
48. Further exploration of this idea throughout Matthew can be found in my *Heaven and Earth in the Gospel of Matthew* (Grand Rapids: Baker Academic, 2009).

In sum, then, to receive the Gospels as Holy Scripture is to embrace their diversity, receiving with joy the different insights and wisdom they provide, while also rejoicing in their complementary univocality. As Stephen Barton writes:

> That there are four gospels standing side by side in the canon, none of which has been subordinated to another, is an invitation to recognize that the truth about Jesus to which the Gospels bear witness is *irreducibly plural* without being either incoherent or completely elastic. The fourfold gospel points to the profundity of Jesus' impact on his followers, the inexhaustibility of the truth about him, and the way in which knowledge of Jesus is necessarily self-involving.[49]

The discrepancies between the Gospels need not cause an angst that raises doubts or overwhelms the joy of the gift of a fourfold witness to the reality of Jesus Christ. We may conclude with wise words from the great scholar Martin Hengel, writing near the end of his life:

> The "multiplicity" of the Gospels may sometimes seem an aporia to us today and perplex us, but in reality—contrary to all false attempts at harmonization—they became an inexhaustible source of power, the power which created true faith, love and hope. . . . Looking back on the history of the church which is now almost two thousand years old we must say that, thank God, the real unity of the churches does not lie in our different, indeed controversial human convictions and efforts, but in the one Lord. . . . By the will of God we have the one—unique—"good news," the one Gospel which stands at the beginning of the church, in sometimes very different human forms. Yet all four Gospels proclaim solely the one Lord of the church and the one salvation brought about by him.[50]

49. Stephen C. Barton, "Many Gospels, One Jesus?" in *The Cambridge Companion to Jesus*, ed. Markus Bockmuehl (Cambridge: Cambridge University Press, 2001), 170.

50. Hengel, *Four Gospels*, 167–68.

5

Texts and History

The Testimony of the Fourfold Witness

An Active Fault Line

The annual Wheaton Theology Conference in 2010 was dedicated to honoring and interacting with the work of the prolific and influential scholar N. T. Wright.[1] The first day of the conference dealt with Wright's work on the historical Jesus, particularly interacting with his massive book *Jesus and the Victory of God*.[2] One of the respondents was the renowned scholar Richard Hays. Hays offered a friendly but substantive critique of Wright's work in his paper titled "Knowing Jesus: Story, History, and the Question of Truth." Hays's paper was in fact a response to a critique Wright had made of Hays's approach at the Society of Biblical Literature meeting in 2008, when a panel was dedicated to discussing Hays and Gaventa's book *Seeking the Identity of Jesus*.[3] Wright had critiqued Hays and others as being too dogmatic in their approach and not sufficiently historical.

The title of Hays's paper indicates that the issue in dispute is not a secondary or tangential topic but instead involves a decision about a major issue

---

1. The papers from this conference are now published in *Jesus, Paul and the People of God: A Theological Dialogue with N. T. Wright*, ed. Nicholas Perrin and Richard Hays (Downers Grove, IL: InterVarsity, 2011).

2. N. T. Wright, *Jesus and the Victory of God* (Minneapolis: Fortress, 1996).

3. Beverly Roberts Gaventa and Richard B. Hays, eds., *Seeking the Identity of Jesus: A Pilgrimage* (Grand Rapids: Eerdmans, 2008).

in Gospels study. To use the language of Hays, this topic of how story and history relate to knowing the truth is a major fault line in biblical studies. A brief walk along this theo/geological outcropping will serve us well as we seek to understand how the Gospels witness to the historical reality of Jesus.

Using Wright's writings, especially *Jesus and the Victory of God* and the methodology laid out in *The New Testament and the People of God*,[4] Hays surveys Wright's historical method, which Wright calls "critical realism."[5] Hays notes what this looks like when applied, particularly Wright's extensive use of the Second Temple Jewish literature to reconstruct a realistic first-century Jewish setting for Jesus. This reconstruction leads Wright to confidently speak about Jesus's intentions and self-understanding and results in his using the (Synoptic) Gospels as windows onto a plausible historical setting. This is how one is to construct theological understanding. For Wright, understanding the Old Testament's story as retold in the Second Temple literature enables us to understand Jesus as a self-consciously eschatological prophet who is proclaiming and in himself bringing about Israel's long-awaited return from exile. From Wright's perspective, his critical realism approach keeps together both historical work and a place for faith and theological understanding. Wright correctly cares about the fact that Jesus came in real space and time in history, and he argues that we need to keep history and theology together because they are in reality integrally related.[6]

Hays does not seem to have a problem with this latter statement, but he goes on to observe that in practice and by Wright's other statements, this marriage of history and theology proves to be an unequally yoked one.[7] That is, in many revealing ways Wright often gives the upper hand to historical grounding and historical reconstruction as the basis for doing theology, even over against a canonical and ecclesial reading. So, as Hays points out, while Wright's work

---

4. N. T. Wright, *The New Testament and the People of God* (London: SPCK, 1992).

5. After surveying alternative approaches, Wright describes critical realism as a way of knowing "that acknowledges *the reality of the thing known, as something other than the knower* (hence 'realism'), while also fully acknowledging that the only access we have to this reality lies along the spiraling path of *appropriate dialogue or conversation between the knower and the thing known* (hence 'critical')." Ibid., 35, italics in original.

6. As an interesting aside, it is helpful to contrast this view with one at somewhat the opposite pole, that of John Sailhammer, as seen in his magnum opus, *The Meaning of the Pentateuch: Revelation, Composition and Interpretation* (Downers Grove, IL: InterVarsity, 2009). Sailhammer's views are at once brilliant and difficult to understand. He admirably argues for a text-preference approach, letting the texts themselves tell and interpret their story as opposed to historical reconstruction constraining the text. Yet at the same time, Sailhammer often inadvertently reintroduces behind the text suppositions that greatly affect his reading. This dialectic is indeed inevitable, but Sailhammer vociferously argues that it should not be, making his inconsistencies all the more perplexing.

7. The metaphor is mine, but a very similar and perceptive critique of Wright on precisely this score was made earlier by Murray Rae in his book *History and Hermeneutics* (London: T&T Clark, 2005).

has many strengths (including his in-depth and plausible reconstruction, coherence, high Christology, and apologetic value), some fundamental problems
arise. Namely, Wright's method often leads him not to hear the individual
(theological) voices of the evangelists because they are drowned out by the
synthetic historical reconstruction behind the text, a reconstruction that is
itself a bit too neat and tidy and overly systematized.[8] As a result the canon
itself loses authority as (Wright's) historical reconstruction becomes a crucial
and even necessary aspect for reading the canonical text correctly. Kähler's
comment then applies to Wright, that the critical historian effectually becomes
the fifth evangelist. Although this is clearly not Wright's intention as it is for
Crossan and others, in effect the Gospels are replaced by a constraining historical reconstruction.

A fundamental problem is the absence of the resurrection in Wright's explication of the historical Jesus. To be fair, Wright dedicates a whole other volume
to the resurrection and makes strong arguments there for the bodily raising of
Jesus and its importance.[9] Clearly he cannot do everything in one book, but
Hays's critique still stands: Because the resurrection is the epicenter of history
and is the beginning of the new creation itself, it must be the starting point
for our theology, our epistemology (i.e., how we know), and any historical
reconstruction.[10] Therefore, we cannot meaningfully or helpfully speak of a
historical Jesus *without* thorough reference to the reality and reality-changing
event of the resurrection. In this Hays seeks to moderate Wright by turning
to Karl Barth for a more balanced approach that still accepts the historical
reality of events but tempers historical reconstruction in terms of theological
articulation. Hays's point is that while historical work is important, apart
from a canonical-theological understanding of Jesus we cannot hope to get the
historical story right. Moreover, we cannot privilege historical reconstruction
as the avenue for doing canonical theology.

On three different occasions at the conference, Wright had the opportunity
to respond. Taking these responses together, we can identify how Wright's
views differ from Hays's.[11] Wright responds that his work does indeed use

8. After the publication of *Jesus and the Victory of God*, a volume dedicated to interacting
with Wright appeared: Carey C. Newman, ed., *Jesus and the Restoration of Israel: A Critical
Assessment of N. T. Wright's Jesus and the Victory of God* (Downers Grove, IL: InterVarsity,
1999). Many of the critiques offered there are worth perusing, including that of C. Stephen
Evans. See below for further discussion.

9. N. T. Wright, *The Resurrection of the Son of God* (Minneapolis: Fortress, 2003).

10. Maryanne Meye Thompson also mentions Wright's lack of resurrection focus in *Jesus
and the Victory of God* in her paper "The Gospel of John Meets Jesus and the Victory of God"
(presented at the Wheaton Theology Conference, Wheaton, IL, April 16, 2010). Again, a very
similar argument has already been expounded in Rae's *History and Hermeneutics*, chap. 4.

11. A similar but not identical response can be found in Wright's essay "In Grateful Dialogue:
A Response" in Newman, *Jesus and the Restoration of Israel*, esp. 244–52. I had the privilege of
being present at this conference, and my comments and summary are based on my own notes. In

much of the method of other historical Jesus studies (such as focusing on the Synoptics rather than John), but he does this for apologetic reasons so that he might get a hearing, especially in a scholarly environment that was formerly dominated by the likes of Robert Funk and John Dominic Crossan. In the modern period, a theological understanding of Jesus has often been rejected on the grounds of history. Wright wants to show the opposite and does so by using the same approaches to present a more plausible case. Yes, Wright says, his project can be seen as a response to eighteenth-century developments in historical Jesus studies, but it could not be otherwise to engage with these influential views. But Wright does not stop there; he does not see his historically grounded approach as adopted *only* for apologetic reasons, but he also argues for the *necessary* role of history in all theological construction. It is dangerous to proceed without doing our history first, Wright argues. Without historical grounding for one's arguments, there is insufficient reason not to doubt (it is mere fideism). Scholars and popular writers often bully churchgoers with their "historical arguments." We should respond with care and clear thinking. History matters, and it is essential that these events happened lest Christianity be only an abstract idea or general truth. Also, without historical grounding we can too easily make Jesus into whatever image and agenda we desire. Wright references the words of Ernst Käsemann, who after World War II argued for the importance of grounding Jesus in his proper historical context, unlike the developments in Germany that had led to a disastrous view of Christianity and Judaism. We can too easily create a nonhistorical, docetic Jesus in our own cultural image. But even more pointedly and aggressively, Wright argues that in fact the creedal tradition has imposed on us a Jesus different from the true one that historical situatedness gives us. Wright does not think he is creating a behind-the-text Jesus; rather it is the church tradition that has tended to do this by emphasizing Jesus's divine identity (which Wright would not deny) rather than what Jesus was actually about: inaugurating the kingdom of God, which is the fulfillment of God's promises to Israel. Creeds like that from Chalcedon effectively "de-Israelize" Jesus and remove him from his Jewish context, precisely what we need to recover to read the Gospels rightly.

These are indeed weighty matters! I offer a survey of this debate because, as Hays rightly notes, this difference of approach and opinion is emblematic of a broader debate that runs through much of biblical studies and academic evangelical understanding. This issue is not only a continental divide; it is an active fault line with tremors (and added man-made explosives) running through and shaking up authors and institutions. These issues are important and will not soon go away. As we will see, they have been with us for a very long time and are worthy of revisiting. We will now dig more deeply into what

---

addition to Wright's earlier essay in the Newman volume, one may also see Wright's comments in the published proceedings from the Wheaton conference, referenced above.

is at stake here and also suggest a way forward that was unfortunately absent from the stimulating discussion at the conference.

The History of History[12]

Ancient History

History—meaning here the writing of history and history as an object of study[13]—has its own colored and varied history, one that continues to be debated to this day. Its story rides the crests and troughs of the waves of theology and philosophy. We may start at least as far back as Plato's famous cave analogy and the subsequent Platonic influence on Greek thought. This dualistic predisposition that separated the human realm of space and time from that of the eternal and unchanging tended to produce an antihistorical approach in much of Greek thought. There were exceptions (e.g., Herodotus, often considered the "father of history"), but in general, truth was thought to be a matter of the eternal world outside this changing one, not contingent on human history, but a matter of philosophical speculation.[14] This is a strong trend in the Western understanding of history that will find continual ebb and flow in subsequent development.

Understanding this Greek cultural and philosophical environment deepens one's appreciation for the titanic struggle the early church faced with its patently non-Platonic, Judeo-Christian understanding of God's real work in history, ultimately seen in the incarnation of the divine Logos. Even though the first two centuries of the church's existence faced stubborn incredulity regarding the claims that the divine could inhabit the earthly, in the fourth century AD the church experienced an unprecedented turn of Roman favor with the conversion of Constantine. Connected to this, along with the rise of great apologists and theologians in the third, fourth, and fifth centuries, most notably Augustine (354–430), the Christian worldview in large part won the

---

12. This is a massive and important area of study on which I can provide only a necessarily cursory discussion. I will refer to several key works, but much of what follows depends on the helpful and readable volumes of Murray Rae, *History and Hermeneutics*, and Thomas Howard, *Religion and the Rise of Historicism: W. M. L. de Wette, Jacob Burckhardt, and the Theological Origins of Nineteenth-Century Historical Consciousness* (Cambridge: Cambridge University Press, 2000). Also very thorough and well-written is Scot McKnight's chapter "The Historical Jesus, the Death of Jesus, Historiography, and Theology," in his *Jesus and His Death: Historiography, the Historical Jesus, and Atonement Theory* (Waco: Baylor University Press, 2005), 3–47. Though coming from a different perspective than my own and with different conclusions, the treatment in Alexander J. M. Wedderburn, *Jesus and the Historians* (Tübingen: Mohr Siebeck, 2010), is also worth reading.

13. Many scholars acknowledge that much confusion has arisen because of our sloppy use of the polyvalent term "history." "History" in current English parlance can mean a range of things including what happened in the past or a retelling and reconstruction of past events.

14. Rae, *History and Hermeneutics*, 5.

day, including its biblical notion of history (cf. Augustine's monumental *City of God*). This shift represented a great reversal concerning the relationship of history to the eternal and the divine. From a biblical perspective God is the author and superintendent of time and history and is intimately involved in it, most notably in the incarnation, and finally at the parousia. In contrast to a Platonic or Herodotian approach, Christian historiography was universal, providential, apocalyptic, and periodized.[15]

Enlightenment Developments

The period from late antiquity through the medieval era and the Reformation were not without epistemic and philosophical changes,[16] but as these impinge on understanding history, a decisive turning point in our story arrives with the developments of the Enlightenment and modernity. With the rise of modernity, especially Descartes (1596–1650) and Spinoza (1632–77), "the Western philosophical tradition began again to question whether truth and history could be regarded as coalescent terms."[17] Though early generations of modernists retained the language of God, the new, real god was reason. Spinoza's influence on theology and biblical studies (and consequently on the understanding of history) was profound. He argued that truth about God was not to be found in historically mediated revelation but through reason. The result was a distinction between the Bible's teachings—which are simply about moral virtues—and its history-like content, which serves no relation to "faith."

Furthering this view is the work of G. E. Lessing, one of the leaders of the German Enlightenment, who argued against the epistemic value of historical testimony, questioned the trustworthiness of the Bible's miracles, and argued that even if we could prove that the Bible's claims were true, this would not justify the belief in its theological claims, such as the divinity of Jesus. This argument is summed up in Lessing's famous remark that "the accidental truths of history can never become the proof of necessary truths of reason." Human autonomous reason reigns supreme and alone is trustworthy. Antiquated notions of revelation (into history) are rejected, as is the central place of history in understanding Christianity. Christianity is now understood as the moral exercise of our rational capacities. This approach is applied to the Gospels in one of the

---

15. This typology comes from the fascinating analysis in Leonard S. Smith, *Religion and the Rise of History: Martin Luther and the Cultural Revolution in Germany, 1760–1810* (Eugene, OR: Cascade Books, 2009), 16–17. In the initial chapter, "A Typology of Classical and Christian Historiography," Smith sees three main stages in the development of historiography: (1) classical, such as the thought of Herodotus; (2) Christian, from Augustine to Voltaire; (3) modern professional, from B. G. Niebuhr and Leopold von Ranke and the founding of the University of Berlin (1810).

16. One may consult the brief but helpful essay by Ellen Charry, "Walking in the Truth: On Knowing God," in *But Is It All True? The Bible and the Question of Truth*, ed. Alan Padgett and Patrick Keifert (Grand Rapids: Eerdmans, 2006), 144–69.

17. Rae, *History and Hermeneutics*, 6.

most influential books of the Enlightenment period, D. F. Strauss's *Life of Jesus* (1835), in which the "historical" Jesus is presented, a Jesus "stripped bare of the accretions of theological dogma."[18] Timeless truth, as revealed in the "real" ethical Jesus, not (unreliable) history, is what matters. Historically mediated truth is seen as a contradiction in terms as God is timeless and ahistorical.[19]

Post-Enlightenment intellectual history is not monolithic, however, especially where it intersects with religion. While one strong trajectory did emphasize reason as the avenue of all truth, another strand of modern thinking instead came to view empirical objective historical study as the way to get at the truth.[20] This approach also had earlier roots, especially in the Renaissance and Reformation cry of "*Ad fontes*" ("To the sources!") as a way of understanding and breaking free from encrusted tradition.

In much of nineteenth-century Germany this "classical historicism" developed and came to dominate. "Historicism" is a worldview or way of understanding reality that in many ways is a response to the dead end realized by taking the supra-temporal reason approach to its logical conclusion.[21] The most famous and influential historicist thinker was Leopold von Ranke, who sought to ground history in the particulars of the past *wie es eigentlich gewesen* ("as they really happened"). Driving this approach to history is the idea that the scholar must be "free from theological and dogmatic presuppositions . . . objective and scientific, and therefore capable of recovering what actually happened in history, rather than imposing later theological categories upon history."[22] This is not just an academic methodology but a view of reality in which historians through their objective ("scientific") work give us the meaning of the world. This "historicism" becomes for many in Germany and beyond a new religion or at least the new epistemic approach to religion.[23] It is difficult to overestimate the significance of this change and the profound impact historicism had on epistemology in the modern period.

18. Ibid., 15. See also Howard, *Religion and the Rise of Historicism*, 80–81.

19. Howard, *Religion and the Rise of Historicism*, 78–79.

20. This is not to say that historical objectivity did not also rely heavily on reason, but to distinguish between (pure) reason as a mode of thinking pursued apart from arguments driven by historical data. Indeed, behind all forms of modern historical criticism, natural reason drives the program. As Plantinga astutely observes, despite the various approaches of "historical biblical criticism," they are all "an effort to try to determine from the standpoint of reason alone what the Scriptural teachings are and whether they are true." Alvin Plantinga, "Two (or More) Kinds of Scripture Scholarship," in *"Behind the Text": History and Biblical Interpretation*, ed. Craig Bartholomew et al., SHS 4 (Grand Rapids: Zondervan, 2003), 27.

21. Howard, *Religion and the Rise of Historicism*, 12.

22. As summarized by G. E. Ladd in his essay "The Problem of History in Contemporary New Testament Interpretation," in *Studia Evangelica*, ed. F. L. Cross, vol. 5 (Berlin: Akademie-Verlag, 1968), 88.

23. Karl Mannheim, reflecting on the development of historicism, remarks that it alone "provides us with a world view of the same universality as that of the religious world view of the past." Quoted in Howard, *Religion and the Rise of Historicism*, 12.

In the twentieth century this "classical historicism" has been called "crisis historicism." Its key influential fi̹ continued with and concretized the scientific methodol but he came to see the inevitable cultural conditioning (including those of the supposed critical historian. Tht cepted historicism's methods, he believed that history w acquisition of meaning (as in classical historicism) but rather that it "progressively showed the relativity and invalidity of the values and beliefs of Western culture."[25] One can see already, then, the first sprouts that will flower into the skepticism of late modernity and postmodernity.

The point for us in this all-too-brief survey is that in both of these approaches to the relationship of history and access to truth (reason and historicism), a less-than-biblical viewpoint develops. The Gospel accounts come to be severely criticized and rejected, either as being irrelevant to true religion (which is the rational ethics of the enlightened human) or as so encrusted with dogmatic tradition that they cannot give us the "real" historical Jesus. This historical Jesus is instead delivered by the new hero, the scientific and objective historian. In either case, herein lies a key turning point in the increasing secularization of Western civilization with its concomitant decline of the place of the church and the Bible's role in society. Note that we are talking here about not just a loss of belief or trust in the Bible's "accuracy" but a foundational epistemic change, that is, a change in understanding how we know and what counts as valid knowledge. First rationalism and then history becomes the reigning god of the mental acropolis.[26] The question to be raised here, but addressed more fully below, is to what extent today's believing readers have adopted these epistemological categories of historicism, unaware of how this conflicts with understanding the Gospels as Holy Scripture.

Responses to Enlightenment Historicism

Such radical developments, of course, did not come without significant detraction. We have already noted that nineteenth-century classical historicism was itself in many ways a reaction to eighteenth-century rationalism,

24. Troeltsch's famous three principles of historicism are criticism, analogy, and correlation.

25. Howard, *Religion and the Rise of Historicism*, 13.

26. Tischendorf, lamenting the Gospels-debasing influence of the Frenchman Joseph-Ernest Renan combined with German rationalism, writes: "Not only is the prevalent rationalism, which places our common human reason above a divine revelation and so sets aside the supernatural claims of the Gospels a product of this French book, but German zeal is aroused, as well, to supply what is lacking of scientific accuracy in Renan's work, and to make his results more trustworthy. And so we have one of the frightful spectacles of our time—French levity and German learning reaching brotherly hands to each other over the fresh grave of the Saviour." Constantin von Tischendorf, *Origin of the Four Gospels*, trans. W. L. Gage (Boston: American Tract Society, 1867), 32–33.

en while the latter continued to have influence in many quarters. The ghosts of old ideas always linger. The twentieth century likewise saw reactions and responses to both rationalism and historicism (in both its classical and crisis forms). Tracing these responses within theological and biblical studies provides a virtual Who's Who of influential interpreters right down to the present.[27] In many ways the debates of twentieth-century biblical scholarship have been framed by decisions about the role of history in this endeavor.[28] Broadly we may describe these as different ways of relating history to theology: "theology versus history" and "theology through history."

THEOLOGY VERSUS HISTORY

At the turn of the twentieth century Martin Kähler provided a strong contrast to Troeltsch and argued that Jesus's uniqueness as the revelation of God means that he cannot be found through historicism, especially its (Troeltschian) principle that all historical events can be analogized to others. Jesus's uniqueness breaks this bond. Rather than seeking a historical Jesus behind the text, we find Christ in the kerygma, the apostolic proclamation found in the church.[29] Key to Kähler's argument and subsequent influence is his distinction between two German words, *Historie* and *Geschichte*.[30] *Historie* is the history reconstructed by the historical-critical method; *Geschichte* is an event of the past known by its impact on subsequent history. Kähler understood the Gospels as presenting us a true *Geschichte*, while he found *Historie* (what we are calling here historicism) to be a *Holzweg*, or blind alley. This is because *Historie*'s product is irrelevant for faith and is based on ideas and principles imported into the text.[31] It is not difficult to detect in this response the seeds of thinking for both Bultmann and Barth, even though they will take them in very different directions.

27. As Patrick Henry said in 1979, and which applies even more so now, "Much Christian theology and New Testament study in the twentieth century has been shaped in response to 'the problem of history.'" Patrick Henry, *New Directions in New Testament Study* (Philadelphia: Westminster, 1979), 28.

28. Very helpful on this topic is the chapter "The War of the Worldviews" in Roy A. Harrisville and Walter Sundberg, *The Bible in Modern Culture: From Baruch Spinoza to Brevard Childs*, 2nd ed. (Grand Rapids: Eerdmans, 2002), 10–29. I will not discuss here the reactions of Schleiermacher or that of the Pietists, both of which can be found in this essay. For a detailed survey of these issues as they relate to the "salvation history" approach, see Robert W. Yarbrough, *The Salvation Historical Fallacy? Reassessing the History of New Testament Theology* (Leiden: Deo, 2004).

29. Rae, *History and Hermeneutics*, 22–23. As above, this section depends heavily on Rae's own survey.

30. Martin Kähler, *Der sogenannte historische Jesus und der geschichtliche biblische Christus* (1892; Munich: Chr. Kaiser, 1956). Translated by Carl E. Braaten as *The So-called Historical Jesus and the Historic, Biblical Christ* (Philadelphia: Fortress, 1964).

31. This understanding of Kähler is provided by the summary in Ladd, "Problem of History," 92–93.

Influenced by both Kähler and Albert Schweitzer,[32] Bultmann similarly argued that the Christian faith could not be founded on such historical research as historicism supplied because Christianity is about God, not humanity, and historicism only supplies information about Jesus the man. For this reason Bultmann rejected the liberal Christianity of his day, because it was anthropocentric. He likewise rejected Troeltsch for making Christianity a phenomenon of this world and for presuming its truth could be exhausted within categories of immanence. Bultmann posited that we need the Christ of faith, not the Christ of the flesh, which he read 2 Corinthians 5:16 to support. Instead of looking to history, Bultmann emphasized finding Christ in the kerygma, something to which historians can contribute little. As Rae notes about Bultmann's kerygma, it is a message that "floats free of the particular circumstances of its deliverance by Jesus, which, in themselves, are merely incidental."[33] The result, then, for Bultmann, is a faith for which history is incidental. Not only did he think we can know little about Jesus historically, he preferred it that way. God is "wholly other," and therefore we cannot identify God and his acts through historical study. "The redemptive acts of God can never become objective events of the past; they can be only present events of my existence."[34] (One can hear the echo of Lessing here.) In fact, to claim that God acts in history is to speak the language of myth, something that modern humans can no longer do. Whence comes Bultmann's famous "demythologizing" project. It should be noted that Bultmann differs from Kähler in that for Bultmann, the *Geschichte* becomes the Christ-event that occurs when we as individuals existentially experience God. We can see then that in his (correct) rejection of historicism and its inability to grasp Christianity and Christ himself, Bultmann swung back to the dehistoricizing pole of understanding (à la Lessing). Rather than finding reason as the way forward, he substituted existentialism as the way to grasp the true essence of faith in Jesus.

More balanced and ultimately more influential is Karl Barth. Unlike Bultmann, Barth did not see a discontinuity between the Jesus of history and the Christ of faith. However, crucial for Barth, in contrast again to historicism, is the fact that revelation of Christ cannot be gathered from doing history, because "revelation is not a predicate of history, but history is a predicate of revelation."[35] In other words, we cannot start with history in investigating the

---

32. In his monumental *Quest of the Historical Jesus* Schweitzer concludes that historical study cannot disentangle the eternal realities about Jesus and the historical forms they took. "The abiding and eternal in Jesus is absolutely independent of historical knowledge and can only be understood by contact with His spirit which is still at work in the world." Albert Schweitzer, *The Quest of the Historical Jesus*, 2nd ed. (New York: Macmillan, 1950), 401.

33. Rae, *History and Hermeneutics*, 25.

34. This is a summary of Bultmann's view from G. E. Ladd in *Jesus Christ and History* (Downers Grove, IL: InterVarsity, 1963), 4.

35. Barth, *Church Dogmatics*, vol. 1, pt. 2 (Edinburgh: T&T Clark, 1956), 64.

Bible's witness to revelation because the order of knowing must be reversed. "Only in light of revelation itself can we properly know what history is."[36] Additionally, it is impossible that historicism's methods, which are antithetical to belief in revelation, will be able to produce for us understanding of God's revelation in Christ. Historical Jesus studies are mistaken precisely because they fail to see Jesus's divinity, but necessarily approach him only as a man. "If, therefore, there is to be an historical-critical method that is true to the reality of Jesus himself, then it must be one that submits itself to revelation, to what is given to be known only by God himself."[37] One can see here that Barth understood more clearly than his modern contemporaries (or at least acknowledged more openly) that the question of history and theology is necessarily one of epistemology. Both antitheological historicists and theological historians have up-and-running systems of presuppositions. For *epistemological-theological* reasons, Barth, who *did* care about real history, perceived that the role of historical research must be one of a servant, not a master. We can see again that Barth's approach is a response to the historicism of his own day. He was reacting—maybe overly so at points—to the modern worldview that had come to dominate biblical studies. He was not denying the importance or relevance of real history like Bultmann did (with whom he had a famous break) but rather emphasizing that historical reconstruction cannot be the basis for understanding revelation.[38]

THEOLOGY THROUGH HISTORY

The "to history or not to history" pendulum swings back again with Bultmann's most famous student, Ernst Käsemann. Käsemann agreed with his teacher that faith is founded on an act of divine revelation. But he decisively broke with Bultmann by arguing that the truth of Christianity *should* have its grounding in the historical reality of Jesus. Käsemann adopted much of historical criticism's method and (subsequently) did not have great hope for the historical reliability of the Gospels. Nevertheless, he thought it important for historical criticism "to be able to show a degree of continuity between the preaching of the early Church and the figure of Jesus himself."[39] The result was

36. Barth as described by Rae, *History and Hermeneutics*, 29.

37. Rae, *History and Hermeneutics*, 30.

38. It is important to note that not everyone interprets Barth as positively on history. The debate continues, especially among evangelical scholars. In reality, due to the voluminous and multifaceted nature of the Barth corpus, there will never be a definitive view; each side has plenty of proof texts regarding Barth's views either for or against the value of history. Although I am certainly no expert on Barth, I lean more on the history-sympathetic interpretation of Murray Rae, Neil MacDonald, John Webster, Bruce McCormack, and Mark Gignilliat. But I also value much the importance of real history, and I understand the hesitation of some who see Barth as not valuing this enough. Ultimately what matters is not what Barth thought but how the Holy Scriptures themselves witness and speak.

39. Rae, *History and Hermeneutics*, 31.

the renewal of the quest for the historical Jesus, now called the "New Quest" of mid-twentieth-century scholarship. It is not clear that Käsemann fully faced or addressed the issue of how revelation fits into this search for the historical Jesus, but in terms of our discussion here, we can still place Käsemann on the historicism side of the debate. The same can be said of other important New Questers such as Günther Bornkamm and James M. Robinson. While seeking a way forward, many critics have noted that the New Quest falls back on "objective history" as the ground for faith.

Responding especially to Bultmann but also disagreeing in part with Barth as well as the New Quest, Oscar Cullmann provided yet another viewpoint in our surveyed debate.[40] Cullmann rejected the dehistoricization of many of his contemporaries because he saw this as conflicting with the view of the Bible that is very much concerned with "salvation history," or "the series of episodes in human history through which God works out his saving purpose for the world."[41] Cullmann accepted Kähler's distinction between *Historie* and *Geschichte* and the notion that historicism's "historical Jesus" is a dead end. Cullmann sought to function both as a historian and a theologian, seeing at the heart of the biblical message the truth that God has acted in historical events to reveal himself and his salvation.[42] Against Bultmann, Cullmann saw the modern rejection of this "God acting in history" view as arising not because we have now arrived at an enlightened scientific worldview, but because of the theological claim and scandal that God has worked in history. This is a scandal intrinsic to the Christian faith and one over which many people in the first through the twenty-first centuries have stumbled. Cullmann sought to keep Christianity planted in the *realia* of God acting in real human history. Herein, however, lies a potential chink in his proposal: in speaking this way Cullmann doesn't really address the problem at stake here. While believing readers (including myself) want to affirm that God is real and really acts in history for our salvation—most climactically in the resurrection—this position does not wrestle sufficiently with the epistemic issues of what history is (including biblical history) and what kind of witness it provides. So, while Cullmann staked out a position that is consciously biblical over historicist, it does not significantly help us move forward at this impasse because it does not address the epistemic issue.[43] Nevertheless, we must not be unfair to Cullman

---

40. Cullmann's two most famous works in this regard are translated as *Christ and Time* (London: SCM Press, 1951) and *Salvation in History* (London: SCM Press, 1967).

41. Rae, *History and Hermeneutics*, 33.

42. Ladd, "Problem of History," 98.

43. Rae's critique is similar, and he also rightly notes the notoriously unclear meaning and definitions of "salvation history." Rae, *History and Hermeneutics*, 34–35. See also Martin Hengel's critique of the phrase in his essay "Salvation History" in *Reading Texts, Seeking Wisdom: Scripture and Theology*, ed. David Ford and Graham Stanton (London: SCM, 2003), 229–44. For a more thorough and generally positive take on the value of the "salvation history" approach in modern scholarship see Yarbrough, *Salvation Historical Fallacy?*

and his learned project. He was not seeking to provide formal epistemological justification for his work, and so he should not be overly criticized for not offering it. In many ways Cullman does model a combination of both theology and history even if it is not sufficiently developed to be fully satisfactory.

Other important scholars who have also wrestled with such issues and reached different conclusions include Adolf Schlatter, Wolfhart Pannenberg, Brevard Childs, Géza Vermes, Joseph Ratzinger, and Francis Watson. But our discussion of Cullmann naturally leads us to mention one who was (and remains) especially influential on the American scene, particularly within evangelicalism: George Eldon Ladd.[44]

Ladd was arguably "the most important biblical scholar" in the postwar evangelical resurgence in America.[45] As one whose experiences spanned the spectrum from fundamentalist church life to heady historical study at Harvard Divinity School and who was influenced by both Kähler and Cullmann, Ladd had much at stake in wrestling with the question of history and its relationship to the Bible. In his magnum opus, *Jesus and the Kingdom*,[46] we find a helpful discussion of Ladd's historical methodology. Ladd was heavily indebted to Cullmann and saw this approach as the solution to the problem of history and theology. Consequently, Ladd valued historical-critical tools but sought to temper them with a refined distinction between *Historie* and *Geschichte*, rejecting closed-continuum Enlightenment historicism in favor of a view of history that includes the notions of revelation and *Heilsgeschichte*. Like Cullmann, Ladd believed that God has acted and will act in history and thus history matters, and that the authoritative record of these acts is found in the biblical record. But Ladd realized that God and the supernatural did not fit within his contemporaries' understanding of what was accepted as (academic) history. Ladd rejected Bultmann's demythologizing solution to this problem and instead argued that the historical-critical method has a place in analyzing "ordinary" history, while faith is required to understand "redemptive" history. Ladd considered the *Heilsgeschichte* approach able to incorporate historical-critical tools for demonstrating and interpreting whatever they are able to measure, while recognizing that "the historical-critical method has self-imposed limitations which render it incompetent to interpret redemptive history."[47] Thus, the solution is to let historical criticism have its place and *also* recognize that this historicism is alien to the Bible and necessarily distorts its understanding. Ladd

44. A fascinating and fair (though tragic) biography of Ladd can be found in John A. D'Elia, *A Place at the Table: George Eldon Ladd and the Rehabilitation of Evangelical Scholarship in America* (Oxford: Oxford University Press, 2008).

45. Ibid., 176.

46. G. E. Ladd, *Jesus and the Kingdom: The Eschatology of Biblical Realism* (New York: Harper & Row, 1964). The second edition was published as *The Presence of the Future: The Eschatology of Biblical Realism* (Grand Rapids: Eerdmans, 1974).

47. Ladd, "Problem of History," 99.

sought to recognize and hold together both of these aspects in his approach, which he called "biblical realism," as highlighted by the subtitle of his book.

It is not difficult to see how this potentially dichotomous position has influenced much of evangelical scholarship, consciously or unconsciously. There is much to be commended in Ladd's work, and on the most sympathetic reading he provides us with a thoughtful attempt at keeping together both history and theological significance. However, along with Cullmann one cannot help but wonder whether this position surrenders too much epistemologically to Enlightenment historicism and is in part motivated by the desire to be accepted as part of the "real" scholarly academy.[48]

RETURNING TO WRIGHT

This discussion of the influential Ladd and his own description of his methodology as "Biblical realism" leads naturally into a discussion of our final scholar to be surveyed, N. T. Wright. Like Ladd in his own day, Wright is one of the most influential New Testament scholars writing today (with a transatlantic appeal that transcends Ladd's), and he has been very invested in the study of the Gospels and their historical setting. As mentioned above, Wright designates his own approach as "critical realism,"[49] and many striking similarities can be found between him and Ladd. This is doubly intriguing because despite the widespread influence of Ladd and the overlap between their approaches and terminology, Ladd appears nowhere in Wright's seminal *New Testament and the People of God* and is mentioned only in passing in the sequel, *Jesus and the Victory of God*. How conscious Wright was of his overlap with Ladd is unclear, but what matters most is the way that Wright lays out his own methodology.[50]

Wright, whose ideas and arguments have been forged in regular debate with contemporary skeptical, historicist Jesus scholars (such as Borg and Crossan), sees historical study as not only possible but also very important. He is not unaware of the modern history of Gospels scholarship,[51] and by his own statements he is seeking instead to bring together again history and theology. In a balanced way he understands that there is no such thing as objective, neutral history and that to read the Scriptures only historically in a Troeltschian, positivistic way ignores the theological import of the text. At the same time, he notes that we

48. This is a weighty charge, I realize, but one that seems amply supported in the case of Ladd by the documentation and his own testimony provided in D'Elia's biography.

49. This terminology precedes Wright, particularly in the application of Lonergan's philosophy of history to the Gospels in the work of Ben F. Meyer. Wright acknowledges his debt to Meyer and has written an introduction to the republication of Meyer's *Aims of Jesus*, Princeton Theological Monograph Series (Eugene, OR: Pickwick, 2004).

50. Wright explains his methodology in his introduction to *The New Testament and the People of God* (Minneapolis: Fortress, 1992–2003), the first volume of his multivolume work, Christian Origins and the Question of God.

51. For example, see his insightful and devastating critique of the Jesus seminar in his *Jesus and the Victory of God*.

cannot avoid the questions of history altogether in our theological reading; to do so is potentially quite dangerous and can lead to mistakes like those of Bultmann and other dehistoricizers. While not fully addressing the epistemic issues at hand, this understanding seems to offer a promising way forward.

However, as several close readers of Wright have noticed, this balanced, two-legged view *in practice* seems to have one much longer and heavier-booted foot. Murray Rae expresses his concerns by quoting several places in which Wright clearly makes historical study the ultimate foundation. As Rae summarizes Wright's view, historians show us who Jesus was and what he thought his aims were; theologians are left to consider the implications. But as Rae points out, one cannot truly address the supposed "historical" questions about Jesus without understanding his resurrection and lordship. As we saw at the beginning of this chapter, Hays makes similar critiques.

Hays and Rae are not alone, however, in raising these same concerns.[52] In an appreciative and balanced essay, C. Stephen Evans likewise observes that in many ways Wright adopts the modern historical-critical method and its attendant commitment to "methodological naturalism."[53] Evans is careful to distinguish between different levels and applications of historical criticism and he does not unfairly or unreflectively heap up modernist boogeyman accusations against Wright. Quite the contrary, Evans's presentation is a model of virtuous argumentation. This makes his observations all the more powerful. Evans points out that while Wright clearly is not committed to *metaphysical* naturalism, his practice ends up revealing that along with John Meier, Wright believes that the historian's job is to explain things *without* recourse to divine activity, but through *natural* means, thus in effect following Troeltsch's principle of correlation.[54] Again, Evans is careful to acknowledge that Wright is mixed in his approach but notes that in many places Wright's rhetoric against traditionalism and his exaltation of historical study as the way forward are overstated and misleading at best.[55] Luke Timothy Johnson is even more

52. In addition to Hays, Rae, and Evans, discussed subsequently, from a quite different perspective we find a similar analysis by Stephen Fowl. When surveying Wright's approach, Fowl concludes that Wright and his frequent sparring partner Crossan end up doing the same thing: trying to fit the data of the Gospels into a framework developed by the demands of history rather than the Gospels themselves. "Thus, in this crucial respect Wright, Crossan and those in between perpetuate that late eighteenth-century shift in reading practices wherein history understood in a particular way is given priority over theology." Stephen Fowl, "The Gospels and the 'Historical Jesus,'" in *The Cambridge Companion to the Gospels*, ed. Stephen C. Barton (Cambridge: Cambridge University Press, 2006), 89.

53. C. Stephen Evans, "Methodological Naturalism in Historical Biblical Scholarship," in Newman, *Jesus and the Restoration of Israel*, 180–205. A much fuller argument for understanding these issues can be found in Evans's brilliant book *The Historical Christ and the Jesus of Faith: The Incarnational Narrative as History* (Oxford: Clarendon, 1996).

54. See esp. Evans's arguments in "Methodological Naturalism," 190.

55. Ibid., 201–5.

pointed in his critique, but the substance is in effect the same. He discerns in Wright's approach that "historical construction is the dominant factor to which theology must conform."[56]

We have now come full circle to the Hays-Wright discussion from the beginning of the chapter. I have spent significant time discussing Wright because of his widespread current influence and because he provides an example of someone consciously seeking to read the Gospels as both Scripture (having been written by real people in a real time in history) and as holy (being a divine and therefore theological word). Wright stands as another scholar in a long line of theologically interested historians (or would he prefer historically interested theologians?) operating in and reacting to the wake of Enlightenment historicism.[57]

This survey helps us see that much of the discussion here at the beginning of the twenty-first century is a continuation of the debate about the role of history in doing theology that began in the Enlightenment. The parameters (or ropes) of the boxing ring were set by the modernist questions. But this issue is not just about whether the Bible is believable and trustworthy; at its core is the question of epistemology.[58] As Luke Timothy Johnson observes about Wright and all the modern quests for the historical Jesus, at their heart "are the epistemological issues that are suppressed or bracketed by Third and New Questers alike" and that "unless and until Questers of any stripe seriously engage the epistemological challenge, conceptual confusion and methodological imprecision will continue to haunt the entire enterprise."[59]

Historicism in Crisis

Rowan Williams, writing in 2002, notes that the historical-critical approach to the Bible, so dominant in the academy for the last 250 years, is now under intense attack.[60] If this was true in 2002, it is doubly so now. Inspection of the self-assured tower of historical criticism has revealed cracks at the foundation

56. Luke Timothy Johnson, "A Historiographical Response to Wright's Jesus," in Newman, *Jesus and the Restoration of Israel*, 206–24, here 209.

57. After completing this chapter I (re)discovered a very good article by one of my former professors, Grant Osborne, "History and Theology in the Synoptic Gospels," *TJ*, n.s., 24 (2003): 5–22. Osborne provides a helpful taxonomy of developments on the issue here, seeing three stages: (1) history or theology; (2) history and theology; and (3) history through theology. In this last (and apparently recommended) stage, he includes the approach of Wright. While the survey and taxonomy provided are helpful, the problems presented here suggest that we have not yet arrived at the best way forward.

58. Though not using this language, Harrisville and Sundberg similarly observe that the difference between premodern and modern reading of the Bible is a difference in worldview. Harrisville and Sundberg, *Bible in Modern Culture*, 10–29.

59. Johnson, "Historiographical Response to Wright's Jesus," 210.

60. Rowan Williams, "Historical Criticism and Sacred Text," in Ford and Stanton, *Reading Texts, Seeking Wisdom*, 217–28.

with few of this generation interested in fixing them, and even the naked eye can see that the edifice is now leaning precariously.

We have already noted that within the first centuries of the Enlightenment, reaction and detraction occurred aplenty. The twentieth-century stage of the development of historicism itself we called "crisis historicism." But today, at an even deeper level we find historicism to be in crisis. Williams identifies the attack as occurring on two fronts—(1) by theologians (both those returning to premodern insights and postcritical scholars) who assert that historical criticism is not as neutral as it claims[61] but rather has an agenda that is hostile to the theological understanding and use of Scripture; and (2) by postmodern literary critics who dispute the "authority of origins" approach of historicism and its "notion that meaning can be secured and decisively defined by discovering the most primitive layer of a text's historical life—ideally the authorial intention."[62] This is well summarized. We might add to it only by making explicit that overlapping and interwoven with these criticisms is the epistemological question.

In the intervening years since Williams made these observations, many developments have continued to advance criticism of historical criticism and to suggest alternative ways forward. One of these is revived interest in and practice of premodern interpretive approaches. The field of patristic studies, for a long time arrogantly derided by modernist scholars,[63] is now bursting with new life and energy, attracting many students and producing many widely read books.[64] Brian Daley observes the same: "Patristic exegesis has become

61. Over forty years ago, and echoing the sentiments of those writing before him, Ladd rightly observed that in the development of the historical-critical method, "what really happened was not the abandonment of dogma on behalf of pure scientific objectivity; it was rather the exchange of one kind of dogma for another. Scientific dogma was substituted for theological dogma." Ladd, "Problem of History," 89. Similarly, Martin Hengel, a German scholar known for his detailed historical work, can write near the end of his career: "Primitive Christianity has no knowledge of the abrupt distinction between 'dogmatics' and 'church history' which is so popular, or even between 'faith' and 'facts of history' in that form. The truth lies between a 'historicism' which is hostile to theology and a 'dogmatism' which is hostile to history." Martin Hengel, *The Four Gospels and the One Gospel of Jesus Christ: An Investigation of the Collection and Origin of the Canonical Gospels*, trans. John Bowden (Harrisburg, PA: Trinity Press International, 2000), 9.

62. Williams, "Historical Criticism and Sacred Text," 217.

63. Typical are the comments of Frederic W. Farrar in his 1885–86 Bampton Lectures in Oxford and their subsequent publication as *History of Interpretation* (London: Macmillan, 1886). He states, "We shall pass in swift review many centuries of exegesis and shall be compelled to see that they were, in the main, centuries during which the interpretation of Scripture has been dominated by unproven theories, and overladen by untenable results." Later Farrar says of the church fathers, "There are but few of them whose pages are not rife with errors—errors of method, errors of fact, errors of history, of grammar, and even of doctrine." Quoted in Brian E. Daley, "Is Patristic Exegesis Still Usable?" in *The Art of Reading Scripture*, ed. Ellen Davis and Richard Hays (Grand Rapids: Eerdmans, 2003), 70.

64. Evidence of this is ample, including the popularity of InterVarsity's Ancient Christian Commentary on Scripture series, its many corollary monographs by the likes of Oden and Hall, and new translations of patristic and medieval commentators coming onto the market.

almost fashionable again. After centuries of neglect, even hostile dismissal, on the part of Christian preachers and scholars of virtually every hue and stripe, the efforts of early Christian writers to interpret the Bible have recently been watered into life again by a small but swelling stream of conferences, scholarly books, and doctoral dissertations." Daley observes that this is true in part because the Enlightenment approach has lost much of its energy and seeming relevance, especially among younger scholars. Instead, "a significant number of Christian theologians and biblical scholars are turning with interest and even respect to the exegetical efforts of the patristic era in the hope of finding there modes for new ways of reading the Bible with both scholarly sophistication and a reverent, orthodox faith."[65]

At the same time, there appears to be renewed interest in the writings and approach of Karl Barth, and somewhat related, Brevard Childs. Interest in Barth has been strong since his earliest days of scholarly output, but with the castle of modernism crumbling from significant postmodern trebuchet attacks, there seems to be a fresh and broader appreciation among many younger scholars for the ways in which Barth sounded an early and prophetic call against the dangers of historicism. The work of a one-time student of Barth's and a very significant scholar in his own right, Brevard Childs, has also found a larger audience among those grappling with how to understand the Bible as Holy Scripture. Childs is now appreciated by many as the (nearly) lone voice that functioned within the academic world of historical criticism but also always boldly asserted that the issues needed a more ecclesial and canonical approach.

Integrally related to and informed by both of these developments is the growing movement that may be called the "theological interpretation of Scripture." Those working in this field generally recognize that this amorphous group has many versions, influences, approaches, and theological and ecclesial commitments; its various manifestations, however, share an understanding that recognizes the weaknesses and dead ends of modernism and particularly historical criticism. Many books and articles are now exploring new ways forward, often by rediscovering voices of premodern interpretation as well as postmodern insights.[66] One central theme is that the meaning and significance

65. Daley, "Is Patristic Exegesis Still Usable?" 69–70. An appreciative and very helpful book to introduce readers to patristic interpretation is John O'Keefe and Russell Reno, *Sanctified Vision* (Baltimore: Johns Hopkins, 2005).

66. To reference particular books in such a burgeoning field is to commit oneself to being quickly outdated. Nonetheless, some of the volumes that I have found helpful entries into this topic are Daniel J. Treier, *Introducing Theological Interpretation of Scripture: Recovering a Christian Practice* (Grand Rapids: Baker Academic, 2008); Joel B. Green, *Seized by Truth: Reading the Bible as Scripture* (Nashville: Abingdon, 2007); Peter J. Leithart, *Deep Exegesis: The Mystery of Reading Scripture* (Waco: Baylor University Press, 2009); and J. Todd Billings, *The Word of God for the People of God: An Entryway to the Theological Interpretation of Scripture* (Grand Rapids: Eerdmans, 2010). The number of articles is legion. One may consult

of Holy Scripture cannot be contained or constrained by the methods and worldview of historicism.

One subgroup that can be classified as advocating the theological-interpretation-of-Scripture approach is the diverse group of scholars who gathered for the multiyear series of conferences under the banner of the Scripture and Hermeneutic Seminar (SHS). Headed by Craig Bartholomew and several other regularly attending scholars, the SHS spent eight years discussing a variety of topics related to renewing biblical interpretation and invited a range of different scholars to address assorted issues. The resultant published volumes of the interactive papers are quite rich, especially volume 4, which addresses particularly the question of history and biblical interpretation.[67] These conferences and volumes have brought to the fore the need to rethink and renew biblical hermeneutics.

Another contributing factor to the crisis of historicism is the postcritical approaches of the so-called Yale school. Although theologians considered part of this "school" generally do not acknowledge that it actually existed as such, key ideas and a certain (unplanned) synergy seem to have occurred among some crucial thinkers connected with Yale's divinity school in the 1980s.[68] One of these thinkers is the late Hans Frei, whose insights detailed in his *Eclipse of Biblical Narrative* have achieved an almost *Rocky Horror Picture Show* level of alternative and abiding influence. Frei recognized that in the developments of historicist eighteenth- and nineteenth-century scholarship the depicted biblical world and the real historical world became separated in thought. During the Enlightenment the task of hermeneutics became to fit the biblical texts—now understood primarily as about their ostensive reference—into the "real" world of human experience. The trustworthiness or truthfulness of the Bible was to be accepted or rejected on the basis of its perceived accuracy (or lack thereof), to be judged by current scientific and historical-critical methods. This position was true for both fundamentalists and liberals, who differed not in their approach but only in their conclusions. This stance is the reversal of the pre-Enlightenment approach, which understood the perceived world in light of the biblical text, often through figural understanding. Recognizing this distinction, especially when that recognition

---

the newly formed *Journal of Theological Interpretation*. A recent issue of the *International Journal of Systematic Theology* (12, no. 2 [April 2010]) was dedicated just to this topic, with several helpful overview articles.

67. Bartholomew et al., *"Behind the Text."* Essays particularly relevant to the discussion in this chapter are those by Alvin Plantinga, Craig Bartholomew, Joel Green, Iain Provan, Murray Rae, and Gregory Laughery. Also on this topic are some essays from an earlier conference volume, Bartholomew, Colin Greene, and Karl Moller, eds., *After Pentecost: Language and Biblical Interpretation* (Grand Rapids: Zondervan, 2001), esp. the essay by Dan Stiver, "Ricoeur, Speech-Act Theory, and the Gospels as History," 50–72.

68. In addition to Hans Frei, discussed here briefly, we can mention the important works of George Lindbeck and David Kelsey. This line of thinking might also be called postliberal.

is wedded to a more robust epistemological stance (see below), proves to be very important in understanding historicism and creating room to move in new directions free from historicist dogma.

Finally, we may also note the crisis facing historicism by observing the unexpected and somewhat sudden decline in vigor of the former Holy Grail of Gospels study, the "quest for the historical Jesus." Unrelated but in the very same month that Hays was questioning Wright's investment in a historical-critical approach, *Christianity Today* released a series of articles on the state and future of historical Jesus studies. The articles were headlined by Scot McKnight's bold and provocative essay titled "The Jesus We'll Never Know: Why Scholarly Attempts to Discover the 'Real' Jesus Have Failed. And Why That's a Good Thing."[69] In a Puritan-like way, McKnight's lengthy title leaves no question about his point. McKnight, himself formerly deeply vested in historical Jesus studies, traces the recent decline in the field and argues that this is okay because the approach has proven to be fundamentally flawed. McKnight mentions the work of several heavyweight scholars who, like himself, have come to see the *Holzweg* of this formerly predominant form of historicism.[70] There are some helpful response articles by Wright, Craig Keener, and Darrell Bock, but none can refute the most obvious point: the kind of historical-critical approach that once dominated historical Jesus studies has been dealt a fatal wound.

Historicism is indeed in crisis. The question for us who desire to read the Gospels as Holy Scripture is how to move forward. It is neither simple, wise, nor possible to try to repristinate the past or act as if Enlightenment developments never occurred. Rather, we must learn from the past and its turns as we find a new way forward.

The point of the preceding discussion of "the history of history" is to understand that how we construe history is itself a historical development, and the modern approaches to doing history are clearly part of the modern epistemological stance. Thus we must be aware that our own approach to history and its relationship to truth and theology must be examined thoughtfully. Specifically, we may assert that the epistemological foundation of modernistic, positivistic history is strikingly different from the biblical understanding. And this leads to our next important point.

---

69. Available online at http://www.christianitytoday.com/ct/2010/april/15.22.html.

70. McKnight briefly discusses James Dunn and Dale Allison. We can add to this list Luke Timothy Johnson. See esp. Johnson's *The Real Jesus: The Misguided Quest for the Historical Jesus and the Truth of the Traditional Gospels* (New York: Harper Collins, 1996). Most recently from Dale Allison, see *The Historical Christ and the Theological Jesus* (Grand Rapids: Eerdmans, 2009) and *Constructing Jesus: Memory, Imagination, and History* (Grand Rapids: Baker Academic, 2010). Other Gospels scholars who would question historical Jesus studies as they have been practiced include Richard Bauckham, Markus Bockmuehl, Richard Hays, and Francis Watson.

The Interpreted Nature of All History Writing

How then shall we now think about history? More specifically, how should one think about the role of historical study in reading the Gospels as Holy Scripture? With the hegemony of positivistic historicism broken, we are now approaching a place where we may once again find a balanced perspective, taking into account the importance of theological understanding in the kind of history the Gospels give us. It seems that even as the last flames of a dominantly historical-critical study of the Bible wane into embers, the time is ripe for a phoenix-like, reborn approach.

One of the most important developments in historiography is the increasing recognition that all history writing is itself an act of interpretation. That is, post-Enlightenment scholars have slowly but surely come to acknowledge that the production of accounts of past events (in this sense, "history") can never be simply "as it really was" á la Ranke. The heady, headstrong, and puffed-up days of the Enlightenment envisioned the historian as the objective scientist poring over the documents and artifacts to ascertain the unadulterated, clear truth of the matter, even if it required torturing and twisting those witnesses to make them yield what they did not want to tell. We might imagine such a noble historian as a white-aproned chemist, carefully mixing two parts potassium with one part sodium, or alternatively, as a well-dressed Hercule Poirot, simply observing and then collecting data until the truth of the whole matter is (magically, it seems) produced out of thin air. These images of the historians' role and achievements linger in popular understanding, as whole television channels dedicated to popularized "history" testify. Likewise, at Easter time, the popular news magazines—always seeking the sensational story—routinely parade before us the supposed historical experts who assure us that Jesus never said anything like we find in the Gospels except the parts that make him sound like an eco-friendly, anti-imperial modern-day prophet.[71]

Nevertheless, within the academy, recognition that history writing is not entirely neutral or "scientific" has long been recognized. As we noted above, Troeltsch himself already came to recognize this, though he saw no way out of this blind alley. Wright also is careful to acknowledge this mistaken approach to historical study. But even more, with the advent of the postmodern understanding of the perspectival nature of all our thoughts and arguments, and

---

71. In his trenchant and profound critique of historical criticism, Levenson points out the irony that an exclusively historical-critical reading of the Bible effactually delegitimizes the reasons for its own existence and at the same time such scholars "have depended for their livelihood upon those who not only rejoice that the Bible survived those worlds [of the ancient Near East and Greco-Roman contexts] but who also insist that it deserved to survive because its message is trans-historical." Jon D. Levenson, "Historical Criticism and the Fate of the Enlightenment Project," in his *Hebrew Bible, the Old Testament, and Historical Criticism* (Louisville: Westminster John Knox, 1993), 110.

with a greater global consciousness of the diversity of worldviews, the belief that the historians' job is simply producing "as it really was" is increasingly seen for what it is, a false (and unnecessary) hope.[72]

For many, the result of this recognition ranges from despair to apathy. There is indeed a wide swath of postmodern thinking that quickly becomes hopelessly nihilistic. Everything is play and meaningless and a power struggle for dominance. If this is indeed the case, then the only proper response would be, it seems, to enter in and try to be the dominant one, if indeed there is no right or wrong and no hope for any better situation.

An alternative to such self-defeating nihilism is a mature, balanced way that openly acknowledges the fool's errand of value-free neutrality yet sees that real growth in thinking and communication and truth-apprehension can be sought, even if not with the simple elegance of $E = mc^2$.

It is now widely recognized that all history retelling is an interpreted affair, not only for the historian writing today but also for the primary documents that are telling us history. There is no such thing as "brute fact" history. The closest one might have to this would be a table of dates and figures, but even this would involve a massive amount of selection and culling of data, the choice of what to include and what to omit. For example, should a simple chart of the "events" of the Battle of Gettysburg (July 1–3, 1863) only include the number of soldiers present on each side and the names of the generals or also potentially significant data about weather conditions, dietary differences, and/or statistics on the quality of canvas used for Confederate cots and so on? Decisions must be made at every turn by the historian lest we fall into the trap of "the democratization of events whereby nothing has significance because everything is of equal consequence."[73]

But even so, a list of dates does not history make. Once one begins the monumental and much more important task of *narrating* past events, a complex series of judgments must be made, not only regarding material to include, but also about cause and effect, motives, likelihood, plausibility, and so on. Moreover, the historian also is trying to make a case for his or her particular interpretation of the events, and so another level of interpretation occurs on

72. The issues and debate here are more complex than they may appear to the nonprofessional historian. They involve the complex matters of the impact of linguistic and postmodern literary theories on the understanding of what history and history writing is. To delve into this topic further here would derail our progress, but the interested reader may pursue the issue in the following books: Georg G. Iggers, *Historiography in the Twentieth Century: From Scientific Objectivity to the Postmodern Challenge* (with a new epilogue), 2nd ed. (Middletown, CT: Wesleyan University Press, 2005); Hayden White, *Figural Realism: Studies in the Mimesis Effect* (Baltimore: Johns Hopkins University Press, 1999); Paul Ricoeur, *Memory, History, Forgetting,* trans. K. Blamely and David Pellauer (Chicago: University of Chicago Press, 2004).

73. Joel B. Green, "Which Conversation Shall We Have? History, Historicism and Historical Narrative in Theological Interpretation: A Response to Peter van Inwagen," in Bartholomew et al., *"Behind" the Text,* 147.

the rhetorical front—which data to present in which order, how to structure the argument, what to highlight, and what to downplay. All these choices are inevitable and a necessary (and not invalidating) part of the historian's job. Once this is acknowledged, the door to a whole new world of understanding of "what history is" is opened.

One theologian who has wrestled with these issues and applied them to biblical studies is Murray Rae, whose book *History and Hermeneutics* we have referenced and relied on above. Here too Rae proves very helpful. He notes that even in the best-case scenario of an eyewitness to a historical event— for example, Thomas touching Jesus's nail marks or a closed-circuit camera installed in Jesus's tomb—merely seeing the phenomenon is not enough for understanding.[74] The judgment or decision about what the historical event/ fact *means* is the result of a series of complex judgments, beliefs, presuppositions, and habits of mind (virtuous or not) on the part of the interpreter. Thus, for example, even a camera recording of the moment of Jesus's resurrection would not in itself compel belief; plenty of alternative theories could potentially explain this event to one not inclined to believe, such as that Jesus only appeared to be dead (the swoon theory) or that someone had tampered with the recording. There is no ultimate "proof" that could convince everyone. On the other hand, if one knows something about Jesus—his manner, his character, other demonstrations of his godliness and power, past experience of his care and faithfulness—then one will interpret this image of Jesus's rising very differently. This must also have been what led Thomas to respond not with more skepticism but with "My Lord and my God!" The point is that interpretation of historical events is a complex activity that is more than merely seeing or experiencing sensate data. As Rae notes: "The perception of historical reality is, irreducibly, a hermeneutical activity. There is no seeing of epistemic worth without the interpretive judgments of observers who bring to the task a range of commitments, beliefs, experience, and so on, that inform the judgments made."[75]

Regarding the Bible, the key notion here is to recognize that theology and divine action can (and even must) be allowed a role when one considers what history is. That is, contra Enlightenment historicism, which requires excluding God (either belief in him personally on the part of the reader or belief in God's intervening actions) from "real" history, we are now in a position to reinsert theology into our articulation of what the Bible's history is giving us. Although all historical interpretation is necessarily a function of one's worldview, we continue to hear from historicists (especially in biblical studies)[76] that we can somehow access the truth without the "interference" of personal interpreta-

74. Rae, *History and Hermeneutics*, 87.

75. Ibid., 96.

76. In his essay critiquing historicism and distinguishing it from the work of real historians, C. S. Lewis wryly notes that it is not usually historians who fall into the arrogant danger of

tion. Not only is this impossible; it is not desirable. The interpretation and writing of history—both by the Gospel writers themselves and by us now as readers—is an act of interpretation; it is a focus on the *significance* of what was said and done. Historians are always sifting and selecting from a vast array of data and offering their interpretation of the significance of events. This does not mean that we are lost in the mire of utter subjectivity. Rather

> this viewpoint and interest of the historian need not undermine the historian's goal of telling the truth about the past. Individual historians may be more or less successful in accomplishing that goal. Of those who are more successful, however, we shall have to say, not that they have better eyesight, but that they are better interpreters. . . . The belief-laden character of seeing and interpreting is a feature of every effort to tell what went on in history.[77]

Thus, history and theology (or historical and theological understanding) should not and cannot be spoken of as if they were distinct, unrelated areas of study or, at best, are connected with the former being the foundation for the latter. Rather, *history in the Bible is theologically interpreted narrative retelling.* As Francis Watson rightly observes, "Even Christian historians who at a personal level accept that Jesus is the Christ, will be subject to the constraints of this methodologically atheistic worldview [of Modernism]—*unless they are prepared to rethink what 'history' is, on the basis of theology.*"[78] The point, then, is that we do not need simply to add belief in accuracy on top of the "solid, modern historical-critical method" inherited from the Enlightenment; rather we need a more solid understanding of what history retelling itself is: an interpreted explication of the meaningfulness of events. And because we understand and believe that the Bible is Holy Scripture, we understand God as the ultimate author of this authoritative, interpreted narrative.[79]

A helpful metaphor in this regard is to think of the Gospels as stained-glass windows onto the inner sanctum of God in Christ. They are not clear-paned windows that we can look through and behind to find the "real" or "historical" Jesus, free from the shackles and framing of the evangelists. (There is no such thing as a clear-glass window onto history, and if there were, we would not necessarily want it.) What we are given in the Gospels are four self-consciously

---

historicism, but rather theologians, philosophers, and politicians trying to do history. C. S. Lewis, "Historicism," in *Christian Reflections*, ed. Walter Hooper (Grand Rapids: Eerdmans, 1967), 101.

77. Rae, *History and Hermeneutics*, 96–97.

78. Francis Watson, "The Quest for the Real Jesus," in *The Cambridge Companion to Jesus*, ed. Markus Bockmuehl (Cambridge: Cambridge University Press, 2001), 164, italics mine.

79. To be clear and fair, Wright clearly views history in this interpreted way, and he is thus not guilty of this egregious error that many before him have made. Nonetheless, as was shown above and will be explored further below, in practice Wright seems to revert to a naturalistic approach to historical reconstruction. The same qualification may also apply to Cullmann, Ladd, and Schlatter; none of them is a historical positivist.

painted portraits and interpretations of the real Jesus. The retelling in narrative form inevitably entails much interpretation on the part of the evangelists. Thus we must be sensitive to and learn from these interpretations, rather than seek to get behind them to "what really happened."

The issue then is not whether the events happened—both the Gospel writers and readers make this assumption, otherwise the whole exercise would be meaningless—but to recognize that what we have are inspired, theologically, pastorally, and at times, even polemically driven accounts. And this is enough.

This realization is an important start in our mental refitting of what history is and what it gives us. But it does not yet provide sufficient grounding for our trust in the reliability and authority of the Gospels as Holy Scripture, nor does it sufficiently address the question at hand: what role does historical reconstruction play in our reading of the Gospels? To complete our refitting, we need to make one more crucial argument.

Rediscovering Our Epistemological Grounding—Testimony

In the massive onslaught of books that pour forth from the publishing houses every year like orcs from the gates of Mordor, only a few will the future look back on as significant. One such book is Richard Bauckham's *Jesus and the Eyewitnesses: The Gospels as Eyewitness Testimony*.[80] Bauckham is a paradigm-shifting scholar who writes clearly, eruditely, and with remarkable common sense. In this book he draws from decades of research to address the question of history and theology at a crucial time in our understanding. He not only critiques past movements in biblical scholarship but also provides a balanced way forward by introducing the category of testimony.[81]

We have noted above that historicism is in crisis, and I have suggested that the various alternatives to it proffered in biblical studies have proved wanting. Bauckham begins his argument by likewise mentioning the inherent problems with the recent centuries' quests for the historical Jesus. He notes the methodological flaws of "naïve historical positivism" and that historical reconstructions of the supposed "real" Jesus are really alternatives to the Gospels.[82] At the same time, he is careful not to abandon the importance

---

80. Richard Bauckham, *Jesus and the Eyewitnesses: The Gospels as Eyewitness Testimony* (Grand Rapids: Eerdmans, 2006). Also very helpful is the work of Iain Provan on testimony applied to the history of Israel, in Iain Provan, V. Philips Long, and Tremper Longman III, *A Biblical History of Israel* (Louisville: Westminster John Knox, 2003), 3–74.

81. Though Bauckham does not reference John Goldingay in *Jesus and the Eyewitnesses*, we should note Goldingay's earlier attempt to marry fact and interpretation in narrative under the category of "witness." See John Goldingay, *Models for Scripture* (Grand Rapids: Eerdmans, 1994), esp. chaps. 2–6, and Bauckham's blurbs supporting the book on the back (and front!) cover.

82. Bauckham, *Jesus and the Eyewitnesses*, 3.

of history—it matters that Jesus really existed and did such things as the Gospels purport—nor historical study of Jesus and the Gospels. He agrees with Wright that such abandonment would be a kind of Docetism. Instead, Bauckham sees that the issue is one of what role historical reconstruction has in our understanding of Jesus. He argues that any such reconstructions (even, presumably, those done by believers) can never provide "the kind of access to the reality of Jesus that Christian faith and theology have always trusted that we have in the Gospels." Instead, all historical reconstructions end up necessarily being reductionistic.[83] He does not call it such, but we can see that he is talking here about the epistemological issue I have raised above.

So what is the solution to this dichotomous dilemma? Should we lean strongly on theology as the skeleton key with some necessary downplaying of the role of history in theological construction? Or should we emphasize that historical work (usually done according to modern standards) must ground all our theological work? Or, as a variation on this theme, should we as believers allow historical work to be as it is and reserve a different part of our approach for issues of faith and salvation?

Instead of these approaches Bauckham, in concert with many other voices, offers a way forward with the category of testimony. Testimony is "a unique and uniquely valuable means of access to historical reality." In its simplest definition, testimony is the account or report of events given from one person to another, with the inherent request to trust the truthfulness of what is said. The most important thing for our purposes is to understand that testimony offers us in one approach a category for reading the Gospels as history and at the same time as theology. Bauckham writes:

> Theologically speaking, the category of testimony enables us to read the Gospels as precisely the kind of text we need in order to recognize the disclosure of God in the history of Jesus. Understanding the Gospels as testimony, we can recognize this theological meaning of the history not as an arbitrary imposition on the objective facts, but as the way the witnesses perceived the history, in an inextricable coinherence of observable event and perceptible meaning. Testimony is the category that enables us to read the Gospels in a properly historical way and properly theological way. It is where history and theology meet.[84]

Later he writes similarly that testimony is

> both the historically appropriate category for understanding what kind of history the Gospels are and the theologically appropriate category for understanding what kind of access Christian readers of the Gospels thereby have to Jesus and

83. Ibid., 4.
84. Ibid., 5–6.

his history. It is the category that enables us to surmount the dichotomy between the so-called historical Jesus and the so-called Christ of faith. It enables us to see that the Gospels are not some kind of obstacle to knowledge of the real Jesus and his history but precisely the kind of means of access to the real Jesus and his history that, as historians and as believers, we need.[85]

Part of the understanding that informs this idea of testimony is that ancient historiography, unlike that which developed in the Enlightenment, consciously valued the report that participants in events provided. The "best practice" for ancient historians was not some supposed "scientific," objective neutrality, but rather their being a personal eyewitness of the events themselves. When the history writer did not personally witness the events he was recounting, the views he valued were those not of a dispassionate observer or other historians but of "one who, as a participant, had been closest to the events and whose direct experience enabled him to understand and interpret the significance of what he had seen."[86] As Samuel Byrskog notes, "Involvement was not an obstacle to a correct understanding of what they perceived as historical truth. It was rather the essential means to a correct understanding of what had really happened."[87]

Here we are clearly addressing the epistemological issue once again. We are talking about what counts as real historical knowledge and how we come to acquire that. Going against modern historiographic developments is a premodern—indeed, ancient—idea of the value of *involved* witnesses to events. One can see how important this move is toward rejoining theology and history, the very thing the Gospels understand themselves to be.

The bulk of Bauckham's book is devoted to detailed arguments concerning how the Gospels present themselves and were regarded as eyewitness testimony in literary form. These arguments go beyond the scope of our study, important though they are. I am interested here in noting the significance of this epistemological stance and how it enables us to move forward through the history-versus-theology impasse surveyed above.

The epistemological question and definition of testimony does not return full force until Bauckham's concluding chapter.[88] Here Bauckham, drawing on the work of philosophers such as C. A. J. Coady and especially

---

85. Ibid., 473.

86. Ibid., 9. In this section Bauckham is appreciatively using the work of Samuel Byrskog in his *Story as History—History as Story* (Tübingen: Mohr Siebeck, 2000). In a later article, Bauckham expands upon the differences between ancient and modern historiography and applies them to evaluation of the Gospel of John. Originally an *NTS* article, it has now been published as Bauckham, "Historiographical Characteristics of the Gospel of John," in his *Testimony of the Beloved Disciple: Narrative, History, and Theology in the Gospel of John* (Grand Rapids: Baker Academic, 2007).

87. Byrskog, *Story as History*, 154, quoted in Bauckham, *Jesus and the Eyewitnesses*, 9.

88. The other significant chapter of this nature is chap. 13, "Eyewitness Memory."

Paul Ricoeur,[89] explores more fully what it means to think of the Gospels as testimony.

Bauckham rehearses the negative view toward testimony as found in important historiographic works such as those of Marc Bloch and R. G. Collingwood. Characteristic of the modern stance in both of these thinkers is a kind of triumphalistic attitude over against the past, from which the modern historian is liberated. For such modern thinkers, the modern historian is like a Baconian scientist who forces the artifacts and testimonies of the past to tell us what we want to know from them, and even more than they want to tell us. As a result, from this perspective testimonial knowledge cannot be valid or trusted as true historical knowledge because it is not neutrally obtained scientific knowledge.[90]

But as Coady and others have now shown, this kind of skepticism and "scientific" approach proves to be ill founded and self-defeating. A far better and more rounded understanding of historiography is that of Ricoeur. Ricoeur understands that testimony is the bedrock of our understanding of history and indeed all reality. Without trusting the testimony of others—regarding everything from major historical events to the true contents of one's toothpaste tube—we cannot have any knowledge other than our own immediate experience (and even that is influenced by our understanding from others). Trusting testimony is the epistemic foundation for knowledge; we cannot get below it nor need we. This does not mean that we trust all testimony equally and uncritically, but it does mean that our knowledge need not be (and in reality, rarely is) based on our ability to verify it, either through reason or historicism. Testimony is irreducible. The assessment of testimony is whether it is trustworthy. We usually cannot seek independent verification of what testimony relates to us; otherwise we would no longer need to rely on testimony. Moreover, we cannot separate out the "brute facts" of "as it really was" from the interpretation or the significance of the meaning. Testimony is—like all historiography—an interpreted account. And this is sufficient. Again, this is not to say that all testimonies are equally good—some can be trusted more than others. Nor is this saying that referentiality is insignificant—it matters that things really happened. Rather, we are talking here about the true nature of (historical and other) knowledge and how we apprehend it: through evaluating and trusting testimony.

89. Coady's work on testimony is considered by many to be seminal: C. A. J. Coady, *Testimony: A Philosophical Study* (Oxford: Clarendon, 1992). Likewise, Ricoeur's *Memory, History, Forgetting*. Also significant on this topic, though not mentioned by Bauckham, are several essays in Bimal Krishna Matilal and Arindam Chakrabarti, eds., *Knowing from Words* (Dordrecht: Kluwer Academic, 1994), used by Rae in his *History and Hermeneutics*, and several works from Robert Audi, one of the leading epistemologists, including his *Epistemology: A Contemporary Introduction to the Theory of Knowledge* (New York: Routledge, 1998), which devotes a whole chapter to testimony.

90. Bauckham, *Jesus and the Eyewitnesses*, 481–85.

To sum up, then, when we read the Gospels as eyewitness testimony (in literary form), we care about real history, but we are not attempting to reconstruct the history *behind* the Gospel texts as if their trustworthiness depended on their verifiability. We are taking "the Gospels seriously as they are" and acknowledging "the uniqueness of what we can know only in this testimonial form."[91] Testimony alone is "the theologically appropriate, indeed the theologically necessary way of access to the history of Jesus, just as testimony is also the historically appropriate, indeed the historically necessary way of access to this 'uniquely unique' historical event."[92]

This introduction of the category of testimony provides a colossal leap forward and helps us lay a firm and level foundation for understanding the kind of historical witness the Gospels provide. We might only add to Bauckham's presentation a more explicit and fuller discussion of the epistemological issue at hand here. This is not a criticism of the book—one cannot do everything in every book, and Bauckham has plowed and planted many other important fields in this work. It is rather to take this category of testimony and round out our own argument for our purposes here.

Specifically, we will benefit from understanding that the category of testimony can be wedded to the notion of "properly basic beliefs." Space does not permit me to delve deeply into the insights of Nicholas Wolterstorff, Alvin Plantinga, Robert Audi, and others on this topic.[93] Suffice it to say that developments in epistemology (as a branch of philosophy) have shown us that the modern turn of the Enlightenment damaged not only our understanding of history but our understanding of understanding itself, specifically, again, on the question of what constitutes proper knowledge. Plantinga especially has argued persuasively that there are many beliefs that are "basic," that is, which are held without other beliefs or arguments underlying them, supporting or verifying them. One can see, I hope, that testimony dovetails beautifully with this same insight; both acknowledge that at the core of our belief systems are irreducible beliefs.[94]

Neil MacDonald has provided a great service in wrestling with this same question in regard to the development of historicism.[95] MacDonald appreciatively reflects on Hans Frei's analysis of the Enlightenment's mistaken focus on

91. Ibid., 506.

92. Ibid., 508.

93. The place to begin such further study is Alvin Plantinga, *Warranted Christian Belief* (Oxford: Oxford University Press, 2000).

94. This is to say not that any particular beliefs based on testimony are "properly basic" but that belief in the irreducibility of testimony is a valid way of knowing.

95. Neil B. MacDonald, "Illocutionary Stance in Hans Frei's *The Eclipse of Biblical Narrative*: An Exercise in Conceptual Redescription and Normative Analysis," in Bartholomew, Greene, and Moller, *After Pentecost*, 312–28.

the biblical texts' referentiality, thereby eclipsing the biblical narrative with a historical reconstruction behind the text. But MacDonald offers a slight critique of Frei and an insightful argument by showing that the shift from precritical to historical-critical approaches entailed at its core an *epistemic* shift from the historical reliability of the Bible being a basic belief to a nonbasic belief. That is, what changed for Enlightenment thinkers—including believing ones such as John Locke—was the shift from "faith seeking understanding" to "faith requiring justification."[96] Thus belief in the Bible's truthful history-telling became a function of verifiability, hence the rise of evidentialist apologetics. Ironically, in this sense, as often noted, the approach of the liberal skeptic and the believing fundamentalist became the same, only with different results. Both adopted some form of the historical-critical approach, which is not just a methodology (that can have harsher or softer versions) but an understanding of how we know knowledge and the role of history in theology and reading the Gospels.

And now yet again we have come full circle. The point of our survey of "the history of history" has been to show that in all these Enlightenment developments and the various responses they evoked, the core issue was always the more fundamental question of how we know. And in this we can now rediscover a way forward that appreciates the insights of historical work but avoids the pitfalls of a modern historical-critical epistemology.

The Truth as a Knife Edge

To conclude this lengthy discussion, get us back on track with the goal of this book, and point a way forward in our reading of the Gospels, we may use the image of the truth as a knife edge—a thin, sharpened line that requires balance and from which one may easily fall in either direction. As it applies to our topic at hand, we may state it this way: *We must not lose history in doing theology, and we must not lose theology in doing history.*

The human spirit regularly tends to extremes and overreactions. We have seen this played out on the question of theology and history. Some have emphasized history at the expense of (and even in opposition to) theological understanding, while others have (often in response) stressed theological understanding in a way that disregards or has little room for historical understanding. In many ways, each of the scholars surveyed in our "History of History" section was planting his flag on one or the other side of this battle line, but always to the detriment of wisdom. I have suggested, along with others, that the peaceful way forward is not siding with one over the other but

---

96. In this argument MacDonald is openly and gladly drawing on the insights of Nicholas Wolterstorff, especially his essay "The Migration of the Theistic Arguments: From Natural Theology to Evidentialist Apologetics," in *Contemporary Classics in Philosophy of Religion*, ed. Anne Loades and Loyal Rue (La Salle, IL: Open Court, 1991).

focusing on the larger issue of what constitutes knowledge and what kind of knowledge the Gospels in particular give us. The answer in short is that they give us witness or testimony to historical realities, inevitably presented as and interwoven with theological interpretation.

To return to the conclusion of the first two chapters of this book, I defined the Gospels as the *theological, historical, and aretological (virtue-forming) biographical narratives that retell the story and proclaim the significance of Jesus Christ, who through the power of the Spirit is the Restorer of God's reign.* Operative here are the first two adjectives, both alive and uncompromised. The Gospels are simultaneously making theological *and* historical claims, not as separate, dual goals but as one exercise, given to us through testimony. Balance is again required. We may so emphasize one of these adjectives at the expense of the other that we cancel out both.

If we approach the Gospels only as repositories of grand theological ideas and ideals, divorced from the historical reality of the incarnation and the resurrection, then we lose the history. Yet if we (even as believers) draw near to the Gospels thinking we must abandon all orthodox, creedal, and ecclesial notions and constraints on our reading or, less strictly, at least grow our theological construction in pure historical soil, then we not only fool ourselves in these possibilities, but we also deny the canonical nature of the Gospels.[97] Reflecting on this tendency, as far back as 1938, C. H. Dodd commended a balanced view, acknowledging that the Gospels give us the Word of the transcendent God, "from faith to faith," and not merely historical information. Yet it matters to Christianity that these events happened in history. Thus "the Gospels profess to tell us what happened. They do not, it is true, set out to gratify a purely historical curiosity about past events, but they do set out *to nurture faith upon the testimony to such events.*"[98]

Part of our continual confusion on this matter is a failure to distinguish between history as real events (that happened and matter) and the retelling and writing of history. "History" can function with either of those meanings in our parlance, but we often do not consider their vital difference. The result is confusion about what matters and what is being said. This confusion, when applied to the weighty matters of faith and religion, unfortunately results in

97. While Bauckham would certainly not deny the canonical nature of the Gospels or fall into this second category, it is important to note that the nature of Scripture as inspired and given by God does not play any explicit role in his formulation of why their testimony is to be trusted; it seems to be based ultimately on historical grounds (not dogmatic/theological ones). This stands in contrast to the lights of the early church (such as Augustine, discussed below) who explicitly base their trust of the Gospels (and all the Scriptures) in the revelatory nature of the apostolic kerygma now inscripturated. This insight comes from Robert Yarbrough.

98. C. H. Dodd, *History and the Gospel* (New York: Scribners, 1938), 15. It remains a question in my mind whether Dodd in practice maintained such a balance, or rather, like his contemporaries, he landed on one side or the other. Nonetheless, this statement presents a balanced perspective.

more grenade-lobbing warfare than constructive building, especially from the more conservative wing of the church. There is often a failure to understand that to reject historicism (or a historical-critical–focused hermeneutic) as a methodology, an epistemology, and a worldview, is *not* the same thing as saying that history is unimportant. For many sincere believers, talk that pushes back against historicism or a historical-critical approach appears to question the historical reliability of the Bible; it sounds and smells only like a denial of the Bible's accuracy and therefore its authority or like a view that history doesn't matter. However, this reaction fails to understand that the issues at stake here are complicated and that again, *to question historical verifiability as the foundation of knowledge is not the same thing as questioning whether history (that is, events) really matters.*

The knife edge is to recognize that it *is* essential that Jesus Christ came in the flesh and truly died and was bodily resurrected—this is a historical (and history-making) reality—while at the same time acknowledging that this belief *cannot* ultimately be historically verified apart from testimony but is a "basic belief" founded on trusting the testimony of the apostles as recorded in Holy Scripture, which itself is understood as the divine Word. And to push this even further, this trusting is ultimately a pneumatological reality: it comes to us only through the work of the Holy Spirit, who reveals to us knowledge of God in Christ.

In light of this realization and at a lower-flying level, we can ask the more practical question: What, then, about historical-critical work? If testimony is irreducible, does all the background and historical work done concerning Jesus and the Gospels even matter for those who accept the Gospels as Holy Scripture? Yet again, a balanced view is in order. *Yes, historical-critically derived information is still valuable, but No, if and when it becomes the sole or even primary avenue through which theological understanding is gained.*

In Rowan Williams's essay on historical criticism, mentioned above, he concludes by arguing that, despite its weaknesses, we should by no means wholly abandon historical-critical scholarship, even though its use within theology needs to be reconsidered. Historical-critical work helps us see, maybe even better than precritical readers did at times, the difference between us and the text. Even more, it imposes on us a helpful discipline:

> While history will not settle issues of meaning, interpretation that is strictly *incompatible* with what we can know of the history of a text's production will not do, to the extent that it trains us to look away from the actual difference of the text. It is not just premature, it is theologically wrong-headed to write off the historical-critical method and its relevance for constructive theology. We may look for a postcritical theology, but it will not be one that ignores the critical moment.[99]

99. Williams, "Historical Criticism and Sacred Text," 228.

Ellen Charry also helpfully reminds us that while the modern epistemological turn has had many negative effects (particularly, the loss of a sapiential
approach), there are aspects of modern epistemology that we abandon only
at our peril. Specifically, "modern empiricism and rationalism meant to curb
authoritarianism, magic, and superstition, and this is something we must not
forget when we attempt to address their weaknesses."[100]

Additionally, we should openly and gladly acknowledge the important role
that historical work provides for the apologetic defense of the faith. Here
we may mention again the excellent essay by C. Stephen Evans in which he
interacts with Wright's approach. At the end of the day, even though Evans
sees Wright as operating within a "methodological naturalism," Evans does
not consider this a devastating criticism. As Evans writes: "There is therefore
nothing objectionable, and possibly a good deal to be gained, when believing Christians who are historical biblical scholars seek to show what kind of
knowledge about Jesus can be achieved, even when one is limited to evidence
that would be admissible to a naturalist."[101] Even a methodologically naturalistic
approach can be justified on the grounds that it can help us see things about
Jesus we would not otherwise see, and it enables us to be part of the scholarly
debate and engage non-Christians by seeking common ground.[102] That is, it has
apologetic value. Wright would undoubtedly concur with these sentiments,
and he has in fact used such arguments to justify his methodology.

Yet, as I have suggested above, Wright often seems to go further than this
and thereby falls off the other side of the knife-edge. Evans concludes the
same. He notes that at times Wright steps over the apologetic line to suggest
a stronger claim, that, in Evans's words, "such a method is the best or even
the only means of ascertaining the historical truth about Jesus of Nazareth."
This seems undeniable from Wright's own statements and practice, especially
where he suggests a historically based critique of traditional orthodox understandings.[103] It may be that Wright sees his audience as the Jesus seminar types,
and therefore he wishes to show himself as a tough-minded historical scholar
willing to break free from theological orthodoxy when history demands it,
thereby earning a hearing. However, as Evans observers, "if that is what is
going on, there is a danger that the rhetoric intended to appease such a reader
will give a misleading impression to his other readers,"[104] especially, I would
add, those looking to understand the Gospels as Holy Scripture.

As a healthy alternative Evans suggests what I have argued above: bas-
ing beliefs not on historical-critical findings but rather on the hearing and

100. Charry, "Walking in the Truth," 148.

101. Evans, "Methodological Naturalism," 200.

102. Ibid., 201.

103. See the number of very revealing quotes from Wright as collected in Luke Timothy Johnson,
"Historiographical Response to Wright's Jesus," 209–10.

104. Evans, "Methodological Naturalism," 203.

believing testimony of the apostles, as well as the testimony of the Spirit and the church. If indeed Jesus is not only a historical person but a theologically and religiously significant one as well, then historical-critical study is not the only or sufficient means of discovering who he is.[105] Evans concludes, "For Christians there is no reason to think that the historical accounts about Jesus produced by this [historical-critical] method, legitimate and valuable as they may be for pragmatic and apologetic purposes, give us our best access to the historical events in first-century Palestine as they actually occurred."[106]

105. Ibid., 202.
106. Ibid., 204.

6

Reading Holy Scripture Well

Three Avenues

The Scope of This Chapter

Writing about issues of hermeneutics in a *concise* and yet *substantial* way has always been a difficult task. I dare say it is even more so now because of recent developments in hermeneutical theory. There are always recurring, inevitable shifts in emphasis from generation to generation, but it seems that the kind of hermeneutical changes happening currently are more tectonic than the normal generational variation. This is perhaps because today's hermeneutical changes are the result of a shift from modernism to postmodernism in a variety of forms. This larger change has already happened in much of the academy and culture but is felt more keenly now in confessional circles, which tend to be a "Johnny come lately" to new insights.

This continental shift means that while the last few hundred years have seen the normal diversity of opinions from generation to generation on how to approach the interpretation of Scripture, the difference now is that modernism (which in many ways can be summarized as a particular hermeneutical stance toward the world, or a worldview) has suddenly become too weak to exercise the intellectual hegemony (and tyranny) it enjoyed for the preceding several generations. The causes of this are many and not all easily discernible. We mentioned some of them in the last chapter when discussing the demise of Enlightenment historicism. What is clear is that we are in a new era for theories of textual interpretation and communication, and this is a positive development overall.

This is certainly true as well of biblical interpretation. The amount of true heat and light being generated now within the confessional academic guild on the issues of what it means to read Scripture well appears to be having a significant impact. Much of this heat and light falls under the rubric of a "theological interpretation of Scripture" and even a "movement" of sorts under the same name (TIS).[1] Indeed, the motivation for this book is in part the same. It comes from my own journey as one trained in academic biblical studies toward figuring out what it means to read the Gospels (and all of the Bible) as Holy Scripture. For those with ears to hear, this book's title also hints at this same shift: my goal in reading is interwoven with the biblical idea of wisdom more than the modern scientific idea of mere knowledge, understood narrowly and impersonally.

This chapter and the one that follows are my attempt at laying a hermeneutical foundation for reading the Gospels wisely. This chapter argues that a multilayered or multi-avenued method is the wisest way to approach Scripture in general. In the following chapter, several specific issues relating to this hermeneutical approach are addressed.

These chapters must inevitably and (for me) painfully be inadequate and cursory. Indeed, I am under no illusion that I can provide a whole hermeneutics course in a chapter or survey and interact with the literature on the subject, even just within the field of TIS, with which I generally identify. Rather, I will simply provide a broad approach to what I consider the most relevant and helpful hermeneutical issues.

Three Avenues of Reading

Let's begin our journey of reading at the very beginning of God's revelation in Holy Scripture, Genesis 1:1. "In the beginning God created the heavens and the earth." The primary (and recurring) question that we want to ask of this verse is simply, "What does this mean?" This may at first appear to be a simple and rather straightforward inquiry. But let's consider the cornucopia of *meaning-laden* statements that might be made about this singular verse:

- This verse uses language similar to other ancient Near Eastern cultures that also make statements about cosmogony (how the world was created).
- The pairing of "heaven" and "earth" tell us something about the kind of cosmological structure the ancient Israelites believed in.

1. Some helpful, introductory reference works include Daniel Treier, *Introducing Theological Interpretation of Scripture: Recovering a Christian Practice* (Grand Rapids: Baker Academic, 2008); and J. Todd Billings, *The Word of God for the People of God: An Entryway to the Theological Interpretation of Scripture* (Grand Rapids: Eerdmans, 2010).

- This opening line presents Yahweh, the God of the Jews, as superior over all other ancient Near Eastern gods and demigods.
- This opening line stands as a header or organizing statement over the rest of this section, which extends through Genesis 2:3.
- In light of the lines that follow, "the heavens" here describes not God's dwelling but the sky and the planetary realm.
- The theme of heaven and earth is central throughout the biblical witness and becomes a predominant motif that has both a cosmological and a theological point.
- The Gospel of Matthew manifests a carefully crafted use of the same heaven and earth theme we find in Genesis 1:1, utilizing it in ways both continuous and discontinuous with the Old Testament tradition.
- Genesis 1:1 has been understood throughout Jewish and Christian history in a wide variety of ways. The church fathers read this text in light of the reality of the Trinity, while much of Jewish interpretation focused on detailed debates over the meaning of each word. Only in the modern period was this text employed as a scientific statement.
- Genesis 1:1 and the whole creation account must be understood in light of the Trinity and redemptive history. It is the first stage in God's dealings with humanity, which finds its apex in the new creation through Christ.

These assorted statements are but a few examples of the many things we could say about this text and some of the many ways we can read it. Which one is right? Or which *ones* are right? Which ones are true to the text? I think the answer is "all of them and many more." The helpful observations that might be made about this verse are truly innumerable. The number only multiplies when one begins to consider this verse not as an isolated statement but as part of a larger literary unit or discourse in Genesis, as part of the Pentateuch, as part of the Jewish Scriptures, and as part of the whole of Holy Scripture (both Old and New Testaments).

Here is the crucial question: How do these assorted observations relate to what the text "means"? And what do *we* mean when we ask what a *text* means? In the modern period "meaning" came to be defined quite narrowly along the lines of "authorial intent," understood as the historically particular intended point that was in the mind of the author. As we will see in the following chapter, this thin and constricted approach has come under significant fire, sometimes justly and sometimes not. *Unjustly*, some have dismissed the role of the author completely from the inquiry into meaning, seeing the meaning as entirely a function of either the autonomy of the text or the community that is reading it. This approach proves to be quite problematic and ultimately *meaningless*. But the modern "authorial intent" approach has also been *justly* criticized with regard to its insensitivity to the nature and function of all communicative events, the fallacy of thinking that we can get into the mind of the author, and the fact that meaning ultimately must be understood as right application and as a function of the fusing of the two horizons of the author *and* the reader via the medium of the text.

To these matters we will return in the following chapter. But to the text at hand, Genesis 1:1, we can begin our inquiry by observing that these offered observations are not all of the same type. Some are *historical*, some are *literary*, and some are *theological*. Some of these statements make claims about the historical setting and context of Genesis 1:1. Others observe how it relates to the surrounding literary structure. Others draw meaningful connections between this verse and other biblical texts such as Matthew. And yet others comment on how it has been read theologically by believing people over time.

In many ways—though not perfectly—these three categories of observations relate to what is now often referred to as the threefold approach of reading *behind* the text versus *in* the text versus *in front of* the text.[2]

With this in mind, we may now turn our attention to the accompanying chart, "Three Avenues of Reading a Canonical Text" (fig. 1), which is schematized in this threefold way. The macro-level point I am making with this schema and this chart is simply that *to be a good and wise reader of Holy Scripture we will, to whatever degree possible, approach a text not just through one or even two of these avenues, but in all three ways.* The way to get at the "meaning" of the text (which I have yet to define more carefully) is via three avenues, not just one.

Behind the Text

In this approach we can focus on the historical matters that stand behind the text, such as the author's identity, his or her social situation, that person's place in history, how he or she used language, the year the writing was composed, the sources of information he or she used. Many of these topics can be considered the "lower critical" issues of authorship, date, and so on. Included here also are the traditional grammatical-historical approaches that focus on the grammar, syntax, and historical background of a text, as far as we can reconstruct this information.

This category also includes most of the modern scholarly/critical approaches to the Bible, including source criticism, form criticism, redaction criticism

---

2. Often in hermeneutical discussions of this sort the "behind–in–in front of" pattern is described as the difference between focusing on the author (behind) versus the text (in) versus the reader (in front of). This is certainly valid and helpful. A very good text that organizes interpretation along these lines is W. Randolph Tate, *Biblical Interpretation: An Integrated Approach*, 3rd ed. (Peabody, MA: Hendrickson, 2008). Also helpful is Jeannine K. Brown, *Scripture as Communication: Introducing Biblical Hermeneutics* (Grand Rapids: Baker Academic, 2007). I choose here to approach and identify the third column in a slightly different way as will be explained below. Issues of the reader's role in interpretation will be addressed in chap. 7.

Fig. 1. Three Avenues of Reading a Canonical Text

"Behind the Text" Historical	"In the Text" Literary	"In Front of the Text" Canonical/Theological
• Redaction, Form, Source criticism • Social-scientific criticism • Historical criticism • Grammatical-historical exgesis • Quest(s) for Historical Jesus	• Literary criticism • Genre analysis • Narrative criticism • Composition criticism • Intratextuality	• History of interpretation • Reception history • *Wirkungsgeschichte* ――――――――― • Biblical theology • Redemptive history • Theological reading • *Regula fidei* • Figural reading • Intertextuality

◄――――――― Human Authorial Intent ―――――――►

◄―――――――――― Divine Authorial Intent ――――――――――►

◄――――― Surface Meaning ◄► Bonus Meanings ―――――►

◄――――――― Mechanics ◄――――――――――► Art

◄――――――― Letter ◄――――――――――► Spirit

(concerning the origins and agenda of the Gospels), and social-scientific criticism (concerning the social setting and sociological factors at the time of writing), all of which are really subtopics under the general rubric of historical criticism. Also included is what is called the quest for the historical Jesus—probably the dominant way in which Gospel studies have proceeded in the last 150 years.

We call this aspect *behind* the text because the focus is clearly on the origins and information that inform the creation of the text and the mind of the author/editor.

In the Text

The second column or avenue, in contrast to the first, approaches texts very differently. Here, instead of focusing on reading the texts through the lens of what is going on behind the text, that is, with the author's situation, this reading focuses on how the biblical texts themselves as literary units develop themes and ideas and how they make their point(s). We may broadly call this a more literary approach, and indeed it comes from the critical study of literature in general.

When reading texts in this way, we develop certain skills for reading them closely, observing literary techniques such as chiasm, repetition, merism, and parallelism and how texts are structured and fit together. This is all the stuff of literary criticism. Narrative criticism is a specific type of literary criticism that examines how plot, characters, and settings are used by the author to craft his story and make his effect. Composition criticism is a related technique that appreciates and employs many of the techniques of literary criticism, yet also with an eye to how other historically related literature might affect and relate to the text at hand. Also included in this way of reading is what may be called intratextuality—that is, how a literary piece picks up and reuses themes, motifs, and phrases in other parts of the same book in an "intratextual" way.[3]

Such "in the text" literary approaches have arisen in the scholarly world especially in the last thirty to forty years, partly in reaction to the super-dominance of the historical-critical approach. In other words, many scholars began applying literary- and narrative-critical techniques in reading the Bible and have shown how much insight they can yield and how focusing on just behind-the-text issues can often obscure and bludgeon a text's meaning.

In Front of the Text

The third column represents an "in front of the text" reading. In reality I have included two somewhat different things in this category, represented by the dividing line.

In the first instance, we can include in this column studies that trace how a biblical text has been interpreted and received throughout time. In this sense they are in *front* of the text, not focusing on what happened during the time when the text was composed or on what is going on in the text. Instead, the history of interpretation traces the different ways in which a text, such as the Sermon on the Mount or the Letter to the Romans, has been interpreted throughout the patristic period, the Middle Ages, the Reformation, and up to the current time. Reception history is similar and focuses on how a specific text was received and appropriated in a particular time by some group of readers. It is similar to the history of interpretation but focuses on a particular time and place (synchronic) rather than tracing a text through time (diachronic). Another, related area of study is what is called *Wirkungsgeschichte*, a German word applied to an approach that treats *the history of the effects* of the text, particularly outside the realm of commentary and preaching. *Wirkungsge-schichte* looks at how a biblical text has reacted to, created, and affected the cultures it was received in, especially in media other than texts, such as art and music.[4] While writing this chapter, I am listening to Handel's oratorio based

---

3. In using "intratextual" in this way I am adopting the insights of Dale C. Allison Jr. as he applies the term to the Gospel of Matthew. See his *Studies in Matthew* (Grand Rapids: Baker Academic, 2005), esp. 79–105.

4. This is the sense of *Wirkungsgeschichte* developed especially by Ulrich Luz both in his celebrated commentary on Matthew and his book *Matthew in History: Interpretation, Influ-ence, and Effects* (Minneapolis: Fortress, 1994). Others such as Gadamer (see below) have used

on the "apocryphal" but very popular story of Susanna (an addition to the book of Daniel). A "history of effects" study might include in its interpretation of this text an analysis of how Handel approached, handled, and interpreted this story in his own musical and lyrical representation.

Studying the history of interpretation of texts in any of these forms can be *very* beneficial for our interpretation for several reasons: (1) it opens up new interpretive possibilities that we have not or were not able to consider; (2) it reveals blind spots and assumptions about ourselves and our times when we see how others have read a text (fighting against what C. S. Lewis has called "chronological snobbery"); (3) it shows that there is really nothing new under the sun. Any time we think we have come up with a new and insightful interpretation, the odds are that someone has already had this insight and expressed it better; (4) conversely, if we do arrive at an entirely new interpretation, then chances are, if none of the tens of thousands of students of Scripture have ever seen things that way, that interpretation may have serious weaknesses and blind spots; and (5) related to number 2 above, learning how a text was interpreted in earlier times, especially premodern times, reveals much about our own hermeneutical approaches to reading Scripture.

Underneath the dividing line in column 3 is a different kind of reading that can still be classified as *in front of the text*. This section includes a number of related ideas that go beyond the authorial origin of any one text or its own literary features. *These ways of reading focus on the placement of a text within the broader canon of Holy Scripture and Christian orthodoxy.* In one sense we could place these within column 2, literary approaches, but it is more helpful to locate them here because the first two columns of our chart are more clearly constrained (in part) by the notion of (human) authorial intent. All the readings in column 3 intentionally look beyond this historical particularity of a text to the interaction between texts and current readers, an inevitable part of the *meaning* of a text.

This second part of column 3 includes what is often now called biblical theology, identified here as tracing a theme or idea throughout the various texts in the Scriptures.[5] Related is a redemptive-historical approach that views the canon as entailing a grand narrative, or metanarrative, that runs through-

---

this term in a broader hermeneutical sense to refer to our own situatedness in the history of the effects of a text.

5. The meaning(s) of "biblical theology" have varied significantly over the course of the last few centuries. "Biblical theology" has been used over against strictly historical analysis or over against dogmatic or systematic theology (a grievous and false dichotomy). Also the expression can be used to mean objective scholarship as opposed to loose or "pneumatic" exegesis. Alternatively it can mean subjective readings when contrasted with interpretation by supposedly theologically distinterested scholars. From A. K. M. Adam in *Reading Scripture with the Church: Toward a Hermeneutic for Theological Interpretation*, ed. A. K. M. Adam et al. (Grand Rapids: Baker Academic, 2006), 19. I am consciously using the term in the way defined here.

out the whole Bible. This confessional assumption and view certainly affect one's reading of any particular text. Also included here is the *regula fidei*. The *regula fidei*, translated as "the rule of faith," is a concept dating back to the earliest days of the church. The basic idea is that our reading of Holy Scripture can and should be guided and "ruled" by a canon and sense of the overall economy or story line of Scripture.[6] Irenaeus provides one of the earliest and best-known explanations of the role of the *regula fidei*. He invites us to consider the many tiles of a mosaic that could be assembled in such a way to make a picture of either a king, a dog, or a fox. To make the proper mosaic picture one needs a key (in Greek, a *hypothesis*) to guide the construction of the picture. This is what the rule of faith is for Christians, the God-given, orthodox understanding of what the content or picture of Jesus in the Bible is. The innumerable bits and pieces or data in the Scriptures can be arranged in a variety of ways, as every Bible-based heresy shows. But the right way of assembling the pieces together is the *hypothesis* that presents the true picture of Jesus Christ as the King who pulls together and completes the whole story of the Bible.[7]

"Figural reading" and "typology" are again very old ideas and approaches that Christians have always used when reading the texts of the Bible as Holy Scripture. In short, there are types or figures in Scripture that relate and connect to other events, people, and places in the Bible. Analogies can be made, under the providence of God, between various, otherwise unrelated realities. Many of these are glaring and obvious and form the substance of the New Testament's witness. For example, Jesus's title of Son of David is obviously intended as more than a statement concerning his genetic ancestral line but is moreover a declaration regarding his role as a fulfilled prophecy, his kingly nature, and what he came to do and establish. More subtle but no less important would be the recognition of the way in which the Old Testament institution of the tabernacle and then the temple finds its transformed fulfillment in both Jesus himself and now in the church. Since the Reformation, "typology" has been used to discuss these matters. I, along with others, prefer the term "figural" because it more readily communicates the atemporal, analogous nature of such connections without tying this nature to a particular historical development (one figure or event being the historical precedent or type of another).

Finally, we can mention here the notion of biblical intertextuality. We will be addressing this more fully in a subsequent chapter, but for now we can

6. One helpful brief discussion of this notion and how it functions within a Protestant understanding of *sola Scriptura* can be found in C. Stephen Evans, "Tradition, Biblical Interpretation and Historical Truth," in *"Behind" the Text: History and Biblical Interpretation*, ed. Craig Bartholomew et al. (Grand Rapids: Zondervan, 2003), 320–36.

7. Treier, *Introducing Theological Interpretation of Scripture*, 58–59. See also John O'Keefe and Russell Reno, *Sanctified Vision* (Baltimore: Johns Hopkins, 2005), 35–36.

note the way in which the texts of the Bible pervasively pick up and embed earlier texts into later ones. That is, a study of intertextuality examines how an earlier text is taken up, transplanted, and transformed in a later text. In some sense this important and widespread phenomenon could be included in either columns 1 or 2, but we are placing it here to emphasize that from the perspective of the *older* text, there is an extension of the *meaning* of that text within the canon once it is transplanted into its new canonical context, although it still also retains its own voice as such in its original context.

Revisiting Genesis 1:1

We have now examined the three different avenues or categories by which we may approach any text of Holy Scripture. If we were to revisit and reexamine the statements we made previously about Genesis 1:1, we would notice that, again, they can be classified into these three different columns or avenues of approach. Some are primarily historical, some literary, some stem from the history of interpretation, and some are intracanonical readings. Each are *meanings* of the text, and we would be impoverished by the lack of any of them. The macro-point again is that a wise reader of Scripture avails himself or herself of all these approaches to ascertain the meaning of God's Word manifested in the present through the witness of the Bible.

We can draw an analogy here to the world of golf. To successfully navigate a golf course (a "good walk ruined," as Mark Twain quipped), one needs different clubs in the bag. Different lengths and conditions and ball placements require the use of distinctive, specifically designed golf clubs. Attempting to play a whole course with a driver or a putter or anything in between would be a difficult and arduous task. Similarly, the varied and beautiful course that the Scriptures encompass requires a variety of appropriately applied tools. Pushing the analogy further, we may observe that if, during the game, a player breaks one of his clubs (or throws it into the pond in frustration), he must continue to play the game but now with a significant disadvantage. As we will discuss momentarily, one of the benefits of this three-avenue approach is that it counters the modernist tendency to emphasize just one "right" approach, summed up in a method. By analogy this approach can be compared to trying to play the glorious Old Course in Saint Andrews with only a six iron. This is an unnecessary, self-imposed limit; it puts chunks in the course; and it makes some shots impossible or nearly so. Many such Gospel-scholar golfers have now hit their whole bag of balls into the lake and don't know how to get around it. Some of them then spend their time instead in the clubhouse only, reading up on the history of golf and its great players rather than playing the game themselves. Using the panoply of clubs available and getting out on the course is the way forward, as we will see.

Spectrum Bars That Span the Chart

Returning to figure 1, in addition to the three columns or avenues of approach, one will notice several bars or spectrums that span all three columns. Discussing these bars will help fill out our understanding of this threefold approach.

HUMAN AND DIVINE AUTHORIAL INTENT

This bar shows that there is still a role for the idea of "authorial intent" (understood as the human author of the text), but that this historically particular author only affects the first two columns of the chart and not the third. The nature of Holy Scripture, by confession, is that there is more than a human author at work in the production of the texts of the Bible. God himself is the first and last Author of all Scripture; Scripture is the record of or witness to God speaking and revealing himself. The role of this divine authorship encompasses not only the first two columns but also the third. On the one hand, it weaves together themes and threads throughout the entire canon of Scripture, and on the other hand, it providentially guides and illumines the church's theological formulations and readings.

We might say that Holy Scripture has both a lowercase *a* author and an uppercase *A* Author. The implications of this dual authorship are the following: We can and should use techniques and skills that we would use on any other (human) literature to help determine the human author's intent—historical and literary. In other words, because the Bible is humanly created literature, it can at one level be read like any other book, using the skills and techniques of columns 1 and 2. Yet at the same time, the divine authorship of Scripture means that the meaning of a text is not and cannot be limited to its human author's intent. This is true even apart from the issues of the nature of meaning itself (see below). Asserting a meaning of the text beyond the historical one is a necessary result of understanding the Bible not just as a mere record of religious beliefs and events but also as the Word or speech of the living God, who continues to speak through and from the Word. Thus believing readers have always naturally read the Bible as God speaking directly to them, making the Psalms their own prayers and making Paul's teachings their instruction.

SURFACE MEANING AND BONUS MEANING

The idea and language of a "surface meaning" and a "bonus meaning" of a text come from an article by the always-insightful biblical scholar R. T. France.[8] France observes that texts (and any form of communication) function on multiple levels. Hearers or readers inevitably receive the message of the text with different degrees of understanding and depth based on their own

8. R. T. France, "The Formula-Quotations of Matthew 2 and the Problem of Communication," *New Testament Studies* 27 (1981): 233–51.

knowledge, experiences, maturity, and skills as readers. And well-crafted texts (such as the Gospels) are capable of sending a message that can be received at varying levels; there is the surface meaning as well as a variety of potential bonus meanings for the keen-eyed reader. As Augustine said when reflecting on his own experience of reading Scripture: "The surface meaning lies open before us and charms beginners. Yet the depth is amazing, my God, the depth is amazing. To concentrate on it is to experience awe."[9]

Thus, as France points out, in the first two chapters of Matthew, where we read the account of Jesus's birth, each small story ends with a "fulfillment quotation," an Old Testament verse quoted to show that this story "fulfills" what was previously spoken. At a surface level, any of us—even our hypothetical alien from chapter 4 of this book, who comes to Earth to study Christianity—can understand the basic point: that Jesus somehow fulfills some older scriptural statement. But for those readers who also know the nuances and turns of the grand story of the entire Old Testament and who know specifically about the passage from Isaiah or Jeremiah or some other prophet whom Matthew quotes, a much richer and more profound depth of meaning is to be had. In fact, that meaning will often be at the level of recognizing the subtle twist and shift of the meaning of the original text now in its new "fulfillment" as used by Matthew. This is a real and powerful "bonus" meaning.

I recall a time when our family was living in Scotland, and I was riding my bike from our house to my office in the college. I would wave several times to my (then) young children, often pretending to ride away and then quickly turning around to wave again. So the children always warmly waved good-bye to me all the way down the hill. One morning I was riding away down the hill, waving, and noticed that my daughter was standing in the dining room, directly below her brother, who was standing in one of the bedrooms on the floor above. Both were looking out their window at me as I waved to them. It struck me that from their perspective, each would think I was waving to him or her personally. But of course, I was in fact waving to both of them, at the two different levels, even though they each perceived it as a wave personally to them. So too readers at different levels will receive what they can from their own perspective of the author's rich and textured meaning.

John Nolland comments on the profound skill and artistry of Matthew to this effect, though what he says could apply to much of the Bible. The strong story line of Matthew suggests that a one-time reading through was intended, yet the density of the teaching discourses also suggests the need for deeper engagement and rereading. Nolland writes, "The subtlety of the allusive quality of so much of the Gospel material is such that most of it would be lost in a single encounter on most of even the most biblically literate of readers or hearers. The complexity of the patterns of cross reference within the Gospel

---

9. Augustine, *Confessions* 12. See also his *De Doctrina Christiana* 4.

itself reveal themselves only to those who give patient and repeated attention to the text."[10] As we increase our biblical knowledge, our skills in reading texts, and our theological understanding, the more *meaningful* they will be.

MECHANICS AND ART SPECTRUM

There is both a skill and an art involved in reading Scripture well. We can and should learn skills and techniques for reading texts, including historical background studies and knowledge of how literary texts function. But ultimately a good reading of Scripture goes beyond mere mechanics; there is an art to reading Scripture well and a level of skill and insight that goes beyond techniques that can be developed. Rarely will a text (or a painting) be good if the mechanics aren't there; the most powerful and effective readers are those who build on a skill set and learn to read creatively and expansively. As we learn to be good readers of Holy Scripture, we must seek the high form of being a craftsman, not just a technician. That is, our goal in reading is not merely to screw down the right bolts in the right places to construct the right reading nor even just to "get the right answer" to the text as if it were a math problem waiting to be solved. We as readers are not mere technicians but those who, with skills in place, are inspired to read well and creatively. And just as in painting, the best way to grow from being a mere technician to a craftsman or even an artist is by learning from the masters. Some people are simply better readers and exegetes than others, and this is okay. Even as art students regularly set up their easels next to a great painting at the Louvre, we too should seek to learn how to read well from our particularly skilled contemporaries and predecessors—those who model moving beyond mere technical and mechanical reading to a skilled artistic and creative reading. This is represented on our spectrum in that the first two columns are generally skills that can be developed by most readers. The third column represents a type of reading that requires a more expanded set of insights and abilities, but it is a goal worth pursuing by all readers.

LETTER AND SPIRIT SPECTRUM

This idea and the language alludes to 2 Corinthians 3:6 and stems from a dominant motif in much of premodern interpretation of Scripture, that of the "literal" and "spiritual" meanings of a text. In his classic book surveying patristic interpretation, Boniface Ramsey identifies as "by far the most significant aspect of the patristic approach to the Bible" the firm belief that Scripture has two senses or two levels of meaning.[11] This belief was, as Ramsey notes, an article of faith not just for Origen but for *all* the fathers across the spectrum of theological and hermeneutical diversity.[12] The simple point here

10. John Nolland, *The Gospel of Matthew*, NIGTC (Grand Rapids: Eerdmans, 2005), 22.
11. Boniface Ramsey, *Beginning to Read the Church Fathers* (New York: Paulist Press, 1985), 25.
12. Ibid.

is that in traveling across our three columns, one can discern a move through and from the "letter" or "literal" sense of a text into its more spiritual/Spiritual sense(s) as manifested in canonical and ecclesial readings. This overlaps with the ideas discussed above about the dual authorship of Scripture (God and human) and the mechanics/art spectrum.

Particularly, this "spiritual" meaning ultimately finds its reality in Jesus Christ, the final Word spoken by God. Thus, a text like Genesis 1:1 has a literal meaning in its own historical setting and literary context but also a spiritual meaning that points to Christ. This dual meaning is a function of the radically Christ-focused nature of the Scriptures and a Christian reading of them. The texts of Holy Scripture ultimately have both a literal and a spiritual meaning because the revelation of Jesus transforms the understanding of the biblical text "just as a complex detective story comes into focus only after the solution to the mystery is revealed and an array of data suddenly fits into a new and intelligible configuration."[13]

Kevin Vanhoozer, when speaking about how the historical particularity and diversity of the biblical texts can still be the one Word from God, uses the related analogy of emerging stratification or complexity that arises in biological situations. In the natural sciences "emergence" is the idea that biological phenomena are dependent on physical phenomena but cannot be reduced to the physical level. "Rather, when physical things reach a certain level of complexity, properly biological phenomena emerge and require the distinct concepts and principles of biology to account for them." Yet the biological phenomena cannot be reduced to their physical understanding (e.g., the brain versus the mind; human thoughts depend on brain states but cannot be reduced to them). Thus, when we confess the Bible to be God's Word, another stratum of divine discourse emerges at a higher, canonical, level of complexity. "What God is doing at this level *depends* on the human discourse, but it cannot be *reduced* to human discourse."[14] This is a very helpful and crucial idea to grasp if we are to be full-hearted, three-avenue readers of Scripture.

Conclusion

There are a variety of avenues and approaches to reading the Scriptures. A wise reader will concentrate not merely on one or even two of these approaches but will seek to learn from and appropriate insights from all three, developing skills and artistic sensibilities to grow in becoming a competent reader.

13. David M. Williams, *Receiving the Bible in Faith: Historical and Theological Exegesis* (Washington, DC: Catholic University of America Press, 2004), 141.
14. Kevin Vanhoozer, "Imprisoned or Free? Text, Status, and Theological Interpretation in the Master/Slave Discourse of Philemon," in Adam et al., *Reading Scripture with the Church*, 69–70.

We might compare this point to a three-part vocal harmony. Together three voices provide a nuance and even synergy that individual melody lines cannot alone produce. In music the whole is indeed more than the sum of the parts. So too is our reading that listens to insights from all three avenues of approach. Each must be allowed to sing its part, not permitting any one voice to dominate or prevent the others from participating and also restraining each with the overall melody and tune.

7

Reading Holy Scripture Well

Intent, Meaning, and Posture

In the last chapter we set out a general approach to reading Scripture that acknowledges the value of following a variety of different avenues of reading—avenues that are "behind," "in," and "in front of" the text.

This discussion leaves several significant hermeneutical issues untouched and indeed raises other important questions. As we round out these two chapters of hermeneutical discussion, we will attempt to address the most important of these issues under the headings of intent, meaning, and posture.

Intent

At the heart and foundation of modern hermeneutics is the notion of "authorial intent." In the late nineteenth century and for much of the twentieth century, pursuing and finding the intent of the writer came to be seen as the gold standard, the basis for a solid grammatical-historical reading and the supposed grounds for a secured, objective reading. Find the author's intent and you have found the meaning, we are told by modern exegesis. In the modern period, hermeneutics focused on method: finding the proper method(s) to assure one has uncovered the intent and thereby the meaning. On the one hand, this rhetoric served as a critique of the ostensibly unscientific readings of precritical and premodern readers. This belief is at the core of the vision of the Enlightenment.[1] On the other hand, and more frequently today, "authorial

---

1. Examples of this view are legion in the literature of modern academic biblical studies from the earliest days of the Enlightenment down to the present. Notice the arrogance and pointed

intent" is the battle cry for conservative readers to hold fast the walls against the perceived even-more-unscholarly readings of postmodernity (whatever that is understood or misunderstood to be!).[2]

Much has been written in recent decades on authorial intent, with some rejecting, some supporting, and some qualifying this notion.[3] Although it is impossible here to comprehensively address or even survey this issue satisfactorily, we can at least make a few crucial points of clarification to guide our wise reading of Holy Scripture.

First, it is important to recognize that while the specific language of "authorial intent" is not frequent in premodern times, the notion was certainly known and valued in patristic and medieval interpretation. In the widely held premodern notion of the literal and spiritual senses of Scripture,[4] the literal sense (*sensus literalis*) corresponded *somewhat* to what we now call authorial intent. That is, what the scriptural human author was saying mattered

---

agenda manifest in a statement such as Farrar's dismissal of nearly all patristic interpretation with a sweep of his pen: "We shall pass in swift review many centuries of exegesis and shall be compelled to see that they were, in the main, centuries during which the interpretation of Scripture has been dominated by unproven theories, and overladen by untenable results." He goes on to observe, "There are but few of them [patristic interpreters] whose pages are not rife with errors—errors of method, errors of fact, errors of history, of grammar, and even of doctrine." From Frederic W. Farrar's 1885–86 Bampton Lectures and their subsequent publication as *History of Interpretation*, quoted in Brian Daley, "Is Patristic Exegesis Still Usable?" in *The Art of Reading Scripture*, ed. Ellen Davis and Richard Hays (Grand Rapids: Eerdmans, 2003), 70. This issue is not dead and indeed in some ways is heating up again in reaction to the rise of more theologically oriented approaches to Scripture. For example, in 2010 there was a vitriolic attack on the organizers of the Society of Biblical Literature meetings for letting so many "nonscientific," "confessional" readers participate in these supposedly academic (translate, "supposedly objective and free from bias") meetings.

2. One of the clearest proponents of scientific method in hermeneutics for the purpose of quelling the "vertigo of relativity" is Wilhelm Dilthey. See the summary and critique of his approach in Merold Westphal, *Whose Community? Which Interpretation? Philosophical Hermeneutics for the Church* (Grand Rapids: Baker Academic, 2009), 29–34.

3. None will deny the categorizing role that E. D. Hirsch has played in his seminal and thoughtful work *Validity in Interpretation* (New Haven: Yale University Press, 1967). In our current time his articulation of modern "authorial intent" has become the flag that has either been rallied behind or used as the target for the antimodernism smart bombs. As usually happens with such pivotal works, his view is discussed more than his book is actually read, which results in misunderstandings and caricatures on both sides. It is always impossible for reductionistic retellings of an idea to maintain the nuance of the original, and it seems that Hirsch is neither as guilty as some charge him nor as flat-footedly supportive as those who have often depended on him. Even more problematic, the discussion of Hirsch does not typically take into account the ways that he revised and shifted toward his opponents in later writing. Significant moves away from the entrenched ideas of *Validity in Interpretation* can be found in his later articles "Meaning and Significance Reinterpreted," *Critical Inquiry* 11, no. 2 (1984): 202–25; and "Transhistorical Intentions and the Persistence of Allegory," *New Literary History* 25, no. 3 (1994): 549–67.

4. Boniface Ramsey, *Beginning to Read the Church Fathers* (New York: Paulist Press, 1985), 25.

and played an important part in interpretation; this is *not* merely a modern phenomenon that was discovered over against precritical interpretation. In the most developed schema of the multiple senses of Scripture—the "fourfold sense"—the human author's choice of language and historical setting was considered an important first step in reading Scripture well.[5] This understanding shares value with modern ideas of "authorial intent."

Yet at the same time, another important point to make is that the human author's role was seen as only *part* of the literal sense; the two were not coextensive. That is, while authorial intent was considered important, it was also understood that by confession God the Holy Spirit is the ultimate Author of Scripture. Therefore, even the literal sense—not to mention the other senses of Scripture—necessarily goes beyond merely the mind of the human author and his historical particularity and limited wisdom. Each text of Scripture is part of God's larger revelation in the canon, and the *sensus literalis* includes what God as the Author intended. Thus, an important distinction remains between the modern notion of authorial intent and the older and broader notion of the literal sense. The latter is more robustly divine, time transcending, canonically sensitive, and applicatory, while in modern hermeneutics, the authorial intent came to be limited to and collapsed into what we may instead call the *sensus historicus*, or historical sense.

The hermeneutical implications of this fuller understanding of the *sensus literalis* were not lost on premodern exegetes. One of the greatest interpreters of Scripture in the history of the church, Thomas Aquinas, following Augustine, wrestled with what the literal sense meant in comparison with the spiritual sense(s) of Scripture, as well as the implication of understanding the *sensus literalis* in a fuller way. Thomas defines the literal sense effectually as the authorial intention, but with this key distinguishing caveat: the primary author is the Holy Spirit. As a result, we cannot collapse the *sensus literalis* into the *sensus historicus*: "Now because the literal sense is that which the author intends, and the author of Holy Scripture is God who comprehends everything all at once in God's understanding, it comes not amiss, as St. Augustine says in *Confessions* 12, if many meanings [*plures sensus*] are present even in the literal sense of a passage of Scripture."[6]

This "multiple senses" view is not just a function of medieval (and earlier) exegesis; this broader understanding of the literal sense is also found in the Reformers, who themselves are much more akin to medieval exegesis than modern. For example, Richard Muller observes that the "literal" meaning

5. The best and fullest introduction to this important idea is Henri de Lubac, *Medieval Exegesis: The Four Senses of Scripture* (Grand Rapids: Eerdmans, 1998).

6. *Summa Theologica* 1. Q.1. art.10, quoted in Stephen E. Fowl, "The Role of Authorial Intention in the Theological Interpretation of Scripture," in *Between Two Horizons: Spanning New Testament Studies and Systematic Theology*, ed. Joel B. Green and Max Turner (Grand Rapids: Eerdmans, 2000), 83–84.

of the text for Calvin included a message concerning what Christians ought to believe, what Christians ought to do, and what Christians ought to hope for.[7] This applicatory reaching forward goes beyond a modernist notion of authorial intent. As Brevard Childs concludes, it is now "abundantly clear that the literal sense was never [before the modern period] confined to a verbal, philological exercise alone, but functioned for both Jews and Christians as a 'ruled reading' in which a balance was obtained between a grammatical reading and the structure of communal practice or a rule-of-faith (*regula fidei*)."[8]

Thus, taking these first two points together we can observe that the intention of the human author has been consistently valued throughout most of Christian interpretation, while at the same time, the modern period marks a significant narrowing and constraining of this sense.

A related, important point to make on the *other* side of modernity is that from a *post*-Enlightenment perspective, the modern, overly narrowed description of authorial intent is inherently problematic in significant ways. In the first instance, we face what has been called the "intentional fallacy," wherein we imagine that we can get inside the mind of the author. As the theologian John Frame argues:

> If [authorial] intention refers to a hidden psychological state of the author, then we have no more access to that than we have to his mental images. . . . And such a hidden psychological state is irrelevant to determining what an author or speaker means as are his mental images. Intentions, of course, may be defined to refer to something other than psychological states, to something objective that it is possible for us to discover, at least provisionally. But such definition of intention makes the search for an author's intention identical with a search for something else [such as the understanding of the original audience or the *use* of the words].[9]

7. Quoted in Daniel J. Treier, *Introducing Theological Interpretation: Recovering a Christian Practice* (Grand Rapids: Baker Academic, 2008), 53n36. This is not mere historical particular authorial intentionality. Treier also points out that, for Frei, Calvin functions as the ideal pre-critical reader who models a sophisticated "figural reading." It is important to note that the Reformers—probably especially Calvin—did not generally speak of "multiple senses" in the medieval sense, though they clearly held to a thicker sense of Scripture than that which develops in the modern period.

8. Brevard Childs, "Does the Old Testament Witness to Jesus Christ?" in *Evangelium, Schrift-auslegung, Kirche: Festschrift für Peter Stuhlmacher zum 65. Geburtstag*, ed. J. Ådna, S. J. Hafemann, and O. Hofius (Göttingen: Vandenhoeck & Ruprecht, 1997), 60, referencing the works of R. Lowe, "The Plain Meaning of Scripture in Early Jewish Exegesis," in *Papers of the Institute of Jewish Studies in London*, vol. 1 (London: Institute of Jewish Studies, 1964), 140–85; B. S. Childs, "The Sensus Literalis of Scripture: An Ancient and Modern Problem," in *Beiträge zur alttestamentlichen Theologie: Festschrift für Walter Zimmerli*, ed. H. Donner et al. (1976), 80–94; Katherine Greene-McCreight, *Ad Litteram: Understanding the Plain Sense of Scripture in the Exegesis of Augustine, Calvin and Barth of Genesis 1–3* (New York: Peter Lang, 1999).

9. John Frame, *The Doctrine of the Knowledge of God* (Phillipsburg, NJ: P&R, 1987), 95–96.

The "psychologism" of modern hermeneutics (coming especially from the highly influential Schleiermacher) has now been critiqued and rejected by many, for many reasons. John Frame provides a comprehensive, "perspectival" theory about all our knowing, showing along the way the weakness and thinness of a modern, scientific, authorial-intent approach.[10] Others, such as Nicholas Wolterstorff, have revealed the problems of psychological authorial intent by exploring the speech-act function of language.[11] He does not reject the role and importance of what he calls "authorial discourse interpretation" but seeks to qualify it more carefully in terms of how language actively and effectively functions rather than attempting to get inside the mind of the author.

Most profoundly, the hegemony of the supposed "authorial intent" and "objective meaning" that comes from it has been critiqued by Hans-Georg Gadamer. Gadamer's thought is complex, but we can summarize his grounds for rejecting authorial intent as follows: the author does not have the ability to impose meaning unilaterally on the text, and expression of inner experience is not the primary function of language.[12] We will return to Gadamer (and Ricoeur) below in discussing "meaning."

Kevin Vanhoozer, from within a confessional perspective, has done a great service in addressing similar issues and revitalizing the importance of a qualified notion of authorial intent. He does so not by simply asserting dogmatically the Bible and our reading of it as free from perspective and interpretation, but by showing the *morality* of doing justice to what the author of a text is saying. From the ethics of Scripture itself—for example, the Golden Rule and the Ninth Commandment—we must respect and listen to what the author of a text is saying. This is not to say that we can recover the psychological intentions an author may have had, but we can describe what an author *did* say by using certain words in a certain way.

These issues are a deep and fast canyon river for which an experienced and thoughtful guide is needed.[13] They go beyond the scope of this present

10. The whole of Frame's scholarly *Doctrine of the Knowledge of God* can be considered in this way. For his particular exploration of the "meaning of meaning" and the problem of authorial intent, see his "Appendix C: Meaning," 93–98.

11. Nicholas Wolterstorff, *Divine Discourse: Philosophical Reflections on the Claim That God Speaks* (New York: Cambridge University Press, 1995).

12. These brief statements come from Westphal, *Whose Community?* 34. A fuller explanation of Gadamer's rejection of objectivism and his critique of its great proponent, E. D. Hirsch, can be found on 45–68.

13. For a big book that delves deeply into the issues of authorial intent, especially from the perspective of speech-act theory, one may consult Kevin Vanhoozer, *Is There a Meaning in This Text? The Bible, the Reader, and the Morality of Literary Knowledge* (repr.; Grand Rapids: Zondervan, 2009). For a small book that surveys these issues and presents a compelling summary of Gadamer's approach, see Westphal, *Whose Community?* For an article-length treatment of the impact of Gadamer and Ricoeur, see Sandra M. Schneiders, "The Gospels and the Reader," in *The Cambridge Companion to the Gospels*, ed. Stephen Barton (Cambridge: Cambridge University Press, 2006), 97–118.

book, and it would take us too far off course to follow the stream any farther. Rather, our goal has been simply to raise the commonly asked question about the significance of authorial intent for our reading of Scripture. My three avenues approach from the preceding chapter typically raises this question, so I have sought to address it briefly here and also to underscore that this question and its answer(s) are much more complicated than modern exegesis often presents them.[14]

In sum, then, the history of Christian interpretation shows us that authorial intent is valuable but not ultimately determinative or all-constraining. The modern notion of discerning objective (human) authorial intent cannot be our main goal, either from a confessional understanding of the nature of Scripture as a divine Word or from the perspective of post-Enlightenment thought that rightly sees the epistemological missteps of modernism. Nevertheless, this does not mean that the notion is completely mistaken or unhelpful. Undertaken in a balanced and contributory way rather than as ultimate and hegemonic, seeking to listen carefully to what an author is saying so as to learn from one other than ourselves can be valuable. And we are listening because we are trying to obtain "meaning," the next topic that we must explore briefly.

Meaning

The question of the "meaning of meaning" overlaps with the topic of authorial intent. That is, as observed above, the modern turn is realized significantly in the assertion that objective meaning—the great goal—is only to be found through a scientific method applied to texts, seeking to understand the historically particular intent of the author. But even if we do not accept this view completely, we still must examine the issue of the meaning of meaning, especially for those of a faith that finds its core testimony in a collection of texts that must be read, interpreted, and applied. The meaning of meaning is as complex as it is important, much more so than it may appear at first glance. For our purposes of learning to read Holy Scripture well, we will approach this subject from two sides: (1) objectivity and the role of the reader; and (2) meaning and application.

Objectivity and the Role of the Reader

In the modern period, hermeneutical development occurred in such a way that texts came to be seen as "free-standing semantic containers in which a

---

14. A very balanced discussion of these matters (including the role of authorial intent, the effect of canonization, and the place of historical criticism) can be found in Max Turner, "Historical Criticism and Theological Hermeneutics of the New Testament," in Green and Turner, *Between Two Horizons*, 44–70.

single, stable meaning was intentionally embedded by the author."[15] The "meaning" that was to be found in the biblical texts was alternatively seen as historical ("what really happened") and/or as what the community that created the text wanted us to understand or believe about the historical facts. However, as was discussed in chapter 5, the problems with this exclusively historical orientation toward texts increased greatly during the twentieth century. A literary focus on the texts themselves and not just viewing them as windows onto historical events broke the autocracy of this kind of "behind the text" reading, resulting eventually in the "turn to the subject"—the awareness that all readers are themselves situated in a time, place, culture, and worldview, and therefore what we understand texts to mean inevitably involves us.

This turn in thinking is the opposite of the modern view of the inherent objectivity of texts and their meaning, to be accessed via proper method, executed by the disinterested, uninvolved, objective interpreter (read: lab-coated technician). On the other hand, it is strikingly similar to premodern reading, which understands the meaning of Holy Scripture to include historical data *and* personal, transformative application (cf. the discussion of the *sensus literalis* above).[16]

This does not mean, however, that all texts—and especially normative texts like Holy Scripture—are simply wax noses that can be bent and manipulated into whatever shape and direction we choose. This "anything goes" approach is a valid cause for concern, especially for people who *do* consider some texts authoritative (and inspired) across all generations of situated readers, hence the continuing role of authorial intent discussed above. However, finding the tensive balance between recognizing our own situatedness, our personal involvement as readers, and the continuing *otherness* of the texts of Holy Scripture as normative is not easy.

Much help can be found in two of the leading hermeneutical philosophers of the twentieth century, Ricoeur and Gadamer. Both of these thinkers can be labeled "postmodern" because they are engaged in a critique of modern hermeneutical approaches. Postmodern here, however, should not be understood as meaning relativistic and lax in their view. Both are committed to the reality of real communication occurring between people across time; there is no hidden power agenda, no conspiracy theory about oppressive regimes that control everything, or simply a playing with texts. Ricoeur and Gadamer

15. Schneiders, "Gospels and the Reader," 97. The remainder of this section closely follows the argument of Schneiders.

16. An interesting article that compares Augustine's premodern interpretation with that of Gadamer's postmodern is Cynthia Neilsen, "St. Augustine on Text and Reality (and a Little Gadamerian Spice)," *Heythrop Journal* 50, no. 1 (2009): 98–108. These approaches, however, are not coextensive; for Augustine and other Christian interpreters there is an inherent, ontological authority resident in the text of Holy Scripture because it is God's speech, despite (and in fact requiring!) its polyvalency.

are not wax-nose promoters. Quite the opposite, both in their own way embrace the situatedness of all readers (including themselves), but believe that real discourse and communication can be obtained through conscious effort to advance along what we may call the "hermeneutical spiral."[17] In this they bear remarkable similarity to the great Christian tradition as exemplified in Augustine, who also saw the "surplus of meaning" in the texts of Scripture but not a hermeneutical free fall.[18]

Ricoeur sees texts—the encoding of discourse in writing—as inherently having some semantic autonomy from their authors. Texts by virtue of being written communication can outlive their authors and interact with readers who could never have been envisioned by the texts' creators.[19] Moreover, unlike oral speech, in which the speaker can correct misinterpretations and clarify intentions, what a text means depends (at least in part) on how various competent readers take it, even if this meaning is not quite what was originally intended. Texts are inevitably *recontextualized* into new environments that go beyond the original situation of their creation; this new environment inescapably affects how they are understood.[20]

For example, during my childhood the expression, "It's not easy being green" evoked only images and sounds of the Muppet Kermit strumming his banjo and singing melancholically from his lily pad. Here in the second decade of the twenty-first century, when being environmentally "green" is

17. For a specifically evangelical appropriation of this idea (and image), one may consult Grant Osborne, *The Hermeneutical Spiral: A Comprehensive Introduction to Biblical Interpretation* (Downers Grove, IL: InterVarsity, 1991), who agrees at least in part with the importance of the reader in interpretation. The summary of his approach in this regard can be found on 411–15. Also similar, though from a Reformed perspective and even more open to the dialogical nature of our interpretation of Scripture, is Richard Pratt's development of the "Authority-Dialogue Model" of interpretation in *He Gave Us Stories: The Bible Student's Guide to Interpreting Old Testament Narratives* (Phillipsburg, NJ: P&R, 1990), 23–42.

18. We typically think of Augustine's *Confessions* as his personal testimony, which it is. However, there he also touches on how to read Scripture, especially in book 12, which explores the multiple valid readings of Gen. 1:1, not all of which are equally good but from which we cannot derive only one (even Mosaic-intended) meaning. As Neilsen comments on this balance in both Augustine and Gadamer: "Clearly, Gadamer is not saying that the interpreter has license simply to ignore the text and to assign it any meaning that she sees fit. Nor does Gadamer believe that the interpreter ought to approach the text neutrally. Rather, the interpreter comes with full awareness (insofar as that is possible) of her own 'fore-meanings' and 'prejudices' and allows the text 'to present itself in all its otherness and thus assert its own truth against one's own fore-meanings.' From what we have seen thus far, I suggest that neither Augustine nor Gadamer seek to promote a hermeneutical free-for-all; however, both reject hermeneutical practices that assume a univocal or flat understanding of meaning and reality." Neilsen, "St. Augustine," 102.

19. In Hirsch's later developments, he comes to acknowledge his move toward Gadamer and Ricoeur on this topic. See the discussion in Scott Blue, "The Hermeneutic of E. D. Hirsch, Jr. and Its Impact on Expository Preaching: Friend or Foe?" *Journal of the Evangelical Theological Society* 44, no. 2 (June 2001): 258–61.

20. Schneiders, "Gospels and the Reader," 104.

suddenly pervasive in society, the meaning of this expression to a hearer (including me) involves the greater cost and hassle—but importance—of living in an earth-friendly way. Indeed, for me, this phrase triggers both of these unrelated thoughts simultaneously. What it might mean in one hundred years is impossible to say. Moreover, for other contemporary hearers, "It's not easy being green" might induce not the recognition of the greater-cost-but-worth-it idea of environmentalism, but rather skepticism and antagonism toward the government sentiment for imposing such ideas on our lives. Alternatively, "being green" may evoke strong anti-big-business feelings for the activist upset with environmental degradation. In every case the *situatedness of the reader* affects how one receives the relatively simple expression at hand, and many of these understandings will have nothing to do with the original authorial intention.[21] Meaning is understanding, and the reader's environment as distinct from the environment of the text's creation inevitably contributes to the meaning. Meaning necessarily involves not only *denotation* (what the other is referencing) but *connotation*, what is evoked in the reader because of his or her own situatedness. Denotation and connotation cannot ultimately be separated in the experience of meaning that a reader/hearer has.

Gadamer uses the analogy of a work of art to explain what happens when a classic text is actualized in the present environment. As Schneiders explains:

> Just as great art (e.g., the *Mona Lisa*) exists, even when it is not being aesthetically appreciated as an art object, but comes into the fullness of being as a work of art only when it is actually engaged by the viewer, so the classic text exists physically as potentially meaningful until it is actualized by a competent reading. The stability of the text as artefact grounds the continuity and family resemblance of subsequent interpretations, which will all be different because of the different circumstances, interests and capacities which individual interpreters bring to the task.[22]

This idea of a family resemblance among interpretations is particularly helpful as we wrestle with objectivity and the meaning of meaning. The artifact of the text—and, I would add, the authorial intent—is a guiding factor in the pluriform readings that any text creates in the innumerable environments in which it is read and interpreted. In this way we can retain an authoritative and even normative role for the original text and its author, including providing some criteria and guidance for adjudicating between assorted readings. At the same time we avoid falling into the errors of objectifying the text and the falsehood of our own supposed objectivity.

21. Some astute readers may object that this is instead an example of "meaning" versus later "significance" or "application." However, as we will discuss, such distinctions are more convenient than accurate.

22. Schneiders, "Gospels and the Reader," 105.

Along with art, musical performance also provides an instructive illustration to understand this relationship between normativeness and openness in texts. A musical performance is normed by the score but can and will be original and fresh in the hands of each musician. Schneiders again is insightful:

> The same score can be played beautifully by a virtually infinite number of talented performers, each of whom contributes with originality to the body of interpretation of the piece, which itself remains identical. Similarly, the integrity of the text is not threatened by the potentially infinite variety of interpretations by readers whose interpretations are creatively diverse but faithful to the text. And just as it is possible to grade musical performances as good or better, flawed or totally inadequate, so it is possible to distinguish good textual interpretation from bad.[23]

So once again we see that the question of meaning must be thought of as an interaction between the author/text and the readers, or said in another way, meaning is the fusing of the two horizons between texts and readers.[24] As the musical illustration intimates, an important balance must be maintained between the norming direction of the score and the creative and individual performances.

We must also recognize that meaning is not completely objectifiable because every text (and event) has its own history, which itself is ever developing and becoming the context for our understanding of it as readers. For example, the meaning of World War II or some detail of the Thirty Years' War continually becomes meaningful in different ways only as subsequent history develops.[25] So too with texts, whose own interpretive history continues to develop and to affect subsequent readers' experience of the meaning of the text. This is to say not that the text or event itself changes but that meaning is understanding, and thus it necessarily involves the context of all readers, including the context of the text's/event's interpretive history. So again, a balance should be maintained between the text as authoritative and the inescapable situatedness of every reader.

Meaning and Application

Later modern hermeneutic work, such as that of E. D. Hirsch (especially his earlier work), sought to address this recognizable, inescapable situatedness

23. Ibid., 107–8.
24. One of the most learned and influential writers on philosophical theory and as it relates to biblical hermeneutics is Anthony Thiselton, such as in his books, *The Two Horizons: New Testament Hermeneutics and Philosophical Description* (Grand Rapids: Eerdmans, 1980); *New Horizons in Hermeneutics* (Grand Rapids: Zondervan, 1997); and now more recently, *Hermeneutics: An Introduction* (Grand Rapids: Eerdmans, 2009).
25. Peter Leithart addresses this topic in his chapter "Texts Are Events: Typology" in *Deep Exegesis: The Mystery of Reading Scripture* (Waco: Baylor University Press, 2009).

of readers by emphasizing that while different readers may perceive different things from a text, the actual *meaning* of the text was stable and objective; all other thoughts that it might stimulate are rather *significances* or *applications*. This understanding is an attempt to preserve the objectifiable and therefore universally applicable meaning of the text from being "changed" over time via recognition of the ways different readers across time and place hear the text. It is itself a late modern reaction to the crumbling edifice of the Enlightenment.

One of the most fundamental problems with this approach, however, is that it cannot account for the vast variety of meanings or interpretations that are constantly produced by contemporary readers, even those with similar backgrounds and methods. That is, if meaning is supposedly stable and objectifiable from a text, obtained by using certain methods, then why does one rarely if ever find two interpreters who agree with each other—even contemporary interpreters with similar convictions, let alone diverse ones? Additionally, if the "objective" meaning of the text according to authorial intent could be discerned once and for all, then certainly we would have done so by now, wouldn't we? This issue is similar to that of Bible translation from a typical layperson's perspective. Why do we need so many translations? Can't we just get enough scholars together, look up all these words, and make *the* right translation once and for all? Anyone engaged in biblical languages and translation—indeed, anyone who is bilingual—knows immediately the impossibility of acting on such a simplistic perspective; translation is an art involving a complex series of judgments that must be sensitive to not only the author's language but also the "target" language of the translation.

Moreover, we must also recognize that such a Hirschian distinction between meaning and application (or significance), while heuristic in value and apparently obvious at first, proves to be an untenable and unreliable way to preserve stable textual authority.

This focus on the "original meaning" and the distinction between "what a text meant" and "what it means" is noble in that it tries to prevent the wax-nose appropriation of texts mentioned above. By limiting the meaning of the text to its historical situatedness, it appears that we can thus protect its stability. But this proposed solution of creating a distance between the *meaning* and the *application* of the text is ultimately very problematic for several reasons.

First, as Thiselton, Vanhoozer, and many others have observed (building on Wittgenstein and Austin), language does not work this way. Language or discourse does not just inform but also has a purpose. Texts not only have a propositional meaning (locution) but also are a call for action, response, change of view, and commitment (illocution). Thus, when Paul writes to Corinth, he is not just writing a series of abstract propositions but is hoping to effect some change in the hearers. Or when Jesus utters the Beatitudes, he does not just "mean" something in his original context; he is also calling for response. Most if not all language works this way. In discourse "meaning and significance are united in a single act of coming-to-understanding. The text not only communicates its meaning but demands response," a response that can be pluriform.[26]

We touched on this topic above with the views of Wolterstorff and Vanhoozer. Both maintain the importance of authorial intent but recognize that the illocutionary nature of language requires that we leave behind the notion that *meaning* can be separated cleanly from *application* or *significance*. This is true for any text. But when we move from talking about just any text to dealing with Holy Scripture, the stakes are raised because ultimately to read the Bible is to hear the Word of God, to discern what God is saying to us. Bible reading is not just informative, but it must be transformative; otherwise its meaning is not truly understood. From the insights of speech-act theory (and simple reflection on how we all use language), we discover that authors not only signify or communicate—in the narrow sense of conveying information—but they *do* various things in, with, and through words (e.g., promise, command, warn, encourage, affirm, deny). This, then, "opens up rich new possibilities for thinking about the Bible as God's word written. Most importantly, it allows us to view interpretation in terms of personal engagement and not merely information processing."[27] The point here for our reading of the Bible is that understanding Scripture must be more than understanding its *locution*; just as important, we must understand its illocutionary point, and to truly "understand" it is to let it have its perlocutionary effect on us (namely, faith in God and all its effects). Thus, to make a sharp distinction between what a text "meant" and what it "means" is mistaken because the "meaning" of a text cannot be reduced to a set of abstract propositions about it. The meaning of a text is the locution, illocution, and perlocution of God speaking to us *now* in Holy Scripture.

For another reason the strong meaning/application distinction is ultimately untenable, we can once again return to the insights of the Reformed theologian John Frame.[28] Frame astutely observes that when we ask for the *meaning* of a text, we are actually already asking for an *application*. It is a false distinction to speak of the meaning of a text being different from its application; in fact, every meaning is an application, and every application is a meaning.

For example, take the Eighth Commandment. The text would be the Hebrew words *lōʾ tignōḇ*. A basic translation would be "You shall not steal." One might say that this translation statement is the original *meaning*. The

26. From Grant Osborne, "Hermeneutics/Interpreting Paul," in *Dictionary of Paul and His Letters*, ed. Gerald F. Hawthorne and Ralph P. Martin (Downers Grove, IL: InterVarsity, 1993), 391.

27. Kevin Vanhoozer, "Imprisoned or Free? Text, Status, and Theological Interpretation in the Master/Slave Discourse of Philemon," in *Reading Scripture with the Church: Toward a Hermeneutic for Theological Interpretation*, ed. A. K. M. Adam et al. (Grand Rapids: Baker Academic, 2006), 65.

28. Frame, *Doctrine of the Knowledge of God*, 82–84, 93–98.

interpretation might be said to be, "Don't take anything that doesn't belong to you." Then one might think of various *applications* such as, "Don't embezzle," "Don't cheat on your income tax," "Don't take donuts without paying," and so on.

But further reflection reveals that such distinctions do not hold water. These various, extended statements seamlessly flow over into one another. For example, what if two scholars or readers agreed that "Thou shall not steal" is a good translation or meaning of the Hebrew words, but then disagreed on its application—one scholar thought it applied to embezzling; the other thought it did not? Could we really say that they both got the *meaning* right even though they disagreed on the *application*? What is the meaning if it is not a right application of the discourse? Meaning is understanding. To give a correct *meaning* of a text is to give a correct application; at the same time, to give an *application* is to give a *meaning*. We cannot ultimately distinguish them.

Similar to Frame and leaning explicitly on Gadamer, Vanhoozer addresses this same issue with a related argument. Vanhoozer understands application not as coming *after* understanding but rather as "constitutive of understanding itself." Law is an easily accessible illustration of this truth that occurs in all discourse. "Judges have to decide what a given law *means* (e.g. how it applies) to particular cases. . . . To understand a law properly, therefore, is to know how to *perform* it in a concrete situation."[29] Judges—or interpreters—cannot make arbitrary applications, simply "what it means to me," divorced from the extended intent or the history of its reading. Rather, application is comparable to the task of translation—"to preserve the original meaning in a new context."[30]

Bringing it back into the realm of theological discussion particularly, Frame sums up the point this way:

1. To ask for the meaning of an expression is to ask for an application.
2. As meanings are applications, so applications are meanings. One does not know the meaning of a text or piece of language if he cannot use it in some way. Scripture makes it clear that those who are unable to *apply* God's Word do not *truly* understand it.
3. Some people find this account too subjective and would like meaning to be the objective *basis* for all application. . . . True enough, application must be the application *of* something! But in my view, the objective basis of application must be the text itself, nothing more and nothing less. . . . If someone wishes to define *meaning* as the text itself, then I can accept a distinction between meaning and application. Meaning is

29. Kevin J. Vanhoozer, *The Drama of Doctrine: A Canonical-Linguistic Approach to Christian Theology* (Louisville: Westminster John Knox, 2005), 327.
30. Ibid., 328.

the text, and application is our use of the text. Those definitions are, however, entirely contrary to normal usage, and that is why I shun them. What we must categorically reject, however, is some mysterious, intermediary thing called "the meaning" that stands *between* the text and its application. Instead of increasing the objectivity of our knowledge, such an intermediary is a subjective construct that inevitably clouds our understanding of the text itself.

4. That sort of subjectivity is especially evident in the theological context. . . . The objective basis of theology is the text of Scripture, not any product of theological endeavor. *Sola scriptura*.[31]

To be painstakingly clear, this "meaning = application" understanding does not suggest that a text can mean *anything*—in fact, just the opposite; there are bad readings or applications of a text that do not cohere with its thrust. Rather, a text's *meaning* cannot be limited to some "original" historical meaning and then all else is *application* or *significance*. Or to put it more positively, a text's meaning is as many right applications as it has. A variety of meanings/applications orbit around a text, not all equally good or beautiful or coherent, but all good ones stemming from the text. We must continually return to the source of Holy Scripture to hear its meaning/application anew. This is what theology is: the reading/applying of Scripture by us as God's people.[32]

As Brevard Childs notes, reflecting on what it means to read the Bible theologically:

It is an important caricature of the relationship between exegesis and theological reflection to suggest that the former is an independent historical and philological exercise which seeks objectively to discover what the text actually says, whereas the latter is a subsequent and subjectively reflective activity, largely of a speculative nature. This misleading mischief goes back at least to the time of Gabler. . . . Rather, I would argue that the relationship between exegesis and theology is a far more complex and subtle one which is basically dialectical in nature. One comes to exegesis already with certain theological assumptions and the task of good exegesis is to penetrate so deeply into the biblical text that even these assumptions are called into question, are tested and revised by the subject matter itself. The implication is also that proper exegesis does not confine itself to registering only the verbal sense of the text, but presses forward through the text to the subject matter (*res*) to which it points. Thus *erklären* [to explain] and *verstehen* [to understand] belong integrally together in the one activity and cannot be long separated.[33]

31. Frame, *Doctrine of the Knowledge of God*, 97–98.
32. An excellent argument for a "pluriformity of meaning within constraints" view can be found in Murray Rae, "Texts in Context: Scripture in the Divine Economy," *Journal of Theological Interpretation* 1, no. 1 (2007): 23–45.
33. Childs, "Does the Old Testament Witness to Jesus Christ?" 60.

To conclude this discussion of meaning, I would suggest that in light of these issues raised against a modernist view of meaning and authorial intent, we should reframe (or re-Frame) our taxonomy or means of approach to our goal in reading Scripture. When reading the Bible our goal is not excavation—to use certain tools to dig *the* point out of a particular passage (though tools are still very important)—but rather we are engaged in *productive* readings, some of which are better and deeper than others. That is, there is no one simple, right way to read a text, as both premodern Christian hermeneutics and Gadamerian postmodern interpretation understand. Instead, there are a variety of more or less *faithful* readings or performances of a text that are closer or farther on a spectrum to the *sensus literalis*. There are also unfaithful readings and misreadings, to be sure. But a richer understanding of what it means for a text to "mean" releases much steam from the pressure cooker of modernist exegesis and its angst-ridden drive to find *the one true, objective meaning*, upon which all applications can then supposedly be built. Those who are involved in preaching—either producing sermons or just listening to them—know this already; there is no *one right sermon* that can be produced for every text, nor can we even say there is one *best* sermon for every text. If this were the case, then certainly by now we could have crafted that sermon (maybe by committee) and codified it as *the right interpretation of each passage*. But alas, then we would have done precisely what we know we cannot do: replace Holy Scripture with our (imperfect) interpretations of it. Rather, the Scripture alone stands unchanged, while our readings of it can be judged only to be more or less faithful and effective, but not to be *the final and definitive correct reading*. Meaning is understanding is application.[34]

Posture

We now come to our third and final hermeneutical issue for exploration, and it is quite different from the others. We have discussed the theoretical issues of what we should be consciously pursuing when reading and what it means to mean. This third topic at hand is a step back into a broader matter. Or put another way, the issue of our *posture* is more foundational than these theoretical issues of authorial intent and meaning, though there is still some overlap. As we conclude our two-chapter discussion of hermeneutics, my final point is

34. Jeannine Brown's hermeneutical text is worth mentioning here again. Her chapter on "meaning" sagaciously offers the following affirmations: (1) meaning is author-derived but textually communicated; (2) meaning is complex and determinate; (3) meaning is imperfectly accessed by readers, both individual readers and readers in community; (4) ambiguity can and often does attend meaning; (5) contextualization involves readers attending to the original biblical context and to their contemporary contexts; (6) the entire communicative event cannot be completed without a reader or hearer. Brown, *Scripture as Communication: Introducing Biblical Hermeneutics* (Grand Rapids: Baker Academic, 2007), 79–90.

that *the most important and determinative aspect of reading Holy Scripture well is not our method or theory but our posture and our goal.*

As mentioned above, reading and studying texts in the modern world became focused on proper method. Method is the avenue through which assured results can be obtained. In one of the most ironic turns in human thought, the notion arose that even when studying Scripture we must employ a nontheological method to assure that we read the Bible properly, free from dogmatic constraints. I say that this is ironic because to do so is to read it against the Scripture's own grain and purpose, as if somehow that would be preferable. Quite the opposite of this approach and in concert with both premodern and some postmodern approaches, rather than a nontheological, nonconfessional method, the most important avenue for reading Holy Scripture involves practicing a posture, or habitus, of reception to the divine Word. Our goal in reading Scripture is not merely to *understand* what God is saying (via helpful exegetical tools) but to *stand under* his Word.[35]

As Joel Green observes in his helpful book *Seized by Truth*, "The best methods rightly used guarantee neither a Christian interpretation of the Bible nor a reading of the Bible as Christian Scripture. Paradoxically, they might even get in the way of a Christian interpretation of the Bible or a reading of the Bible as Scripture."[36]

Green is not here (or elsewhere) denying the importance of exegetical tools and skills, but he is arguing against the danger of focusing on method. This danger is a paradox in that, while we can and should develop our skill set to being competent readers of Scripture—even as this book is trying to teach!—this method and even these skills can distract us from focusing on the most important thing, reading the Bible as Holy Scripture.

Unfortunately the scientific methods that we have developed in recent centuries tend to "objectify the text—that is, they turn the biblical materials into an object to be examined."[37] Rather than emphasizing a separation and distance between us and the texts of Scripture—a distance that can be transcended only by an elaborate set of exegetical tools—we must come to see that the biggest difference is our lack of knowing and loving God; the real divide is between us and God in the text.[38] Green sums up the problem this way:

35. Joel Green uses this terminology, which appears to be originally a Vanhoozerism. See Kevin Vanhoozer, "The Reader in New Testament Interpretation," in *Hearing the New Testament: Strategies for Interpretation*, ed. Joel Green (Grand Rapids: Eerdmans, 1995), 318.

36. Joel Green, *Seized by Truth: Reading the Bible as Scripture* (Nashville: Abingdon, 2007), 10.

37. Ibid., 13.

38. Dostoevsky perceived this many years ago: "The science of this world . . . has examined everything heavenly that has been bequeathed to us in sacred books, and, after hard analysis, the learned ones of this world have absolutely nothing left of what was once holy. But they have examined parts and missed the whole, and their blindness is even worthy of wonder. Meanwhile the whole stands before their eyes as immovably as ever." Fyodor Dostoevsky, *The Brothers Karamazov*, trans. Richard Pevear and Larissa Volokhonsky (New York: Random House,

Critical exegesis today tends toward a hermeneutical theory that presumes that we must make pilgrimage into the world of the biblical text in order to ascertain its truths, then return to our world in order to transform those truths into contemporary thought and language forms. The exegetical vision I am sketching presumes that the idea of "pilgrimage" is thus wrongly applied. "Pilgrimage" is more appropriately a description of the character of our lives in this world, with our status as strangers in the world attributable to our making our home in the world of Scripture. In this hermeneutical scenario, it is not the message of the Bible that requires transformation; it is we who require transformation.[39]

Our emphasis, therefore, should be on our dispositions and obedience to live and love according to the teachings of Scripture, which is certainly the grandest and deepest reason for God's inscripturation of his Word into the Bible. "Accordingly, more necessary than familiarity with ancient peoples and their cultures, more basic than learning the biblical languages, and more essential than good technique in interpretation are such dispositions and postures and gestures as acceptance, devotion, attention, and trust."[40]

This may sound like an overstatement. I am not suggesting, however, an either/or choice (rarely is this helpful) between a humble, faithful, open reading and a skilled, rigorous, exegetical reading. Both are to be sought in full. But the priority is the posture. A person who is deficient in skills—and who is not?—but seeks to read with an openness to learn from the otherness of the text (and the God behind it) can be a better reader than a methodologically skilled exegete who reads without a posture and disposition of humble teachability, the greatest of the intellectual virtues. Here again premodern Christian exegesis and the insights of Ricoeur and Gadamer agree. Our disposition and our willingness to learn from the otherness of the text are the necessary starting point to progress in understanding.

To return to our use of a music analogy, New Testament scholar Markus Bockmuehl notes the problem with reading Scripture scientifically but without spiritual goals and application:

> To read Scripture predominantly as a document of ancient religion, or as an instrument of repression and exclusion, is to commit an elementary category mistake. Such interpretation confuses genesis with meaning, or finds fault with a design for how it is abused and for what it is not. The former reading resembles restricting the study of a Stradivari to the alpine soft-wood industry of Trentino; the latter, reducing the story of the instrument to who was prevented from

---

1991), 171. Similarly, Kierkegaard says: "He who can sit with ten open commentaries and read the Holy Scriptures—well, he is probably writing the eleventh, but he deals with the Scriptures *contra naturam*" (*Søren Kierkegaard's Journals and Papers*, ed. and trans. Howard V. Hong and Edna H. Hong [Bloomington: Indiana University Press, 1967], 1:210).

39. Green, *Seized by Truth*, 56.
40. Ibid., 11–12.

playing or hearing it, how it was played badly, or what was *not* played on it. That sort of analysis can be intellectually respectable, and may even have a certain complementary scientific or sociological interest. But it has by definition little light to shed on the instruments actually played by an Itzhak Perlman or a Yo-Yo Ma. So too the historic significance of the ancient biblical texts is inseparable from the space they have inhabited, and continue to inhabit, as the canonical Scripture of the Christian Church. Critical readings outside that perspective are of course possible and may often provide important historical, literary or ideological insights. . . . Nevertheless, what such external discussions cannot manage is a "thick" reading of the biblical texts that accounts for the ecclesial dynamics of life and worship in which those texts have in fact had their existence. For that, Christian Scriptures must be read in the context of Christian faith.[41]

The Mother-in-Law–Jeremiah 29:11 Refrigerator Magnet–Diet Principle

To conclude, we may illustrate this ecclesial or Christian reading of Scripture with what I call the "Mother-in-Law–Jeremiah 29:11 Refrigerator Magnet–Diet Principle." Imagine yourself as a seminary student. Now imagine yourself as a young, male seminary student with a semi-educated, somewhat emotional, faithful churchgoing but biblically untrained mother-in-law. You like her well enough, but as your own seminary training has increased your exegetical skills, knowledge of church history, and theological acumen, you have found a corresponding increase in discomfort when talking to her about God and the Bible. She is very passionate about the latest devotional book she is reading and the new insights she has gained into passages of Scripture from looking up Greek words in *Vine's Expository Dictionary*. Every time you see her, you sense with increasing intensity that she could be on the cover of the next edition of Carson's *Exegetical Fallacies*. On your better days you just nod and smile politely. In your grouchy moments you daydream about ripping the books out of her hands, mocking them, stomping on them a few times, and throwing them into the fireplace while quoting Greek paradigms. But then when you arrive at her house one Thanksgiving, you see something that pushes you over the edge. On the refrigerator, holding up her unrealistic diet plan, is a magnet with a nice flowing script of Jeremiah 29:11—"For I know the plans I have for you," says the Lord. "They are plans for good and not for disaster, to give you a future and a hope." It is obvious that this verse and this diet plan are organically related in her mind. She is taking this verse to heart every day as a promise from God for her success in shedding a few pounds.

How will you respond? Your exegetically and theologically trained mind immediately populates a list of problems with her use of this verse: this is a

---

41. Markus Bockmuehl, "Reason, Wisdom and the Implied Disciple of Scripture," in *Reading Texts, Seeking Wisdom*, ed. David Ford and Graham Stanton (London: SCM, 2003), 53–54.

horrible translation of the Bible; this verse is taken out of context; this is a word spoken to the nation of Israel in the Old Covenant and therefore can't apply to her; God doesn't care about her diet, and on and on. Thankfully, you have enough sense and wisdom not to attack or mock her and her refrigerator magnet, but in your quiet moments later you face a couple of crucial questions. These questions are ours as well when we read Scripture and when we read and hear interpretations of Scripture. First, what is wrong with her interpretation/reading/application of this verse? And second, should you say anything to her about it? Our answers to both questions can be helped by all that we have said in this chapter.

What is wrong with this use of Jeremiah 29:11? In the first instance, we are right to emphasize that what a text or verse means is best approached in its own literary and theological context. Her ignorance of the overall story of the Bible and the fact that this verse is from a letter that the prophet Jeremiah sent to the elders and priests of Jerusalem who were then in exile in Babylon is a regrettable oversight. This knowledge would deepen and contextualize the significance of these lines. We may also register some concern that not every word to the nation of Israel necessarily has a *direct* application to the individual Christian. Other examples come to mind including details of the Mosaic law concerning diet and clothing or promises of physical blessing for obedience to Torah.

However, we must also ask what might be good about her reading. And herein lies much that we might initially overlook. Even though her reading and application of this verse may not be very sophisticated or theologically astute, I would suggest that ultimately what it possesses is greater than this deficiency. At one level her reading is in fact more theologically perceptive than our systematized view might be. That is, in a very real sense a promise like Jeremiah 29:11 *does* apply to the individual who is in Christ (in whom "*all* the promises of God are Yes and Amen"; 2 Cor. 1:20). Jeremiah's words are God's words; they reveal God's heart and disposition toward his people, who are now defined no longer ethnically but based on faith response in Jesus—that is, all Christians. To read Jeremiah Christianly is to receive this as God's promise *to us*, albeit in light of the full picture of Scripture in which the church is now in a time of sojourning exile awaiting the return of the Son.

Moreover, what is good—even glorious—about her reading of Jeremiah 29:11 as applied to her diet is that she has the right posture toward God and Holy Scripture as she reads. That is, she is going to the Bible looking for God to speak and guide and direct her life very personally. She expects the living God to speak to her, and she is willing to listen. She has chosen the better part. Certainly we might want her to grow in her theological knowledge and interpretive skills, but not at the expense of this simple God-ward faith and posture.

We as trained exegetes and theologians can and should also have this posture, but honest self-reflection reveals that for most of us, our learning often creates layers of distance between us and hearing the Bible as God's Word to us. Although it was obtained for the supposed goal of bridging the gap between us and the biblical text, our training in fact often creates in our hearts and minds an elaborate structure of paper walls and divisions that create a maze of distance between us and Scripture. Relegating meaning to the *sensus historicus*, obtained through the employment of an elaborate skill set, and making understanding and application secondary steps only opens the door for this deferral more widely. Instead, we can learn from our faithful mothers-in-law that to read Scripture is to seek to hear and obey God now in very practical ways. Anything less is not reading Holy Scripture according to its purpose.

If we've made it this far in our thinking, then the second question posed to ourselves becomes a little clearer. We should not say anything to her about her refrigerator magnet if that conversation will be a lecture on improper exegesis or the foolishness of such mistaken theological reading. If we discourage her devotional reading of Scripture and/or sow seeds of doubt in her mind about reading the Bible as God speaking to her, then we are certainly doing more harm than good and likely we should be put into the category of "causing those little ones to stumble"—not a positive place according to Jesus. Yet at the same time, this does not mean that she is free from the need for instruction and guidance in reading. This is, after all, why God has always given teachers, preachers, and prophets to the church: to guide how we read and understand and apply the Scriptures. And herein lies a beautiful balance worth pursuing: developing skills as readers (whether professional or lay) while also keeping the true goal always in sight—hearing, reading, and applying the Holy Scriptures to our lives. This is understanding. This is wisdom.

This same situation was already pondered and illustrated by the great theologian and hermeneutist Augustine in his textbook on how to read Scripture. His illustration has stood the test of time and indeed has experienced a renaissance recently through the rediscovery of a theological reading of Scripture. Augustine promotes a balance between reading the Scriptures for the sense that the author (including God) intended and yet recognizing that the ultimate purpose is to build up "the twin love of God and neighbor." Thus a reading that results in greater love for God and for neighbor, no matter how poor the exegesis, is in some real sense good. Those who read in this way—maybe our mothers-in-law—are mistaken, Augustine says, "in the same sort of way as people who go astray off the road, but still proceed by rough paths to the same place as the road was taking them to. Still, they must be put right, and shown how much more useful is it not to leave the road, in case they get into the habit of deviating from it, and are eventually driven to take the wrong direction altogether."[42]

---

42. Augustine, *De Doctrina Christiana* 1.36.41, from the translation, *Teaching Christianity*, trans. Edmund Hill (Hyde Park, NY: New City Press, 1996), 124.

Good exegetical skills, reading for the authorial/Authorial intent, are important guidelines for our reading now and in the future, and thus they should be learned and taught to others. But we must never mistake these means for the real end—developing a posture and practice of love for God and neighbor. And to the question of *how* we speak to our mother-in-law about her reading, Augustine would be the third person, I'm sure (after Jesus and Paul), to remind us to speak in such a way that we too promote the twin love.

We have sought in this chapter to explore important hermeneutical issues that relate at the broadest level to what it means to read Holy Scripture well. We have seen that ultimately these theoretical issues about what we are doing when we read and the skills that we should develop in our reading must all be subsumed under the greater issue of our posture and goal in reading Scripture. We can now turn our attention to applying these insights to our reading of the Gospels in particular, which is the focus of the following chapter.

8

Foundations for Reading
the Gospels Well

Our Goal in Reading the Gospels

We are now at the final chapter in our preparatory discussion for reading the Gospels wisely and well. The stated goal of this lengthy section of the book is to clear ground, dig deeply, and lay a solid foundation for good Gospel reading. After this chapter, we will turn to the second, shorter part of the book and focus on the practical matter of how to read the Gospels as theological stories. But first, it will benefit us to pause, take a few steps back, survey the foundation we have laid, and remind ourselves of where we are going before we finish the house itself. This exercise is like pulling out a picture of the final home that we are building to remind ourselves of the whole picture before we proceed. We need to cast a final, keen eye over the ground we have covered (or uncovered) and consider more deeply the implications for our practical reading. The goal for this chapter, then, is to bring together the previous seven chapters into a clear statement of our goal in reading the Gospels. To do so, we will summarize, condense, and deepen the implications of what we have discussed previously, in three sections covering the preceding chapters in groups. And then we will address head-on the question of what our goal in reading the Gospels should be.

Revisiting Our Definition of the Gospels (Chaps. 1–3)

In the first two chapters we addressed the big question of what the Gospels are, both in terms of why the New Testament authors use this term and what literary genre the Gospels appear to be. From those two chapters we produced a concluding definition: *Our canonical Gospels are the theological, historical, and aretological (virtue-forming) biographical narratives that retell the story and proclaim the significance of Jesus Christ, who through the power of the Spirit is the Restorer of God's reign.*

This definition has two significant implications that affect our goal in reading the Gospels. First, whatever else we may get out of the Gospels, we must understand them as a message—indeed, they claim to be *the final message*—about God's kingdom coming from heaven to earth in the person of Jesus the Christ. Focusing initially on the last part of our definition above, we learn that the Gospels have a *purpose* in communicating that includes both storytelling and meaningful, applied proclamation. The fourfold Gospel book is a message that is staking and making a claim upon its hearers. The Gospels cannot be regarded as "mere" historical data or only the backdrop to the apostolic proclamation, but they themselves are homiletical and exhortational in nature.

This purposeful message of the Gospels has a specific, Christ-centered, and kingdom-centered content. This message concerning God's kingdom is both *good* news and *restorative* in nature. To proclaim the arrival of God's reign in Jesus is to announce that the favorable day of the Lord has come (cf. Jesus's use of Isaiah in Luke 4), a time wherein the brokenness and injustice and death of this fallen world are overturned. Thus to read the Gospels in line with their purpose is to hear them with a focus on the restorative, Jesus-centered, kingdom-oriented message of God's work in the world.

This, then, also encompasses the first half of the definition. As purposeful documents they are simultaneously theological and historical—they are about what God did in real history through Jesus and what he is continually doing until its fruition. This is a theologically freighted and focused understanding of history.

The second implication we can derive from our definition of the Gospels is that their biographical nature means that in large part they exist to invite us into emulation of the good characters and avoidance of the bad; they are aretological (virtue-forming). Narratives—especially *bioi*—serve to inculcate virtue in their readers via the powerful medium of story. As discussed in chapter 3, the vehicle of story is so transformative because it engages our whole being, enables us to have life experiences vicariously, and provides us with a real, experiential encounter with Christ. Therefore, a significant part of our goal in reading the Gospels must be to experience transformation and growth in God-ward virtue. We cannot simply read the Gospels for historical data or even theological information if these are divorced from the ultimate goal of learning to live differently as followers of Christ.

We might label and explore these two implications with the terms "gift" and "example." In the early years of the Protestant Reformation, Martin Luther penned "A Brief Instruction on What to Look for and Expect in the

Gospels."[1] Rather than being an introduction on how to read the Gospels, as the title might imply, this short address is really an emblematic presentation of Luther's strong argument that "the gospel" (as opposed to "law") is to be found anywhere in the Scriptures where God's grace shines forth and invites us to trust in him and not ourselves. Luther is concerned that his contemporaries have turned the Gospels (and the Epistles) into a religion in which Jesus is at best merely an example and at worst a new law-giving Moses. If we read the Gospels in this way, Luther argues, then we read the Bible as if it were "simply a textbook of teachings or laws," and we miss the great truth that Christ is given to us as a gift. This is why the gospel is *good news*, and why in it our hearts sing with assurance: because the gospel is the message of God's gift of overwhelming goodness and grace to us in Jesus. "The gospel is not really a book of laws and commandments which requires deeds of us, but a book of divine promises in which God promises, offers, and gives us all his possessions and benefits in Christ."

Once we have grasped Christ at this "higher level," we can also understand the Gospels as providing us an *example* to follow in Christ. Luther is opposed to seeing Jesus as a new Moses, yet he perceives clearly that once we have received Christ as gift, we *can* find in the Gospels clear models to follow in our own growth in grace. For example, we should learn from Jesus's example in the Gospels what it means to love our neighbor—"how he prays, fasts, helps people, and shows them love." If we *only* have Jesus as an example, then "Christ is no more help to you than some other saint." But once we have him as gift, "it is necessary that you turn this [gift] into an example and deal with your neighbor in the very same way, be given also to him as a gift and an example."

This understanding is a wise and beautiful balancing and ordering of Christ as gift and example. So, too, the two implications we have identified above can be joined together as an inseparable pair of gift and example, with the first as the foundation and the second as the result. That is, the Gospel is first and foremost the good news of the *gift* that God is now in Jesus Christ restoring his heavenly reign on earth in society and in our individual lives. In Jesus the favorable day of the Lord is being proclaimed and given to us by faith. This is nothing of our own doing; it is the gift of God—as Paul would describe it.

Building on this foundation, the Gospels then also give us clear examples in Jesus (and other characters) of how to live according to God's coming, eschatological kingdom. They are examples of what we may call God-ward virtue, given to us through the powerful medium of story.

---

1. Written in 1521 while in exile at Wartburg Castle, this piece served as an introduction to Luther's commentary on the various texts of the Wartburg Postil. This "Brief Instruction" can be found in translation and with comments in Timothy F. Lull, *Martin Luther's Basic Theological Writings*, 2nd ed. (Minneapolis: Fortress, 2005), 93–97. All quotations below come from this translation.

Thus, in this summary we have pulled together the implications of the first three chapters of this book. The Gospels are a deeply profound and universally wide theological message embedded in the most powerful medium, that of a story.

Exploring the Implications of the Gospels as History (Chaps. 4–5)

In chapters 4 and 5 we explored the historical witness of the Gospels. In the definition above, we have emphasized both their historical and their theological character. These elements are worthy of greater exploration, including the way in which these two categories prove to be integrated and inseparable. Chapter 4 surveyed at the more mundane level the angst often created by the simple fact of our having not just one Gospel account but four. Several solutions were offered for this potential anxiety; going further, we discovered the great joy and value in having a fourfold witness rather than a monographic one.

More weighty is the topic explored in chapter 5, in which we delved into what it means to write and read "history"—an issue that itself has its own varied history. I argued that we must acknowledge that all history writing is itself consciously interpreted and purposeful. There is no such thing as value-free history retelling; it always involves selection, deselection, and purpose; otherwise it is incoherent and meaningless. Biblical history, by extension, is theologically interpreted narrative retelling. The historical narratives in Scripture are a selected, interpreted explanation of events with a God-focused agenda and worldview. They are testimony that calls us to believe and trust. They are not value free either in their composition or in their purpose; they are calling us to belief and personal transformation. Thus, to return once again to our Gospels definition, they are simultaneously making historical, theological, and aretological claims, given to us through the only epistemological avenue ultimately available for accessing history, testimony.

In this my arguments are similar to those of William Placher, who has also addressed this question in brief. In his discussion of "how the Gospels mean," he proposes that the Gospels are "history-like witnesses to truths both historical and transcendent."[2] He unpacks this first by talking about what the Gospels are not. They are not fiction, myth, or the history of a modern historian.

The Gospels are not fiction in that they do not operate in their own secondary world but rather purport to define our reality and give us the *real* history of the world as we know it. The Gospels relate stories that took/take place in our real world, and they make universal claims that reach out to their readers. Moreover, unlike fictional literature—such as Homer—into which we might

---

2. William C. Placher, "How the Gospels Mean," in *Seeking the Identity of Jesus: A Pilgrimage*, ed. Beverly Gaventa and Richard Hays (Grand Rapids: Eerdmans, 2008), 27.

simply escape for a while, the Gospels "do not flatter us that they may please us and enchant us—they seek to subject us."[3]

The Gospels are also not myth in that they narrate datable events and do not read like primordial stories.[4] Nor, on the other hand, are the Gospels the kind of history that a modern historian might attempt to write. Placher means by this that they are rather minimalist in the sense of being stories about a particular human life not distant from the author, with the details rearranged.

Put positively, Placher argues that the Gospels are "history-like witnesses to truths both historical and transcendent." They are testimony to real events even though they are casual about chronology and details and "far more willing to include their understanding of the events' ultimate meaning in the telling of their stories."[5] Additionally, they make claims that are not *only* historical in nature but are also history-making and history-transcendent, such as the resurrection.[6]

Placher's arguments overall correspond quite closely to my own, except that I think he overstates his view in suggesting that the evangelists wrote "without worrying overmuch about the accuracy of the particular stories."[7] In rightly moving away from modern historicism as I do as well, he seems to teeter on the other edge here in a way that does not correspond to the Gospels' own emphasis on the *trustworthiness* of their testimony. Additionally, by calling the Gospels "history-like" Placher perhaps unwittingly concedes too much to the modern historicism he is critiquing. "History-like" suggests that the Gospels' different way of presenting history as interpreted and transcendent is somehow only partially *real* history; it is only *like* history as we know it. But this would be the case only if one concedes the idea of history to modern historicism. Better to simply call the Gospels *history* while carefully redefining that term according to its premodern sense. But if we cannot simply rescue the word "history" from modernism and do need to qualify it, then a better term might be "testimonial history" rather than the diminished "history-like."[8]

3. Ibid., 30, applying to the Gospels Auerbach's words about all the stories of Scripture from his *Mimesis: The Representation of Reality in Western Literature*, 50th anniversary ed. (Princeton, NJ: Princeton University Press, 2003), 15.

4. Placher, "How the Gospels Mean," 31.

5. Ibid., 37.

6. Ibid., 38–39.

7. Ibid., 34.

8. In light of Placher's other writings on Hans Frei, it seems almost certain that he borrows this terminology from Frei, who describes the Gospels as "realistic narrativity" and "history-like." For all the good in Frei's (and Placher's) approach, the question remains of whether this formulation takes sufficient account of their historical referentiality. As Turner notes, "In sum, if Frei was right in 1974 to complain about the eclipse of the narrative by historical criticism, Watson may have had justification in 1997 to complain about the eclipse of history by at least some 'narrative' approaches." See Max Turner, "Historical Criticism and Theological Hermeneutics of the New Testament," in *Between Two Horizons: Spanning New Testament Studies and Systematic Theology*, ed. Joel B. Green and Max Turner (Grand Rapids: Eerdmans, 2000), 60–67, quote from 64.

This leads us, then, into a focused examination of the implications of our discussion of history in chapters 4–5.

Five Overlapping Implications for Our Understanding of the Gospels as Testimonial History

There is a limited and circumscribed role for historical Jesus studies

The most developed version of modern historicism applied to the reading of the Gospels is the field of inquiry known as "historical Jesus studies." This massive scholarly machine has produced countless works and summaries of such works, complete with its own recognized phases or "quests."[9]

We mentioned in chapter 5 that modern historicism, including the world of historical Jesus studies, is in crisis. This does not mean that no one is engaged in such activity or that *Time* magazine will stop running to the "Jesus Seminar" when looking for a provocative Easter-season article. But if Scot McKnight and other leading scholars are right, the former dominating influence of the historical Jesus approach to the Gospels is now clearly on the wane.[10]

For our purposes in this implication-driven chapter, we may note that our understanding of the Gospels as testimonial history means that modern historical Jesus approaches have only a circumscribed and limited value. Their value is that of any historical information: it can provide a positive "thickening" of our understanding of the context of the composition of the Gospel documents and the oral and literary context of Jesus's own day. It may deepen and expand our understanding of what is being communicated in a text.[11] However, as Richard Bauckham observes, better than the supposed "historical Jesus" is the "real Jesus," "since historical reconstruction cannot render the full reality of any persons or events, still less the religious significance of this historical person."[12] As Murray Rae notes, following the lead of Barth, the problem with modern historical study is that there is much more to real-

9. Some introductory orientations to this field include James Carleton Paget, "Quests for the Historical Jesus," in *The Cambridge Companion to Jesus*, ed. Markus Bockmuehl (Cambridge: Cambridge University Press, 2001); James D. G. Dunn, *New Perspectives on Jesus: What the Quests for the Historical Jesus Missed* (Grand Rapids: Baker Academic, 2005); chaps. 1–3 of N. T. Wright, *Jesus and the Victory of God* (Minneapolis: Fortress, 1996).

10. In addition to the references given in chapter 5, one may also consult the article by Joel Willits, "Presuppositions and Procedures in the Study of the 'Historical Jesus': Or, Why I Decided Not to Be a 'Historical Jesus' Scholar," *Journal for the Study of the New Historical Jesus* 3, no. 1 (January 1, 2005): 61–108.

11. A fine recent article that explores the continuing importance of historical questions along with other, more theological ones in reading the book of Acts is Eckhard J. Schnabel, "Fads and Common Sense: Reading Acts in the First Century and Reading Acts Today," *Journal of the Evangelical Theological Society* 54, no. 2 (2011): 251–78.

12. Richard J. Bauckham, from a lecture titled "The Johannine Jesus and the Synoptic Jesus." Available at http://richardbauckham.co.uk/index.php?page=unpublished-lectures.

ity than historical inquiry could ever supply, even if done fully and perfectly.[13] Or as Donald Bloesch argues, "For biblical evangelicals [how Bloesch would classify himself], the truthfulness of the Bible cannot be determined by historical investigation since this truth is inaccessible to human perception and conception (cf. Ps. 139:6; Job 42:3; Dan. 12:8; Rom. 11:33–36; Phil. 4:7). The truth of the Bible is the revelational meaning of the events that are described, not the events in and of themselves."[14]

To clarify, I am suggesting here not that *no* help can be found in historical Jesus studies or historical background work overall, but simply that such work is at best limited in what it can tell us about the real Jesus and his theological significance.[15] At their worst, historical Jesus studies give us only a reconstructed, behind-the-text, theologically and ethically vacuous data set of information about the man Jesus—a far cry from who Jesus is and from the whole purpose of the Gospels.

WE SHOULD FOCUS ON VERTICAL OVER HORIZONTAL READINGS OF THE GOSPELS

In previous chapters I mentioned the difference between a "vertical" reading of the Gospels and a "horizontal" one. Vertical reading focuses on reading the individual Gospel accounts as wholes, following their narrative structure and development, as one reads from top to bottom on the page of a book. This is normal reading of any literature and would not justify a label such as "vertical" if it were not for the tendency of many Gospel readers to read horizontally instead. To read horizontally is to always have an eye toward parallel passages from the other Gospel accounts. This kind of reading is made easy (and almost mandatory) through a four-column synopsis of the Gospels, which rearranges the stories to show parallels. When any passage is read, one looks to the left and right horizontally to compare any parallels.

Although it is certainly useful to engage in horizontal, comparative Gospel reading, this approach should not be preferred over vertical reading. Both the principles of literary analysis and our conclusions about the kind of testimonial history the Gospels are giving us justify this conclusion. That is, a horizontal reading of the Gospels tends to focus less on what the individual evangelists

13. Murray Rae, *History and Hermeneutics* (London: T&T Clark, 2005), 69–71. Rae also rightly emphasizes the history-transforming nature of the resurrection, which must be taken into account in any rendering of history.

14. Donald G. Bloesch, *Holy Scripture: Revelation, Inspiration, and Interpretation* (Downers Grove, IL: InterVarsity, 2006), 19.

15. Francis Watson reviews different ways that people might respond to the quests for the historical Jesus and argues for a balanced view between a supposedly neutral, nontheological, and nonmiraculous history and a de-emphasis on the historical reality of Jesus. He argues that a critical dialogue with historical scholarship can be positive and constructive theologically if used correctly. See Francis Watson, "The Quest for the Real Jesus," in Bockmuehl, *Cambridge Companion to Jesus*, 156–69.

are saying (their "testimony") than on a reconstructed history *behind* the text, the "what *really* was said" or "what *really* happened." A horizontal reading does not necessarily or always do this, but this is, nonetheless, its observable tendency. Our exploration above of the kind of history retelling that the Gospels are encourages us to focus instead on what each evangelist is saying rather than primarily on the referentiality of their discourses (true or false, according to one's opinion) or their comparison. Both horizontal and vertical reading are beneficial, but we must prefer the latter.

WE SHOULD READ THE GOSPELS AS WITNESSES

Closely related to and overlapping the preceding point, understanding testimonial history means that we should focus our reading of the Gospels on reading the texts themselves as witnesses, not using the Gospels as windows onto other events and realities.

While affirming the essential historical veracity of the Gospel accounts *and* the importance of real history to which they testify, we must not in theory or in practice supplant the text with our reconstruction of the events behind it, *nor* should we make this reconstruction the end goal of our reading. We have no access to the events behind the text other than the testimony of the Gospels themselves, and to avidly seek such data would be to deny what we *do* have in the canonical, inspired Gospels: testimony to those events. To seek the behind-the-text realities is to fall back into the errors of modern historicism, which eschews testimony, distrusts witnesses, and desires to reach the supposed, original, objective truth of the matter. But this, as we have argued, is epistemologically and historically naive and impossible! One must finally trust testimony, or not; we can evaluate the trustworthiness of a witness, but we can never objectively get beyond the irreducibility of testimony.

As Murray Rae notes, we must realize that the biblical writers are themselves tradents who have gathered, organized, and interpreted previous layers of tradition that are no longer available to us. "For this reason their testimony functions, for us, as the first layer of tradition and so constitutes an authority behind which, for the most part, we cannot go."[16] That is, it is the interpretations provided by the evangelists—not our reconstruction of it or our thoughts on the significance of the event—that matter. The evangelists' interpretations of the events and their purpose in writing should be our focus.

WE SHOULD RECEIVE THE GOSPELS AS TESTIMONY—A BLENDING OF FACT AND INTERPRETATION

Stemming from and again overlapping the previous point, to receive the Gospels as testimony means to understand that they provide us with the blending of fact and interpretation. It is impossible for history retelling to do

---

16. Rae, *History and Hermeneutics*, 125.

otherwise. The best history writing consciously marries event and meaning. This is what it means to provide testimonial history. Conscious, intentional retelling of events with a purpose is what good history is, and this is not to be dismissed as "unscientific." Quite the opposite, as Richard Bauckham observes, the blend of fact and interpretation is "our best way of access to the history *and* significance of Jesus, better than some minimal recitation of mere facts reported without any reason for doing so."[17]

This is what makes testimony such an important and powerful idea and reality. Testimony moves us beyond the mere referentiality of events to a claim of authority and the author's *purpose* in writing. By providing an interpretation of events, the evangelists are fulfilling their purpose in writing, which is obviously not merely informative, but exhortational, pastoral, and homiletical.

WE SHOULD READ THE GOSPELS ACCORDING TO THEIR PURPOSE— THEOLOGICAL AND TRANSFORMATIONAL

Our final implication, then, is that we should read the Gospels according to their testimonial purpose, which is both theological and transformational. In chapter 3 I noted the tendency among many believing readers to prefer Paul and the epistolary literature over the Gospels. This preference stems from a variety of reasons, including the fact that direct moral instruction, rather than narrative, is easier to apply to real life.

A negative consequence of this tendency is that such readers relegate the Gospels to the realm of "historical data," and consider the epistolary literature to be the site where the theology, exhortation, and application of the New Testament are given. Consciously or unconsciously many readers slot the Gospels into the position of "transitional documents" that simply provide information about Jesus's life, which the apostles, especially Paul, use to teach and preach the full gospel. The Gospel materials become the backdrop or stage setting for the *real* action, the apostolic proclamation understood as something like the Romanesque forensic justification by faith. To use another analogy, in this view the Gospel stories are seen as concrete footings and foundations, but the actual house of New Testament theology is found in the Epistles, where the significance of Jesus is explicated. Those who consciously pursue this line of thinking may even argue that the pre-Pentecostal nature of the Gospels' historical data requires this lessened role for the Gospels; they come from an earlier "epoch" in salvation history, some would argue.[18] All these notions are radically mistaken and unfortunate. Quite the opposite, the Gospels are not

---

17. Richard Bauckham, "In Response to My Respondents: Jesus and the Eyewitnesses in Review," *Journal for the Study of the Historical Jesus* 6 (2008): 229.

18. The most extreme form of this line of thinking is classical dispensationalism, which overtly states that the NT and the church begin with the apostolic teaching as found in the Epistles while the Gospels are relegated to the OT era. Thus, for example, the Sermon on the Mount applies to Jewish believers in the future millennium, not to Christians in the New Covenant era.

mere "transitional" documents to get us to the real meal of the Epistles; rather, they are the highest and fullest form of witness to God's work in the world through Jesus the Christ, upon which the Epistles base their applications and exhortations (see chap. 12).

Watching the Gospels and the Kentucky Derby

I argue in the final chapter of this book that this diminished role for the Gospels is unfounded in light of church history and many theological considerations. But for now we can address this issue through an informative illustration of my experience with the Kentucky Derby. Rather than being merely foundational, past-era historical data, the Gospels are more like a television viewing of the annual Kentucky Derby horse race.

I am not a native of Kentucky, but having lived for several years in horse country and in the city of one of the world's most famous horse races, I have come to appreciate the enthusiasm and hoopla surrounding the Kentucky Derby. Soon after I moved to Louisville, I was invited to a derby party, which I attended with much apathy to the supposedly exciting event; I went dutifully as a matter of fellowship, not personal interest. But as the horse races leading up to the derby race were shown, I began to see the thrill of those fast-paced two minutes. Finally, the actual derby race came, and rather than remaining apathetic, I found myself on the edge of my seat cheering passionately for my chosen horse. It was all over in a matter of seconds (and I did not win). But then what happened next greatly struck me: after the live flurry of the actual two-minute event, the race was rebroadcast, but now with expert commentary and analysis, since the winner was now known. That is, once the race was completed and the commentators knew the outcome, then (and only then) were they able to provide insight into what was happening at certain points in the race—which moves at turn three or what action of the winning jockey in the last straightaway proved significant. The nonlive televised reshowing enabled the commentators to gray out the insignificant events and horses and highlight the winning horse and trace his activities throughout the whole race. This was all possible, of course, because they knew the outcome, which was uncertain at the time of the actual event. Indeed, it is often impossible in the midst of the race to predict who will win or even the general placement of any horse; many times a horse in the back of the pack surges to be the winner, and an apparent leader fails at the end.[19]

This postevent television viewing is precisely what we have in the Gospel accounts: expert commentary and analysis of the events after their conclusion and based on knowing the final outcome and goal of the story. Jesus's

---

19. In the 2010 race, the winner, Super Saver, pulled ahead only at the end, while the leaders (and favored horses) for most of the race ended up finishing in the upper teens in rankings, including my chosen horse, Line of David.

actions and teachings were typically misunderstood by those who heard him, including his inner circle (e.g., Matt. 13:10, 36; 14:14–17; 16:5–12)! And when he did speak clearly and was understood, his plan was opposed by his own disciples (Matt. 16:21–23). Moreover, Jesus's death was confusing, dismaying, and inexplicable at the time of the event, and even after the resurrection there was still no small amount of fear and uncertainty about how to proceed. Despite the promises of resurrection and the appearance of the resurrected Christ to several of the disciples, Jesus's followers remained fearful (cf. John 20:19) and rather inward focused (Acts 1:12–14) until the giving of the Spirit. But once the Spirit of power and revelation had come upon the disciples at Pentecost, they understood the significance of all that Jesus had taught and done beforehand (cf. John 2:22).

Pentecost and the giving of the Spirit is crucial, but this fact does not relegate the Gospels to an earlier, transitional epoch. Rather, the evangelists were writing their accounts *precisely with this post-Pentecost perspective and expert analysis and commentary*. Because of the centrality of the death and resurrection in salvation history, the Gospel accounts were written from the perspective of this historical-theological event. They were written with the purpose of giving theological interpretation and transformational exhortation. In no way do they ever present themselves as providers of "just the facts, ma'am," upon which the apostles build and apply. They are comprehensive, applied narrative theology. This is precisely what all testimonial history is. Thus, for us to read the Gospels well means to read them with the grain of this same purpose. The point of a Gospel story is not *primarily* or *ultimately* to convey historical information (though history matters and the stories indeed do provide this) but to teach, explain, and exhort us God-ward, toward transformation through virtue.

In this sense the Gospels are really like the rest of biblical narrative in that, as Leland Ryken points out, they intermingle three ingredients:

1. the historical impulse to record facts;
2. the theological and didactic impulse to teach religious truth;
3. the literary impulse to re-create experiences in our imaginations.[20]

Therefore, the combination of these ingredients and impulses means that the Gospel stories are realistic stories pointing beyond themselves to spiritual realities, all the while seeking to engage us at a personal level. The Gospels are not just bald, objective video recordings of the life and teachings of Jesus; rather they are inspired, theological retellings/interpretations *after the crucial*

---

20. Leland Ryken, *Words of Life: A Literary Introduction to the New Testament* (Grand Rapids: Baker, 1987), 29. This book is now revised as part 4 of the 2nd ed. of Ryken's *Words of Delight: A Literary Introduction to the Bible* (Grand Rapids: Baker, 1987).

reality of the death and resurrection of Jesus. God raising Jesus from the dead changes everything for the Gospel writers. Once they were writing after this fact and the giving of the Holy Spirit at Pentecost, they could see significance in things that Jesus said and did that they could not have seen previously.[21] And this is precisely what is given to us in the testimonial history of the Gospels.

Hearing from Hermeneutics (Chaps. 6–7)

Chapters 6 and 7 endeavored to wade into the deep and fast-moving waters of hermeneutics. I attempted not a deep-sea excursion but rather a day trip along the shore, seeking to examine the contours and point out some landmarks and sights of interest. Some implications of my hermeneutical approach were broached in those chapters, especially as it relates to our posture. It will be worth our while now to pull together some ideas from both of these chapters and relate them to our goal in reading the Gospels as Holy Scripture.

In Chapter 6 I emphasized that the meaning of any textual communication is best pursued not through simply one approach or method but by examining the text through the three avenues of "behind," "in," and "in front of" the text. Chapter 7 took up some remaining hermeneutical issues regarding authorial intent and the meaning of meaning.

I have argued that authorial intent is an important aspect of our pursuit of hearing what a text is saying, with the important qualifier that we recognize that the meaning of the text is not limited to and compressed into the historical sense of the text nor is figuring out what was in the mind of the author our primary task. Moreover, when we seek to hear from Holy Scripture, we must recognize that, rather than a merely human author, God the Holy Spirit is in the truest and deepest sense the Author; hence, the intent goes beyond the limited perspective and situatedness of the writer.

On the issue of the meaning of meaning, in chapter 7 I argued that the meaning of a text is its right performance or application, in all its glorious pluriformity. Rather than an excavatory model that seeks to uncover the artifactual sense of the text, good reading pursues a faithful application and listening to the meaning. This is the meaning of meaning: its application, which is pursued through good reading skills, including sensitivity to the authorial intent.

This leads into the final and most important idea from these hermeneutical chapters, the vital principle of posture. I proposed in chapter 7 that the single

21. As Chris Seitz observes, "History writing is reporting past events, to be sure—but from a perspective that the future alone can grant." Seitz, *Prophecy and Hermeneutics: Toward a New Introduction to the Prophets* (Grand Rapids: Baker Academic, 2007), 191. See also Richard Hays, "Reading Scripture in Light of the Resurrection," in *The Art of Reading Scripture*, ed. Ellen Davis and Richard Hays (Grand Rapids: Eerdmans, 2003), 216–38.

most determinative and essential element of reading Holy Scripture well is having a proper posture toward God. To read Scripture as God's Word requires that we approach the Triune God with humility and with a willingness to be read by the text, to stand under it, not simply to seek to understand it.

Words of Life

One helpful recent book along these lines is *Words of Life* by Timothy Ward.[22] In this thoughtful book on the doctrine of the nature of Scripture and how Scripture relates to God, Ward concludes with a chapter titled "The Bible and Christian Life: The Doctrine of Scripture Applied." The final pages of this chapter discuss the aim of Bible reading. In light of his discussion of the nature and purpose of Scripture, Ward rightly states that "the most appropriate question to ask ourselves when we open Scripture to read it is: *What is God wanting to do to me, and in me, through the words I am reading?*"[23] He notes that this does not mean that the text means simply whatever it means to me, because Scripture is God's speech acts. Therefore, the semantic content is important. However, interpretation of this content is not an end in itself. "Reading the Bible is not fundamentally a comprehension exercise. Interpretation should serve only to lead us to an encounter with God as he actually presents himself to us in Scripture." If our reading of Scripture stops at the comprehension stage, we have "made the mistake of exalting Scripture's content over its purpose. It has ripped apart in Scripture two things that ought not to be ripped apart. Therefore we must also ask: And what, in this part of Scripture, is the Lord wanting to *do* with that teaching, to me and in me?"[24]

Ward observes that many believing readers worry about "getting Scripture wrong." We *should* be concerned with interpreting the meaning of Scripture well, of course, for we should forever be growing in the knowledge of God. "However, our greater concern should be the ease with which we can content ourselves with *learning* the truth, while refusing to let God act in us with that truth as the sharp sword he intended it to be."[25] Ward states well the tension that must be maintained between a skilled reading and a proper posture.

Spiritual Reading

This approach can also be described with the expression "spiritual reading," an idea that has dominated most Christian reading of Scripture throughout history. Engaging in "spiritual reading" means two things. First, underlying

---

22. Timothy Ward, *Words of Life: Scripture as the Living and Active Word of God* (Downers Grove, IL: InterVarsity, 2009).
23. Ibid., 174–75.
24. Ibid., 175.
25. Ibid.

all our reading is a conviction as well as an assumption that we read Holy Scripture for a personal application to Christian life and obedience. To do less is not to read Scripture according to its purpose. As Augustine famously wrote, "Whoever, therefore, thinks that he understands the divine scriptures or any part of them so that it does not build up the double love of God and neighbor does not understand it at all."[26] Since Holy Scripture is divine pedagogy, the instruction of wisdom from the heavenly Father to his children, we must read it accordingly and with this personal and pious purpose in mind.

Brian Daley, a leading scholar of early church interpretation, notes this important difference between the reading practices of earlier Christianity and our tendency in the modern period. Spiritual reading of Holy Scripture

> receives it not simply as a historical document but as a revelation of God's will to heal and transform the hearer. Put another way, because the Bible is not just a book of texts but is *Holy Scripture*, the concern of the ancient exegete was not simply, or even primarily, to reconstruct the *Sitz im Leben* of the text being studied but to elucidate its *Sitz in unserem Leben*, its situation in *our* life; the hearers' faith is the living context in which its scriptural meaning—its meaning for our salvation—is to be found.[27]

Second, to be a good reader of Holy Scripture one must personally pursue this same God of Scripture in holiness, obedience, and piety, and above all, faith. Personal spiritual devotion is essential to good exegesis because it is the pure in heart who will see God (Matt. 5:8).[28] This assumption corresponds to the ancient notion of virtue, which understands the person as a whole and acknowledges that even as there are virtuous and unvirtuous ways of behaving morally, so too are there intellectual virtues and vices. Moreover, the intellectual and moral lives interact and influence each other. Thus, one's personal life inevitably affects how one reads, what one finds in Holy Scripture, and how one appropriates the text, which is true understanding. We are embodied knowers, and this embodiment affects and is affected by our virtues or lack thereof. Rather than approaching the interpretation of texts with a modern notion of "meaning" as a disinterested, scientifically discernible entity that can optionally be "applied" or not, spiritual reading sees the meaning or proper reading as a spiritual matter—affected by one's own spiritual life and applying directly to it.[29]

---

26. Augustine, *On Christian Teaching* 1.36.

27. Brian E. Daley, SJ, "Is Patristic Exegesis Still Usable?" in Davis and Hays, *Art of Reading Scripture*, 77.

28. For a stimulating and helpful survey of the meaning(s) of this verse in the history of interpretation, see Dale C. Allison Jr., "Seeing God (Matt. 5:8)" in his *Studies in Matthew* (Grand Rapids: Baker Academic, 2005), 43–63.

29. Daniel Doriani provides an insightful chapter on the role of the interpreter in understanding and applying Scripture. Doriani, *Putting the Truth to Work: The Theory and Practice of Biblical Application* (Phillipsburg: P&R, 2001), 59–80.

Taking Our Mother-in-Law's Diet Magnet to the Prayer Meeting

This idea of spiritual reading reminds us of the concluding illustration from chapter 7, what I referred to as the principle of our mother-in-law's refrigerator magnet. The point of this illustration and principle is that once again our receptive posture is the most important instrument in our toolbox of interpretive practices.

I used an Old Testament example of this principle from Jeremiah 29:11. We may revisit and deepen our understanding of this issue with another example, this time from the New Testament. If the refrigerator magnet is the high-water mark for gauging the popularity of a Bible verse personally applied, then the comparable corporate gauge would be the verse most regularly used for the Wednesday night ladies' prayer circle. And the uncontested winner here would be Matthew 18:20: "For where two or three are gathered in my name, there am I in the midst of them."

On the surface Matthew 18:20 seems like a wonderfully encouraging promise concerning the effectiveness of gathering together corporately for prayer. The preceding verse, if read, would seem to confirm this interpretation, with its reference to Jesus's disciples agreeing with one another about whatever they ask the Father. But a broader contextual and literary-theological reading of this verse reveals that it is in the first instance a statement not about prayer but about the unprecedented and unexpected authority that now resides in Jesus's disciples as gatekeepers of the orthodoxy and orthopraxy of the church's members. Jesus is radically proclaiming that *his* disciples—as opposed to the trained rabbis and hereditary priests—have the power to loosen and bind regarding entrance into the kingdom of heaven. This authority does not reside in their own will but rather is a ratification on earth of what God is doing already in heaven (18:18). This authority is a function of Jesus's fundamental redefinition of the people of God based on faith response to him, not ethnicity or outwardly pious "righteousness."

This is a rather sophisticated understanding of the verse based on taking Matthew as a literary and theological whole and knowing something about first-century rabbinic language and practices. But it is unlikely that the members of our Wednesday night prayer circle have discerned this interpretation. So what is the young pastor to do when he is invited to lead the devotion at the prayer meeting and is given this text as the cherished verse for that purpose? Should he, for the sake of proper exegesis and hermeneutics, quickly pour cold water on the fires of their fervent prayer-meeting hopes and expectations? Should he explain that choosing this treasured prayer-meeting verse is a huge mistake? Or maybe he is more pastorally sensitive than this—or at least wise enough not to make enemies with these matriarchs of the church!—and instead he goes along with their naive interpretation, all the while laughing inside at their simpleness and lack of exegetical skill.

Or maybe—and hopefully—his understanding of what it means to read Scripture well, wisely, and spiritually will lead him to something greater: approaching this text and his fellow believers with a proper posture. With a posture of humility and an awakened awareness of the rich fullness of Scripture, our pastor may be able to see some significant ways in which this text *is* being heard correctly and should be encouraged, even while he may redirect and shape that reading.

Although the use of this verse as a direct promise of Jesus being somehow extra-present in the prayer meeting—is Jesus somehow *not* present when one prays privately?—may not be the *most skilled* reading, there are valid ways of hearing this text and reading it for the prayer meeting that are *organic extensions* of the text's initial *sensus literalis* and almost certainly Matthew's "authorial intent." Namely, Jesus is teaching here that there is a God-sanctioning and approving of the Spirit-led words and deeds of his disciples; it is not difficult to apply this to their prayers. Additionally, reading this text in prayer meetings is an understandable extension or application of the fact that, as the gathered people of Christ on earth, we do bind and loosen realities through the gift of prayer in the Spirit. And even beyond these intracanonical readings, what is most laudable is that those gathered for the prayer meeting are doing so with expectation, hope, and confidence—in short, faith—that Jesus here in Matthew 18 and beyond is certainly commending. Their posture is one of hearing from God through his Word and approaching him with humble confidence.

I believe if Augustine were the young pastor invited to that week's First Church of Hippo prayer circle, he would reflect on all of this and conclude that the most important thing in reading, explicating, and applying Matthew 18:18 is keeping the principle of the double love central. The double love—love for God and love for neighbor—as the pairing of the first and the second greatest commandments is the ultimate guiding, constraining, and directing criterion for good Scripture reading.[30] The double-love test applied to this situation confirms the appropriateness of this reading of Matthew 18:18. Ultimately, those involved are built up in greater love for God by this reading of Scripture, and its interpretation is also being guided by a love for others and a desire to see them thrive. All the while, we may also direct our listeners to a deeper and fuller understanding of what this text means in its broadest context. There are indeed even more riches to be brought out of the treasure house of this text that the wise teacher-disciple will open up for his or her hearers (Matt. 13:52).

This double-love criterion and goal lead us to the final and consummating section of this chapter and this first part of the book: examining what our goal in reading the Gospels ultimately is.

---

30. Augustine, *On Christian Teaching* 1.35–40.

Our Goal in Reading the Gospels Summed Up: Revelation and Identification

A repeated thread that has appeared in the summaries given above is that our goal in reading Scripture must be more than informational; it must be transformational. Therefore, our hermeneutical approach and methods must be more than excavational; they must be personal and application driven. When we apply all of this specifically to our reading of the Gospels, we can sum up our goal under the categories of revelation and identification. Taken together these two foci will give us clear and organized direction as we enter the practical world of reading the Gospels.

Revelation

The first and determinative aspect of the Gospels is that they are a revelation of who God is in Jesus Christ. At the fount and all throughout, the Gospels are a revelation concerning Jesus as God's Son, as the Messiah, as the fulfillment of Israel, David, and the promise to Abraham.[31] Thus, our first and determinative goal in reading the Gospels should be to discern and explore how any passage in the Gospels reveals who God is for us in Christ. The primary and controlling focus should be on the Gospels as revelation.

This is the radical Jesus-centeredness of the entire apostolic witness, especially of the four, lengthy testimonies that stand at the head of the New Testament. As a result, when we read a passage such as the story of Jesus walking on the water and Peter going out to him (Matt. 14:22–33), our first and foremost reactions to it should be centered on Jesus, not on Peter or ourselves or the mechanical possibilities of such a miracle and so forth. There is a place for all these other considerations, but only in their proper order, with the focus on the revelation of God in Christ being kept central.

This revelatory focus guides us to see that this story is primarily telling us something, indeed, many things about who Jesus is. He is more than human in his ability to tread on the waters, something reserved in identity for God himself and something that God does in rescuing his beloved people (cf. Job 9:8; Ps. 77:19; Isa. 43:16). Jesus also demonstrates his divine power over nature by giving Peter (by faith) the ability to walk on water. Then, upon Jesus's entrance into the boat, the strong and contrary winds cease (14:32). Yet even in this majestic display of his power over nature, Jesus is also shown to be caring and compassionate. His words to his shocked and scared disciples are, "Take heart, it is I; have no fear" (14:27). The reader of Greek will also see an intentional heightening revelation here that is lost in translation. Jesus's words, which are fairly translated "it is I," are not accidentally the important revelatory words of God's name, *egō eimi*, "I am" (cf. Exod. 3:14). Jesus uses these evocative

---

31. Thus I argue below that the Gospels have a central place in all Scripture. See chap. 12.

words several times, and the Gospel of John develops this repeated usage as a major theme and organizer with its many "I am" statements. Jesus's compassion also shines forth when Peter's boldness is followed by weak-faithed, sinking failure, and Jesus kindly reaches out his hand in rescue (14:31).

Thus, we can see more clearly that the "revelation of God in Christ" is what Matthew wanted us to see as primary in this text. For precisely this reason, the story ends with the disciples worshiping Jesus and declaring, "Truly you are the Son of God" (14:33). It is difficult to miss the revelatory focus.

This revelation of God in Christ reminds us again that the Gospels are first and foremost a divine Word, given to us as a gift. We should not think of this revelation aspect as merely informational. The revelation of Christ in every Gospel passage is more than mere knowledge; it is a personal encounter with the risen Christ. We emphasized above that we must first receive Jesus as gift before we can have him as example. So too here. We must first read and receive the Gospels as a revelatory act of God on our behalf in which we are given Jesus himself.

Identification

Once we have in place the central Christ-revelation function of the Gospels, we can turn to the ways in which the Gospels focus on us as readers, on how they invite us to identify with the characters in the stories, including Jesus himself. The genre and purpose of the Gospels, discussed earlier, mean that we cannot stop simply at the revelation in them but must press on to their virtue-forming (aretological) purpose and effect. Again, Luther's categories of gift and example are helpful and overlap with my own. His emphasis on the example given in the Gospels corresponds in part with my suggestion that we are intentionally meant to identify with the characters in the stories.

In the following chapters we will discuss what it means to read the Gospels as narratives. But we can anticipate that a bit at this point by mentioning one crucial element of good narrative reading and analysis: focusing on the characters of the story. Just as a story is not a story without a plot, so too we do not have a narrative without characters, even if those characters are animals or space aliens. For there to be plot, there must be characters who do something or respond to something done to them by others or the environment or the gods. A mere description of a place over time does not a narrative make—at least not one that most of us would want to read. The geological account of a natural disaster, such as the earthquake and tsunami in Japan in 2011, becomes *a story* when we hear of tragic losses, heroic efforts, and the experience of the people (or even cats) involved. This character necessity and character focus is heightened with regard to our study of the Gospels because they are biographies (which by nature focus on at least one main character) and because they are directed to "disciple-readers" for whom the characters serve as models.

This identification function of the Gospels occurs at two levels or on two axes: imitating Jesus and responding in kind to good and bad characters in the stories.

Imitatio Christi

Throughout most of the church's reading of the Gospels, imitating Jesus in his actions and attitudes has played a prominent role. For some this goes as far as physically reenacting elements of Jesus's life, such as the *Via Dolorosa* and the stations of the cross at Eastertide. But more generally for all Christians, the Gospels have served as a picture of who Jesus is so that we as his disciples might live in imitation of him. Again, this is why the narrative, biographical nature of the Gospel accounts is so important. One writes a *bios* so that the readers will be inspired to emulate the good in the main character. The apostles could have simply given us doctrinal statements, theological abstractions, and moral instructions—and this they do give us—but they primarily give us stories of Jesus, so that we can follow his example and learn from him.[32] Indeed, in the Gospels themselves, the disciples' actions are shown to be conscious imitations of what Jesus himself has already done[33] or at times their failure to do what he does.

Throughout history, and especially at times of social crisis and change, biographies have served to guide people in the way they should now live. Biography is the most moral type of literature in its effect. Since ancient times it has been recognized that through imitation one learns how to live; hence the central place that character stories have always played in society.[34] For Christians this is already explicitly stated in the New Testament, as in Paul's exhortation to imitate him while he imitates Christ (1 Cor. 11:1). And in early Christianity a large body of literature developed that presents to the reader the life of some saint worthy of imitation. This tradition continues into the present.[35]

But the primary focus has always been on how Christians should follow the example of Jesus himself. Unfortunately, for some, especially some

32. For an excellent and succinct discussion of this idea, complete with many great historical quotes on the power of biography, see Dale C. Allison Jr., "Structure, Biographical Impulse, and the Imitatio Christi," in his *Studies in Matthew*, 142–55. For an excellent treatment of the power and importance of the narrative form of the Old Testament, see Richard Pratt Jr., *He Gave Us Stories: The Bible Student's Guide to Interpreting Old Testament Narratives* (Phillipsburg, NJ: P&R, 1990).

33. A prime example is Matthew 10, which includes detailed instructions for the missional life of the disciples, all of which involve things that they have seen Jesus do or which he will do in the subsequent chapters. Allison, "Structure," 151, provides a comparative chart of this.

34. For example, Seneca notes, "The way is long if one follows precept, but short and helpful if one follows patterns." *Ad Lucilium* 6.4, quoted in Allison, "Structure," 154.

35. Early examples include Athanasius on the life of Anthony, Pontius on Cyprian, and Jerome on Malchus. At the time of the Reformation, Foxe's *Book of Martyrs* became standard reading. And this tradition continues today with the popularity of John Piper's Swans Are Not Silent series of biographies.

contemporary conservative Protestants, talk of following Jesus as an example sounds dangerous. They fear that focusing on Jesus's example of humanity risks diminishing his divinity. Indeed, many orthodox believers are rightly concerned that some forms of Christianity have made Jesus into *merely* an example of perfect humanity and have rejected his divine nature and salvific role. As a result, these believers have overreacted by shying away from speaking of Jesus as the New Testament also does, as the "pioneer and perfecter of our faith" (Heb. 12:2, following the catalog of other faithful people) and the one to be imitated. Some, especially in the Lutheran tradition, also worry that talk of imitating Jesus will lead us into moralistic human effort. This too is a valid concern, but one that was already addressed in balance with Luther's conjoined ideas of gift and example, as we have seen. As with all virtue and wisdom, the *via media* is the way forward, maintaining a balance between Jesus as the revelation of God and as the model for identification.

Outside the Gospels, one finds this balance pictured beautifully in the First Epistle of Peter. When exhorting various members of the church to live in certain ways, Peter appeals to Jesus as both the Savior, who is unlike us, and as the model for us to imitate. We are told that Jesus "bore our sins in his body on the tree" and that "by his wounds you have been healed" (1 Pet. 2:24). And in the same breath Peter says that Jesus suffered unjustly, thereby "leaving you an example, that you should follow in his steps" (2:21). This example is one not of reviling those who reviled him but of being silent and submissive, doing so by trusting his just Father. Thus, both slaves of ungodly masters (2:18–23) and wives of ungodly husbands (3:1–6) can be exhorted to follow Jesus's model.[36]

Disciples of the Disciples

We have mentioned already how insightful Luther's gift and example categories are and how they correspond closely (though not coextensively) with mine of revelation and identification. The biggest difference is that while Luther rightly acknowledges the role of Jesus as an example in the Gospels, he does not mention the fact that the *other characters* in the Gospels also serve as exemplars, either good or bad. This may be simply a function of the brevity of Luther's remarks. Or perhaps Luther consciously or unconsciously wanted to exclusively maintain the Christo-centricity of the Gospels' witness. Maybe he was reacting against the rather overwrought veneration of the saints during much of medieval Christianity. Nevertheless, a crucial part of understanding the identification role of the Gospels is recognizing that other characters

36. Jeff Dryden has provided us with a very insightful book that shows how 1 Peter seeks to develop character in his disciple-readers not merely through moral exhortation but by providing a distinctly Christian narrative worldview and corporate identity and by upholding Christ as both saving and a moral exemplar. Jeff Dryden, *Theology and Ethics in 1 Peter: Paraenetic Strategies for Christian Character Formation* (Tübingen: Mohr Siebeck, 2006).

in the stories provide important models either for emulation or avoidance. Indeed, even though Jesus is undoubtedly the central character in the stories, the other characters in the Gospels most readily provide the opportunity for identification with them as illustrations of God-ward virtue (or lack thereof). Additionally, it is from the other characters that we often learn how we should or should not respond to the main character, Jesus.

Not many contemporary treatments of the Gospels explore the importance of the role of the other characters in the story, but one happy exception is Timothy Wiarda's book *Interpreting Gospel Narratives: Scenes, People, and Theology*.[37] The subtitle reveals in part that Wiarda sees significance in the "people" of the Gospels. The opening chapter addresses the question of whether the Gospel writers were interested in individual characters, and Wiarda notes potential pitfalls in either de-emphasizing or overemphasizing characters other than Jesus in the Gospels. But he wisely observes that yes, indeed, the evangelists do take care to depict other characters in the Gospels with purpose and in a variety of ways. Much good can be gleaned from the tradition of reading the Gospels in this way.[38]

Chapter 4 of Wiarda's book, titled "Individuals and Other Interests," takes a thoughtful approach to the role of characters in the Gospel narratives. Wiarda argues that a reading sensitive to a focus both on Jesus *and* on the disciples is ideal, and he suggests Mark 4:35–41 as a particularly good example of a story that presents to us this balance in a clear way.

Wiarda observes that secondary characters can play a role in Gospel narratives in two different ways. Sometimes they contribute to the portrayal of Jesus by providing an occasion for who Jesus is to shine through, and at other times they "model attitudes and behaviors the author wants readers to emulate or avoid." The first he calls christological and the second exemplary. In the stilling of the storm story in Mark 4:35–41, Jesus's disciples perform both of these roles. Their fear and their awe of Jesus at the end of the story serve a christological purpose. At the same time, "the disciples' fear in the face of the storm functions as an example (in this case of behavior to avoid) through which readers learn about how they are to live as Jesus' followers."[39]

My point here is that, in accord with the purpose and function of biographical narrative, the Gospels give us many models of a wide variety of characters who serve as direct examples of what a disciple should or should not look like. We are organically connected to these first disciples both by virtue of the God-given, Spirit-wrought faith in Christ that we share with them and through the long chain of history by which disciples have passed on the faith to the next generation of believers all the way down to us. We are disciples of the disciples.

37. Timothy Wiarda, *Interpreting Gospel Narratives: Scenes, People, and Theology* (Nashville: Broadman & Holman, 2010).

38. Ibid., 8–10.

39. Ibid., 138.

Thus our direct identification with a Peter or a Thomas or a Matthew or a Simon of Cyrene is both natural and commendable in accord with the purpose of the writing of the Gospels. The stories of the Gospels regularly present reactions and responses to Jesus that are calls to us to respond properly as well. Whether it be the younger son in the parable of the prodigal son, the older brother who remains angry at his brother's return, or the self-righteous Pharisees to whom Jesus tells the parable, we are given many characters whom we can identify with and learn from.

The category of identification gives us an avenue of thought in reading Gospel stories to help us consciously look at the characters and ask ourselves how we are like these characters (good and bad) and in what ways we might grow in faith, hope, and love.

When focusing on the characters in a story, one always risks lapsing into moralism and preoccupation with mere human-based, faithless virtue. We will return to this issue in chapter 11 of this book. But if we maintain the revelation focus along with that of identification, we can avoid this error by keeping the centrality of Jesus as gift foremost before the also-important function of the characters (including Jesus) as example.

We may now briefly return to the story mentioned above from Matthew 14 and see how the identification aspect emerges in it. We noted that this story teaches us much about who Jesus is: he is divine in nature and displays power over nature, yet is compassionate and kind toward his friends of weak faith. This revelation of God in Christ must be kept central in our reactions to and explications of this story. Thus we cannot make this story simply one about the five faith steps you and I need to make to be successful in ministry in a storm-tossed world or some such pithy approach. If we preach or teach Matthew 14:22–33 without focusing first on Jesus's power, divine nature, and Sonship, then we have certainly missed the boat (pun intended). This is the error of human-based moralism, which has caused some careful readers to shy away from *any* focus on the human characters. We can see why some want to throw Peter out with the bathwater, lest all we have is what Peter did, devoid of the right centrality of Jesus in this story and who God is for us in Christ.

But if we do keep the revelation and gift of Jesus at the forefront of all we say and do, we can see that much help comes from identifying with the characters in the story. For example, we can see that Jesus's disciples, just like us, are truly fearful of their seemingly dire situation. They are, after all, facing possible death on a storm-tossed sea, and then, in the midst of this stress and anxiety they see what appears to be a ghost coming toward them on the water! Fear and doubt are completely normal and to be expected here. To this any honest reader can relate. Then, after some realization of their security through Jesus's kind words, bold Peter does step out (literally) in Jesus-centered faith, only to stumble again when his focus returns to the direness of the waves. So too is our fickle and imperfect faith, which is strong one moment yet quick to disappear. So too do we need to hear Jesus's words of kindness and calm, tinged as they are with a smiling reproof of our little faith.

Again, the category of identification with these characters enables us to enter into the story at a deeper and more personal level, feeling with the characters and applying their reactions and responses to our own lives. This is not simplistic "spiritualizing" (as if that were a bad thing anyway, to read the text spiritually!) but is precisely what stories invite us to do and why they are so powerful: we find and understand our own story in the stories of others. So, while "Five Steps of Faith in a Storm-Tossed World" may be a trite and moralistic reading of this story, the impulse to identify with the characters and apply their experience to our own "storm-tossed" lives is indeed a right posture, attitude, and habit. It only needs to be married carefully to the revelation of who God is for us in Christ Jesus and applied carefully as we seek to identify honestly with the experiences of the characters of the story.

PART 2

Building the House
through Wise Reading

Reading the Gospels as Stories

*The "Whatever Strikes Me" (WSM) Hermeneutic
versus Narrative Analysis*

Now that we have provided layers of foundation for our Gospel-reading building, we can move into more practical matters of method. Continuing our analogy and metaphor, we may think of this chapter and the two that follow as the walls and roof of our wisely built Gospel-reading house. Our discussion of how to read and analyze the Gospels as narratives will cover two chapters, followed by a summary chapter that pulls everything together by considering how to teach and preach from the Gospels. First, we will discuss the need for narrative analysis and offer a model for doing so. In the following chapter we will broaden our purview beyond the individual story to look at the series of contexts in which the Gospel episodes exist.

Reading Luke 7:1–10

To enter into this discussion and wrestle with what it means to read Gospel narratives as stories we would be wise to begin with an actual story, this one from Luke 7.

> After he had ended all his sayings in the hearing of the people he entered Capernaum. Now a centurion had a slave who was dear to him, who was

sick and at the point of death. When he heard of Jesus, he sent to him elders of the Jews, asking him to come and heal his slave. And when they came to Jesus, they besought him earnestly, saying, "He is worthy to have you do this for him, for he loves our nation, and he built us our synagogue." And Jesus went with them. When he was not far from the house, the centurion sent friends to him, saying to him, "Lord, do not trouble yourself, for I am not worthy to have you come under my roof; therefore I did not presume to come to you. But say the word, and let my servant be healed. For I am a man set under authority, with soldiers under me: and I say to one, 'Go,' and he goes; and to another, 'Come,' and he comes; and to my slave, 'Do this,' and he does it." When Jesus heard this he marveled at him, and turned and said to the multitude that followed him, "I tell you, not even in Israel have I found such faith." And when those who had been sent returned to the house, they found the slave well. (RSV)

Whether we are reading this story for personal devotion, academic study, or sermon preparation, we naturally want to ask, "What does this story mean?" From our discussion in the preceding chapters, we are likely aware that in part the answer to this question will lie in our own goal and posture toward the story. That is, what we "get" out of the story is inevitably linked to and affected by the kind of questions we ask of it, how developed our reading skill set is, what we are seeking to find, how we regard the validity and authority of the text in which the story is located, and even the spiritual state of our souls. But beyond these issues the basic question remains: "What is the point of this story?" Assuming we are focusing on the story itself and not just on questions of its historicity, accuracy, or sources, we may rightly query about Luke's intention in giving us this story: Why did he craft the story in this way? Or to push the meaning question most practically: If called upon to preach or teach this passage, what would we say? What is the "big idea" of this story?

Here are some potential answers to this important question:

- Jesus cares about military personnel as seen by his willingness to help a centurion.
- Good things happen in Capernaum!
- Jesus always goes to a new place for a purpose.
- Those who do good things for God will find his favor. (This is the logic of the argument in v. 5.)
- Even if you are worthy to receive help (such as the centurion here, according to v. 4), you should act like you are not.
- We should keep Jesus at a distance out of humility, as modeled by the centurion's unwillingness to have Jesus come to his home.

- Humility is the right response to Jesus as modeled by the centurion.
- Jesus is human like us—he is even surprised. (Jesus "marveled" in v. 9.)
- Jesus has the authority (and compassion) to heal.
- If you want to get things accomplished, it is good to develop relationships with those in authority. The centurion's past generosity inclines the Jewish elders to speak to Jesus on his behalf.
- Jesus often heals by touching people but sometimes by just "saying the word" (v. 7).

These are but a few of the many textually based meanings or applications one might take from this story. Some of them are patently trite and strike us as misreadings, even laughable at points. Others are more serious yet still don't feel quite right, though we may not be sure why. Others seem to be sound and appear to be good interpretations.

But the question remains about how we determine which are good or bad statements or which are better readings than others? Some of the suggested responses just seem wrong and misplaced, but on what basis do we make this judgment? And how do we adjudicate between those possible readings that do seem valid and true enough? Even if we understand that a story by its nature rarely has only one point and if we rightly adopt a multilayered perspectival reading of Scripture, most of us would not say that *all* possible readings of this text are *equally* valid, good, and beneficial.

As discussed earlier, authorial intent does matter, even if it is rightly understood in a broader canonical and theological sense than modernism's conception. Even if we cannot ever definitely determine what Luke meant in an absolute sense, it does not follow that his story means simply *anything we might say about it*. No one would suggest that the point of Luke 7:1–10 is that we should systematically engage in genocide or make laws that require all popsicles to be cherry flavored. Why? Because there must be something *in the story* that inclines us toward a certain interpretation.

But *what* is it in the story that guides us? For many readers of narrative the meaning one comes away with is usually based on what we may call the "WSM Hermeneutic"—"Whatever Strikes Me." That is, most readers—whether brand-new to the Gospels or lifelong readers—simply read the stories and take away from them whatever comes to mind, whatever stands out to them this time. At times this approach will be sufficient, thanks either to luck or to the intuitions of a generally skilled reader. But overall, for wise reading we need a more solid understanding of how stories work—how they speak and communicate—so that we can learn to read the Gospel narratives well and to adjudicate wisely among various good readings. We need a model for narrative analysis.

What Stories Are and How They Work

The discussion of what stories are and how they work goes back at least to Aristotle, who in his famous work *Poetics*[1] provides a basic analysis of the necessary elements of a story. As Aristotle explains, story is built upon plot, and a plot must have a beginning, a middle, and an end. This is the most basic structure necessary to all stories, and the plot that goes through these stages must have a unity or consistency. A story's plot will usually have some kind of reversal and/or moment of realization as well as some suffering on the part of the characters. The two main forms of plot, then, are tragedy, wherein the important reversal turns the story toward suffering, and comedy, wherein it turns the story toward fortune.

Aristotle's book is considered the earliest work of literary criticism, and it significantly influenced both Europe in the Middle Ages and the Arabic literary tradition. His analysis continues to form our basic understanding of how stories work. But in the modern period, following the trajectory of Aristotle, another work has been equally influential: Gustav Freytag's *Technique of the Drama*.[2] Freytag provides an analysis of the basic plot and structure of stories as seen in the common pattern of the five-act play. According to Freytag's analysis, premodern dramas include an introduction or exposition, rising action, a climax or turning point, falling action, and a denouement or resolution, a structure that constitutes the dramatic arc. The plot development is driven by tension or conflict that is set up, rises to a climactic or turning point, and then is finally resolved (for good or for ill). Without such a tension, there is no plot and therefore no story.

Freytag's analysis has resulted in a very common pictorial diagram, called Freytag's Pyramid, that clearly shows this rise and fall of tension and plot structure (see fig. 2).

Although this model has its critics, its basic idea is sound and valid for most narratives even today. In the modern period many stories provide variations on this pattern through some twist but rarely a wholesale break with the model. For example, many stories add another rise of tension or conflict during the falling action and thus reset and twist the climax that leads to another and unexpected climax. But even in this variation the basic insights of both Aristotle and Freytag still stand. Plot built on tension with a beginning, middle (albeit varied), and end is the core of all stories. Grasping this is a crucial first step toward reading narratives well.

---

1. This classic work appears in many translations and editions. A standard scholarly edition is the translation of Stephen Halliwell in the Loeb Classical Library (Cambridge, MA: Harvard University Press, 1995).

2. Original titled *Die Technik des Dramas* (1863), Freytag's work has been translated into English several times. The most recent translation is *Freytag's Technique of the Drama: An Exposition of Dramatic Composition and Art*, trans. Elias MacEwan (Charleston, SC: Biblio-Bazaar, 2008).

Fig. 2. Freytag Pyramid

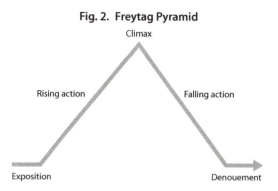

In large part the meaning of a narrative comes through paying attention to its form. We discussed at the beginning of the book the importance of understanding the genre of the Gospels. In a similar vein, to wisely read any narrative or story we must be sensitive to the form that stories take and how they function. The use of a narrative analytic tool, then, as opposed to the "whatever strikes me" approach, can help us greatly to understand how any particular story works.

A Narrative Model for the Gospel Stories

When analyzing and interpreting the stories in the Gospels, we must first decide what unit of text we will engage. This is usually a fairly straightforward decision in that the Gospel stories tend to be short episodes with clear boundary markers. Our translations generally do a good job of separating these episodes into paragraphs. In the modern period these individual Gospel stories or episodes have come to be called pericopes. Though the terminology of "pericope" is modern, the episodic nature of the Gospels was recognized in the early days of the church; already by the time of Eusebius the individual Gospel stories had been broken up, numbered, and categorized.[3] It is valid and helpful to analyze these individual pericopes with a narrative model.

Building on the basic insights of Aristotle and Freytag, we can offer a modified model for analyzing Gospel narratives. It follows the same core idea of tracing the arc of the plot or tension but with adjustments to the parts and some additions to the model.[4] The following pictorial diagram describes this model:

3. Eusebius's *Canons* comprise a numbering of the individual Gospel episodes as well as a categorization of these episodes according to the Gospel(s) in which they appear. Ten possible permutations are used in the schema. This analysis is an early effort at what will much later be called source criticism.

4. I am indebted to several sources for the model pictured and developed here. The basic idea and "roller coaster" depiction comes from Daniel Doriani, *Getting the Message* (Phillipsburg, NJ: P&R, 1996). Dr. Keith Johnson and I together modified this schema over several years as

Fig. 3. Story Line Development

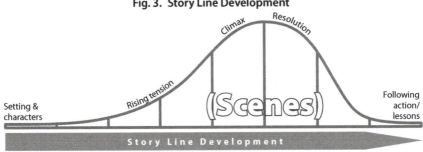

Explanatory Notes:

The basic building blocks of any story are the setting, characters, and scenes, all used to develop the plot. Usually setting and characters are established at the beginning of a story. Sometimes they need to be supplied by the surrounding context. We begin our analysis by identifying the setting and characters, apart from the plot.

It is very helpful to break a story into scenes. Scenes generally involve a change in characters or setting or the introduction of a new character or element. Sometimes it is helpful to think of scenes as different camera shots in a movie or TV show. However, with dialogue this can be misleading if we break the scenes too minutely each time someone speaks. Breaking the story into discrete units or scenes helps one read it more slowly and thoughtfully and begin to arc the plot.

The rising tension does not necessarily refer to a physical or verbal fight between characters; rather it is the development of some problem, conflict, or dilemma. This tension or conflict may be stated at the very beginning of the episode, or it may creep in as the story unfolds. Either way, the rise and increase of this tension develops the plot. With no conflict/tension, there is no plot, and with no plot there is no story.

Climax here refers specifically to the climax of tension, where the conflict or plot reaches its highest point from which the whole story will turn one way or another. The climax of tension is the place in the story where one is holding one's breath to see what will happen, where one is on the edge of one's seat, where the outcome could go either way.

The resolution is the solving of the problem or the release of the tension that has been rising to the climactic point. At the resolution one feels that some kind of solution has dissipated the tension. On the diagram the climax and the resolution are intentionally paired together at the "top" of the plot's arc. Together these straddle the high point of the plot.

---

part of our course development for the theological education program of Campus Crusade for Christ. The exact origin of particular points and ideas is now impossible to pinpoint.

As an illustration of the climax and the resolution coming together, w might imagine the last few seconds of a great basketball game, perhaps during the NCAA's March Madness. It's the championship game, and your small-town, underdog team is down by two points. They have fought hard through injury and loss to get to this point. (This is the setting and the rising tension in summary.) There are now three seconds left, and your team gets the ball and heads down the court. A moment before the buzzer, the ball is released from the shooter's hands and is soaring toward the basket. *Stop right there!* This is the climax, the moment of highest tension. The story could go either way right here. If it is a comedy, the resolution occurs when the ball sails through the net, and the crowd explodes. If it is a tragedy, the ball hits the rim, rolls around, and pops out. (And if this were a nihilistic Kurt Vonnegut story, a tornado would blow through and wipe out the gymnasium at this very point. Thankfully, the Gospel stories never take this turn!)

The following action/interpretation is the ending of the story that ties up any loose ends, with a level of tension like that of the introduction. To continue our basketball analogy, the following action is the camera shot of the coach hugging the star player and the words that appear on the screen filling us in on the later careers of the characters. In the case of the Gospels this may be an action such as "the woman went home healed," or it may be a theological statement—an interpretation of the situation—provided by the narrator, such as, "Thus, he declared all foods clean" or "I tell you, this man went down to his house justified rather than the other."

A (Partial) Method for Using This Model

When applying this model to an individual Gospel episode, we may use the following method. This is not the complete method, which must wait until the next chapter, hence the "partial" qualifier here. But we can trace the arc of the plot using the following steps:

1. Isolate the Literary Unit
   First, we need to determine the parameters of the story. What is the proper demarcation of the episode? Usually in the Gospels this will be clearly indicated by the paragraph breaks given in our Bibles.
2. Read the Story Multiple Times
   We must keep the whole experience of the story at the forefront rather than simply jumping right into analysis. Read it slowly. Read it quickly. Read it silently. Read it aloud. (If you can read it in Greek, all the better!)
3. Identify the Setting and the Characters
   It is helpful to simply state what the setting is and to list all the characters. Who is here and where is this story happening?
4. Observe the Story

Are there key words or phrases or repeated ideas? Are cause-and-effect relationships stated? What illustrations are used, if any? Noting all these things will help you pay closer attention to the story. Ask questions of the text and write them down. Explore the text with an open mind. There are no stupid questions or observations!

5. Isolate the Different Scenes

   At this stage it is helpful to take the whole pericope and simply break it up into different scenes (note above comments). The first scene will usually be the setting.

6. Analyze the Narrative:
   - Identify the Rising Tension
   - Identify the Climax
   - Identify the Resolution
   - Identify the Following Action/Interpretation

Because when reading the story one does not know exactly where the rising tension ends until the climax and resolution are discerned, it is often easier to find the climax and resolution pair first and then back into the rising and falling tension.

The Benefits of This Kind of Narrative Analysis

This process may seem like an overwhelming amount of work just to read a short and simple Gospel pericope. Some readers may be tempted to return to the WSM approach instead! Indeed, there is a danger that in submitting a story to such analysis, putting it on the scientist's table and dissecting it like a formaldehyde-pickled frog, we rob it of its power and effectiveness *as a story*.

Nonetheless, although we should consciously resist doing *only* such an analysis, exploring and investigating Gospel episodes in this way yields great benefits. At the simplest level, approaching the text with this method forces us to slow down and read carefully and with new eyes. Moreover, *the most important thing we gain from doing narrative analysis is that we can see that the main point of a passage is usually found in the climax and resolution and/or the following action/interpretation*, not in any particular detail that may strike the reader's fancy. The best narrative reading is sensitive to the development and resolution of the plot/tension of the story. By forcing us to think carefully about how any particular pericope is structured, narrative analysis gives us greater confidence that we are grasping the main thrust/ideas of the story.

By way of illustration, we may think of this narrative analysis tool as comparable to making a thermographic map of the story. A thermographic map indicates relative heat emission from objects or areas under its purview. The hottest areas are represented by red and the coolest by blue. In between, the relative heat emissions are shown by the spectrum of colors ranging through orange, yellow, and green. It is helpful to imagine a story as a thermographic map. Where are the hottest, red spots, and where are the cold, blue areas? Where are the most relevant and important points, and where are the details that serve only to set up and frame the story? The most important ideas/elements of the story are those that are reddest in color, and they will usually be found at either the highest point of tension (the climax and resolution) or the closing comment (the following action/interpretation), or sometimes at both.

Thinking of a story in this thermographic way helps us see the relative value of different aspects of the story: not all parts of a story are equally "hot." This analogy serves our reading of stories well because, even as a map may have more than one area of heat and will have a range of thermal areas, so too a good story is not monolithic in its depth. Rather, most stories have a range of relatively important points and may even have more than one "hot spot." Generally, one idea or part of the story will stand out as more relevant than all others, but the illustration of a thermographic map helps us see the depth and variety of points that a good story communicates.

The Fine Print: Limitations to the Model and Some Final Clarifying Notes

It is important to remember that this narrative analysis tool is just that, a tool or a model. Just as a hammer serves many purposes but does not work as the best instrument in every situation, so too this narrative model provides a generally helpful framework but will not always work perfectly. This is partly a function of the limits of any model imposed on a variety of texts and partly the result of some unique elements of the Gospels as literature. It is worth our while to explore these exceptions because they offer an opportunity to understand important aspects of how the Gospels function as stories.

At the most general level we must keep in mind that there is no single correct or accurate way to analyze the narrative. Certainly some analyses will be better than others if they seek to be sensitive to the plot arc, but deciding how to break down the scenes or where to place the various scenes in the plot arc is an art, not a science; there is room for disagreement and difference of opinion.

Additionally, as observed above, stories rarely have only one, singular point or effect. Rather, there are typically several points of varying levels of "heat" on the thermographic map of the story. Various interpreters will be inclined to highlight some elements over others in their readings, and this is understandable and valid. Although the narrative model is more helpful than a purely WSM approach, it cannot provide a definitive or comprehensive analysis.

It is also important to note that while this model will generally help with the narrative portions of the Gospels and the books as narratives overall, the

Gospels themselves are comprised of a variety of subgenres. We have observed that in general they are *bioi*, but the Gospels also consist of other types of literature such as parables, aphorisms, and lengthy didactic discourses, as well as specific types of narratives such as conflict stories, encounter stories, miracle stories, and pronouncement stories. The point, then, is that a narrative model will obviously not work on a didactic section in the Gospels such as the Sermon on the Mount, which is not constructed on a plot arc but communicates through other literary means such as repetition and link words. Sometimes Jesus's parables can be analyzed through the narrative model, but sometimes not, depending on where they lie on the broad spectrum of what a "parable" is—whether more narrative, more allegorical, or more aphoristic.

Related to the preceding point, at times the narrative model is less effective when applied to the Gospels because of their Jesus-saying focus. That is, the radically Jesus-centric nature of the Gospel biographies means that at times the stories are given primarily or even exclusively to communicate some theological or moral statement from Jesus's lips. In such instances, the plot-tension arc is often left underdeveloped. Even if the text is still technically a narrative, the overriding concern to relate some particular pronouncement diminishes the normal story-tension element and therefore the value of the model.

This often happens in the Gospel of Matthew, which seems less concerned with providing well-told stories about Jesus than with using narratives to relay certain teachings about Jesus. Of course, there are exceptions, but such a tendency can be seen, for example, in the first two chapters of the First Gospel. All the stories in Matthew 1:18–2:23 are unmistakably selected and given because they serve as evidence of the ways in which Jesus's history "fulfills" the words of the Jewish Scriptures; each story ends with a formulaic statement to this effect: "This took place to fulfil what the Lord had spoken by the prophet. . . ." As a result, the plots within the individual stories do not play as significant a role as the concluding statement. Our model can still account for this because, as we have observed above, the main point will at times be found in the following action/interpretation. Yet we must acknowledge that the rest of the model will not prove as relevant in these scenarios. Matthew does little by way of developing tension in these stories; he has a different overriding goal in mind: the fulfillment quotation. Thankfully, even Matthew moves away from this overly pedantic style after he has established his "fulfillment" point in the prologue. Nevertheless, throughout each of the Gospels the stories relayed to us sometimes lack narrative development.

It is also important to realize that the model must be used in a flexible way because at times a storyteller will intentionally break the normal plot arc for the sake of variety or to heighten the tension. For example, at times a story will end precisely *without* a resolution, leaving the characters and the plot up in the air as an effective means of communicating and heightening the overall drama of larger narrative. For example, the well-known story of the prodigal son in Luke 15:11–32 ends without resolution. This story, which is itself part of a threefold cycle of stories (15:1–7, 8–10, 11–32), leaves the reader with the question in the air, "How will the elder son respond?" We are never told. This is a very effective invitation to Jesus's original hearers and to all subsequent readers to enter into the story and the ongoing tensive question of how they as individuals will respond to the radical grace of the Father as pictured in this story—either with joy or with anger. Thus, our narrative model *is* still helpful in reading the story carefully and experiencing the plot and the hot spots of the text, as long as one does not feel compelled to find in every story all the elements in toto or without variation. Doing the latter would make the model a master rather than the servant it is meant to be.

Also, we must remember that the individual Gospel stories are always part of a larger whole. They are individual stories with a self-contained unity with beginning, middle, and end, but they come to us in a broader literary context. Thus, when analyzing an individual Gospel narrative episode, we must also remain sensitive to the whole from which this part has come and recognize that there is plot development at a level larger than the episode.[5] This is an important matter worthy of more consideration; thus we will explore it more fully in the following chapter.

Finally, and speaking most broadly, we must recognize the potential danger in doing analysis like this if we come to substitute it for actually reading and experiencing the story. If we cease to read the Gospel accounts—or any narrative—as stories and instead become lab-coated technicians, we will miss the greater point. We will be the literary-analysis equivalent of Martha instead of Mary. While narrative does follow a pattern of plot development that can be helpfully analyzed, stories are not merely reducible to their structure or their ideas. This is an inherent danger in analyzing stories: approaching them as if the story itself is dispensable once the "idea" is discerned. Readers with a propensity toward the analytic and not the poetic should be particularly aware of this pitfall.

But stories do more than transfer information as in an exposition or argument. Rather, they invite us to experience the created world of the narrative, calling us to use our God-given gift of imagination. As Leland Ryken notes, stories appeal to our image-making capabilities such that we can understand, feel, and sympathize with the characters and their experience of the plot. As a result, we are able to connect with broader human experience through the

---

5. Fokkelman, speaking of OT narratives, argues that "because of the fact that the single story forms part of these greater wholes, it need not always have a plot of its own, and discussing the theme will in that case only be possible if we go up one or two levels and read the entire act or cycle first." J. P. Fokkelman, *Reading Biblical Narrative: An Introductory Guide* (Louisville: Westminster John Knox, 1999), 156. This applies to the Gospels in that it is important to read stories as part of the whole, but the *bios* nature of the Gospels makes the individual episodes slightly more independent than those in books like 1–2 Samuel.

story and to make sense of our own experiences. "A literary narrative . . . is primarily interested in getting us to relive an experience, not [merely] to grasp an idea."[6] Thus, a good story (such as we have in the Gospels) resists our impulse to merely reduce the story to abstract propositions, while inviting us to relive and enter the experiences presented. A literary text "invites us to enter a whole world of the imagination and to live in that world before we move beyond it."[7]

When we analyze stories without experiencing them, or if we approach them only on a nugget-hunting search for the truths buried there, we undercut the essence of the genre of the story itself. To reduce a story to its "ideational content is to rob [it of its] power, distort its true nature, and make it finally unnecessary. If the ideas are the important thing in a work of art [or story], we obviously do not need the work itself once we have deduced the ideas."[8]

Recall the illustration I used in chapter 3 about the young couple planning to go on a dinner-and-movie date. The woman desires to see the latest romantic comedy on offer at the local theater. The man agrees but then has the brilliant, time-saving, and money-conserving idea of instead finding a video store (if any still exist!), going to the "Rom-Com" genre section, and together reading the synopses on the backs of the many DVD cases. Why is this not the same, and why would this night likely end up as a failure in the final reckoning of the history of dating? Because the story is not only about the analysis of the plot or the idea or truth that may come from the story—though those can all be important—but rather the story itself is to be experienced, and therein lies its power and effectiveness.

Returning to Our Reading of Luke 7:1–10

To conclude this first chapter on reading the Gospel narratives as stories, let's return to our Luke 7 example and see what the results of our method might look like at this stage of our yet-incomplete analysis:

1. Isolate the Literary Unit—Luke 7:1–10
2. Read the Story Multiple Times
3. Identify the Setting and the Characters
   * Capernaum
   * centurion, his slave, his friends, Jesus, Jewish elders, crowds around Jesus

6. Leland Ryken, *Words of Life: A Literary Introduction to the New Testament* (Grand Rapids: Baker, 1987), 17.

7. Ibid., 23.

8. Leland Ryken, *The Liberated Imagination: Thinking Christianly about the Arts* (Eugene, OR: Wipf & Stock, 2005), 128.

4. Observe the Story
  • This story has a change of place in verse 1, following Luke's sayings similar to the Sermon on the Mount.
  • This is an interesting cross-section of first-century, Roman-controlled Judaism, with a centurion, elders of the Jews, and people of different socioeconomic statuses, such as a slave.
  • Notice the repeated theme throughout the story of "worthy."
  • It is surprising and unexpected for the Jewish elders to actually ask for Jesus's help. Maybe these leaders weren't necessarily opposed to Jesus and maybe even ultimately followed him. Does Luke intentionally call them "elders" and not "Pharisees" for a reason?
  • This story reminds me of the healing of Jairus's daughter, with Jesus being on the way to the healing and then getting word from the house where he is going (v. 6). I sometimes confuse the details of these stories with each other, though they are quite distinct.
  • I had never noticed that it appears Jesus didn't end up actually going to the centurion's house, or at least we are never told that he did. Instead, it seems from verse 10 that the messengers returned and found the servant healed *without* Jesus going there! Did he ever meet the centurion? This story doesn't tell us that he did, though it seems likely that Jesus would have liked to speak with this centurion who had some kind of faith. Luke's point, then, must be something other than the conversion of this centurion, of which we're never told anything.
5. Isolate the Different Scenes
     Scene 1—vv. 1–2 (setting)
     Scene 2—v. 3
     Scene 3—vv. 4–6a
     Scene 4—vv. 6b–8
     Scene 5—v. 9
     Scene 6—v. 10
6. Analyze the Narrative
  • Identify the Rising Tension—vv. 2–6a
  • Identify the Climax—vv. 6b–8
  • Identify the Resolution—v. 9
  • Identify the Following Action/Interpretation—v. 10

Conclusion

We are not yet finished with explaining and applying our narrative model. This requires a bit more discussion to follow in the next chapter. But the essential idea and the basic plan are laid out here. This model for narrative analysis is not perfect or universally applicable, but it is a great resource for approaching texts with direction and guidance that enable wise reading far better than simply "whatever strikes us." Most important, although there is no one right way to analyze a narrative, this model will help us slow down and read carefully with new eyes while giving us a means of getting at the most important points of a text.

So far in this example from Luke 7 we can see that rather than the assorted statements we made at the beginning of this chapter, the main points likely involve Jesus's authority and/or the faith of this non-Israelite centurion, both of which are found at the climax and resolution.

But before making this judgment we must expand and deepen our narrative analysis by looking at the circles of contexts in which this particular story is set. For that we must turn to the following chapter.

10

Reading the Gospels as Stories

Circles of Contextual Meaning

Fiddling on the Roof

I love musicals, both the classic American ones of the Rodgers and Hammerstein vintage and modern masterpieces such as *Les Misérables* and *Wicked*. I have happily infected my children with the same love for musicals. Several summers ago I brought home the sound track to the classic *Fiddler on the Roof*, and it did not take many listenings in the van and at home for all of us to fall under its spell, memorizing, singing, and dancing to all the songs and plucking them out on the piano and the violin.

It had been some years since I had seen the musical myself, so I couldn't quite remember the whole story line. The rest of the family had not seen the film, though this did not prevent them from enjoying the sound track. However, as we continued to listen to the songs, some questions began to arise. At times the children asked what a particular line in a song meant or even the meaning of a whole song. I tried to fill in the details but could never do so completely; it had been too long since I had seen the whole musical. For example, in the song called "The Dream," the main character, Tevye, relates to his wife a scary dream he had informing him that he should let his daughter marry not the old butcher, Lazer Wolff, but instead the young tailor. The children were confused by this song, and I was able to explain that, if my memory served me, Tevye actually *made up* this dream as a way to break the news of his change of plans to his wife in such a way that she would take it as a sign from God and not kill him as a result!

Some weeks into owning the sound track, the family surprised me by purchasing the movie version for Father's Day. With great anticipation—and a sense of familiarity even though only one of us had seen it—we watched this lengthy film. What we experienced was remarkable. When hearing each of these songs now *in their narrative context* of the whole story, we found that several different things happened. In some cases, our guesses about what a song meant were confirmed, such as with "The Dream." In other cases, it turned out we were totally mistaken about what a song meant, such as learning that "Matchmaker" was being sung (and acted out) sarcastically by the daughters *to make fun of the matchmaker* and in poignant fear of who their matches would be. But in *every* case, the meaning, nuance, significance, and effect of the songs were greatly deepened when we experienced them in the midst of the story line from which they came. We now knew the characters and the whole journey of the story, and this greatly affected our ability to receive and experience each song.

This is an appropriate and instructive illustration of our experience of reading the individual stories of the Bible, including those in the Gospels. Most of the stories can be enjoyed, appreciated, and even learned from when taken in isolation. But the best, most powerful, and deepest reading will come when they are read and experienced *in the narrative story line of which they are a part.* Our approach to and knowledge of the Bible's stories tend to be like listening to a sound track: we listen to individual songs, isolated from their context. Some parts we understand; some we completely misinterpret; and most we have only a limited appreciation of as a result. But the best and wisest way of reading the Gospel episodes is in the context(s) in which they come to us as part of a larger story.

In this second chapter on how to read the Gospels as narratives, we will seek to both deepen and broaden the narrative model given for individual

Fig. 4. Range of Contexts

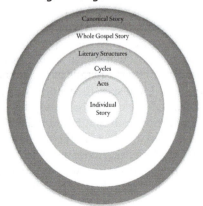

pericopes in the previous chapter. This deepening and broadening occurs through learning to read the individual songs of Holy Scripture's stories in their immediate and far-reaching narrative-musical contexts. Any particular story in the Gospels (or elsewhere) sits in a story line that ranges from its immediate context to broader literary structures to the whole book of which it is a part, as well as its place in the canon of Scripture itself. We may think of this range of contexts as a series of concentric circles (see fig. 4). Moving beyond our narrative plot arc, we can and should learn to read Gospel episodes in light of their place in cycles, acts, and the macro-plot of the Gospels, as well as part of the entire canon of Scripture.

Acts, Cycles, and Literary Structures

In the preceding chapter we emphasized that the individual Gospel pericopes can be analyzed and interpreted as coherent stories within themselves. As is appropriate to the genre and purpose of the Gospels as *bioi*, these books focus on the identity of the Son of God as exemplified through his actions and teachings. Therefore, individual episodes often serve a particular purpose of revealing some character trait or saying of the main character, Jesus, and they can thus stand alone. Their independent nature means they can also be put into different places in the overall story, as in fact we see happen in the different Gospel accounts.[1] Additionally, sometimes one episode does not depend *directly* on the one(s) that come before it. The Gospels are largely episodic in nature.

In this sense, we may draw an (imperfect) analogy to some contemporary television sitcoms versus the traditional TV soap opera. A television soap opera is not episodic in that each one-hour slot of viewing is not a self-contained story with a clear beginning, middle, and end. Just the opposite, this type of narrative subgenre seeks to keep the story line(s) going ad infinitum with a never-ending series of cliff-hangers, love interests, and plot twists. Quite the reverse is the case with a contemporary narrative comedy. Although character development occurs across the weekly episodes and some arcs might be traced from week to week or even season to season, each episode can stand on its own with a setting, rising tension, climax, resolution, and following action. Granted, one's experience of an individual episode will be inevitably shallower if one does not know what happened previously in terms of character development; events, interactions, and statements made in the episode will be much more meaningful if one knows something about the characters and their relationships beforehand. Nonetheless, even without watching all the installments,

---

1. For example, Matthew has clearly collected together a series of healing stories in Matt. 8–9, even though these stories appear in different places in the other Gospel accounts, such as the healing of Peter's mother-in-law (Matt. 8:14–17; cf. Mark 1:29–34; Luke 4:38–41).

one can still understand the story of an individual episode. Generally, this is how the Gospels read as well. They are in many ways episodic in nature. This analogy is imperfect, however, in that because the Gospel accounts are biographies, they also have a wider story to tell that spans the life (and death) of the main character. But this episodic nature does enable the evangelists to teach us many different things about Jesus's character and his teaching and to picture him in many different settings with materials arranged according to the evangelists' pedagogical purposes.

This recognition is helpful yet should not be overdone. An emphasis on the episodic nature of the Gospels will eventually prove too limiting. Reading the individual episodes only as independent pearls on a string is not wise Gospel reading. Our fourfold Gospel book is not merely a sketchbook of assorted sayings or episodes; rather it is a narrative biography with other literary structures and plans and an overall purpose as well.[2]

Moving beyond the level of the individual episodes, we can observe broader units that also have intentional literary and narrative structure and plot developments. In terms of broader narrative structure and plot, we can identify both *acts* and *cycles*. An act consists of several sequentially related stories together, and a cycle, a number of acts strung together.[3] For example, in the Gospel of Luke we may observe that 15:1–32 consists of a series of episodes (15:3–7; 15:8–10; and 15:11–32) that are meant to be read and interpreted together as a unit (an act). The famous prodigal son parable of 15:11–32 is best read not only as a great story in and of itself but as the third and climactic story in a series of lost/found parables. Likewise, there is a pattern and structure to the series of stories at the beginning of Luke's Gospel (1:5–25; 1:26–56; 1:57–80; 2:1–20) that show these stories are not only episodes but are also part of an act. Each of these acts, then, exists within larger sections or cycles in the book. One such cycle is Jesus's journey to Jerusalem (9:51–19:27). This "journey to Jerusalem" cycle, together with Jesus's ministry in Galilee (4:14–9:50), his passion and resurrection (22:1–24:53), and others comprise the whole of the Gospel of Luke.

Related to the notion of acts and cycles, we may also observe that the evangelists often combined several pericopes into literary structures in such a way that when we pay attention to the clues given, we see a greater meaning being communicated than the individual episodes can give us. In this sense, the whole is indeed greater than the sum of the parts.

For example, in the latter part of Matthew we find a highly structured series of pericopes that together make a larger point. After Jesus's publicly disruptive

---

2. This basic observation is the most striking difference between the canonical Gospels and a text like the Gospel of Thomas, whose nearly random collection of 114 sayings/stories reveals that the title "Gospel" is clearly a misnomer. Thomas is not a narrative at all, not even an episodic one.

3. This terminology follows that of J. P. Fokkelman, *Reading Biblical Narrative* (Louisville: Westminster John Knox, 2000), 156.

arrival in Jerusalem, his authority is questioned by the Jewish leadership (21:23–27). What follows is a series of seven interrelated episodes. First, Jesus responds to the authorities by telling three increasingly provocative parables all involving sons: (1) the story of two sons, one who said he would be obedient and then was not and the other son who rebelled but then repented and did what his father asked (21:28–32); (2) a retelling of the parable of the vineyard and the unfaithful tenants from Isaiah 5, which is expanded by Jesus to include the climactic element of the sending of the son (21:33–46); and (3) a lengthy parable about a king whose wedding feast for his son is disregarded and dishonored by his subjects (22:1–14). Then the Jewish leadership ask Jesus three pointed questions, each of which is designed "to entangle him in his talk" or "with a word" (22:15). These three questions are (1) whether faithful Jews should pay taxes to Caesar (22:15–22); (2) concerning the nature of the resurrected state (22:23–33); and (3) which is the greatest commandment in the Law (22:34–40). After successfully refuting each question, for the seventh pericope in the series Jesus turns and asks *them* (the Jewish leadership) a pointed question that is at the same time theological and about a son, particularly the identity of the Son of David (22:41–46). Although the obvious answer to us is that Jesus is the Son of David who is also called his Lord, Matthew wryly informs us that "no one" from among Jesus's interlocutors "was able to answer him a word" (alluding back to their plans in 22:15), "nor" from that time on "did anyone dare to ask him any more questions"!

We can discern a consistent theme and structure in this series of seven pericopes:

Three Sonship Parables—21:28–32 / 21:33–46 / 22:1–14
Three Challenging Questions—22:15–22 / 22:23–33 / 22:34–40
One Ultimately Challenging Sonship Question—22:41–46

It is not difficult to see that Matthew wants us to perceive the structure of two sets of three (a Matthean favorite)[4] followed by a climactic seventh story (an obviously important number of completion), which itself brings together the theme of sonship with the challenging theological questions, with Jesus shown to be the Son of David.

Yet the structural indicators don't stop there. When we pan out a bit further, we see that this highly structured set of episodes is itself nested in another unit that also focuses our attention on Jesus as the Son of David. This section consists of all of chapters 21 through 23. Chapter 21 marks the final stage of Jesus's life and Matthew's account, with Jesus's triumphal (and disputed) entry into

---

4. On the significant use of literary sets of three in Matthew, see Dale C. Allison Jr., "The Configuration of the Sermon on the Mount and Its Meaning," in his *Studies in Matthew* (Grand Rapids: Baker Academic, 2005), 173–215.

Jerusalem, the city of David. Without doubt Matthew wants us to see this entry as underscoring Jesus's lineage and connection to David (which was already highlighted in Matt. 1:1–17), with the children crying out, "Hosanna to the Son of David" (21:9), which is repeated again at Jesus's cleansing of the temple (21:15). This leads into the structure of seven detailed above, which is itself followed by Jesus's series of woes upon the faithless Jewish leadership (23:1–36). This larger unit of chapters 21–23 is then concluded and brought together by Jesus's lament over Jerusalem (23:37–39), described as now forsaken and desolate (cf. the temple and the fig tree). They will not see Jesus again, he proclaims, until they say, "Blessed is he who comes in the name of the Lord," now used for the third time (21:9, 15; 23:39) and providing a key inclusio with the triumphal entry at the beginning of chapter 21. Thus, the overall structure looks like this:

Jesus's entry into Jerusalem, emphasizing him as the Son of David (21:1–11)

    Jesus's cleansing/cursing of the temple and the authorities' challenge (21:12–27)

        Jesus's three sonship parables, which speak of the rejection of the Jewish leadership (21:28–22:14)

        The Jewish leadership's three questions to Jesus and his responses (22:15–40)

    Jesus's question about David's son (22:41–46)

Jesus's woes/curses on the Jewish leadership (23:1–36)

Jesus's lament over Jerusalem, emphasizing him as the Son of David (23:37–39)

Thus a close and careful reading reveals an intentional literary artistry on the part of Matthew. My point is not so much to emphasize a chiasm present in this example, though one could make this argument effectively, but to observe that, when taken together and analyzed, this series of episodes itself has a point and a theme that goes beyond any individual pericope. Clearly, chapters 21–23 teach us many particular things, but the overall point must be the focus on Jesus as the Son of David, with a closely related theme of the rejection of the Jewish leadership in Jerusalem, who themselves reject the Son. Thus Matthew's major points are embedded in a literary structure.

This is but one of many examples that could be given to demonstrate the importance of reading with sensitivity to structures and connections between pericopes that go beyond the individual story. *The Gospel writers cared about literary structure, and to read their works well is to read in this way.* Along these lines, the work of Timothy Wiarda is helpful. Though he does not provide a narrative analysis model as we have here, Wiarda is very insightful on this issue of the interconnectedness of individual episodes. He observes that there are various forms of interconnection between individual pericopes and their overall narratives. He outlines and illustrates seven ways in which this interconnection occurs in the Gospels:[5]

1. individual stories arranged thematically around a common theme;
2. stories linked by narrative analogy, that is, different episodes spread throughout that should be read as connected (e.g., Peter in Matthew);
3. interwoven tapestry of thematically linked episodes;
4. stories linked by special patterns of literary arrangement (e.g., chiasm, parallel structuring);
5. individual stories that contribute to an unfolding story thread;
6. two stories connected through intercalation;
7. several adjacent episodes that work together to present a unified and progressing story, with a developing plot or developing characters.

Wiarda gives helpful examples for each type of interconnection. To read the Gospels well and wisely is to be sensitive to this kind of structure that goes beyond the individual pericope, as I have modeled with Matthew 21–23, and in a variety of other ways, as Wiarda points out.

The Whole Gospel Story

We can also view the Gospels beyond these literary patterns and acts and cycles. As observed above, we must not forget that the biographical genre of the Gospels means that they are intended to tell us the overall story of Jesus's life and death and their aftereffects. Thus we must always read the individual pericopes, the larger literary units, the acts, and the cycles as part of a macro-plot that spans the entirety of the Gospel. This next level of concentric circles of context is very important. The whole-Gospel-reading sensitivity should be pursued along the lines of intratextuality, the fourfold Gospel book context, and the whole-Gospel plot line.

Intratextuality

First, as we read individual episodes, we should be aware of allusions to any particular story elsewhere in the same Gospel, thereby indicating that we should read these accounts in light of each other. That is, often some element or idea in a story is reused; its thread is pulled, sometimes ever so slightly, so that the sensitive reader can see connections between stories and thereby sense a deeper issue and levels of meaning. This phenomenon is sometimes called "narrative analogies," defined as when "a particular motif or combination

5. Timothy Wiarda, *Interpreting Gospel Narratives: Scenes, People, and Theology* (Nashville: Broadman & Holman, 2010), 187–93.

of narrative elements recurs in a literary work."[6] Wiarda gives the example of tracing the series of Peter appearances in Matthew, wherein we can see a pattern: "Peter says or does something with good intentions, but then immediately encounters correction or failure."[7] This goes beyond just looking at the immediate literary context of a story to observing how separate episodes form themes larger than themselves.

We may also call this phenomenon "intratextuality."[8] This term refers generally to the intentional but often subtle connections that an author makes to earlier parts of his work in later sections. Or to borrow language from the scholarly discussion of intertextuality, intratextuality occurs when an author embeds phrases and ideas from his own earlier story into later texts within the same work.

One simple example, which is more on the explicit side, is the use of literary foreshadowing. When Jesus three times predicts his own future suffering and death in Jerusalem, while on the journey to Jerusalem (Mark 8:31–38; 9:30–32; 10:32–34; and parallels), we as readers are meant to see these statements as hints about where the story is going. Only after the story reaches its end can we fully see that some previous reference was indeed a foreshadowing, but that is the nature of good storytelling always; its subtleties and skillfulness are manifested increasingly on subsequent readings. There are also more subtle forms of foreshadowing, such as how the use of the appellation "king of the Jews" is used in the first chapters of Matthew with regard to Jesus as the true King instead of the worldly King Herod (2:2). When one then reaches the end of the First Gospel and three times hears this applied to Jesus again—the Roman soldiers mock him thus (27:29); Pilate insists the title be put above Jesus's head, "This is Jesus the King of the Jews" (27:37); and the Jewish leaders scorn his weakness by repeating this claim (27:42)—it is not difficult to see that Matthew was setting up this crucial idea from the very beginning.

Related but subtler than foreshadowing is a type of intratextuality in which one can see themes and ideas worked out in more than one story throughout the narrative, often providing consummation of an earlier idea in a later

6. Ibid., 180. Wiarda borrows this helpful term from the OT narrative critics Robert Alter and Myron Sternberg, as applied to the Gospels by J. Williams.

7. Ibid. On the pages that follow he unpacks each of these episodes involving Peter, showing the pattern there.

8. Different terms are used to describe this phenomenon. For example, in describing Matthew's literary techniques John Nolland gives examples of this with the somewhat laborious description of "Internal Cross-Referencing by Means of Language Echoes." Nolland, *The Gospel of Matthew*, NIGTC (Grand Rapids: Eerdmans, 2005), 27. I am here borrowing the term from Dale Allison's usage in his *Studies in Matthew*. As used here, the term is intentionally connected to the popular word "intertextuality," referring to the way texts allude to and use a variety of earlier works, but with the constraints here being within one particular work, hence *intra*textuality.

pericope. For example, John Riches observes several intratextual ties between the climactic conclusion of Matthew (28:18–20) and several earlier Matthean texts:[9]

- It breaks the ban on gentile mission found in 10:5, 6.
- It clarifies and transcends the titles given to Jesus at the beginning: Son of David, Son of Abraham; the Son of David will rule not only over Israel but all the world/all nations, Jews and gentiles.
- It picks up the theme of God with us in 1:23.
- It reverses Satan's offer of authority over all kingdoms (4:8–9).
- It connects with the hidden wisdom given by the Father to Jesus (11:25–30) and now to the disciples.
- It brings together Jesus as the Son of Man with Daniel 7:13ff.

I would also add:

- It consummates and brings full circle the language of "genesis" and "beginning" from Matthew 1:1 with its reference to "the end of the age."

This is but one example of many such intratextual threads in Matthew. The nature of good storytelling, especially that which has the conscious goal of presenting to us transformative truths, such as we have in the Gospels, is that it contains levels of interconnectivity within the story line. These interconnections deepen and expand the meaning of any individual pericope such that reading them together gives a fuller sense of what is being communicated. Discerning the "accuracy" of such interconnections is not mechanistic but is a matter of judgments made as we read more and learn to be sensitive readers. As Richard Hays observes:

> The identification of allusions and especially echoes is not a strictly scientific matter lending itself to conclusive proof, like testing for the presence or absence of a chemical in the bloodstream. The identification of allusions, rather, is an art practiced by skilled interpreters within a reading community that has agreed on the value of situating individual texts within a historical and literary continuum of other texts (i.e., a canon). The "yes" or "no" judgment about any particular alleged allusion is primarily an *aesthetic* judgment pronounced upon the fittingness of a proposed reading.[10]

9. John Riches, "Matthew's Missionary Strategy in Colonial Perspective," in *The Gospel of Matthew in Its Roman Imperial Context*, ed. John Riches and David Sim (London: T&T Clark, 2005), 128, 137.

10. Richard B. Hays, *The Conversion of the Imagination: Paul as Interpreter of Israel's Scripture* (Grand Rapids: Eerdmans, 2005), 30.

Thus our goal as wise readers of the Gospels is to develop certain skills of attention, such as we are discussing in these chapters, and to have our antennae increasingly tuned to hear the music of the theme and variation of episodic interconnections.

The Context of the Fourfold Gospel Book

Throughout this book we have emphasized that from the earliest days the fourfold book, the Tetraevangelium, was considered the *one* Gospel that has come down to us "according to Matthew," "according to Mark," "according to Luke," and "according to John." One implication of this for our canonical-contextual reading is that any particular passage or episode in the Gospels resides in the context of the whole Gospel story that is the fourfold book. That is, the meaning/significance of any passage is in some ways significantly affected by the rest of the pericope's brothers, sisters, and cousins in the other evangelists' writings. Since what we are given in the Holy Gospels is not just individual stories or even individual books but rather a fourfold book, the best readings of any episode take into account relevant information from the rest of the Gospels canon.

At the most basic level this means that reading any Gospel pericope well includes examining places in the other Gospels where a parallel or related story is told. For this, owning a good synopsis of the Gospels, in which the stories are placed in corresponding parallel columns, is very valuable.

This kind of examination corresponds to what we discussed earlier as horizontal reading. That is, when reading a Gospel story, we may with great benefit glance to the left and to the right and see how the story at hand is presented by the other evangelists, if at all. We call this horizontal reading because of the visual effect created by producing a synopsis of the Gospels. The parallel columns enable one to easily see comparable passages. We also call this horizontal reading to contrast it with vertical reading, whereby we read each Gospel focusing instead on how that particular evangelist develops his plot and motifs.

It is important to note that this sideways glancing, or horizontal reading, must always be held in balanced tension with a more literary, vertical reading. Ultimately, the latter is more important and will produce the best and ripest fruit. Reading that is exclusively or even primarily horizontal will result in distorted, misshapen produce: "behind the text" readings that are based on our own reconstructed "what really happened" rather than the witness of the sacred texts themselves. (Balance must always be kept here between a canonical and a historical reading; see chap. 5.)

Nevertheless, as observed in previous chapters, looking at other parallel texts—especially with canonical-theological questions rather than historical ones—can indeed provide great insight into particular emphases or points that the present evangelist is making. For example, there are good reasons to suppose that the Gospel of John reflects knowledge of and interaction with some form of Mark, so we can with benefit compare stories in the Second and Fourth Gospels. Going beyond such historically based approaches, however, all the Gospels can and should be read with one another because they have been canonized into one book; we are meant to receive them as one. As a result, looking at parallel passages—some nearly identical, some more conceptually related—is an important part of the circles of context within which any Gospel pericope resides.[11]

Recently a colleague of mine expressed to me his discomfort about a sermon we both heard wherein information about Mary's and Martha's different character traits (via Luke 10:38–42) was used to explain their different reactions to Jesus at the death and raising of Lazarus (in John 11). That is, Mary's reaction to Jesus in John 11 was assumed to be the proper response, while Martha's was not. This interpretation was based on importing the differing character traits of these two women from the well-known story in Luke 10. This example provides an excellent argument for reading both horizontally-canonically and vertically and keeping the two approaches in tension. My colleague was concerned that this famous Lukan story about Mary choosing the better part and sitting at the Lord's feet while Martha busied herself with housework should *not* be used to interpret these actions of these same women at the raising of Lazarus. My colleague argued that they come from a different Gospel and there is nothing in John's account that inclines us to see Mary as the "good guy" and Martha as the "bad guy" in John 11.

In this scenario both the preacher in question and my colleague were partly right. On the one hand, we are right to be hesitant about flatly and unthoughtfully assuming that Luke's recounting of this story of Mary and Martha becomes the paradigm through which we should read every other story in the Gospels in which these characters appear. That is, we should let the primary source of information about Mary and Martha in John 11 be John the Evangelist in the rest of his Gospel. If there is nothing in John overall or in the immediate context that inclines us to read Martha's response to Jesus as mistaken and a model of faithlessness (as many are inclined to do via Luke 10), then we should at least be quite hesitant to make this view of Martha a major or solid fact in our overall interpretation of John 11. The vertical reading

---

11. In speaking of the habits of ancient commentaries on the Gospels, Bockmuehl observes that "the patristic commentators took it for granted that the normative text should be interpreted in the first place with reference to itself." As a result, for many centuries "gospel commentaries tended to draw heavily on cognate or parallel passages in the other gospels" not to compare synoptic differences but to enrich our full understanding of what the Gospels overall are teaching. Markus Bockmuehl, "The Making of Gospel Commentaries," in *The Written Gospel*, ed. Markus Bockmuehl and Donald Hagner (Cambridge: Cambridge University Press, 2005), 284–85.

must take precedence. In his reticence to simply import Luke 10 into John 11 in an unexamined way, my colleague is certainly right.

Yet, at the same time, we cannot suggest or argue that Luke 10 and John 11 *must* be kept far from each other and *necessarily* have no mutual bearing. To do so is to read them *only* historically and not canonically. Quite the opposite, the canonical shape of the fourfold Gospel book exhorts us to read texts, characters, events, and theological ideas across all the accounts, or at least invites us to consider this possibility. The effectiveness and benefit of any particular example must be examined on a case-by-case basis, sensitive to the voice of each evangelist. Maybe it is too much to assume that Martha's misplaced affections in Luke 10 result in a faithless response in John 11. But we cannot reject the possibility of this kind of reading out of hand just because the stories are in different Gospels. We as Christian readers have been given the gift of the fourfold Gospel book, and to read any story isolated from this canonical context is to live in poverty with an uncashed inheritance check in hand. Moreover, in this particular case a good argument can be made that canonically the Gospel of John evinces awareness of the Synoptic tradition and serves to complement, fill out, and thoughtfully transpose those accounts; hence awareness of Luke 10 may indeed inform John 11.[12]

The Gospels' Macro-Plot

In addition to reading the Gospels as wholes in terms of intratextual connections, we must also always keep in mind the overall story of these biographies. Particularly, we should note that each of the Gospels places primary emphasis on Jesus's death and resurrection. In one sense, this is not unlike other ancient Greek *bioi*, which typically desire to use the "biographee's"[13] manner of death and last words as a crucial witness to his character. But according to the evangelists (as well as the rest of the apostolic witness), Jesus's death and resurrection are not just the final part of the story of a great man. Rather the New Testament documents make it very clear that the last week of Jesus's life and his subsequent death and resurrection are the reason for his coming and are the epicenter of history itself. In this emphasis all four Gospels are entirely consistent, despite their many other differences. This macro-truth must certainly affect our reading of any individual episode or portion of the Gospel accounts.

12. An exploration of this kind of canonical shaping (to use Childs's and Seitz's term) is found in Richard Bauckham's essay "Mark," in Richard Bauckham, ed., *The Gospels for All Christians: Rethinking the Gospel Audiences* (Grand Rapids: Eerdmans, 1998): 147–71. For the idea of John "transposing" Mark and possibly Luke, see Andreas Köstenberger, "John's Transposition Theology: Retelling the Story of Jesus in a Different Key," in Michael F. Bird and Jason Matson, eds., *Earliest Christianity: History, Literature, and Theology—Essay from the Tyndale Fellowship in Honour of Martin Hengel* (Tübingen: Mohr Siebeck, 2012).

13. I borrow this helpful term referring to the subject of a biography from Richard Bauckham in his lecture series "The Gospels as Histories," delivered at Southern Seminary in February 2011.

It has long been recognized that the Passion Narratives of the four Gospels are central in terms of sheer space allocated to them in the Gospel accounts. When read in their entirety, it is very clear that the pace of each of the Gospel accounts slows significantly at the end of Jesus's life. The passion week takes up considerable space and provides many more details than the earlier parts of the Gospels, which generally travel at a breakneck speed, providing, as it were, a highlight reel of Jesus's ministry. But once we arrive in Jerusalem for the last week of Jesus's life, we as readers sense the change of pace and the importance of what is happening.

This is especially true in the Gospel of Mark, with its constant sense of urgency (cf. his famous repetition of "immediately"), which suddenly slackens, unexpectedly resulting in seven of Mark's sixteen chapters being given wholly to the last week of Jesus's life. In this Mark is closest to John, who, while much more paced and patient in the earlier part of his Gospel, nonetheless gives a full ten of his twenty-one chapters (including the postresurrection appearances in the epilogue) to the events in Jerusalem at the end of Jesus's earthly life. Matthew and Luke also give more time to Jesus's passion week than they do to any other topic or event, though due to their other goal of providing significant portions of Jesus's teachings, their relative space is less than Mark and John, though still significant: Matthew dedicates eight of his twenty-eight chapters to the passion and resurrection, Luke five and a half of twenty-four. In every case any reader of these biographies would sense that *the events surrounding Jesus's final week are meant to be understood as the focal point of the narratives.*

The implication of this for our reading of any pericope or portion of the Gospel is that the significance of Jesus's death and resurrection must weigh heavily on our overall interpretation of the episode, act, or cycle. If we fail to give due weight to this mandate, we run the risk of reading any given passage in a thin and distorted way.[14]

A classic example is the way in which Jesus's famous Sermon on the Mount (Matt. 5–7) has been misread. A very common misreading of the Sermon on the Mount results from approaching it as a stand-alone unit, as the epitome of Jesus's worldview and teaching. Although the sermon is canonically and theologically one of the most important instances of New Testament teaching and is worth a very close reading and application in and of itself, Matthew clearly never intended it to be excerpted and read apart from the whole Gospel narrative in which it is situated. This is evident first by the many ways in which the teachings of the sermon are revisited, unpacked, and modeled by Jesus in

14. Richard Hays has written a very insightful essay that argues for the centrality of understanding the resurrection in our biblical interpretation, including an exploration of some of the implications of doing so. Richard Hays, "Reading Scripture in Light of the Resurrection," in *The Art of Reading Scripture*, ed. Ellen Davis and Richard Hays (Grand Rapids: Eerdmans, 2003), 216–38.

the rest of Matthew.[15] Nearly everything Jesus teaches in the sermon is given fuller explanation elsewhere in the Gospel, so to read this portion divorced from that context is to cut oneself off from wise reading. Moreover, the overall context for the sermon is one in which the very Teacher of the sermon goes on to die and rise again for those who cannot possibly fulfill its commands and ideals themselves. The rest of Matthew, including especially Jesus's death and resurrection, reveals that the kingdom of heaven that Jesus proclaims in the sermon is inaugurated by and entered into only through Jesus's dying and rising. Crucial to interpreting the sermon's vision of God's coming kingdom is the later explanation that "my Father's kingdom" is given through Jesus's covenant with his people via his own blood (Matt. 26:27–29). Matthew wants us to understand that the sermon is meaningless and impossible idealism if the eschatological realities of which it speaks are not actuated by the One who is teaching it.

Another Matthean example of the importance of the Gospel's macro-plot is his use of Isaiah 53:4 in Matthew 8:17. This verse from Isaiah is part of the important Suffering Servant idea that the New Testament authors understand as fulfilled in Jesus the Christ. Most Christian readers can quite easily read the description of the Servant in Isaiah 52:13–53:12 and understand it as pointing to Christ's rejection, ill-treatment, anguish, and, ultimately, atoning death for the sins of God's people. Indeed, this understanding has a strong tradition in both the New Testament and the history of Christian interpretation. Thus Matthew's use of Isaiah 53:4 is all the more perplexing. After describing a number of Jesus's healings (8:1–16), Matthew uses his familiar "fulfillment quotation" formula to explain Jesus's actions as the completion of Isaiah 53:4, "he has borne our griefs and carried our sorrows." That is, Matthew seems to be reading this text as anticipating physical healings, not atonement for sin per se, by virtue of where he uses it in his own Gospel story. Scholars have offered strong arguments that, in fact, Isaiah 53:4 here does not refer to atonement.[16] However, when one resists the temptation of such a reading focused only on pericopes and considers the whole Gospel, with its clear and consistent focus on Jesus's death and resurrection, it becomes apparent that the use of Isaiah in Matthew 8 cannot be interpreted in this narrow and exclusive way. Rather, the series of healing stories in Matthew 8–9 are intimately connected to Jesus's death and resurrection, which we have already been told is to "save his people from their sins" (1:21; cf. 26:28).[17] It is too thin a reading to pit physical heal-

15. See Allison, "Structure, Biographical Impulse, and the Imitatio Christi," in his *Studies in Matthew*.

16. For example, Morna Hooker, *Jesus and the Servant: The Influence of the Servant Concept of Deutero-Isaiah in the New Testament* (London: SPCK, 1959), 21–23, 83, 149; Richard Beaton, *Isaiah's Christ in Matthew's Gospel* (Cambridge: Cambridge University Press, 2002), 114–15.

17. Fuller argumentation for this conclusion can be found in Mark Jackson, "Atonement in Matthew's Gospel" (PhD diss., Southern Seminary, 2011), 66–74.

ings and forgiving salvation against each other. The Gospel as a whole and its overall point must be considered in interpreting chapters 8–9 in Matthew.

To reiterate, when reading any individual pericope in the Gospels, we must keep the end of the story in mind because the authors have intentionally placed great interpretive weight on Jesus's death and resurrection. In this sense reading the Gospels is analogous to reconsidering the whole of a mystery or detective novel after reaching its climactic and revealing end. Only after the final scene has unfolded and we understand the secret motives and the identity of the true criminal can we look back on events and statements in the novel and see them with clarity.[18] Our reading of the Gospels is similar in that it is the passion week events that bring ultimate insight into all that Jesus said and did up to that time. "But he spoke of the temple of his body. When therefore he was raised from the dead, his disciples remembered that he had said this," as John records for us (2:21–22). This analogy breaks down only in the sense that most of us do not reread detective novels or murder mysteries; doing so would often be uninteresting because it is that last bit of information revealed at the end that cracks open the whole story.[19] The Gospels are not like this, however. Once one sees what happens at the end—which *is* surprising and unexpected in some ways—multiple rereadings are only deepened by this knowledge.

We may recall the Kentucky Derby example I gave in chapter 8. In the Gospel accounts we have expert commentary and analysis of the events based on knowing the final outcome and goal of the story. Jesus's death was confusing, dismaying, and inexplicable at the time of the event, and even after the resurrection there was still no small amount of fear and uncertainty about how to proceed. Despite the promises of resurrection and the appearance of the resurrected Christ to several of the disciples, Jesus's followers remained fearful (cf. John 20:19) and rather inwardly focused (Acts 1:12–14) until the giving of the Spirit. But once the Spirit of power and revelation came upon the disciples at Pentecost, they understood the significance of all that Jesus had taught and done beforehand (cf. John 2:22). The evangelists then write their accounts with this post-Pentecost perspective and expert analysis and commentary. Because of the centrality of the death and resurrection in salvation history, the Gospel accounts are written from the perspective of this historical-theological event. Therefore, as readers we need to follow the lead of the evangelists and trace

18. David Steinmetz uses this experience in describing "traditional exegesis" over against a historical-critical approach. See his "Uncovering a Second Narrative: Detective Fiction and the Construction of Historical Method," in Davis and Hays, *Art of Reading Scripture*, 54–65.

19. The exceptions, of course, are novels of this genre that are also rich in description, place, and character development, such as Umberto Eco's famous *The Name of the Rose*. A rereading continues to return abundantly on the investment of time spent in its pages. But even so, the nature of this genre and its twist at the end mean that it can never quite be enjoyed or experienced in the same way after the first reading.

the same trajectory in our reading, interpreting all the pre-passion stories through the post-Pentecost perspective motivating the authors.

The Whole Canonical Story

Yet one more concentric circle of meaning is very significant in our reading of the Gospels: the overall story of the whole canon, of God's work in salvation history from Genesis to Revelation, from creation to new creation. Even as the meaning of any individual pericope is understood and deepened when considered in its whole Gospel context, so too when we read the Gospels in light of the entire canon, we see that even the elaborate and complex stories of the Gospels do not exist in a vacuum but are clearly situated as part of the larger story of the whole Bible.

As mentioned in the opening illustration of my family's experience of *Fiddler on the Roof*, our tendency as readers is toward isolation of stories and abstraction of meaning. But as we have discussed in previous chapters, the bulk of the Bible consists of narrative, the stories of real people and God's work in history. Although theological propositions certainly can and should be distilled from the Holy Scriptures, the primary theology of the Scriptures is a story. This is patently true especially for the Old Testament. At its core/essence, talk about God in the Old Testament Scriptures is the narrative of what he has done, is doing, and will do in the world. Approaches that seek to organize and interpret this reality are often called "biblical theology" and/or the study of "redemptive history."

One helpful way of thinking about the grand story, or metanarrative, of the Old Testament is to conceive of it as a drama with several distinct acts. There is a growing trend of thinking about the Bible this way, as "a unified and progressively unfolding drama of God's action in history for the salvation of the whole world."[20]

Underlying this reading of the Bible as a whole is the understanding that because the author of the Scriptures and of history itself is ultimately God, we can rightly assume an order, purpose, and design to the whole story. Of course, the meaning of every twist and turn of the drama will not be immediately apparent to us, but there is ultimately a coherence that adheres to God's sovereignty and purpose. This notion of being guided by an overall *hypothesis* or narrative understanding of all God's work (the *economy* of Scripture) was a dominant aspect of premodern reading and one from which we should learn.[21]

---

20. Craig Bartholomew and Michael Goheen, *The Drama of Scripture: Finding Our Place in the Biblical Story* (Grand Rapids: Baker Academic, 2004), 12.

21. See esp. chap. 2 of John J. O'Keefe and R. R. Reno, *Sanctified Vision: An Introduction to Early Christian Interpretation of the Bible* (Baltimore: Johns Hopkins University Press, 2005).

If this is so, we may next ask what the organizing rubric or theme is that holds together this grand drama of Scripture. Many theologians, including Craig Bartholomew and Michael Goheen, have suggested that the kingdom or reign of God is the most helpful thread that can be traced through the entire Bible, which is certainly correct. The only other possible meta-theme would be that of covenant, but as Bartholomew and Goheen observe, the idea of covenant can and should be subsumed under that of kingdom, as covenant is a kingdom-based idea itself.[22] God is depicted as a king who first establishes his rule and vice-regents in his royal garden. He makes a covenant with his subjects, first Adam and Eve and then even with his rebellious subjects whom he rescues—as a warrior king does—time and again. Even though all the different parts of the Old Testament at times look like a jumbled mess of strings and knots going every which way, in reality, when one turns the well-designed tapestry of the Bible over and looks at it clearly, we can see that the seeming mess is really a clear, intricate, and beautiful picture. And there is flowing throughout this woven picture a dominant purple thread, that of God's kingdom from creation to new creation.

Thus, built on the central notion of God's reign, Bartholomew and Goheen lay out the story or drama of the Scriptures in six distinct acts:[23]

Act 1   God Establishes His Kingdom: Creation
Act 2   Rebellion in the Kingdom: The Fall
Act 3   The King Chooses Israel: Redemption Initiated
Scene 1   A People for the King
Scene 2   A Land for His People
Interlude   A Kingdom Story Waiting for an Ending: The Intertestamental Period
Act 4   The Coming of the King: Redemption Accomplished
Act 5   Spreading the News of the King: The Mission of the Church
Scene 1   From Jerusalem to Rome
Scene 2   And into All the World
Act 6   The Return of the King: Redemption Completed

For a more detailed explanation and unpacking of each of these acts and scenes, one must consult Bartholomew and Goheen, in addition to similar works. But for our purposes we can see that recognizing this meta-story of the kingdom of God affects our reading of the Gospels significantly. This background and backstory provides depth and setting for Jesus's own preaching, teaching, life, death, resurrection, and ascension. As we have observed earlier

---

Also Richard Bauckham, "Reading Scripture as a Coherent Story," and Steinmetz, "Uncovering a Second Narrative," in Davis and Hays, *Art of Reading Scripture.*

22. Bartholomew and Goheen, *Drama of Scripture*, 22–25.

23. Ibid., 27.

in this book, the indisputable major theme of the fourfold Gospel book is the kingdom of God preached, explained, and inaugurated by Jesus the Christ.

If indeed, then, the entire story line of the Bible focuses on the reign of God over the false rulers of this world—Satan and sin and death—then Jesus's actions and message make much more sense; they go from being a black-and-white picture to a full-color drama. When Jesus goes about casting out demons and healing the broken, this itself is kingdom work, anticipating the consummation of the story line begun in creation. These actions do not merely serve as apologetic proof for Jesus's identity as a dispensable run-up to his death on the cross. Rather to cast out demons is to dethrone the false ruler of the world now in the name of the One who is truly and will finally be the king of the world (cf. "if it is by the finger of God that I cast out demons . . ."), precisely what has been hoped for and prophesied since Genesis 3. This is all part of the story of redemption that Jesus has come to complete once and for all, fulfilling all the promises of God that go back to the fall in the garden. Redemption is the restoration of creation itself, what the Scriptures anticipate as a new creation.[24] As Norman Klassen and Jens Zimmerman rightly observe: "If the New Testament is right, Christ did not come to pluck souls from an evil and worthless creation and transport them to an angelic existence; instead he came to announce the beginning of the world's renewal."[25]

It is not difficult to see how understanding this meta-story of the whole canon makes sense of and greatly enhances our reading of the Gospels. The Gospels' focus on the kingdom is not an anomaly or a unique aspect but rather consistent with all of Scripture. An understanding of the kingdom–redemptive-history concentration of Scripture elevates our encounter with the Gospels from mere sound track listening to experiencing the whole of the narrative.

We may conclude our argument for the importance of whole-canon context by offering a negative example. That is, when we compare the use of a familiar parable in the canonical Gospels with its usage in another text, the Gospel of Thomas, we can see firsthand the danger of de-storying, or removing the Gospels from their canonical story line.[26]

In each of the Synoptic Gospels we have the story that is usually called the parable of the wicked tenants (Matt. 21:33–46; Mark 12:1–12; Luke 20:9–19). This parable, like much of Jesus's teaching, strongly alludes to, quotes, and evokes important Old Testament stories and ideas. The setting of the parable

24. For a compelling argument that redemption should be understood as the restoration and completion of the creation order and mandate, see Al Wolters, *Creation Regained: Biblical Basics for a Reformational Worldview*, 2nd ed. (Grand Rapids: Eerdmans, 2005).

25. Norman Klassen and Jens Zimmermann, *The Passionate Intellect: Incarnational Humanism and the Future of University Education* (Grand Rapids: Baker Academic, 2006), 162.

26. The following example comes from Richard Hays's essay "The Canonical Matrix of the Gospels" in *The Cambridge Companion to the Gospels*, ed. Stephen Barton (Cambridge: Cambridge University Press, 2006), 53–75.

clearly comes from Isaiah 5:1–7, known as the Song of the Vineyard. Jesus's retelling of this parable intentionally begins with the same details about the planting and preparation of the vineyard. Jesus adjusts and modifies the story to heighten its point and focus the attention on the killing of the vineyard owner's "beloved son," but this change only heightens the Old Testament evocations with reference to texts such as Genesis 22:2; Psalm 2:7; and Isaiah 42:1. One with knowledge of the Jewish Scriptures will also not miss how the tenants' declaration, "Come, let us kill him," in Jesus's parable echoes Joseph's brothers in Genesis 37:20. And most explicitly, Jesus's parable concludes by quoting Psalm 118:22–23 about the builders rejecting the cornerstone.

As Richard Hays has observed:

> By evoking this canonical memory, the synoptic gospels press us to interpret the parable as a word of judgment on the leaders of Israel for their failure to yield the vineyard's grapes to its rightful owner. The parable thereby places the story of Jesus within the unfolding story of Israel and presents his death as the climax of a pattern of unfaithfulness and judgment familiar to any reader of Israel's prophetic literature. At the same time, the identification of Jesus as the "beloved son" (Mk 12:6; Lk 20:13)—linking him both to Isaac and to the Davidic king—hints that his death is to be understood not merely as a tragic episode of violence but as an event of saving significance for Israel. . . . Thus, the canonical synoptic versions situate the parable of the wicked tenants within a larger narrative context and present Jesus' death and resurrection as the climax of the story of Israel. The canonical matrix provides both hermeneutical guidance and theological depth.[27]

Hays here puts his finger precisely on what we have argued above, a point further supported when one compares the very different way that the noncanonical, second-century AD Gospel of Thomas picks up and adapts the same parable. Unlike the canonical Gospels, the Thomas version systematically strips away all the Old Testaments allusions and references, as we see in saying 65:

> He said, A . . . person owned a vineyard and rented it to some farmers, so they could work it and he could collect its crop from them. He sent his slave so the farmers would give him the vineyard's crop. They grabbed him, beat him, and almost killed him, and the slave returned and told his master. His master said, "Perhaps he didn't know them." He sent another slave, and the farmers beat that one as well. Then the master sent his son and said, "Perhaps they'll show my son some respect." Because the farmers knew that he was the heir to the vineyard, they grabbed him and killed him. Anyone here with two ears had better listen![28]

27. Ibid., 54.
28. Note that Thomas saying 66 does have a more veiled allusion to Ps. 118—Jesus said, "Show me the stone that the builders rejected: that is the keystone"—but it is undeveloped and does not seem to be connected to Thomas's version of the parable.

The difference is striking and not without significance. This stripped-down version of the parable is colorless and enigmatic, and by eradicating the Old Testament connections it is divorced from the story of Israel. For Thomas, this enables the writer to co-opt this saying of Jesus into a gnostic message of detachment from an evil world. That is, the decolorizing and detaching of this parable from its context in Israel's history and story enable the creators of the Gospel of Thomas to reappropriate it and commandeer it into a gnostic derivation of Christianity. To quote Hays again, "Thus, Thomas's editorial de-judaizing of the parable illustrates the loss of meaning—or better, distortion of meaning—that occurs when the gospel traditions are artificially removed from the canonical matrix of Israel's story."[29]

While most readers of the present book will not likely be tempted to become gnostic believers, this illustration is still instructive for us. It is very easy to read the Gospels in such a way that we de facto interpret the Gospel stories outside their ultimate and most important context, the whole story of God's work in the world from creation to new creation. When we do so, we risk intentionally or unintentionally co-opting those stories into our *own* worldview and theological construct rather than that of the canonical Scriptures. The safeguard against this tendency is to read the Gospel episodes conscious of their many concentric circles of context, from the immediate literary context to that of the metanarrative of the canon.

Revisiting Our Narrative Model (Finally) for Active Reading

In the preceding chapter we presented a model and method for analyzing the plot arc of a story. We may now add to this model the penultimate step of reading this story in light of its various concentric contexts as discussed above. This results in the following suggested pattern for reading Gospel pericopes well:

1. Isolate the Literary Unit
2. Read the Story Multiple Times
3. Identify the Setting and the Characters
4. Observe the Story
5. Isolate the Different Scenes
6. Analyze the Narrative:
   - Identify the Rising Tension
   - Identify the Climax
   - Identify the Resolution
   - Identify the Following Action/Interpretation

---

29. Hays, "Canonical Matrix," 55.

7. Think about the Contexts
- Acts, Cycles, and Literary Structures
- The Whole Gospel Context Including Intratextuality, the Fourfold Gospel Book, and Jesus's Death and Resurrection
- The Kingdom-Focused, Redemptive-Historical Context of the Whole Canon

8. Summarize the Pericope

The final stage, then, is to write a brief summary of the story, sensitive to its narrative flow, its characterization, and its various contexts as they affect its meaning. This paragraph requires careful thought and editing, but it will serve the interpreter well by forcing him or her to articulate what is most significant in this particular story. As discussed in the previous chapter, this précis, or summary, of the story should never *replace* the actual story, either in our reading, interpretation, or exposition, but it does point us toward a good interpretation/application of the story, which is, of course, the overall goal in the experience of these Gospel stories.

Reading Luke 7:1–10 Again

We may now return to our story from Luke 7 and fill out our analysis. It is appropriate that we consider the actual text again:

> After he had ended all his sayings in the hearing of the people he entered Capernaum. Now a centurion had a slave who was dear to him, who was sick and at the point of death. When he heard of Jesus, he sent to him elders of the Jews, asking him to come and heal his slave. And when they came to Jesus, they besought him earnestly, saying, "He is worthy to have you do this for him, for he loves our nation, and he built us our synagogue." And Jesus went with them. When he was not far from the house, the centurion sent friends to him, saying to him, "Lord, do not trouble yourself, for I am not worthy to have you come under my roof; therefore I did not presume to come to you. But say the word, and let my servant be healed. For I am a man set under authority, with soldiers under me: and I say to one, 'Go,' and he goes; and to another, 'Come,' and he comes; and to my slave, 'Do this,' and he does it." When Jesus heard this he marveled at him, and turned and said to the multitude that followed him, "I tell you, not even in Israel have I found such faith." And when those who had been sent returned to the house, they found the slave well. (RSV)

We are now ready to return to our analysis:

1. Isolate the Literary Unit—Luke 7:1–10
2. Read the Story Multiple Times
3. Identify the Setting and the Characters

4. Observe the Story
5. Isolate the Different Scenes
6. Analyze the Narrative:
   * Identify the Rising Tension—vv. 2–6a
   * Identify the Climax—vv. 6b–8
   * Identify the Resolution—v. 9
   * Identify the Following Action/Interpretation—v. 10

At this point we suggested that, based on the climax and resolution, the main point of this story likely concerns Jesus's authority and/or the faith of this non-Israelite centurion. Let's go on to the next stages and see how this idea might be confirmed and/or deepened by further analysis.

7. Think about the Contexts
   * Acts, Cycles, and Literary Structures
      In terms of immediate literary context this story seems to begin a new section, following some of Jesus's teachings that do not appear to be intimately connected with this particular story, except that this story could be seen as an example of the contrast pair in 6:46–49. The story that follows (7:11–17), however, is another demonstration of Jesus's authoritative and compassionate healing power. Together these two healing accounts, which take place as episodes in two different cities (Capernaum and Nain), serve as the reason for the reentry of John the Baptist into the story line. These healings and manifestations of Jesus's power lead John's disciples to report to him, resulting in John's own query to Jesus (7:18–23).
      Panning out more broadly, we can discern a structure of Jesus's healings and preaching that spans from 4:38–41 to 7:18–23, pericopes that both describe in summary form Jesus's healing of many people, as does one in the middle, 6:17–19.
      Looking back even further in Luke, we find yet another concentric circle of interest: reference to Isaiah seems to frame a larger section of which our story is a part. Particularly, the very beginning of Jesus's ministry, 4:14, is said to take place in Galilee, as the fulfillment of Isaiah's prophecy of good news coming to the poor, release of captives, and recovery of sight to the blind (Luke 4:18, from Isa. 61:1 and 58:6). The first healing miracle of Jesus then occurs in Capernaum, "a city of Galilee," as Luke informs us (4:31–37). What follows is preaching and healing all around Galilee and the calling of the disciples (5:1–11; 5:27–32; 6:12–16). Now, after much teaching Jesus enters Capernaum again and heals a non-Jew. To the inquiry of John the Baptist's disciples, Jesus responds by returning to Isaiah with language reminiscent of 4:14–19, quoting from

a compilation of Isaianic verses: "the blind receive their sight, the lame walk, lepers are cleansed, and the deaf hear, the dead are raised up, the poor have good news preached to them" (Luke 7:22, from Isa. 26:19; 29:18; 35:5, 6; 42:18; 61:1)—precisely summarizing the stories that Luke has just given us about Jesus's activity throughout Galilee.[30]

We may recall also at this point that this all takes place in the cycle of Jesus's ministry in Galilee (4:14–9:50), which is one of several large cycles in Luke, preceding his journey to Jerusalem (9:51–19:27) and his passion and resurrection (22:1–24:53).

Note that these observations about context come simply from scanning the surrounding stories, looking for similarities in structure, ideas, and wording. This is a function of reading closely and with a curiosity that assumes some coherency to the evangelist's choices.

- The Whole Gospel Context Including Intratextuality, the Fourfold Gospel Book, and Jesus's Death and Resurrection

Some of the observations in the preceding section inevitably bleed into this discussion as well. Our story takes place in a broader literary context going back to the very beginning of Jesus's ministry, with its emphasis on the fulfillment of the Isaianic prophecies and ministry in Galilee, with its association with gentiles.

But even more broadly, when reading Luke overall one of the themes that stands out is "salvation for all and healing." There are a great many words in Luke orbiting around the ideas "save," "savior," and "salvation." These words have a variety of nuances, including to rescue from danger and restore to safety and to cause someone to experience divine salvation. Intimately related is the idea of healing, which overlaps significantly. Luke also particularly emphasizes the universality of the gospel of salvation. When reading Luke, one gets the impression that Jesus's actions in this far-off corner of the Roman Empire are actually at the center of history: Jesus's genealogy is traced all the way back to Adam (3:23–38); his birth is set into the context of world history (2:1–2); and his saving work includes Jews, Samaritans, and gentiles, and reaches even to the outcasts and marginalized in society, such as the poor and women, who loom large in Luke's account. Luke's companion second volume, Acts, unpacks and illustrates this expansive view of salvation, based as it is on the rubric of Jerusalem, to all the world. Sensitivity to this intratextual theme in Luke's Gospel deepens the importance of this particular

---

30. We may observe that Matthew does the same thing, more succinctly and clearly, in Matt. 8–9, followed by the use of the same Isaiah references as a summary in Matt. 11:2–6. This seems more than coincidental, and either Matthew is following Luke, or vice versa, or they are both following some tradition that precedes them.

story, in which healing comes to a gentile and, even more outside the pale, a professional soldier of the empire that is oppressing the Jewish people. Jesus's statement, "Not even in Israel have I found such faith" proves to be a clue to a greater part of the story, footprints that mark a track to an understanding of salvation that goes beyond Israel.

When we consider this story in light of its placement in the Tetraevangelium, several interesting observations can be made. We can see first that this episode has a parallel twin in Matthew 8:5–13. This is clearly the same story with almost no differences and the identical climactic declaration, "Not even in Israel have I found such faith." However, Matthew also gives us Jesus's explanatory words that follow this declaration: "I tell you, many will come from east and west [i.e., outside Israel] and sit at table with Abraham, Isaac, and Jacob in the kingdom of heaven, while the sons of the kingdom will be thrown into the outer darkness; there men will weep and gnash their teeth" (Matt. 8:11–12). Although this dominical saying is not attached to the story in Luke, it seems to be an expanded explanation that is completely in accord with what Luke records for us and indeed helps us understand what Luke is saying. Moreover, Luke does give us these same sentiments and almost identical wording from Jesus in another place, in Luke 13:28–29, as the climax to Jesus's exhortation to enter the kingdom through the narrow door (13:22–30).

Mark does not record this story for us, though we can see similarities in the healing of the Syro-Phonecian woman's daughter, which appears in both Mark (7:24–30) and Matthew (15:21–28), but not in Luke or John. Both compassionate healings were done on behalf of another, were done from afar, involved some dialogue with Jesus, and most strikingly, were done for someone radically outside of Israel's pale.[31]

Also interesting, and somewhat unexpected, there appears to be another version of the same story, or at least a similar one, in John 4:43–54. This healing account also takes place in Capernaum in Galilee and emphasizes Jesus's authority in healing from a distance, at the exact hour. It also involves an "official," not identified as a centurion, and the healing is of this official's son, not his servant.[32]

31. In a tongue-in-cheek, biblically allusive way, Matthew particularly emphasizes the Syro-Phonecian woman's outsider status by calling her a "Canaanite" woman (15:22), an expression that is not contemporary like Mark's more geographical description but instead clearly recalls the Israelites' enemies when they entered the promised land.

32. Matthew's story could be read as referring also to a "son" (Greek *pais* could be rendered "son" or "servant"), while Luke's would seem to require instead a "servant" or "slave" (Greek

The story is also somewhat different in that the official comes to Jesus personally and interacts with him. Traveling servants play a role as in the Lukan account, but their part occurs after the healing, not before. Most important, though, the story emphasizes the same point about the believing or faith of the official.[33]

More briefly, when this story is considered in light of the Gospels' emphasis on Jesus's death and resurrection, we may observe the connection between Jesus's healings and the salvation that he procures through his passion. These are connected for us already by Isaiah 40–66, which forms the bedrock of Jesus's mission: Jesus's self-defined calling (Luke 4:14–20) comes as the fulfillment of the vision of the Second Exodus of Isaiah, which itself highlights the Suffering Servant and atoning death of the Servant on behalf of his people (Isa. 52:13–53:12). Thus, the saving and healing work that Isaiah foresees and for which Israel is longing is precisely how the evangelist(s) portrays Jesus's own work from beginning to end.

- The Kingdom-Focused, Redemptive-Historical Context of the Whole Canon

  We have now again inevitably moved organically from one section to another, and that is fine and good. These circles of context are tools to help us read deeply, not orbits that never cross for fear of collision. Related to what we have just observed about the Isaianic context is the kingdom focus and overall redemptive-historical thrust of the Scripture's message. One reason that Isaiah's prophetic vision is so important for the New Testament writers' understanding is because of its outward focus on the light of the good news ("gospel") coming to the gentiles. We see this theme coming to light here in Luke's brief story. It is a gentile who is commended for having faith in God's Servant Jesus, while Israel is given a sideways rebuke for not manifesting such faith.

  Also related at a general level is the fact that again Jesus's healings are themselves kingdom work. To heal anyone, and with such definitive authority, is a sign that God's redemptive-historical plan is now finally being consummated in Jesus's work.

8. Summarize the Pericope

---

doulos), which is why most translators understand Matthew's reference to be a "servant" in parallel with Luke.

33. Scholars do not agree whether this is the same story in a different form or a different story in similar form and with overlapping sentiments. It is fair to consider this question on both sides, but in accord with the arguments concerning "texts and history" and "behind the text" questions earlier in this book, the most important question is how the individual pericopes communicate and function in their own literary and canonical-theological context.

Our initial narrative analysis of this story suggested that Jesus's authority in healing and the faith of this gentile centurion were at the core of the main idea of the story as Luke has given it to us. The reflections above wherein we examined the series of concentric circles of context confirms, deepens, and expands this preliminary reading. Luke 7:1–10 is but one story of many that depict Jesus's compassionate and powerful healing authority in the context of his stated mission as the fulfillment of the Isaianic hope of the coming "day of the Lord." The "gospel," or "good news," Luke informs us at the beginning of Jesus's ministry, is that in Jesus the time of restoration and healing for *all* people, Jew or gentile, has come. Thus, the significance of this particular healing story takes on deeper hues when read in this broader redemptive-historical context.

We may summarize the story thus:

> Jesus manifests his power and compassion as the Isaianic Servant by miraculously healing a Roman centurion's slave. Jesus does so in response to faith in him, a faith that he commends as greater than what he has found in Israel. This commending of faith points us to the theme of God's universal redemptive plan at work here as he heals a gentile by faith, even while the Jews in the surrounding stories often fail to believe.

This summary paragraph is not perfect, I'm sure, nor does it tell us how to preach or teach this passage effectively. For the latter we must wait until the next chapter. Nevertheless, it does help us wrestle with the main thrust and idea of our passage, read in its context.

Conclusion

Even as a story gets its meaning from its greater context, so too these two chapters on narrative reading must be received in the framework of this whole book. This narrative analysis is not a magic trinket by which all Gospel texts may be subjugated nor a sword by which all exegetical, historical, and homiletical dragons may be slain. But it may be compared to learning a skill set at a technical college. A degree in automobile repair does not make one a good (or honest) mechanic, but most of us would rather take our car to such a trained person than a friend of a friend who might know something about radiators. It is true that a person without such training but who has spent his or her life around vehicles and car repair, and who is honest, is preferable to a random person off the street or a first-year automotive student. However, the ideal is to have both/and. Similarly, a lifelong practice of and dedication to wise Gospel reading is the most important qualification, and when combined with the skills of narrative analysis, offers great hope for effective interpretation.

As we conclude this second section of the book, it is important to note how this narrative model connects with the broader hermeneutical discussion of chapters 6 and 7. In the first instance we can observe that this narrative model overlaps most with columns 2 and 3 of the "Three Avenues" approach. That is, the method of reading presented above focuses on the story itself all the way up through a canonical reading. This is the heart of column 2 ("In the Text") and a portion of column 3 ("In Front of the Text"). In giving the eight-step narrative model above, I am not suggesting that we should ignore column 1 ("Behind the Text") or other broader theological aspects of column 3. Undoubtedly, the best reading of a Gospel pericope will be informed by historical background and grammatical-historical work, the stuff of column 1. Such information will be part of the close and careful reading of the story (step 4 in the model) and will often be obtained by reading good commentaries. I have not spelled this out in the model to avoid making it overly cumbersome and also because of my conscious emphasis on the plot line of the story itself (and its concentric circles of context). That is, we should preference hearing the story carefully as this narrative model emphasizes, but not to the exclusion of the insights found in column 1. A wise reading will, as argued in chapter 6, seek to hear the text in its fullness.

Similarly, we should also note how the narrative analysis tools of chapters 9 and 10 interact with the pluriformity of meaning in texts described in chapters 6 and 7. We may illustrate this interaction with the image of a seed-corn bagging table. One of the assorted enjoyable jobs of my younger days was in the agricultural business, where I spent some months running a large, two-story machine that sorted seed-corn kernels into different sizes and shapes. This task was necessary so that the planter attachment on the back of a tractor could be calibrated to release seeds at the proper intervals. Some corn seeds are flat, some are round, and they come in a variety of sizes. It is essential, then, that the planting machine be set to the right size so that one seed and only one will be dropped into the soil. Thus, the seeds must be sorted and marked according to size and shape and sold accordingly, hence the seed-corn sorting and bagging machine. The most important part of this machine was the final shaking table. It consisted of an angled platform that would gyrate and force the seeds along its declining plane. Holes of increasing size covered the table so that the smaller seeds would fall through the table earlier into the bags labeled for their size, and the larger seeds would only fall through once they reached the end of the table, into their own labeled bags. The point is that this shaking table enabled a discerning or judging of relative size and weight of kernels.

When we think of the manifold kernels of truth that we might discern and articulate from a story, we want to have some mechanism for determining which are weightiest. A great story communicates many good insights and truths, even if they are not all equally significant. The discussions in these two chapters, I hope, has made clear that the shaking table we should use in our Gospel reading consists of two parts: one is the logic of the text itself, and the other is the various circles of context. Thus the pluriformity of meaning in the texts stands, and there is value in many of the good things we might discern from a Gospel story. Yet at the same time, the tools presented in these chapters help us make judgments about the *most important things* to take away from the text—aspects of the story that are emphasized via the plot arc and that correspond with the larger context of the story itself.

As I observed at the end of chapter 9, the amount of work required to do what I have suggested in these two chapters is great, maybe overwhelmingly so. As an author writing to distant readers, I realize that it will be all too easy to passively read my instructions and suggestions in these chapters and go on happily reading the Gospels without adopting the practices outlined here. That's not the end of the world—as long as we are still reading the Gospels!

However, to quote C. S. Lewis's joyful horse as he stands on the cusp of the new creation, "Come further up, come further in!" This kind of slow, careful, and active reading of the Gospel stories can indeed extract a pound of flesh and hours of precious time, but it is a worthwhile investment, not a sacrifice. It is an invitation to a deeper and further experience of the Gospel stories. My own experience and the testimony of countless students of mine affirm that if we work at reading the Gospels well, we are paid back richly.

This does not mean that a reader will use all the detailed work presented above or that it will all be equally relevant in the final product of the sermon or Sunday school lesson. Indeed, I hope that much of this material will *not* appear there, or most hearers of those sermons and lessons will be lost in the details and leave hungry (and confused)! But the teachers/preachers/leaders who do this kind of work will have dug for themselves a deep well from which to draw living water for their people, both now and for years to come. Impactful preaching and teaching come from the overflow of insights from and experience with a passage, not the surface skimming that follows merely glancing over a text with the WSM method. Raking the surface of the ground of the text will produce only piles of leaves and dead grass; digging deeply may very much result in gold.

PART 3

Living in the Gospels House

11

Summing It All Up

Applying and Teaching the Gospels

Where We've Been

This penultimate chapter is really the last in the main argument and purpose of the book. The following chapter argues for the central role of the Gospels in the church's life, but in many ways it is an independent statement. This current chapter is intended to provide a summarizing overview of the ground we have covered so that we can conclude with a discussion of applying and teaching the Gospels. The review portion can be rather brief because chapter 8 has already summarized and drawn out the implications of most of the book. We have now added two practical method chapters on how to interpret the Gospels as stories. It remains only to consolidate all of this into a workable tool for us to use in wise Gospel reading. Then we can explore our final, practical topic of applying the Gospels to our lives and the lives of others.

It is appropriate that we once more reiterate our definition of what the Gospels are. *Our canonical Gospels are the theological, historical, and aretological (virtue-forming) biographical narratives that retell the story and proclaim the significance of Jesus Christ, who through the power of the Spirit is the Restorer of God's reign.* The nature of the Gospels as theological, testimonial, biographical history means that they make a claim on us, calling us to believe, trust, and follow Christ. Their purpose is not just information but transformation through the postresurrection witness to who God is for us in

Christ Jesus. This purpose means that our goal in reading must be the same: to hear God speaking to us in this way.

Jesus is given to us in the Gospels first as gift and then example. When reading the Gospel stories, these two ideas are helpful and important to keep in their proper order. We can approach the Gospel stories best through the categories of revelation and identification. The Gospels first reveal to us who God is in Christ and, second, call us to identify with the characters in the story as models to emulate in virtue or avoid in vice.

While it is helpful to read the Gospels from many vantage points—including historical background studies and using various critical theories—the most beneficial way of reading focuses on receiving the Gospels as stories, as theologically loaded and application-freighted narratives. Thus, chapters 9 and 10 provided insight into interpreting literary narratives and provided an analytic method focused on multiple circles of context.

We are now in a position to integrate the goal discussion from chapter 8 into our narrative model from chapters 9–10. After engaging in active reading using the eight-step model given in chapter 10, we should step back, scan the whole story, and ask the big questions of revelation and identification. An active reading of the text as outlined above should make the exploration of the revelation and identification rather easy; the main digging work has been done, one need only know how to articulate and describe what has been discovered. Thus, we might describe our overall reading strategy as consisting of two steps. The first is to read actively, and the second, to articulate the revelation and identification:

I. Read Actively
   1. Isolate the Literary Unit
   2. Read the Story Multiple Times
   3. Identify the Setting and the Characters
   4. Observe the Story
   5. Isolate the Different Scenes
   6. Analyze the Narrative
      • Identify the Rising Tension
      • Identify the Climax
      • Identify the Resolution
      • Identify the Following Action/Interpretation
   7. Think about the Contexts
      • Acts, Cycles, and Literary Structures
      • The Whole Gospel Context Including Intratextuality, the Fourfold Gospel Book, and Jesus's Death and Resurrection
      • The Kingdom-Focused, Redemptive-Historical Context of the Whole Canon
   8. Summarize the Pericope

II. Articulate the Revelation and Identification
   1. The Revelation of God in Christ
   2. Identification of Character Traits to Be Emulated or Avoided

Applying This to Luke 7:1–10

In the previous two chapters we examined the story of Luke 7:1–10 through this narrative-analysis tool for active reading. We may now also put on the bifocals of revelation and identification and read this text once more. As is often the case when applying this method, there is some overlap in what we discover in both steps I and II. That is, our careful reading and narrative analysis of this story already noted Jesus's compassion and power. These same revelations about who Jesus is are rightly reiterated at this second stage in our reading. This repetition of observations is a good thing and suggests that we are on the right track. The point of emphasizing the revelation at this later stage, even if it proves repetitive, is to safeguard us from a nonchristological or nonchristocentric reading of the story. In this particular pericope we should note that Jesus is revealed to us clearly as one who cares about people's needs, has the authority to heal (even from afar), and values and praises a faith response in him.

When we consider the category of identification, we find an overlapping and related emphasis. That is, the most important character trait to be emulated in this brief story is undoubtedly the *bold faith* of the centurion. Most of the speech in this story is devoted to emphasizing the centurion's very confident belief in Jesus's abilities, a faith that seems amazingly knowledgeable and full hearted; Jesus himself marvels at such confidence in him. At the human level this faith is undeniably what the evangelist is recommending to us as the right way of being in the world.

What about the other characters in the story? Many stories include other characters who serve as foils or bad examples and thus provide a contrast to the virtue commended. This seems to be the case here with the Jewish elders, who appeal to Jesus in a rather mechanistic rather than faith-based way—"This man has done good things for us, therefore you should heal him." This reading may not be entirely clear from reading only this story. Broader reading in Luke, however, would incline us to see the elders as the opposite of the centurion in his faith response. They regularly appear as characters who oppose Jesus rather than believing and trusting in him. If so, then the other identification aspect to highlight in this story is the mistaken belief and behavior in approaching God in such a mechanistic and legalistic way rather than by faith in God's undeserved compassion and goodness.

One can see, I hope, that the categories of revelation and identification find their content close at hand from the narrative analysis we have already done.

There will be a natural, organic connection between a close and active reading of the story and the more directed and personal move toward revelation and identification. In many ways these two steps, though different in focus, provide a mutual checking and reinforcing role. Reading actively will generally bring us quite close to the story's revelation and identification. And asking the revelation and identification questions stimulate further active reading.

Going Forward—Applying and Teaching the Gospels

We are now at a final and crucial stage in our overall quest to read the Gospels wisely: application to ourselves and subsequently to others through teaching, preaching, and soul care based on the Gospels. As argued in chapter 7, in reality meaning and application overlap coextensively (or nearly so). Thus, all our work to this point in discerning the thrust and emphasis of a Gospel story—its main intended "meaning," as it were—has already in large part been an exercise in application; we cannot ultimately separate meaning and application. An active reader listening to the text of Holy Scripture with a right posture is inevitably and rightly already applying the text to himself or herself, at least at the heart level of asking probing questions. This is the Spirit's work; the sense of conviction and openness to be convicted, corrected, guided, and consoled are Spirit-wrought applications of the text even while the reader is in the midst of identifying the climax of tension or considering doctrinal points of revelation. We can see that in the Luke 7 example above, the active reading and the revelation and identification are already bleeding into what we might traditionally call "application." Nonetheless, it is helpful conceptually and heuristically to consider briefly how to *apply* Gospel narratives in terms of method and potential pitfalls.

Although countless books and articles have been written on hermeneutics—either theoretical or practical—few authors and scholars have explored the method and theory of *application*. A brief mention is usually made in hermeneutical discussions, but it is at best quite cursory. The best teachers and preachers model the practice of application, but few can or do explain how one moves from analysis-meaning to application-meaning; it is usually something done intuitively and assumed to be a "caught rather than taught" skill.

Applying the Gospels

The most notable exception to this lacunae is the book by New Testament scholar and pastor (and that combination is the key) Daniel Doriani titled *Putting the Truth to Work: The Theory and Practice of Biblical Application*. We have had opportunity to mention Doriani earlier. But here at the end of our discussion, we will be wise to apply some of his insights to our own discussion of reading the Gospels.

Doriani emphasizes above all that in applying biblical narrative we must be God-centered. Whatever other points and applications we make from a text, "the prime responsibility is to discover the way God accomplishes salvation and reveals himself."[1] In this we must "dare to be boring," not tiring of proclaiming the main thing over and over: God's love, grace, and holiness.[2] This corresponds to my emphasis on revelation as the necessary first and foremost idea to take away from a narrative in Holy Scripture. Thus, when we move specifically to *applying* a Gospel story, our first and foundational point(s) of application should be about God and his gracious presence with us, not about human response. Human response will be important, but only once the God-centered focus is made explicit. To fail in this is to put the example before the gift and thus lose grace.

God-centered application statements often begin with imperative phrases such as "Know that God . . . ," "Expect God to . . . ," and "Hope in God because . . ." These may not seem as immediately practical as some other points of application, but it is essential that we start here and maintain this God-centered focus and feel.

For our example from Luke 7, we could offer application statements such as "Take courage in God's love of simple faith" or "Know that Jesus combines perfectly great authority and humble compassion." These statements are not all that we can and should say in applying this story, but we should start here before moving on to application points more focused on human response.

Doriani goes on to argue that once we have in place the God-centered thoughts—which will inevitably overlap from text to text, hence our need to be willing to repeat ourselves—we will find a great diversity of practical applications by considering the various ways in which people respond to God in the story.[3] This corresponds to our category of identification.

People today are no different from those in biblical times in their reactions to seeing God and his work: some respond with faith and belief; some are skeptical; some resist and rebel; some vacillate and avoid. Once we have established the God-centered point(s), we should make explicit application statements based on the various reactions of the characters identified in the story. From our Luke 7 story we might offer statements such as, "Because God loves simple faith, we should give ourselves over to a wholehearted belief in God's power and love for us," which reflects the response of the centurion. Or, "We should fight against our natural tendency to approach God in a mechanistic, business-transaction kind of way," which comes from the mistaken attitude of the religious leaders.

There is much more worth exploring regarding practical applications from biblical texts, and Doriani's extensive discussion is a must-read on this score. If

1. Daniel Doriani, *Putting the Truth to Work: The Theory and Practice of Biblical Application* (Phillipsburg, NJ: P&R, 2001), 168.

2. Ibid.

3. Ibid., 168–69.

possible I would provide a block quote of about eighty pages of his wisdom in this regard![4] He explores seven different ways in which texts generate applications, which when combined with four different kinds of questions people ask, result in twenty-eight different avenues for exploring the relevance of a text. These are not to be taken as a formulaic mechanism; rather they are different tools for identifying and applying the relevant points of a text.

This then leads us to a final comment about applying Gospel stories: There is no single right application. As argued in our earlier discussion, narratives never have only one point or effect or benefit. Rather a good story provides a map of the terrain of reality. Some points will be at a higher altitude and supply a richer view, but they are never the only view. It is wise to recognize the "hottest spots" on the thermographic map of a text lest we miss the most important things. But a place is not a point but rather a space to be occupied. The "meaning" of a story is necessarily manifold, even if we might identify some "meanings" as weightier than others.

This polyvalence of narrative meaning expands and grows exponentially when we seek to explore practical application statements from a story. When we run the diverse richness of a story through a grid of many potential questions and audiences, the result is a wide range of potential relevant ways in which a text can be applied. Granted, the best and wisest applications will be those that grow organically out of the soil of the revelation and identification of the text. But as with interpreting meaning itself, so too when exploring application statements, we must keep in mind that our goal is not backward-looking, archaeological excavation, but outward-focused, transformational exploration. Rather than seeking to find the one "right" reading or application (complete with its constricting anxiety about getting the singular "right" meaning), we should investigate different hearings or readings of a text. Some of these hearings will be closer to the main ideas and some less so. This is okay because meaning itself, and even more so, applied meaning statements, are in part generated by the questions and needs of the hearers. We might use the image of concentric circles once again, now applied to the various ways in which texts radiate application statements.

To revisit Luke 7 once again: in any particular, audience-specific reading of this story, we may choose to draw out and emphasize Jesus's power to heal, or instead his compassion, or yet again, maybe both. And we may explore the faithless response of the Jewish leaders and/or the great faith of the centurion, though probably the latter is weightier than the former. But beyond these things, we may also instead choose to emphasize God's care for all people, as exemplified in the hint in this story that God's grace is spreading to the gentiles, not just the Jews. Or at the same time, we might explore the virtue of humility, which the centurion exhibits in his dialogue with Jesus, a humility

4. Particularly helpful here are chaps. 4–6 of his book, 50–121.

that results from understanding Jesus's great authority. Or yet again, we could speak of modeling Jesus's own compassion for others, especially outsiders. These types of applications may not be on the closest rings of orbit around our narrative analysis of the text, but they are on what could be deemed fair trajectories from the text and should not be dismissed as inappropriate.

There is an art here and a necessary discernment that one can only gain through practice. Holy Scripture—most especially its highly "open" texts such as narrative and poems—invite many hearings and readings, and a pluriformity of meaning spills over into a wide range of doctrinal discussions and personal applications. This rich understanding of Scripture marks premodern and precritical reading (and much of contemporary preaching) in its strong intracanonical dialogue. The loss of this kind of figural, canonical reading represents a great deficit for the church. At the same time, listening carefully to the specific voice and thrust of the particular text that stands before us— with its main emphases of revelation and identification—is to be valued and sought. A good and wise reader keeps these opposing tendencies in balance and healthy tension.

With these comments about articulating the meaning/application of a text, we are now moving into our final area of discussion, how to most effectively preach and teach from Gospel stories.

Preaching and Teaching the Gospels

Most readers of this book are likely engaged not only in the study of the Gospels for personal reading and application but also in preaching and/or teaching from the Gospels in some type of church setting. Space does not permit me to provide a full exposition on how to preach or teach narrative texts effectively, so I must offer only a few notes on this matter.[5] Nevertheless, we should not consider a discussion of preaching and teaching the Gospels a mere bonus track on the "director's cut" of this book. Quite the contrary, preaching and teaching the Gospels is ultimately the reason for their existence and should not be relegated to an optional dessert on the menu of hermeneutical theory. I take guidance and courage here from the model of Augustine, whose one-thousand-year best-selling textbook on hermeneutics has for its final, climactic section, a lengthy discussion of how to preach.[6] Proclamation is always the goal of hermeneutics; otherwise we have missed the point of Holy Scripture and have failed to read it with the direction of its purpose.

5. Outstanding in this area is Bryan Chapell, *Christ-Centered Preaching: Redeeming the Expository Sermon*, 2nd ed. (Grand Rapids: Baker Academic, 2005). Also helpful is Joel Green and Michael Pasquarello III, eds., *Narrative Reading, Narrative Preaching: Reuniting New Testament Interpretation and Proclamation* (Grand Rapids: Baker Academic, 2003).

6. Augustine, *De Doctrina Christiana* 4.

Moreover, my personal experience repeatedly teaches me that only when I am preparing a Gospel story for preaching or teaching do I begin to feel a real ownership of the depth of the story, or better, its ownership of me. I have come to believe that this is a function of the particular questions that I am forced to ask when preparing a Gospel text and the pressure I feel to read and explain it in a theological and aretological way. Without this pressure it is all too easy to read the stories passively, with "objective" disinterest, and purely for information download. But reading the Gospels with theological and virtue-forming goals and questions—which I have argued correspond directly to the purpose and goal of the Gospels' existence—is the doorway into an impactful and applicable exposition of the text. At the same time, reading for the purpose of teaching and preaching to real people opens up great insights into the text.[7]

The steps of analysis given above take us far into the questions of how to preach or teach from the Gospels, at least in terms of the content of that preaching or teaching. That is, stemming from an active narrative and theological reading, the main ideas that present themselves to us from the text will be concerned with who God is in Christ and how the characters in the story serve as models for us. These will provide the main points—at least in terms of application—from our exposition of the story.

But when we consider the even more practical technique questions of how to preach or teach the Gospels, we encounter two outstanding subtopics to explore. The first is a framework for asking good homiletical questions. The second concerns how to structure a sermon or lesson from the Gospels.

FRAMING QUESTIONS

For many years I preached from narrative texts, stumbling upon an approach that, I gather, was generally effective and beneficial to my hearers. But from my side of the pulpit, it was somewhat haphazard and not driven by clear principles beyond homiletical technique. However, through my experience of teaching not only about the Gospels but also a narrative homiletics course, I discovered the practical wisdom of the approach offered in Bryan Chapell's *Christ-Centered Preaching*, and for the first time I understood a clear set of questions to frame my approach to preaching and teaching.

Chapell's widely read book on preaching provides a basic structure for asking the right kind of questions of a biblical text, focusing on how the text

---

7. J. I. Packer argues that right understanding of a text of Scripture entails proclaiming it since this is its very purpose: "The Bible being what it is, all true interpretation of it must take the form of preaching," because "Scripture is the God-given record, explanation, and application of God's once-for-all redemptive words and deeds on the stage of space-time history, and that its intended function is to 'instruct . . . for salvation through faith in Christ Jesus' (2 Tim 3:15)." J. I. Packer, "Preaching as Biblical Interpretation," in *Honoring the Written Word of God*, vol. 3 of *The Collected Shorter Writings of J. I. Packer* (Carlisle: Paternoster, 1999), 317. Thanks to Daniel Patterson for this reference.

reveals our brokenness and how it describes Jesus as the solution in every way. Chapell terms these the fallen condition focus (FCF) and the Christ solution (CS). When one goes to Holy Scripture with these categories, the texts open up in significant practical, personal, and spiritual ways, as they are intended to do. One can likely see how the FCF and the CS dovetail nicely with my own revelation and identification, though not coextensively and not with quite the same purpose.

Through my teaching experience using Chapell's material, in conjunction with that of others, I have modified these helpful framing questions into a threefold set: fallen condition (FC), redemptive solution (RS), and virtue formation (VF).[8] Thus, when moving from the analysis of the Gospel text to preparing to preach or teach it, it is extremely helpful to frame one's approach by asking these three questions in turn: What fallen condition does it reveal? How does God in Christ and the Gospel provide a redemptive solution to this condition of brokenness? And what virtue does this text exhort me to pursue as a result?

A few clarifying notes are in order. The fallen condition to be identified in a text can be a straightforward sin such as lust or rebellion or pride. But often it will be rather a condition of our brokenness or even simply limited creatureliness. Doriani describes it as "Any aspect of human nature that requires God's grace."[9] So, the FC might be fear or lack of understanding or anxiety. These are not "sins" in the normal sense of that word but rather are results of our broken humanity. The redemptive solution, then, stems from identifying an FC; the two dance in time together. The question to explore here is, in light of the FC being discussed, how God's grace in the gospel of Jesus meets and covers this need and brokenness. How is the gospel (perhaps presented elsewhere in Scripture as well) "the remedy for our experience of sin, immaturity, suffering, and brokenness" in this world?[10] This is the RS. Close to hand, then, is the most practical step of application for the hearers, the call to respond, or the virtue formation. This is not a call to mere behavioral change or an exhortation for humans to pull themselves together and simply "stop it!" It is not a message of "God did his part, now you do yours." Rather, the VF is the upholding of some particular God-ward and grace-based character trait in which we should as followers of Christ seek to grow. It is a virtue or habit of character that involves the whole person, one learned over time through trial and error and that has the mark of temperate wisdom. Classic Christian virtues include faith, hope, love, temperance, self-control,

8. Credit for the FC and RS language goes to Keith Johnson and the teaching materials he has developed for Campus Crusade for Christ. The addition of the third category is my own extension of this work.

9. Daniel Doriani, *Getting the Message* (Phillipsburg, NJ: P&R, 1996), 171.

10. Ibid.

and gentleness.[11] Identifying the VF from a text is usually much easier than detecting the deep-level FC and RS. The VF will typically be apparent as the tandem opposite of the FC (courage vs. fear, faith vs. hopelessness, etc.).

When we run our previous story from Luke 7 through this framework of questions, we can identify several potential FC-RS-VF sets. For example, we can note the universal human experience of sickness and death and the fear and anxiety that come with this. The Gospel speaks to this FC here in this particular passage through a miraculous healing. But of course, this is not all that can be said on this score. Not every sickness is healed, and even this sick servant did eventually die of something, even in faith. We must understand the ultimate RS here to be Jesus's healing of our sin-sickness (through faith) and ultimately the healing of our bodies through the resurrection (his and ours to come). The virtue to be inculcated here would be courage and hope, even in the midst of trial and despair.

Another framing of this text would emphasize the FC manifested by the Jewish elders' apparently mechanistic view of God and his blessings. This tendency toward relating to God in a legalistic, business-exchange way is a universal human problem and one the Scriptures constantly address. It is worthwhile to explore this as a fallen condition and then, digging more deeply, to ask what underlies this sin. That is, often there is a "sin beneath the sin" that pushes the FC deeper into the soul's experience. The tendency to relate to God in a legalistic way often has beneath it pride and self-reliance, which could be identified as functional FCs here. The gospel solution to this mechanistic approach to God is radical and beautiful. Indeed, this solution is at the heart of the gospel of grace: crying out to God in faith, not attempting to cajole or persuade him based on our goodness or behavior. This response is right at the center of the story, with its emphasis on the faith of the centurion in Jesus's power and compassion. The corresponding VF for this FC is the obvious pursuit of living by faith in God's goodness, not living in a legalistic way.

As these two examples show, we can likely identify more than one FC-RS-VF set and indeed we will often benefit from doing so. As with all the other stages of reading the Gospels wisely that we have explored, one must choose which to pursue in one's appropriation of and listening to the text. An abundance of meaning and application can be gleaned. When it comes to preaching or teaching the text, we are free to pursue and emphasize different FC-RS-VF frames, or even more than one.

One point of clarification is in order. These framing questions do not replace the revelation and identification categories, though there will inevitably

---

11. From the beginning I have identified the Gospels as aretological, or virtue forming, in goal. For more on how to understand Christian virtue or character formation, one may consult Doriani, *Putting the Truth to Work*, 97–113, 122–45; N. T. Wright, *After You Believe: Why Christian Character Matters* (New York: HarperCollins, 2010).

be much overlap. The FC-RS-VF framework helps one move from analysis to exposition. Thus, we can consider it as a third and final step in our overall method:

I. Read Actively
II. Articulate the Revelation and Identification
III. Use the FC, RS, and VF to Form a Message

Of course, one's experience of the story and its meaning does not follow such a linear, static course; rather one dives in and out and at various depths, exploring all aspects in a circular fashion. Nevertheless, it is helpful to demarcate some direction for crafting a message, after the more analytic work in the first two stages.

I spend much of my prep time in preaching and teaching from the Gospels simply with the Gospel text open with a pad of paper and pen at hand, prayerfully pondering these questions. Throughout the process of reading and studying the passage, I try to articulate both revelation and identification points as well as an FC, an RS, and a VF. Because discerning and expressing these points is my goal, I keep these questions in my mind (and in scribbles on my papers) from the beginning. I have found again and again that in preaching the time taken to explore the text with these practical and personal questions often makes a critical difference in the effectiveness of the message. That is, when I have not spent much time thinking about the fallen condition and redemptive solution of the passage—which is hard, spiritual, honest soul-searching work!—I find that my message and teaching tend toward mere information. It may be good, literarily astute, and doctrinally orthodox information, but it ultimately falls short of the faith-eliciting and virtue-forming goal of the Gospels. But when I am willing to read the text in these more personal ways—or better, to be read by the text—I find I have something meaningful and life-giving to offer my hearers.

CRAFTING THE FORM

Once all this work has been done, the content of the message is basically in place. What remains is the question of how to craft the form or shape of the sermon or lesson based on the Gospel passage. As any good homiletics textbook or practitioner will tell you, there is no one right, universal technique or form for a sermon, homily, or lesson. Indeed, run far away from any textbook or practitioner who *does* tell you this, especially when it is accompanied by the rhetoric that the only "godly," "right" way of teaching the Bible is verse by verse. This approach is insensitive to the wide variety of genres that comprise Scripture, many of which do not communicate in a "verse by verse" kind of way. Additionally, it confuses method with message and limits the creative process that communication is. Crafting a message or lesson is a function of the whole person and thus manifests the great diversity inherent in the variety of people created in God's (manifold) image. A strict cookie-cutter approach produces cookie-cutter (internet marketable) sermons and cookie-cutter Christians.

Rather, sensitivity to genre helps one read wisely and will make the communication of a Gospel text flow more easily. With biblical narrative, including Gospel narratives, noting the way that stories unfold along a line of plot development can help in crafting the message as well. That is, employing the narrative arc, with its building tension and final resolution, is a very effective way of preaching narrative texts.

Thus, one of the best ways to craft a Gospel text sermon is with the following form:

1. Introduce the situation—This introduction could set up the story you are about to retell, or it might be an illustration from life in general that gets at the same issue you are going to address from the Gospel story. Either type of introduction can work very well. In both cases you are setting up the actual story, just like a story's introduction does.

2. Retell the story—Most of the sermon or lesson should be given to a Technicolorized, illustrated, unpacked retelling of the story itself. Recall the video-store movie-date analogy. A condensed, summarized précis of the story violates its very existence and function; stories exist to be entered into and experienced! We should not just recap the given story as if it exists only to be discarded once its ideational content is extracted. It is a sad irony when narrative texts (which comprise the bulk of the Bible) are preached in a way that never invites or allows the hearers to *experience* the very reason the texts are given in this form. Our re-proclaiming of the Gospel text should consist mostly of a retelling of it *as a story*. All that the speaker or teacher is doing at this point is serving as a midwife to help deliver the story to the current hearers by explaining, clarifying, highlighting, and giving skilled interpretive insight. But the story itself should not be set aside or lost in the midst of supposedly teaching it. The speaker should labor hard at his or her own storytelling skills, developing ways to help the modern hearer feel the tension, anxiety, and uncertainty that the characters in the story themselves must have felt.

3. Draw out the main point(s)—After retelling the story, the teacher should then transition smoothly from this story to the "Why is this story here?" question. This is where the hard work of identifying the plot arc and the revelation and identification begin to translate and transform into pulpit and lectern fruit. The skilled speaker will help the hearers see how the story they have just experienced is related to what he or she has identified as the significance of the story, why it is here in the evangelist's intent and, moreover, God's design.

4. Apply the story with illustrations—With the story retold and the significance(s) identified, it is time for the framing questions of FC-RS-VF to appear, at least implicitly if not explicitly. This is not to say that elements of the FC or the RS cannot be present earlier; they may be in the introduction and/or the retelling of the story. In fact, Chapell suggests that it is often helpful to use the introduction of the message to present the FC. This method can work, though I generally prefer to save this element till the end. Regardless, we must move toward practical application at the conclusion of our message, and the FC-RS-VF pattern can be very beneficial to this end.

This is a simple and straightforward way to structure a narrative message and one that I have found to be very effective. It is not the only way, of course. You must make it your own. The greatest advantage of this approach is that it gives proper attention to the form and power of stories and thereby avoids the worst kind of moralistic preaching, wherein the message is simply about what the hearers must now do. Unfortunately, narrative texts are often presented in quite the opposite way. Thus, a verse or two of the story is read; the teacher explains what it means and applies this nugget, and then moves on to the next. As we saw in chapter 9, this is not how stories communicate. Moreover, the beauty and power of the *tension* of the story are lost. Instead, when preaching or teaching narratives such as in the Gospels, we have the wonderful opportunity to be glory- and grace-giving bards, singing out a story not of our own making, greater than any of us, and more than merely entertaining, a story that is life transforming!

An Encouraging Conclusion

This chapter has reiterated key ideas from the whole book and brought together still disparate parts into a (hopefully) coherent whole. This "whole" finds its consummation in applying the Gospels through preaching and teaching. If the Gospels (like all of Holy Scripture) have a transformative, disciple-making, faith-building goal, then to perform them in this way is to ultimately read them with wisdom.

All the steps that have now been presented for analyzing and applying the Gospels can seem, I realize, quite overwhelming. If the "read actively" and "articulate the revelation and identification" stages seemed like a herculean task, how much more the deeper hard work of forming and crafting a message from the Gospels!

Let me conclude this chapter with three images or illustrations that may be encouraging. The first image is that of building a sanctuary. When a young, vibrant church is growing and has a vision for more ministry and kingdom work, it will usually come to a point of needing to build a church or maybe expand the existing church building. When building and expanding, one would only foolishly build to meet the current need; rather a congregation must look ahead and, in faith to be sure, plan for greater and larger things in the future. That is, a growing 250-member congregation doesn't build in faith a sanctuary to fit 250. It builds a 500-seat facility, which provides the resources and opportunities for future growth and ministry. So too we may consider the labor outlined above to be a faith-based building for the future: one's own future ministry. The pastor or teacher or seminary student reading this book may feel that he or she does not have time to do all this work and may also wonder whether it is really necessary for good preaching or teaching from the Gospels. On the first score, I understand that in any given week or season it may be difficult, even impossible, to spend adequate time preparing. Indeed, this will always be the case! No careful preacher or teacher ever feels that everything is perfect and there is no room for deepening and improvement; there always is. So I am not suggesting a new law that requires all this analytical work be done for good teaching from the Gospels to occur. Our prep time will never be enough, and God will still be glad to speak through Holy Scripture to his people. But it is nonetheless a worthy goal to aim for this kind of preparation, in hopes that even falling short will still get us far. On the second matter of whether all this is necessary, the image of the expanded sanctuary comes to our aid. The preacher or teacher who builds a large and deep foundation of experience in the Gospels through the methods I have outlined here is one who is building in faith for his or her future ministry. That is, one is investing in one's own future potential ministry by sacrificing time now for future abilities.

The second image is a spectrum of different types of workers or artists. On one end of the spectrum is the technician, somewhere in the middle is the artisan, and on the other end is the master.[12] When we think of being Gospel readers and interpreters, we should use this scale to guide our goals. That is, much of exegetical method and homiletical skill is taught in a way that consciously or unconsciously promotes the development of technicians. The emphasis is on skill sets and methods producing certain tangible results. It is mechanistic, and although it works in part, it misses the higher goal. Thus, one could take all that I have presented above, diligently adopt it, and become a mere technician who performs the method accurately. On the other end, however, is the master teacher. We have perhaps heard this person on the radio or online or have read a book of his sermons. These are the masters; when you hear them preach or teach, you are transfixed. You can't even analyze the intellectual, rhetorical, and theological moves because they are so smooth and natural and convincing. This is teaching and preaching at its highest level:

12. Credit for this image initially goes to friend and scholar Sean McDonough, though which parts are original to him and which are of my own doing I can no longer recall.

transforming the hearer in a way that seems beyond method and skill sets. This is the ultimate goal for any teaching of the Gospels, though few of us will ever really be that kind of teacher. More realistic is the goal of being an artisan, always seeking to grow toward mastery. An artisan has certain skills and through practice has learned techniques and can perform them with ease, but he or she is being more than an efficient technician. Unlike that of the technician, the artisan's work evidences personality, variety, diversity, and creativity. This should be our goal in reading and teaching the Gospels: to be skilled through practice, but with joy to creatively explore them for ourselves and as guides to others.

The third and final image is another scale, and it is related to the preceding one. This scale or pattern of learning applies to all our education, including that of becoming a wise Gospel reader. It consists of four stages:

Unconscious Incompetence
Conscious Incompetence
Conscious Competence
Unconscious Competence

Whether it be playing golf, learning Portuguese, or becoming a competent reader of Holy Scripture, all human learning follows this pattern. At first a person is incompetent in some area of knowledge and skill but doesn't even know this is the case. Maybe he has some distant knowledge of what it means to be a financial planner or surfer or mountain climber. But until he begins to try these things, he is incompetent without being aware of it. The next stage is the beginning of all learning—and it is the most painful. It is the crucial and necessary step of becoming conscious of one's incompetence. I see this transition every day in my seminary teaching, especially in the area of biblical languages such as Greek. On the first day of class, everything is "all Greek" to my students, and by the end of the second week it has begun to dawn on them how clueless they have been. By the end of the first year, this sense has only deepened as they have been exposed to whole caverns of unsearched knowledge and as they come to try their own hand at developing Greek reading skills. This is the stage where most readers of this book will find themselves now if they take seriously what I have presented here. Any reader who has made it this far has likely grown in knowledge of how much more there is to know and how much more complicated the issues of reading the Gospels well are! And at the same time, many will feel overwhelmed by this same knowledge and experience. This is a painful place to be but take heart; this is the beginning of growth. This stage is the necessary and beneficial "cognitive dissonance" (to use a term from cognitive development theory) that precedes the next step, that of conscious competence.

As people continue to wrestle through the second stage of learning and seek to apply what they are learning, over time they will phase into the third stage. The golf pro initially completely deconstructed your swing, and for the next several months on the course, all you could do was think about the angle of your wrist and knees, and it wasn't very enjoyable. But now, finally, while you are still conscious of a few basic mantras when you are on the links, you are starting to see the benefit of straighter, more consistent, and controlled shots. You are not a pro, but you are growing. My hope is that this book will lead my readers from stage 1 into the beginnings of stage 3 through practice. Finally, for many areas of our lives (but not all), we will eventually reach the fourth stage, wherein we are free from being overly conscious, but we still function smoothly and well. Driving a car is a good example. At first driving is a scary and sensory-overloading experience, but few of us who have been driving for twenty-five years or more think anything about it. Quite the contrary, we may (foolishly) talk on the phone, eat a cheeseburger, and try to break up a spat between the kids in the backseat all at the same time—while driving with our knees. This does not mean that when reading the Gospels we should expect to reach a place where we can completely abandon the techniques and methods discussed above, even as we should not in driving! But it does mean that if practiced over time our reading can become more natural, even second nature, and thereby reduce our preparation time without sacrificing great benefit and effectiveness in teaching. My hope and desire is that this book might serve as a catalyst toward greater effectiveness and wisdom in reading and hearing the Gospels both personally and for the benefit of others in our lives.

12

The Gospels as the Archway
of the Canon

Canons in Canons, Keystones in Archways

Among those who study, teach, and write about the Bible, especially in the modern period, there is a label that is usually considered quite negative, restrictive, and a sign that one is no longer doing "good, solid, objective work": the label of having a "canon within a canon." This charge implies that one is not letting the whole of Scripture's data inform one's understanding, that one is overly and unduly favoring a particular passage or book or theological construct to the detriment of others, or, in its worst version, one is using some portions of the canon to the exclusion of other parts. As a result, other important ideas, books, and passages within Scripture are being neglected such that one's overall reading and understanding is provincial, imbalanced, and twisted.

This accusation gets its greatest traction in the hard ground of the scientific, modern study of the Bible. That is, if one's stated goal is to discern the objective and objectifiable true "meaning" of the text—a singular, historically reconstructed, unapplied object—then the greatest exegetical sin one could commit would certainly be to skew the data by too closely holding to one's pet ideas. Put this way, having a "canon within a canon" raises the emotional ire associated in a free, democratic society with anything that smells like nepotism.

Now certainly there is some truth in this concern, even if one is not a hermeneutical modernist. After all, in any hermeneutical understanding, reason and good argument certainly play an important part, such that an intentional skewing of the data or an unintentional assumption that wrongly controls one's reading in a myopic way should be avoided. For example, one might be rightly concerned about a stringent Lutheran reading that takes up, analyzes, and applies every text according to a strict law/gospel dichotomy. One might fairly object that a Lutheran "canon within a canon" that reads every text, whether it be Genesis 6, Hosea 2, or Matthew 5, solely through the grid of Pauline justification by faith versus justification by works may at times distort what God is speaking through these passages.

On the other hand, there is an unavoidable and harmless way in which we all do and should operate with a "canon within a canon." We would be quite mistaken if we extrapolated the "canon within a canon" charge to mean that there should be no constraining or guiding rule for our reading and understanding. The idea of canon itself represents a decision to hold some ideas, books, and texts as more important than others. To have a canon, as the church does, is to set aside or sanctify as Holy Scripture those very few writings out of the myriad things said and written about Jesus and God.[1] These writings are given special treatment and a special hearing, consciously so.

So our objection to a "canon within a canon" cannot be that some writings or theological ideas are given preference over others. This objection might be valid only if certain texts or ideas *within* the recognized canon are favored to the neglect of others in the canon. Yet even in this, as we learn from Irenaeus's idea of the *regula fidei* in his fight with the gnostics, the development of the canon alone was not sufficient. The church recognized the need for a "ruled reading," or *regula fidei*, that guided the proper reading even of the canonical texts.[2] Any heretic can use the same canon and come up with a heterodox reading by not letting key canonical ideas and texts shape and constrain others.

I raise this issue of a "canon within a canon" and its unavoidability because in this concluding chapter I want to make a bold suggestion: namely, we should have a conscious canon within the canon, that is, a group of texts that guide and direct our overall reading of Scripture. And if you've read this far, you are probably not surprised that I believe this group of guiding texts is none other than the fourfold witness of the Gospels. I am suggesting not that the Gospels in any way exclude or mitigate against the witness of the rest of the Scriptures, but that they do hold a privileged place and controlling position.

---

1. Cf. the helpful notion of the sanctifying of Scripture in John Webster, *Holy Scripture: A Dogmatic Sketch* (Cambridge: Cambridge University Press, 2003).

2. Joel Green, afterword, in *Reading Luke: Interpretation, Reflection, Formation*, ed. Craig Bartholomew, Joel Green, and Anthony Thiselton (Grand Rapids: Zondervan, 2005), 444–45.

I like to think of the fourfold Gospel book, or Tetraevangelium, as the keystone in a Roman archway. The keystone is essential for holding together both sides of the archway, and it alone enables the arch to stand and serve as an entryway. So too, the fourfold Gospel book functions as the portion of Holy Scripture that is so fitted and placed that it holds together the archway with its two sides—the Old Testament Scriptures on the one side and the rest of the New Testament writings on the other. The Gospel accounts complete and make ultimate sense of the story of God's work in the world as found in the Jewish Scriptures, while at the same time they serve as the fountainhead for the rest of the apostolic witness and teaching. The fourfold witness of the Gospels provides the guiding principle (even *regula fidei*) and lodestar for understanding and standing under all of Holy Scripture. The Gospels providentially and uniquely stand at the interpretive fulcrum for reading all of the Bible, for they focus on the revelation of God in Jesus Christ, the final Word spoken by God.

I have sought throughout this book to urge readers to rediscover the joy and power of the canonical Gospels. In this concluding chapter I will make a twofold argument—historical and canonical-theological—for the centrality of these Gospels within the canon and the church. Then we can explore what the implications that such a view might have for our reading of all of Holy Scripture and their function within the life of the church and its people.

Historical Argument

The first part of my argument calling for the keystone position of the Gospels comes from the central role they have always played in the church, at least until recently in some circles. This is a straightforward historical argument based on the widespread role that the Gospel materials (both the Jesus traditions and the canonical four) played in the formation of the church's identity, liturgy, worship, and teaching.

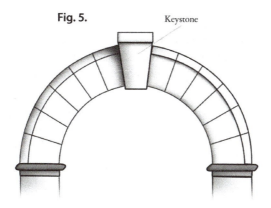

Fig. 5.   Keystone

Keepers of the Story

Among the myriad Bible materials for children one could find in our home, one cartoon series stands out: a thirteen-episode program called *The Story-keepers*.[3] The story line of the series centers on a group of Christians in Rome in the mid-first century and how they navigated their growing faith under the increasing persecution of Nero and the Roman Empire. There is plenty of action and lots of close calls as these Christians seek to promulgate the faith while barely escaping the always-present boots of Roman centurions ready to stomp out this new sect. The main protagonist is a Roman baker named Ben who coordinates an underground network of believers and who takes in several orphans and teaches them the way of the faith. This is where the "story keeping" comes in. Each episode continues the overall story line of the series in its post-Pentecost Roman context while also cutting away to cartoon segments from the pre-Pentecost Gospels in which the stories of what Jesus said and did are retold to the children.

The series is well done and apparently well researched. I enjoyed watching the whole series with my children. However, I began to be concerned by what seemed to be a form-critical assumption behind the project. That is, the series seemed to promote a view of the stories of Jesus as free-floating pericopes (a term that originated in form criticism) divorced from the canonical Gospels and their literary structure. Form criticism is particularly problematic with its assumption and conclusion that these free-floating Jesus traditions were the independent, localized creations of individual churches based on their own ecclesial and theological needs. This view is very misguided and does not correspond with the production, distribution, or use of the Gospels in the early church.[4]

But further reflection on the series made me realize that, without adopting the mistaken assumptions of form criticism, one can learn much from the insights of the fictional but true-to-life account of early Christianity found in *The Storykeepers*. That is, I came to realize that rather than having to dismiss this idea as form criticism, the notion that the early Christians were most interested in and driven by the stories of what Jesus said and did must be exactly right. The keeping and retelling of the Jesus traditions must have been the primary means of explaining and promulgating the faith, not only among children, but for all people. The explanation and proclamation of

3. *The Storykeepers* (Grand Rapids: Zondervan, 1995–97).

4. Many critiques of the form-critical approach have been leveled over the decades, and few if any Gospels scholars today would identify themselves with this methodology and approach, despite the lingering ghosts of some of its terminology and assumptions (e.g., "pericope" and "*Sitz im Leben*"). But definitive work at the historical level has now demonstrated that the free-floating approach to the Jesus traditions is untenable. See Richard Bauckham, ed., *The Gospels for All Christians: Rethinking the Gospel Audiences* (Grand Rapids: Eerdmans, 1998); and his *Jesus and the Eyewitnesses* (Grand Rapids: Eerdmans, 2008).

Christianity were always centered on who Jesus was and what he did as seen through his life and teachings. As Lee Martin McDonald has observed, "Given the fact that Jesus was the final authority, that is the final *canon* for the church, it would be strange if the early church had ignored the various witnesses to his life, ministry, death, and resurrection that were in circulation in the first two centuries of the church's life."[5]

This may seem obvious, but it is precisely this fact that has been so revolutionary in my own thinking and that I believe must be rediscovered in the church. Namely, in our own later and "downstream" ecclesial experience, the Gospels—and in reality, the life and teachings of Jesus—have often played only a secondary and subsidiary role. The real bread and butter of our Christian experience, teaching, and worldview formation has come from the Epistles and orthodox doctrine. A focus on the death of Jesus (and to a lesser degree his resurrection) has been the extent to which the Jesus traditions have impacted our thought, but even this is primarily mediated through the Epistles' summations and applications. The actual life and teachings of Jesus have not been the center. We take occasional forays into the Gospels at Christmas and Easter time, but few of us could say that the Gospels form the basis of our approach to understanding the New Testament; the Epistles often own this place.

But again, this certainly was not the case for early Christians—they were keepers and retellers of the traditions about Jesus. To be sure, they did so valuing eyewitnesses (contra form criticism) and following apostolic authority (which was clearly respected both in person and in letter form), but the stories about Jesus's life and teachings were always central to Christian identity and promulgation. Even during Jesus's own day, the things he said and did were so amazing and memorable that the stories immediately spread far and wide—to such an extent that very soon Jesus's movements were restricted by the constant crowds (Mark 1:45). What drew the crowds to seek out Jesus? Certainly it was the telling and retelling of the stories about what he said and did.

In fact, the dying off of the eyewitnesses and apostles was the primary impetus, it seems, for the final *written* production and distribution of our four canonical Gospels. One would be mistaken to think that only with the production of the Gospels did the Jesus traditions become dominant or influential. Quite the opposite: the dominance and influence of the stories about Jesus, combined with the tarrying of the Lord's expected return, led to the creation of the fourfold Gospel book as the authoritative, eyewitness-based account to summarize and codify the church's understanding about Jesus for future generations. To speak in marketing terms, the four Gospels were finally produced as the authoritative account(s) of what was already well known and cherished by the Christian populace. The Gospels did not suddenly "create a

5. Lee Martin McDonald, "The Gospels in Early Christianity: Their Origin, Use, and Authority," in *Reading the Gospels Today*, ed. Stanley E. Porter (Grand Rapids: Eerdmans, 2004), 150.

market" for Jesus traditions; they met the existing desire for this information and the practice of its adherents.

Along these lines, we must recall that members of this sect began to be called *Nazarenes* at times and *Christianoi* (Acts 11:26) at others precisely because they were followers of a particular man understood to be from Nazareth and who bore the title of the Christ. The sect was understood to be a religion based on a person, not just a set of beliefs, philosophies, purity regulations, and so on. As we have noted previously, this is one of the most striking differences between the two sisters born out of Second Temple Judaism, rabbinic Judaism and Christianity. The former is book and teachings based (*halakah* and *haggadah* both) while the other is person based. Rabbinic Judaism produces the Mishnah. Only Christianity, however, produces the genre of the *bios* to broadcast its faith, because Christians understand their entire faith to stand or fall based on this one man. Based on these assumptions, we see that the stories about what Jesus said and did—not just the theological implications of his death and resurrection—must have been at the core of all of Christian experience. Ancient biographies are the means through which one learns not only the teaching and philosophy of a great man but also how to emulate the person's life. This is what the early Christians must have cared most about.

Thus even though the epistolary literature of the rest of the New Testament canon predates most of the Gospels, *the Jesus traditions* in oral forms (and some written; cf. Luke 1:1–4) that were eventually codified in the four eyewitness Gospels and the Tetraevangelium book *must have been the main avenue of propagating the new faith as well as the focus of its teaching, reflection, and worship experience.* Although this seems an unassailable, logical assessment, we may fairly ask whether historical evidence from the literature of the early church supports it. The answer, I believe, is a resounding yes.

Witnesses to the Centrality of the Jesus Traditions and Gospels in the Early Church

The most obvious witness to the early church's focus on the life and teachings of Jesus is the fact that it produced, valued, and disseminated four lengthy biographies of him.[6] Contra Bultmann and others who would understand Paul and the church as focusing on mystical union with a "resurrected" Christ divorced from the person of Jesus, the historical Jesus and what he said and did were of utmost importance to Christians from the beginning. As Robert Kysar rightly

---

6. I have not spent time in this book arguing for the validity of these four canonical Gospels over other possible contenders, because, in addition to the consistent testimony of the church to this effect, the historical arguments for these four Gospels and not others are very strong. I would highly recommend the clear and thoughtful arguments to this effect in C. E. Hill, *Who Chose the Gospels? Probing the Great Gospel Conspiracy* (Oxford: Oxford University Press, 2010).

queries, reflecting on the Gospel of John, "the simple fact that the evangelist has chosen to express himself through the means of a gospel indicates that there is a real historical human life at the root of the central character of his witness. If flesh is irrelevant to the evangelist or if the revealer in no sense really took upon himself fleshly existence, why did the evangelist write a gospel?"[7]

We may also note that the dominance of the Jesus traditions is apparent from their frequent appearance throughout the rest of the New Testament documents. We will return to this point more fully below when discussing the theological and canonical argument I am making here. But for now, we can simply note that the Jesus traditions, which were eventually codified into our canonical Gospels, were clearly informing and influencing the epistolary authors. The apostles assume knowledge of the Jesus traditions when they write to the churches, and they all allude in varying degrees to aspects of Jesus's life and teachings. One can think of the obvious influence of something very similar to the Sermon on the Mount on James and the many allusions to the Gospels (again, probably especially Matthew) in 1 Peter. And when Paul applies the practice of the Lord's Supper to the matter of disunity in the Corinthian churches (1 Cor. 11:17–34), he describes it not as if it were a new idea but rather reiterates what the Corinthians had already been taught and applies it to their current poor practice.

Again, we will return to these reflections below. The historical argument to be made at hand particularly concerns whether there is evidence *outside* the canon in the early church for the use of the Gospels in such a way that would support my keystone-role thesis.

The Centrality of Gospel Materials in Early Christian Literature

We can begin with the evidence from manuscript production and transmission. This line of inquiry clearly indicates that the Gospels played the predominant role in the book-loving and book-producing first-century Christianity. In chapter 1 I mentioned the work of David Trobisch and the data he presents concerning the binding together and dissemination of the four-part Gospel book in the manuscripts.[8] Similarly, in his *Introduction to the New Testament Manuscripts and Their Texts*, David Parker observes:

7. Robert Kysar, *The Fourth Evangelist and His Gospel: An Examination of Contemporary Scholarship* (Minneapolis: Augsburg, 1975), 191, quoted in Burridge, *What Are the Gospels? A Comparison with Graeco-Roman Biography*, 2nd ed. (Grand Rapids: Eerdmans, 2004), 249.

8. David Trobisch, *The First Edition of the New Testament* (Oxford: Oxford University Press, 2000). Lee Martin McDonald also observes that the canonical Gospels "have the place of priority in all of the surviving lists and catalogues of Scriptures in the fourth and fifth centuries and generally in the order currently found in our New Testaments." McDonald, "The Gospels in Early Christianity: Their Origin, Use, and Authority," in *Reading the Gospels Today*, ed. Stanley E. Porter (Grand Rapids: Eerdmans, 2004), 152.

The Four Gospels, the Tetraevangelium, is *the* book of Christianity—not four books, but one codex. Such manuscripts comprise more than a half of all continuous-text Greek copies of New Testament writings. In every ancient language of Christianity, copies of the Gospels predominate among what survives. And in case this preoccupation is seen as an ancient phenomenon, be it noted that the Gospels in these ancient languages are traditionally far better served with editions and results of research than is any other part of the New Testament. Moreover, more editions of the Gospel manuscripts have been published, in facsimile or in some other form.[9]

This central role of the Gospels is apparent not only from this indirect evidence of the dominance of the Gospels as manuscript artifacts but also from explicit statements made by many church fathers. For example, in *Against Heresies* (ca. AD 180) Irenaeus describes the four Gospels as being the four pillars of the church. His poetic words are worth recording at length:

> The Gospels could not possibly be either more or less in number than they are. Since there are four zones of the world in which we live, and four principal winds, while the Church is spread over all the earth, and the pillar and foundation of the Church is the gospel, and the Spirit of life, it fittingly has four pillars, everywhere breathing out immortality and revivifying men. From this it is clear that the Word, the artificer of all things, being manifested to men, gave us the gospel, fourfold in form but held together by one Spirit. As David said, when asking for his coming, "O sitter upon the cherubim, show yourself." For the cherubim have four faces, and their faces are images of the activity of the Son of God. For the first living creature, it says, was like a lion, signifying his active and princely and royal character; the second was like an ox, showing his sacrificial and priestly order; the third had the face of a man, indicating very clearly his coming in human guise; and the fourth was like a flying eagle, making plain the giving of the Spirit who broods over the Church. Now the Gospels, in which Christ is enthroned, are like these.[10] (3.11.8)

While the modern mind is not accustomed to this kind of figural analogy argument and may be inclined (and trained via the Enlightenment) to dismiss it, we must not miss the more important point here: the fourfold Gospel is

9. David Parker, *An Introduction to the New Testament Manuscripts and Their Texts* (Cambridge: Cambridge University Press, 2008), 311. I was alerted to this quote by Michael Bird, who goes on rightly to observe, "Though Protestants, esp. those of the evangelical and reformed variety, have a special affection for Paul, that should never interfere with the special and devout attention that Christians have for the story and teaching of Jesus." *Euangelion* (blog), http://euangelizomai.blogspot.com/2010/04/four-gospels-as-one-book.html.

10. Among other things, we see here a very early example of the association of each of the Gospels/evangelists with a particular animal, a tradition that will become nearly universal in its application in sacred art, architecture, and manuscript illumination. In fact, the predominance of images of the four evangelists and their symbols in church architecture and art is another bit of evidence for the high value the church has always placed on the Gospels.

central to the life of the church because Christ is enthroned in it as nowhere else.

Similar sentiments can be found in the opening remarks in Origen's commentary on the Gospel of John (ca. AD 231). Instead of using a four winds/ four pillars analogy, Origen speaks of the biblical idea of "first fruits." After reflecting on the meaning of this important idea, he suggests that those who dedicate themselves to the study of Scripture are the spiritual version of Israel's priests, with Jesus as the high priest (*Commentary on John* 1.3). It follows, then, that those dedicated to understanding Jesus and the Scriptures must start with the first fruits of the Scriptures, the Gospel book:

> Now our whole activity is devoted to God, and our whole life, since we are bent on progress in divine things. If, then, it be our desire to have the whole of those first fruits spoken of above which are made up of the many first fruits . . . in what must our first fruits consist . . . but in the study of the Gospel? For we may venture to say that the Gospel is the first fruits of all the Scriptures. Where, then, could be the first fruits of our activity, since the time when we came to Alexandria, but in the first fruits of the Scriptures? It must not be forgotten, however, that the first fruits are not the same as the first growth. For the first fruits are offered after all the fruits (are ripe), but the first growth before them all. Now of the Scriptures which are current and are believed to be divine in all the churches, one would not be wrong in saying that the first growth is the law of Moses, but the first fruits the Gospel. For it was after all the fruits of the prophets who prophesied till the Lord Jesus, that the perfect word shot forth. (*Commentary on John* 1.4)

Some might read Origen's reference here to the "Gospel" as the general message about Jesus and the new covenant. But the following sections of his argument make clear he is distinguishing the four Gospels here—or better, the Gospel book—from the rest of the New Testament canon (*Commentary on John* 1.5–12). He observes that some might refer to the entire New Testament as "Gospel," but it is the four that are most clearly the "Gospel" and the first fruits, because they narrate to us the arrival of the promised good thing (1.7), Jesus, who is himself the Gospel (1.10).[11] Thus, once again we see clearly that in the early church it was understood that the Tetraevangelium, received as the Scriptures, plays the consciously central role in understanding all the Scriptures.

Another important early interpreter, Cyril of Alexandria, also argues for the utmost importance of the Gospels. He writes that "all Scripture, indeed,

---

11. Origen also takes the analogy one step further to argue that in the first-fruit Gospel book, the Fourth Gospel is the first fruit above all (1.6; 1.14). For more on Origen's use of Scripture in the church, see Ronald Heine, *Origen: Scholarship in the Service of the Church* (Oxford: Oxford University Press, 2011), esp. 77–78, where he discusses Origen's view of the central role of the Gospels.

is inspired of God; but this is especially true of the proclamations in the Gospels," using Hebrews 1:1–2 as the proof text.[12] Similarly, Eusebius of Caesarea intimates that the Gospels were the primary instruction for early Christian catechumens. In his commentary on Psalm 22 (LXX), he says that the "grass" and "water" of the psalm are the "holy gospels," which are like "food" for the catechumen, who has yet to be baptized and thus cannot yet partake of the Eucharist.[13]

Going back before Irenaeus, Origen, Cyril, and Eusebius, we find more evidence for the dominant and authoritative use of the Gospels in some of the earliest postcanonical literature, from the early second century. For example, the well-known but mysterious and at times peculiar work known to us as the *Didache* (ca. AD 100) makes constant reference to Jesus's teachings.[14] When one reads this little document, the overwhelming impression is that it is a pastiche of well-known and well-worn Jesus traditions. Nearly every line can be traced to some Gospel passage, and those that cannot are usually somewhat quirky and provincial statements.[15] Additionally, several times this book of instructions for the church refers explicitly to its source being "the gospel" or "the Lord's Gospel" (11.3; 15.3–4). A good case can be made that these are not just references to the Jesus traditions in general but often to Matthew itself. For example, something nearly identical to Matthew's "Lord's Prayer" (Matt. 6:9–13) is the basis for the Didachist's instructions to the church on how to pray (*Didache* 8.2). The overall point here is that once again, in a very early Christian document, one cannot deny the dominance and centrality of the Jesus traditions as the conscious source to which earliest Christianity looked for its understanding and practical instruction.

In the collection of writings generally known as the Apostolic Fathers[16] the Jesus traditions and the canonical Gospels appear in a variety of ways, but throughout it is apparent that the Gospels are well known, highly regarded, and well used.[17] Although the Apostolic Fathers do not offer detailed or sustained

12. From his twenty-ninth homily on Luke, repeated again in his fifty-second homily. Both can be accessed in English translation at http://www.tertullian.org/fathers/cyril_on_luke_00_eintro.htm.

13. I am indebted to Matthew Crawford for these references to both Cyril and Eusebius.

14. For general works on the Didache, one may consult Kurt Niederwimmer and Harold Attridge, *The Didache: A Commentary*, Hermeneia (Minneapolis: Augsburg Fortress, 1998). In recent years the dating and shaping of the Didache have been debated again, and while there is no consensus, many would agree that the origins of the book go back to the first century, while the final form likely comes from the second century.

15. For example, in 8.1 we are told that our fasts are not to be identical with the hypocrites. "They fast on Mondays and Thursdays; but you should fast on Wednesdays and Fridays."

16. Which books should be included in this categorization is not entirely clear. Recent collections and translations can be found in Michael Holmes, *Apostolic Fathers: Greek Texts and English Translations*, 3rd rev. ed. (Grand Rapids: Baker Academic, 2007), and Bart Ehrman, *The Apostolic Fathers*, vols. 1 and 2 (Cambridge, MA: Harvard University Press, 2003).

17. Murray Smith does a good job of succinctly addressing the problems associated with identifying specific sources of quotes and allusions to the Gospels in the Apostolic Fathers. Murray

commentary on the Gospels, the gospel materials obviously are very important. For example, in the early document called *1 Clement*, the author quotes "the Holy Spirit" as giving us the words of Jeremiah 9:23–4 and 1 Samuel 2:10 but then goes on to say, "Most of all, let us remember the words of the Lord Jesus, which he spoke as he taught gentleness and patience." Following then is an amalgamation of quotes from Matthew 5:7; 6:14; and 7:1–2 (parallel Luke 6:31, 36–38).[18] Likewise, in 46.7–8 Clement exhorts his readers to "remember the words of Jesus our Lord, for he said . . ." with words apparently from Matthew 26:24 // Luke 17:1–2. There are also assorted allusions and references throughout this letter to Gospel materials, whether from oral or written tradition.[19]

This is but one example of the pervasive reference to the Gospels in the Apostolic Fathers. Though not as explicit as later writers, they "weave gospel traditions into the fabric of their works—often without even acknowledging the source—and use them, as Joseph Trigg notes, as a kind of 'specifically Christian language.'"[20]

Additional, less direct evidence for the influence of the Gospels in the early church comes from observing how a wide variety of other Gospel-derived works developed in the second and third centuries. That is, because of the dominance and widespread use and interest in the Gospels and their subject, Jesus, both orthodox and heterodox groups begin to produce a substantial amount of literature that is clearly Gospels dependent. On analogy we might compare this to the numerous derivative materials that a phenomenon like the Harry Potter books has produced as compared to the unlikely prospect that the book in your hands now will result in a movie contract, a Broadway musical, action figures, an amusement park, or a spate of books about it. Widespread popularity produces imitation.

And so it was, we can see, with the tendency in early Christianity to produce both a multiplication of apocryphal Gospels as well as Gospel-derived harmonies. Alternative, "apocryphal" Gospels such as the Gospel of Thomas, the Gospel of Peter, the Protoevangelium of James, the Gospel of Judas, and others come from a variety of provenances, dating anywhere from the second century onward, and most are apparently dependent on the canonical Gospels.[21] At the

---

Smith, "The Gospels in Early Christian Literature," in *The Content and Setting of the Gospel Tradition*, ed. Mark Harding and Alanna Nobbs (Grand Rapids: Eerdmans, 2010), 199–207.

18. *1 Clement* 13.1–2. Translation from Michael Holmes, *The Apostolic Fathers: Greek Texts and English Translations*, 3rd ed. (Grand Rapids: Baker Academic, 2007).

19. Examples include Gospel material references in *1 Clement* 24.5, 48.4, 49.6, and others. Also in many other places the life and death of Jesus are simply referred to as a foundational reality, apart from specific allusions to Gospel materials, such as 16.1–17 and 49.6.

20. Murray Smith, "Gospels in Early Christian Literature," 203, quoting Trigg.

21. Ibid., 189–90. The standard collection of the apocryphal Gospels still remains that of Wilhelm Schneemelcher, *New Testament Apocrypha*, vol. 1, *Gospels and Related Writings*, rev. ed. (Louisville: Westminster John Knox, 2006). Much work has been done recently on several of these ancient documents, and there is regular debate about the dating, origin, and meaning of

same time, the tendency to produce harmonizations based on the four canonical Gospels is also found multiple times, most famously in Tatian's *Diatessaron*,[22] and down to the present day. Clearly it is the popularity and widespread use of the Gospels that results in both of these alternative tendencies.

THE CENTRALITY OF GOSPEL MATERIALS IN EARLY CHRISTIAN WORSHIP

In addition to the predominance of the Gospels in early Christian literature, we can also observe the role that the Gospels played in the worship of the earliest church. To this day the reading of the Gospels in church services remains an important and revered part of the liturgy. For example, in the Scottish Episcopal tradition, a separate portion is given to the lectionary reading from the Gospels, in addition to the New Testament and Old Testament readings. The same is true for other liturgical traditions, including the Eastern Orthodox. In the Roman Catholic tradition the homily is generally expected to be based on the Sunday's Gospel reading. These traditions are rooted deep in history, as our examination of the role of the Gospels in early Christian worship will show.

We can and should address the role of the Gospels in early Christian worship because it is in the everyday, non-council-level practice of Christianity that we can glimpse what ordinary Christians valued and practiced.[23] We are addressing here not the high-level, polemical discussions about which books were canonical and which view of Christ's nature was orthodox but rather the daily reproduction and reenactment of the Christian life and the role the Gospel materials played in this.

---

each of these alternative Gospels. On the knowledge and use of the canonical Gospels in a wide variety of early noncanonical documents, see the survey in Hill, *Who Chose the Gospels?* 151–206.

22. A standard work on the *Diatessaron* is W. L. Petersen, *Tatian's Diatessaron: Its Creation, Dissemination, Significance, and History in Scholarship* (Leiden: Brill, 1994). McDonald notes that "the influence of Tatian's *Diatessaron* was known as far to the east as China and as far to the west as England and was cited authoritatively as recently as the fourteenth century." McDonald, "Gospels in Early Christianity," 175. Murray Smith observes, "Tatian's Diatessaron, composed c. 170, presupposes both that its author had access to the four canonical gospels, and that he considered them authoritative in some way, even if his work sought to surpass the four gospels by resolving their differences." Smith, "Gospels in Early Christian Literature," 194.

23. Larry Hurtado remarks how puzzling it is that many scholars of early Christianity fail to see the importance of early Christian worship practices for understanding the history and development of the faith. In the ancient world worship was seen "as the characteristic and crucial expression of one's religious orientations and commitments." Evidence of this is seen in the basis for much of early Christian persecution, which was prompted not so much by unacceptable doctrinal positions as by Christians' refusal to conform to cultic practices and gestures in Roman society. Thus, to understand early Christianity historically we must recognize as central "the devotional practices and scruples of Christians." Larry Hurtado, *At the Origins of Christian Worship: The Context and Character of Earliest Christian Devotion* (Grand Rapids: Eerdmans, 1999), 2–3.

This kind of information is then necessarily more difficult to access because it is assumed and not often addressed directly and not often in writings that have been preserved as significant. But we do have many hints at what early Christian worship looked like, and we find therein a key role for the Gospel materials.[24]

One of the most important keyhole views into early Christian worship comes from a well-known quote from Justin Martyr in his *First Apology* (ca. AD 150). He writes:

> And on the day called Sunday, all who live in cities or in the country gather together to one place, and the memoirs of the apostles or the writings of the prophets are read, as long as time permits; then, when the reader has ceased, the president verbally instructs, and exhorts to the imitation of these good things. Then we all rise together and pray, and, as we before said, when our prayer is ended, bread and wine and water are brought, and the president in like manner offers prayers and thanksgivings, according to his ability, and the people assent, saying Amen. (*Apology* 1.67)

This is a fascinating and important account of what early Christian worship assemblies looked like, in apparently widespread practice by at least the mid-second century and likely reflecting an early time.[25] Just before this quote, Justin also mentions the sharing of wealth among the needy within the congregation, and in the preceding chapter, there is a fuller discussion of the partaking of the Eucharist mentioned here in passing.[26]

What stands out as central is the function that the reading of the Gospels plays in the assembly. Scholars have noted that Judaism and its daughter Christianity are unique relative to Greco-Roman and other ancient religious practice in that they are religions in which a Holy Scripture became the central focus.

---

24. Paul Bradshaw, *The Search for the Origins of Christian Worship: Sources and Methods for the Study of Early Liturgy* (Oxford: Oxford University Press, 1992), cautions us that the evidence for a comprehensive reconstruction of early Christian worship is too slim. Yet D. Moody Smith is certainly right that the assumption of the Gospels' use in public reading and liturgy is sound. Smith, "When Did the Gospels Become Scripture?" *JBL* 119, no. 1 (2000): 5–6n10.

25. As Murray Smith notes, "There are no hints in Justin's account that the practice was a recent innovation; it may well have been characteristic practice amongst the churches for decades." Smith, "Gospels in Early Christian Literature," 198. Hengel says that Justin's form of liturgy represented here "goes back a long time before Justin, since for him it is already recognized Christian usage. It may have been the case at least for Asia Minor, Rome and the rest of the West." Martin Hengel, *The Four Gospels and the One Gospel of Jesus Christ*, trans. John Bowden (Harrisburg, PA: Trinity Press International, 2000), 163. D. Moody Smith concurs: "Justin's description implies that they were functioning as scripture although neither term (Gospels or scripture) is used. Quite possibly this practice was established well before the time of Justin." D. Moody Smith, "When Did the Gospels Become Scripture?" 5.

26. *Apology* 1.66 is concerned completely with the Eucharist and its practice, and we may also note that in this regard the Gospels are mentioned explicitly as the source of this practice: "For the apostles, in the memoirs composed by them, which are called Gospels, have thus delivered unto us what was enjoined upon them," followed by a quote from Luke 22:19.

Bernhard Lang observes that "in the ancient Mediterranean and Middle Eastern world, only the Jews compiled sacred scriptures and instituted a ritual that features their recitation, translation, explanation, and homiletic elaboration."[27] This is not to say that Judaism and Christianity appropriated this characteristic in the same way. Quite the opposite as observed above, Christianity became about a person, while Judaism remained Torah-centric.[28] Nevertheless, the reading of the Scriptures, here especially those concerning the person of Jesus, are clearly central. Similarly, in his work on early Christian worship, Oscar Cullman argues that the preaching of the early church was concerned with tracing "the history of salvation from the Old Testament to the event of Christ in the present."[29] It is reasonable to assume that the Gospel materials play a major role in this mode and manner of preaching, which sees its "endgame," or telos, in the person of Jesus. This kind of preaching certainly finds encouragement in the way that Jesus taught his disciples to read the Jewish Scriptures, according to Luke 24:27. This practice continues clearly in the second and third centuries, as Christian preachers continued to witness that Christ is the fulfillment of the Law and the Prophets. As Hughes Oliphant Old remarks, "This was the heart of the earliest Christian preaching."[30]

This public reading of the Gospels that Justin mentions in addition to the Jewish Scriptures speaks volumes about the high regard for the Gospels as Scripture and for their central role in teaching the essence of Christianity as instruction toward "the imitation of these good things."[31] This practice reflects the understanding that the Gospels are the means of divine revelation as they focus on the final Word spoken by God, Jesus Christ. Martin Hengel observes:

It is interesting that Justin here already mentions the Gospels before the prophetic writings, i.e., the Old Testament, which was understood throughout as

27. Bernhard Lang, *Sacred Games: A History of Christian Worship* (New Haven: Yale University Press, 1997), 139–40.

28. In addition to sources referenced earlier, we may note the work of Hurtado, who argues persuasively for the fundamental christocentricity of early Christian worship. See Larry Hurtado, *Lord Jesus Christ: Devotion to Jesus in Earliest Christianity* (Grand Rapids: Eerdmans, 2005).

29. Oscar Cullman, *Early Christian Worship*, trans. A. Stewart Todd and James B. Torrance (1953; Philadelphia: Westminster, 1978), 12.

30. Hughes Oliphant Old, *The Reading and Preaching of the Scriptures in the Worship of the Christian Church*, vol. 1, *The Biblical Period* (Grand Rapids: Eerdmans, 1998), 251.

31. Smith observes, "Significantly, the fact that the 'Memoirs of the Apostles' (= gospels) were being read in worship, in concert with the prophetic literature, speaks volumes for the status accorded to the gospels, at least in the Christian communities known to Justin." Murray Smith, "Gospels in Early Christian Literature," 198. C. E. Hill concludes similarly, and he does a thorough job of examining the evidence for Justin's knowledge, use, and high opinion of the four canonical Gospels and none others. See Hill, chap. 6, "Preaching and Teaching the Gospels: Justin Martyr and the Apostles' Memoirs," in *Who Chose the Gospels?* As Mary Ann Donovan also notes, Justin "gives evidence that by the mid-second century the worshipping community used the gospels liturgically (thus as Scripture)." Quoted in Hill, *Who Chose the Gospels?* 149.

a prophetic work focused on Christ. One might almost assume that already in his time in Rome the reading of the Gospels occupied a role like that played by the Torah of Moses in Jewish worship, and that this reading had already had such a role for a considerable time. . . . The designation "reminisces of the apostles," skillfully chosen in this particular context, presupposes that the Apologist understood the reading of the Gospels to be a normative testimony of the messengers of Christ to their Lord in the worship of the community.[32]

The Gospels were apparently read aloud, and even within the Gospel texts themselves we can see evidence of this intended function.[33] Certain verses, such as Mark 13:14, indicate at which point the reader likely raised his voice.[34] This may also be the function of the many narrative voice-over moments in the Fourth Gospel especially.[35] The public reading of the Gospels may also be in view when we read in Colossians 3:16, "Let the word of Christ dwell in you richly, teach and admonish one another in all wisdom."[36] This public reading of the Gospels was required because so few members of the community could read or write; it was their means of understanding the Scriptures.[37]

This is not to say that other readings didn't occur in the assemblies, as for example, the letters of Paul to churches in general (e.g., Col. 4:16) or even to individuals like Philemon.[38] These letters were meant to be read aloud in the gatherings, and eventually they would come to be expounded and reflected on like the Gospels were.[39] But the point here is that the Gospels quickly and effectively became the Scriptures for the earliest Christians, both guiding their interpretation of the Jewish Scriptures and providing a lens for understanding and applying the apostolic injunctions of Peter, Paul, James, and others.

It seems clear from the historical witnesses to early church practice that Gospel materials played an essential and formative role in the church from its

32. Hengel, *Four Gospels*, 37–38.

33. Graham Stanton famously argues this for Matthew, and Michael Knowles has furthered this suggestion. Graham Stanton, *A Gospel for a New People: Studies in Matthew* (Louisville: Westminster John Knox, 1992), 73–76; Michael Knowles, "Reading Matthew: The Gospel as Oral Performance," in Porter, *Reading the Gospels Today*, 56–77.

34. Hengel, *Four Gospels*, 37.

35. For example, John 2:21–22; 12:6.

36. Hengel, *Four Gospels*, 269n397, refers to Hartman's work, which emphasizes the liturgical function of Mark and refers to Col. 3:16 in this regard.

37. Hengel, *Four Gospels*, 27. See also Knowles, "Reading Matthew," 56–57.

38. Hengel notes that all the NT documents come to us in the end precisely because they were the ones used in worship. "The important thing here is that all these writings including the Gospels grew out of worship, the focal point of the earliest church, and were written to be used in worship (1 Thess. 5:22)." Martin Hengel, *Between Jesus and Paul: Studies in the Earliest History of Christianity* (Minneapolis: Fortress, 1983), xii.

39. Additionally, we know other letters were also occasionally read during Christian gatherings, such as 1 Clement, though it by no means follows that they were regarded as Holy Scripture. See Hill, *Who Chose the Gospels?* 147.

earliest days. McDonald sums it up this way: the Gospels "were utilized in the church's worship and catechetical instruction, its defense of the 'gospel' in the pagan world, and in its response to the heretical challenges it faced by the end of the first century and beyond."[40] They were so used because "all writings of the New Testament and early Christianity have a derived authority from the church's one true Lord, even Jesus the Christ."[41]

Canonical[42] and Theological Argument

So far I have argued that strong evidence exists for the central and defining role of the Gospel materials in the life, thought, and experience of earliest Christianity.[43] The early church, of course, could have been mistaken in this, and some might be inclined *not* to follow its example. But I think most who consider these issues would be disposed to at least respect this clear pattern in the church's history. To further my argument (and hopefully persuade any still-reluctant fellow readers of Scripture), I will now turn to more canonical and theological reasons to adopt the Tetraevangelium as the archway into Holy Scripture.

The Pervasive Use of the Jesus Traditions in the Rest of the New Testament

I mentioned as part of the historical argument that the Jesus traditions are pervasively found throughout the rest of the New Testament documents. This phenomenon serves not only a historical argument but can also be considered a canonical issue. That is, when we take the New Testament canon as a whole, we see that the Gospel materials provide the bedrock and are the consistent element throughout. The Jesus traditions form the backbone and context for the early church's and our reading and comprehension of the epistolary literature.

40. McDonald, "Gospels in Early Christianity," 150.

41. Ibid., 178.

42. I do not mean to imply by the category "canonical" that I will argue which books should be included in the canon or even that our four Gospels are the right canonical ones. Rather I want to explore the role that the Gospel materials play within the canon that has been received and passed down to us through the church. If the canon itself seems to presume a central role for the Gospels, then this provides additional argument for us to adopt the same view.

43. I have concentrated above on the earliest centuries of the church, but other time periods also reflect the same attitude, some surprisingly so. For instance, I was happy to discover that some key Reformers also emphasized the central role of the Gospels. For example, Martin Bucer, who strongly influenced Calvin, argued that to read the Bible well it is necessary to begin with the Gospels, then move to Paul, and then on to the Old Testament. Richard A. Muller, "Biblical Interpretation in the Sixteenth and Seventeenth Centuries," in *Dictionary of Major Biblical Interpreters*, ed. Donald K. McKim (Downers Grove, IL: InterVarsity, 2007), 25.

Though modern scholarship has at times denied Paul's knowledge and use of the Jesus traditions, the predominant and most persuasive view is that one need not dig very deeply to find the Gospel materials under every epistolary rock. To varying degrees and in different ways, we can see the influence of the Jesus traditions on all of the Gospels' canonical brothers.

At first glance this statement does not seem self-evident. One *could* read the epistolary literature as if it ignored the stories about and teachings of Jesus, and it is true that we are initially surprised not to find more explicit reference to the historical Jesus. This absence has thus led some scholars to suggest that Paul did not care for Jesus the man or his teachings, and that he established the earthly church, whereas Jesus meant to bring about the kingdom of heaven. But as is now widely recognized, much more of the Jesus traditions can be found in the Epistles than first meets the eye.[44] Moreover, the very presumption of knowledge of and familiarity with the oral and written traditions about Jesus enables the other apostolic writers to only allude to and mention in passing this shared knowledge about the centrality of Jesus. This is true even of the major and most obviously dominant facts about Jesus's life: his baptism, transfiguration, and passion. As Norval Geldenhuys observes about the Last Supper, "Ever since the beginning of the existence of the church of Christ the celebration of Holy Communion has occupied such a central place in the life of the faithful that the history of its institution by the Saviour that last evening before the crucifixion was undoubtedly one of the first things in which every new convert to Christianity had been thoroughly instructed."[45] This same insight can easily be extrapolated to the Jesus traditions overall, but especially to the best-known events in Jesus's life. That is, these über-events find little to no explicit mention in the rest of the New Testament, *not* because they are irrelevant or unknown or eclipsed by Pauline theology, but precisely because they *were* such foundational knowledge, the regular items of discussion and teaching within Gospel presentation and knowledge for the new convert, the catechumen, and the daily teaching ministry of the church.

Although this may seem like a convenient argument from silence, it is not based merely on wishful thinking, nor is it a solitary element in the overall picture being reconstructed. As mentioned, many significant studies have shown the pervasive influence of the Jesus materials on the other New Testament writers (and beyond into the Apostolic Fathers), and my arguments here seem reasonable in light of these other studies.

44. The secondary literature on this topic is vast. Some helpful works include David Dungan, *Sayings of Jesus in the Churches of Paul* (Minneapolis: Fortress, 1971); Todd Still, ed., *Jesus and Paul Connected: Fresh Pathways into an Old Debate* (Grand Rapids: Eerdmans, 2007); David Wenham, *Paul: Follower of Jesus or Founder of Christianity?* (Grand Rapids: Eerdmans, 1995).

45. Norval Geldenhuys, *Commentary on the Gospel of Luke* (Grand Rapids: Eerdmans, 1952), 552–53.

The Providential Placement of the Gospels at the Head of the Canon

The argument here is a straightforward theological and confessional one. Namely, even as the church has a doctrine of the inspiration and authority of individual books within the Scriptures, we must have a thoughtful corresponding doctrine of the providence of the canon. That is, by confession we understand that God the Holy Spirit was active in the church, guiding it to recognize and accept the books to be included in the canon and comprise the church's Scripture.

If we accept this argument, then clearly the fourfold Gospel book has always stood, consistently and significantly, at the head of the New Testament canon, providing the linchpin between the Testaments. As we saw earlier, the early church looked to the Gospels as the documents that unlocked the explanation of all of God's works in the world because they directly bore witness to the Key himself, Jesus the Christ.

Likewise, it is no accident that these primary New Testament documents were titled very early on with the term that was already used to describe the apostolic proclamation: the *euangelion*. These documents alone are given this crucial and revealing title; they alone can be described as the summary of the apostolic kerygma.

The Gospels' Self-Understanding as the Consummation of the Biblical Story

A third canonical and theological argument in support of my keystone theory is that the Gospel writers see themselves as providing the consummation of the biblical story. In his article "When Did the Gospels Become Scripture?" D. Moody Smith has rightly argued that the evangelists wrote with the idea of producing authoritative guides to the Christian faith and with the idea of continuing the biblical story.[46] Other scholars have observed the same for particular books.[47] In their own way each of the evangelists provides a capstone

46. D. Moody Smith, "When Did the Gospels Become Scripture?" 12–19. Smith writes, "Although the narrative of the Tanak does not require the Gospel narrative of the NT as its completion, that narrative presupposes what has gone before. Moreover, the early Christian claim that the narrative and prophecies of old are fulfilled and continued in Jesus and the church pre-figures, perhaps even demands, the production of more scripture, which will explain how this happened. Such scripture is required to explain this not first of all to outsiders but rather to Christians themselves. It becomes an essential part of their identity and self-understanding" (12).

47. For example, Allison remarks that Matthew likely intended "his gospel as a continuation of the biblical history—and also, perhaps, that he conceived of his work as belonging to the same literary category as the scriptural cycles treating of OT figures." W. D. Davies and Dale C. Allison Jr., *A Critical and Exegetical Commentary on the Gospel according to Saint Matthew*, ICC (London: T&T Clark, 2004), 1:187. I have argued similarly with regard to Matthew's use of both Genesis and Daniel. Jonathan T. Pennington, "Heaven, Earth, and a New Genesis: Theological Cosmology in Matthew," in *Cosmology and New Testament Theology*, ed. Pennington

or completion to the story of God's work in the world. This is not to say that they would be opposed to *other* apostolic preaching, writing, or explanation, including those apostolic writings that precede them. But rather, their goal of writing a continuing and consummating story is revealed through the way they have approached their task: the Gospels are written in the narrative form of most of the Jewish Scriptures, conscious of and clearly mimicking[48] these stories, intertextually and figurally explaining the events of Jesus's life as the goal and telos of the story of God. This purpose is manifested implicitly in the ways in which Jesus reenacts and completes Israel's history such as with his water crossings and wilderness feedings (Matt. 14:13–33) as well as in more explicit comments such as the hermeneutical procedure Jesus gives for reading the Jewish Scriptures in Luke 24:27. The rest of the apostolic witness clearly reads the life of Jesus the same way, as a reading such as Paul's in 1 Corinthians 10 reveals.

Related to this is the important insight of recent scholarship that, contrary to twentieth-century assumptions, the Gospels were from the beginning composed and circulated for the whole church, not just for specific communities.[49] That is, they do not just reflect particular and provincial concerns, motivated in polemic ways to address local ideological matters. Rather, they manifest broadly understood and cherished ideas concerning the Lord whom their readers are seeking to follow. This insight is founded not only on historical studies about the interrelatedness of the early Christian communities but also on the way that the Gospels themselves read as comprehensive portraits or biographies of Jesus.

If it is true that the evangelists understand themselves as writing the consummation of the biblical story, then the implication is that the Gospels serve a skeleton-key role in unlocking the understanding of the whole Bible. Even as the last chapter—even the last paragraph or line—of a well-written story has the power to affect and effect an understanding of the whole, so too do

---

and Sean McDonough (London: Continuum, 2008), 28–44; and Pennington, "Refractions of Daniel in the Gospel of Matthew," in *Early Christian Literature and Intertextuality*, ed. Craig Evans and H. Daniel Zacharias, vol. 1 (London: Continuum, 2009), 65–86.

48. On the notion of mimesis as an important part of ancient literary techniques, see the classic by Erich Auerbach, *Mimesis: The Representation of Reality in Western Literature*, 50th anniversary ed. (Princeton, NJ: Princeton University Press, 2003); and Dennis MacDonald, ed., *Mimesis and Intertextuality in Antiquity and Christianity* (Harrisburg, PA: Trinity Press International, 2001).

49. The seminal work in this regard, which has now found widespread support, is Richard Bauckham, *Gospels for All Christians*. Martin Hengel expresses it this way: "Contrary to a widespread view, none of the four Gospels was written only for one particular community; far less do they simply reproduce the views of one individual community. They give primarily the views of their authors. We cannot even say with certainty whether they ever came into being only in one community, for the missionaries of the early church travelled a great deal and could be authoritative teachers at different places." Hengel, *Four Gospels*, 106–7.

the consummating narratives of the Gospels provide the interpretive key to the whole story. One might reject this notion, but if this was indeed the evangelists' self-understanding and if we believe that these books are rightly part of Holy Scripture, then it is unavoidable that we follow their lead in interpreting all of Scripture through the final Word spoken by God.

The Gospels as Comprehensive (Narrative) Theology

Finally, and connected with the preceding argument, I suggest that the Gospels provide the closest thing we have to a comprehensive theology of the Scriptures. They see themselves as bringing the whole story of God's redeeming work to its focal point in the final Word, the Son of God, and they provide a well-rounded picture of the Christian faith.

We should note, as many have observed, that there is no systematic theology of the Jewish Scriptures, at least not in the sense of a rationalized, didactic, clearly structured, and organized statement of beliefs. The closest one gets to this is the Shema (Deut. 6:4–5). Rather, the "theology" of the Old Testament and Jewish experience was a story—particularly the worldview-forming narrative of God's redeeming work on behalf of his people in history. Of course, there are nonnarrative portions of the Scriptures—as is to be expected and welcomed—but the overarching ethos and framework are that of the narrative of God's work from creation and the exodus to the expected new creation and new exodus (especially in the vision of Isaiah).

One could argue that the same is true for early Christianity. This is clearly the case for the apostolic writing and preaching, whose theology is also wrapped up in a story. One immediately thinks of Paul's narrative summary of what the gospel is in 1 Corinthians 15:1–11 or the first Christian sermon at Pentecost (Acts 2:14–40). This narrative aspect continues into the postapostolic church, which, even in the midst of specific doctrinal and theological disputes, produces creeds, which are themselves still narrative in nature.[50]

With this in mind, when we return our gaze to the Gospels, we can see that like no other portion of Scripture they are uniquely poised to provide a "systematic" or comprehensive theology, albeit one that is narrative in form. Indeed, as I have suggested earlier, the genre of narrative stands alone in its capacity to engage the whole of reality and human experience; hence we should not resist that notion of narrative as providing the most comprehensive form of theological revelation.[51]

---

50. See, for example, Paul Blowers, "The *Regula Fidei* and the Narrative Character of Early Christian Faith," *Pro Ecclesia* 6 (1997): 199–228.

51. This position also consciously depends on an epistemological understanding that does not see as exclusively valid nor even privilege a certain type of knowledge (*scientia*) over narrative and other discourses of truth such as story. See chap. 3.

None of this is said to diminish the role, importance, and canonical authority of the rest of the New Testament writings (or the OT writings for that matter). Rather it seeks to recognize that not all writings are meant to be as comprehensive and universally applicable as others; some writings simply have more weight than others, and some texts and ideas provide guiding light to understanding other ideas. Few would argue that the books of Numbers or Ruth or Haggai bear equal weight or have equal "value" in our understanding of the whole of Scripture and its weightiest matters. But to say this is not to deny their canonicity or the important—albeit subservient—role that they play. When it comes to the Epistles, while they have a supra-historicized value and application by virtue of their canonization, they are still on one level occasional documents whose application must be more specifically analyzed and applied. By analogy we might compare the Epistles' usage of the fine surgical tool to the Gospels' more complete and wide-ranging manual of medical instruction. Of course, all analogies break down and so too this one, but the comparison has some value. The thesis I am advancing here is not a diminishment or denigration of any portion of Scripture, but rather a recommendation of the benefit of seeing the Gospels as the most comprehensive introduction to an explanation of the whole of Scripture.

Commenting on the nonoccasional nature of the Gospels relative to the Epistles, Craig Keener (following Talbert) makes a similar observation:

> Large, premeditated narrative works like the Gospels are not mere occasional documents like letters. As Charles Talbert points out, "Foundation documents like the canonical gospels (and Acts) seemed more analogous to systematic theology, albeit in narrative form"; they are more shaped by the foundational events they report and less shaped by their local situations than letters are. . . . To require an unimaginative choice between literary strategies and narrative cohesiveness on the one hand, and substantial genuine information on the other, is to impose categories unworkable in ancient literature (particularly historiography and biography).[52]

This language of "premeditated foundation documents" is very informative and insightful. The Gospels are cornerstone documents that guide the thoughts and *theo*-logical understanding of who God is and our relationship with him as the new/renewed people of God in Christ (who claims for himself the role of cornerstone), while also serving as the capstone of all of God's revelation from Genesis 1:1 onward. Thus, we might lift up and transform these

---

52. Craig Keener, *The Historical Jesus of the Gospels* (Grand Rapids: Eerdmans, 2009), 74, quoting Talbert, "Reading Chance, Moessner, and Parsons," in *Cadbury, Knox, and Talbert: American Contributions to the Study of Acts*, ed. M. C. Parson and J. B. Tyson (Atlanta: Scholars Press, 1992), 230. See also David W. Pao, *Acts and the Isaianic New Exodus* (Grand Rapids: Baker Academic, 2000), for discussion of Acts as a "foundation story" for the church.

metaphors into a more comprehensive and active one: to think of the canon of Holy Scripture as an archway with the fourfold witness of the Gospels as the God-set keystone that holds together this arch and entrance.

Theological, Hermeneutical, and Ecclesial Implications

We have now finally reached the point where we can explore some of the implications of the argument presented here. If the church were to adopt (or better, rediscover) a central and guiding role for the fourfold Gospel book, what would the implications be? Although this discussion must necessarily be suggestive rather than exhaustive, we can observe many significant implications.

The Gospels Can Best Guide Us into a Christian Reading of the Whole Bible

I began this chapter with an argument for the possibility—even necessity—of having a canon within a canon, by which I mean simply a lodestar to guide our reading of Holy Scripture. One reason the Gospels serve this role so well is that they alone provide a comprehensive picture of the whole story of the Bible. Closely related is the implication that the Gospels can best guide us to a Christian reading of the whole Bible. It is precisely here that the archway analogy proves so helpful. On one side of the arch is the witness of the Old Testament Scriptures, beginning with Genesis, while on the other side is that of the rest of the New Testament canon, ending with the comparable bookend, Revelation. The Gospels, again, are the keystone that holds this archway together.

On one side of the arch, Jesus fulfills, explains, and consummates the story of the Old Testament Scriptures. The evangelists explicitly connect the events of Jesus's life to the "fulfillment" of the Scriptures.[53] This at times refers to "fulfillment" in the sense of prophecy completed but more often means rather that Jesus deepens, explains, fills out, and reveals the true intent. Implicitly, as noted above, the evangelists tell the stories of Jesus in ways that mimetically correspond to events in Israel's history. The tools and habits of reading intertextually help us unearth these riches.

The linchpin text for all of this is found in the first part of the first major discourse in the first book of the New Testament canon, in Matthew 5:17–20. In these verses the New Testament's understanding of Jesus's relation to the Old Testament is summed up crucially. "Think not that I have come to abolish the law and the prophets; I have come not to abolish them but to fulfil them." We cannot here even begin to survey the full implications of this or

---

53. For example, in Matthew some version of the saying "this happened to fulfill what the Lord had spoken through the prophet" appears as a repeated formula: 1:22; 2:5, 15, 17, 23; 3:1, 14; 8:17; 12:17; 13:14; 21:4; 27:9.

the important role these verses have rightly played in the history of Christian interpretation. But we may provide a brief summary in saying that in these verses we see that Jesus is both in continuity with the old covenant and at the same time transcends and transforms it. The New Testament's witness is clear—as also understood in the early church—that a proper reading of the Jewish Scriptures is one that reads them as fulfilled in Christ (otherwise it is a sub-Christian reading) while also not denigrating or denying the continuing validity of the Old Testament's own witness (as opposed to Marcion's famous heretical view). "Fulfillment" is the key idea here.

One way that the apostolic witness describes this view is by referring to Christian teaching as the "law of Christ" (Gal. 6:1; 1 Cor. 9:21; cf. James 2:8–13). This potent phrase seeks to maintain a sense of the universal continuity of the "law" (or better, "instruction") given by God while also showing its radical and transforming christocentricity. Indeed, as Hughes Oliphant Old has suggested, the Gospels themselves were likely produced at least in part to fulfill the need to have a *written* version of this apostolic "Law of Christ" for liturgical purposes.[54] That is, the Torah was read and explicated regularly in Jewish synagogue life; it was central. Torah, however, is supplanted and reinterpreted in the church by the "memoirs of the apostles," the Gospel materials. The focus of revelation became christianized, emphasizing Jesus as the fulfillment of all of Torah and adding the new revelation of Jesus's own teachings and actions. As a result, the verbiage of the "Law of Christ" served well to pull these two threads together. Thus, the Gospels take their place as the central means of revealing God's will for his people.

We see that the Gospels particularly—leading the charge with the rest of apostolic witness in tow—enable us to read the Old Testament in a properly Christian way: as focused on Jesus as the key to interpreting Torah while still upholding the value of the Old Testament's witness per se.[55]

On the other side of the archway, it is the Gospels that provide us with the key to properly reading the epistolary literature of the remaining New Testament documents. That is, the perspective and overall picture of God's saving work found in the Gospels enable us to understand the rest of the New Testament's witness and theology.

This is particularly discernible with reference to the Gospels' clear eschatological kingdom focus. Without doubt, the central theme in the Gospels

---

54. Old, *Reading and Preaching*, 263.

55. Of course, this could also be said of Paul's writings, which share the same canonical and Christian perspective. But the point here is that the Gospels' more comprehensive and nonoccasional nature enable them to witness to this reality most clearly and consistently. For a deep exposition that maintains the balance of the per se voice of the OT with its place as part of Christian Scripture, one cannot do better than Brevard Childs's *Biblical Theology of the Old and New Testaments* (Minneapolis: Fortress, 1992).

and Jesus's preaching is the inbreaking of God's reign established through Jesus's sacrificial death and resurrection. With this perspective it is not difficult to discover and discern the same in Paul's writings and the rest of the New Testament. But if we approach the situation the other way around—starting with the epistolary literature—we may get a somewhat skewed picture of the main point of the new covenant. This does not mean that our perspective will necessarily be erroneous or incompatible but rather slightly unbalanced. For example, as is typical in much of the Protestant tradition, the eschatological kingdom of God is not a major theme when "the gospel" is discussed, but rather justification by faith or something similar. But when we begin with Jesus's own teaching and the focus of the Gospels, we can rightly read and understand the rest of the New Testament as an outworking and application (in specific polemical situations) of this same perspective.[56] The Gospels provide the proper set of lenses to enable us to read with the proper focus the remainder of the New Testament canon. Or to return to our main metaphor, it is the keystone of the Gospels that enable the rest of the New Testament writings to stand in their proper shape.

The Centrality of the Gospels Points toward a Different Kind of "Biblical Theology"

One implication of the overall thesis here and the preceding point about a Christian reading of the Bible is that it provides us with a different and potentially rich way of thinking about what it means to do New Testament or "biblical" theology. Specifically, thinking of the Gospels as the supporting stone and fulcrum for the rest of the Scriptures encourages us to read the Old Testament and the rest of the New Testament in intracanonical and cross-canonical ways with the Gospels as the primary lens. We will consciously seek to understand the rest of the Scriptures through the perspective of the Gospels, seeking and seeing connections across the canon that provide a whole-Bible reading.

We cannot here delve into the debates and contours of the discussion concerning the validity of "biblical theology"—what it is or is not, nor its myriad approaches. But in short, the way that many practice biblical theology today is by tracing themes or trajectories through various eras of the overall story of biblical history. An alternative approach (though not contradictory) is the practice of "New Testament theology." This method typically takes each individual book on

---

56. Even more strongly, Lemcio argues that if one has only heard the "gospel" defined exclusively in Pauline terms "then the Gospels will never be regarded as gospel. The teaching and actions of Jesus will be seen as preparatory, secondary, and doctrinally optional." Lemcio laments that in light of the Gospels' central place, there is no justification "for the church's proclaiming the gospel about Christ without proclaiming the gospel of the kingdom that Jesus proclaimed." Eugene E. Lemcio, "The Gospels within the New Testament Canon," in *Canon and Biblical Interpretation*, ed. Craig Bartholomew et al. (Grand Rapids: Zondervan, 2006), 129.

its own and examines its historical background, literary shape, and theological contribution. After this work is done, the various books are lined up and read together—resulting in either a contrast and diversity of views or a consistent, unified message, depending in large part on one's confessional assumptions. Both the approaches of biblical theology and New Testament theology are valid and can provide avenues of insight into the richness of Holy Scripture.

However, in concert with these other approaches, and more boldly, in a way that rises above them, we can reenvision a theological reading of the Bible by starting rather with the fourfold Gospel book as the guiding and constraining approach. That is, rather than relegating the Gospels to a pre-Pentecost "epoch" as some have mistakenly done or starting with the historical background and uniqueness of each individual book, it is better to let the Providence-provided and church-recognized Gospel book organize our thoughts and approach to what it means to do New Testament or biblical theology. This means starting with the main ideas, concepts, and emphases of the Gospels—and of course, with Jesus the Christ as well—as we foray into the rest of the Bible to understand theological constructs and concepts.

This approach is really not new but is more in accord with the sensibilities and practices of pre-Enlightenment reading, and even post-Enlightenment for many believing communities. Beginning with the Gospels we should read "outwardly" in both directions, toward the Old Testament Scriptures and the rest of the New, seeking intracanonical connections guided by the Gospels.

The Gospels Highlight Certain Theological Foci That Affect Our Reading of the Whole Bible

Closely related to these preceding points, an important implication of the argument here is that if we begin our inquiry into the meaning of the new covenant with the Gospels, then certain theological focal points will surface and affect our reading of the whole. This again touches on our initial idea of a "canon within a canon." That is, any theological understanding, whether called "systematic" or "biblical," has some ideas or foci that are more central and controlling than others. Even if one does not believe that there is a single "center" to biblical or New Testament or Old Testament theology, most would recognize some ideas or cluster of ideas as more guiding and organizing than others. I recommend that we find these guiding ideas primarily from the focal fourfold Gospel book.

If we were to do so, what effect would this have? Most obviously, the focus on the eschatological kingdom of God would be the focus of our theological constructions as well. As we have said and as is widely accepted, the message of the kingdom is clearly the focus of Jesus's ministry. This message is not simplistic or thin but rather rich and varied. It is necessarily inaugurated and empowered by Jesus's death and resurrection. It is interwoven intimately with the coming of the promised new covenant. It is a fulfillment of God's promises to Adam, Abraham, David, and beyond. It necessarily involves and grants the forgiveness of our sins (Isa. 52:13–53:12; connect Mark 1:4 and 1:15). But it is a message most fully understood as concerning the reign of God. This is certainly not absent in the rest of the New Testament, from Romans through Revelation, but it is most clearly seen and upheld by reading the New Testament through the lens of the Gospels. That is, one could come to an understanding of the kingdom centrality from Paul but could also easily miss it without the focusing role of the Gospel materials.

The Gospels also grant a more central role to the Lord's Supper than we might discern by reading the rest of the New Testament. That is, apart from 1 Corinthians 11 there is little in the epistolary literature that would incline us to see the Last Supper/Lord's Supper as a significant part of Christianity. But we know from hints in the book of Acts and especially from the earliest Christian practice that the Lord's Supper became a focal point of Christian worship and theology. It is in the Gospels alone that we find the same kind of emphasis and certainly the source of this Christian practice.[57] The Gospels consistently make this practice a major theme. In the Fourth Gospel it comes to us in the form of Jesus's famous "bread of heaven" discourse in John 6. For the Synoptic tradition it is the defining and explicating event for passion week. That is, it is notable that although Jesus's crucifixion, death, and resurrection are clearly the most important events in the Gospels (and in history itself!), neither are given an explicit theological interpretation when they are retold. Rather, the meaning and explanation of these events to which all the Gospels point are found in Jesus's teaching and elucidation at his last (Passover) meal with his kinsmen-disciples. At the Lord's Last Supper we are given the clearest teaching about the new-covenant-effecting work of Jesus's broken body and spilled blood. Thus, apart from this emphasis in the Gospels, we would not likely come to see the central role that the Lord's Supper should play in our Christian experience and theology, nor would we be able to explain why it became such a vital part of Christianity.

Similarly, along with the Lord's Supper/Eucharist, another early and dominant aspect of Christianity is the role of the Lord's Prayer (Matt. 6:9–13; Luke 11:1–4) in forming the church's liturgy and self-understanding.[58] Sadly, in much of church life and individual Christian practice today—perhaps especially in Low Church Protestantism—the Lord's Prayer is little more than something children memorize in Sunday school. But within the Lord's Prayer, especially

57. For a survey of the issues involved in the Gospels' retelling of the Last Supper and its theological meaning, see my "The Lord's Last Supper in the Fourfold Witness of the Gospels," in *The Lord's Supper: Remembering and Proclaiming Christ until He Comes*, ed. Thomas Schreiner and Matthew Crawford (Nashville: Broadman & Holman, 2011), 31–67.

58. Some recent secondary literature on the influence of the Lord's Prayer includes G. O'Collins, *The Lord's Prayer* (New York: Paulist Press, 2007), and Kenneth W. Stevenson, *The Lord's Prayer: A Text in Tradition* (Minneapolis: Fortress, 2004).

the Matthean version, we find a rich theological perspective that has shaped and should continue to mold Christian understanding at the core. Particularly, we see in the Lord's Prayer a forward-looking, kingdom-focused faith that seeks provision from God, focuses on God's forgiveness of our sins and his protection from the Evil One, and includes an important note on the nonnegotiable aspect of relationships of love and forgiveness in the community. All of this is repeated and affirmed in the rest of the Gospel materials. Although one would not want to equate this with the entirety of the Gospel, it is not far from the same. Once again, we can see that the Gospels provide this theological focus. This perspective or vision of the Christian life is certainly woven throughout various parts of the epistolary literature, but it is the Gospels that help us place these ideas in proper perspective. After all, this is how the Lord taught the church to pray.

The Gospels Reveal How We Should Explain and Teach "the Gospel"

Currently there is no small debate in some circles about the age-old question of what exactly "the gospel" is. In the opening chapters of this book, I sought to address this question with my own arguments from the Isaianic background and genre study of the Gospels. It is appropriate to bring this view into the discussion here as well. In short, if we understand the Gospels as the central and guiding perspective of the whole Bible, then this can and should affect what we describe as "the gospel."

Specifically, as just discussed, the Gospels clearly present Jesus's life and teaching as focusing on the coming reign of God inaugurated and opened by his sin-forgiving sacrificial death and his death-defeating resurrection. As documents that present history as consummated in him, the Gospels help us see that to present the "good news" to people means providing an understanding of God's whole work in the world as completed in Jesus the Christ. "The gospel" is not just a message about the forgiveness of sins but rather a whole worldview. Thus, while it is certainly not wrong to think of the gospel in terms of God-man-Christ-response, it is better to conceptualize and present it in salvation-historical categories of creation-fall-redemption-consummation. The Gospels certainly help us see this broader perspective.

Likewise, the Gospels also provide a more narrative approach to thinking about how to present and explain the work of Jesus. As we have said, the theology of the Bible is primarily a story about what God has done in real history and what he will do in our real future. Therefore, a presentation of the gospel that fails to speak of Christ in narrative or historical terms violates the form and essence of the biblical presentation. More positively, many have found that a narrative presentation of "the gospel" based on the Gospels proves to be the effective way. A prime example is the missionary and theologian F. D. Bruner, who came to love and value Matthew because of its ability to communicate the gospel of grace to those outside traditional

Western cultures. Speaking of his experience of teaching theology in the Philippines, he writes:

> I soon discovered that the great Christian doctrines connected more pictorially and "asiatically" when I used the classical biblical stories than when I used contemporary (and mainly Western) systematic theologies. Matthew, the most systematic of the Gospels, proved to be the ideal vehicle for teaching the major, Orthodox, Catholic, and Reformation convictions. . . . I found the earthy Gospels to be much closer to my Asian students than the profound yet more abstract Paul.[59]

Bruner's experience is not unique nor does this insight apply only to non-Western societies. All societies are story societies, and every generation rightly and naturally flocks to the genre and style of the Holy Scriptures: narrative. Most of the New Testament (not to mention the OT) is composed of the narratives that profoundly give us Jesus: the Gospels.

The Gospels Should Guide Our Worship Services and Preaching

A rediscovery of the central role of the Gospels in the church will affect our worship services and preaching. As noted above, most liturgical traditions maintain a special regard for readings and expositions from the Gospels. I have been encouraged lately by the greater use of the Gospels in preaching even in Low Church settings. But in general, the Gospels have tended to play a lesser role in much of American evangelicalism. There "the gospel" has often been boiled down to "justification by faith," which is then fed to people in moralism-dusted bouillon cubes on a pilaf of pietism. If indeed the Gospels are significant in the ways I have argued in this chapter, this approach will not do if the church is to thrive. Both in our worship-service Scripture readings and in the content of our preaching, the Gospels themselves must play the dominant role. And when the Gospels are read and preached, they must not be used merely as springboards to other doctrinal ideas. Rather, honoring the narrative form of the Gospels, we must enter into the power and tension of the story and apply this to the lives of believers by focusing on the final Word, Jesus the Christ.

The Gospels Provide a Clear Picture of the Centrality of Discipleship

As we have discussed in several places in this book, one of the most important aspects of the narrative and biographical genre of the Gospels is the inherent power of story through which they call us to follow the real person of Jesus the Christ. That is, the narrative form and content of the Gospels are designed to call forth a response of following—the very essence of what it

---

59. F. D. Bruner, *Matthew: A Commentary*, vol. 1, *The Christbook: Matthew 1–12* (Grand Rapids: Eerdmans, 2007), xviii.

means to be a disciple. No servant is greater than his teacher and no disciple than his master. To be a believer in Jesus Christ is to be a follower of him. One might be tempted by reading the Epistles—though this would certainly be a misreading—to believe that being a Christian is simply believing in certain doctrinal truths and/or having some mystical spiritual experience and/or adopting a certain worldview and set of moral and cultic practices (such as the Lord's Supper). While indeed believing certain truths, having an experience of the Spirit, and following some new worship practices are part of what it means to be a Christian, it would be a skewed view to forget the central notion of discipleship. Without a clear understanding of being a *follower* of Jesus, Christianity can, on the one hand, easily dissolve into mere moralism or a new religious practice or, on the other hand, create great confusion when one tries to marry the mutual teachings of grace and the necessity for a holy life. That is, in reference to this last point, confusion can result from reading in the Epistles of both our salvation as a gift through being "in Christ" and the call for a necessary obedience in the Christian life. Only the notion of grace-based calling and discipleship holds these twin truths together. Christianity must never be construed as merely intellectual and moral assent, on the one side, or as earning or keeping oneself in a covenant through obedience, on the other. The tendency toward either extreme is ever-present. But keeping these tendencies in balanced tension is the notion of *following* or *being a disciple*, which maintains the vision of constant learning and growing in knowledge and greater virtue by following the example of the One who has called us by grace.

Thus although one can and should read the epistolary literature with this Christian discipleship mind-set, it is most clearly and helpfully presented to us in the fourfold Gospel book. In the Gospels the understanding of Christianity as following the Master in knowledge and obedience shines clearest. And at the same time, any notion that this following is simply the same as following Moses or Plato or any other teacher is consistently critiqued and ultimately destroyed: Jesus is repeatedly presented as *more* than a mere teacher to emulate, and the Gospels each are at pains to show us that the end of this teacher's story is his dying and rising on behalf of his people to make them born again by the eschatological work of the Spirit of God.

Again, this is the entire New Testament's understanding. It is not unique to the Gospels, and the rest of the New Testament documents rightly reflect and imply the same. But in the Gospels the notion of discipleship as the constraining picture of the faith is clearest and brightest.

A Concluding Conclusion

One of my former teachers and mentors wisely taught me that in making arguments it is best to hold back a bit, even at the end, to avoid overextending oneself and thereby diminishing one's overall effectiveness and persuasiveness. I have sought over the years to follow this advice. Awareness of this makes the boldness of the arguments in this final chapter cause me some occasional hesitation. That is, while I believe that my arguments for the central role of the Gospels are true and meaningful, I would be unhappy to learn that any reader, if not entirely convinced by my thesis in this final chapter, might leave this book with a less than positive experience and thereby miss my greater point.

My desire for this book—more than that anyone be convinced of every detail or even this final chapter's thesis—is that readers will be invited into the joy of studying the Gospels more deeply and more often. And most of all, my desire is that readers will be not merely hearers of but responders by faith to the clarion call of the love of God in Jesus Christ as presented in the Gospels. To do less than this would be, according to the most important idea of the book, to fail to read the Gospels wisely.

Scripture Index

Old Testament

Genesis

1 43
1:1 20, 28, 109, 110, 111, 116,
  120, 249
2:3 110
3 200
6 230
22:2 201
37:20 201

Exodus

3:14 159
20:15 133, 134

Deuteronomy

5:19 133, 134
6:4–5 248

1 Samuel

2:10 239

2 Samuel (2 Reigns)

4:10 13n32
18 15n36

Job

9:8 159
42:3 149

Psalms

2:7 201
77:19 159
118:22–23 201
139:6 149

Proverbs

1:1 8n13
10:3 21
10:4 21

Ecclesiastes

1:1 8n13

Song of Solomon (Canticles)

1:1 8n13

Isaiah

5 187
5:1–7 201
13:6 208
13:9 208
26:19 205
29:18 205
35:5–6 205
40–66 12n31, 15, 16, 16n39, 207
40:1 15
40:1–5 15n38
40:2 15
40:9 16
40:11 15
40:29–31 16
41:6 16
41:10 15
41:17 16
42:1 201
42:1–4 16
42:7 144
42:9–10 16
42:13–17 16
42:18 16, 205
43:5 15
43:8–10 16
43:10 16
43:16 159
43:18–19 16
44:8 16
44:22 16
45:4 16
45:14 15
47:1–15 16
48:6 16
49:3–5 16
49:8 16, 144
49:22–26
51:5 15
52:7 16
52:9 15
52:12 15
52:13–53:12 16, 16n39, 196,
  207, 254
53:4 196

53:4–6 16
53:10–12 16
54:7–8 15
55:1–2 16
55:3 16
55:7 15
58:6 144, 204
58:13 208
59:21 16
60:6 16
61 15, 44
61:1 11n29, 12, 13, 14, 16, 204, 205
61:1–2 144
61:2 14
61:2–3 15
65:17 16
66:15–17 16
66:22 16
66:24 16

Jeremiah

9:23–24 239
29:11 139, 140, 157

Daniel

7:13 191
12:8 149

Hosea

1:2 8n13
2 230

Joel

2:31 22

New Testament

Matthew

1–2 28, 56n14, 118
1–12 256n59
1:1 8n13, 10, 20, 191
1:1–17 56, 188
1:18–2:23 55–56, 62, 178
1:21 31, 196
1:22 28, 178, 250n53
1:23 30, 191
2 117n8

2:2 190
2:5 250n53
2:15 28, 178, 250n53
2:17 250n53
2:23 118, 250n53
3:1 250n53
3:1–17 56
3:2 13
3:14 250n53
3:15 56
3:17 57, 60
4:1–11 64, 69, 72
4:8–9 191
4:17 13
4:18–20 190
4:23 10n22, 11n29, 12, 14
4:23–25 12, 12n30
5 230
5–7 ix, 12, 14, 37, 68, 113, 151n18, 178, 181, 187n4, 195, 196, 235
5–9 12
5:1 68n36
5:3 72
5:3–12 132
5:7 239
5:8 156
5:17–20 250
5:20 37
5:21–48 30
6:9–13 238, 254, 255
6:14 239
6:14–15 37
7:1–2 239
7:11 63, 64
7:24–27 ix
8–9 12, 14, 185n1, 196, 197, 205n30
8:1–4 69
8:1–16 196
8:5–13 206, 207
8:6 206n32
8:10 206
8:11–12 206
8:14 69
8:14–15 190
8:14–17 185n1
8:17 28, 196, 250n53
8:23–24 69
8:23–27 61
8:28–34 57
9:18 57

9:18–26 57, 181
9:35 10n22, 11n29, 12, 12n30, 14
9:35–38 12
10 68, 161n33
10:1–4 190
10:5–6 191
10:40 30
11:2–6 205n30
11:5 11n29, 12, 13, 14
11:25–30 191
12:17 28, 250n53
13 68
13:10 38, 153
13:10–17 38
13:14 250n53
13:35 28
13:36 38, 153
13:52 158
14:13–33 247
14:14–17 153
14:22–33 159, 164, 190
14:27 65, 159
14:31 160
14:32 159
14:33 160
15:21–28 206
15:22 206n31
16:5–12 38, 153
16:13–23 190
16:21–23 153
16:21–28 190
17:1–13 190
17:5 57
17:22–23 190
17:24–27 190
18 68
18:6 141
18:12–13 65
18:18 157, 158
18:20 30, 157, 158
18:21–22 190
19:16–17 60, 64
19:23–30 190
20:1–16 37
20:17–19 190
20:29–34 61
21–23 187, 188, 189
21–28 195
21:1–11 188
21:4 28, 250n53

21:9 188
21:12–17 61
21:12–27 188
21:15 188
21:23–27 186–187
21:28–32 187
21:28–22:14 188
21:33–46 187, 200
21:38 201
22:1–14 187
22:15 187
22:15–22 187
22:15–40 188
22:22–33 187
22:34–40 187
22:36–40 39
22:41–46 187, 188
23–25 68
23:1–36 188
23:37–39 188
23:39 188
24:14 9–10n22, 11n29, 12, 12n30, 14
26:13 8, 9–10n22, 11n29, 12, 12n30
26:17–29 58
26:24 239
26:27–29 196
26:28 31, 196
26:31–46 190
26:57–58 190
26:69–75 190
27:9 250n53
27:29 190
27:37 190
27:42 190
28:18–20 191
28:20 30

Mark

1:1 7, 8, 9, 10n26, 11, 11n28, 20
1:1–11 56
1:1–12 11
1:4 254
1:13–14 66
1:14 10n26, 11n28
1:14–15 7, 10, 11
1:15 10n26, 254
1:29–31 69
1:29–34 185n1
1:40–45 69

1:45 233
4:21 65
4:35–41 61, 163
4:35–5:20 69
4:41 30
5:1–20 57
5:21–43 57, 181
5:23 57
5:36 58
5:41 63
6:50 65
7:24–30 206
8:31–38 190
8:35 10n26
9:7 57
9:30–32 190
9:42 141
9:42–10:31 65
10–16 195
10:17–18 60, 64
10:29 10n26
10:32–34 190
10:45 31
10:46–52 61
11:15–19 61
12:1–12 200
12:6 201
12:7 201
13:10 10n26, 11n26
13:14 243
14:3–9 66
14:9 8, 10n26, 11n26
14:3–9 61
14:12–25 58
15:34 63
16:9–17n26
16:15 11n26

Luke

1:1 40, 59n16
1:1–2 10
1:1–4 20, 234
1:5–25 186
1:5–80 56
1:19 13
1:26–56 186
1:32–33 13
1:57–80 186
2:1–2 205
2:1–20 186
2:1–52 55–56, 62

2:10 13, 208
3:1–22 56
3:18 13
3:22 56, 57, 60
3:23–38 56, 205
4 44
4:1–13 64, 69, 72
4:14 14, 204
4:14–19 204
4:14–20 207
4:14–9:50 186, 205
4:18 14, 204
4:18–19 144
4:19 14
4:21 14
4:23–27 14
4:28–30 14
4:31–37 204
4:38–41 185n1, 204
4:43 13, 13n33
5:1–11 204
5:27–32 204
6:12–16 204
6:17–19 204
6:20 72
6:31 239
6:36–38 239
6:46–49 204
7:1 181
7:1–2 181
7:1–10 169, 170, 171, 180, 182, 203, 207, 208, 215, 216, 217, 218, 222
7:2 206n32
7:2–6 181, 204
7:3 181
7:4 170
7:4–5 215
7:4–6 181
7:5 170
7:6 181
7:6b–8 181, 204
7:7 171
7:9 171, 181, 204, 206
7:10 181, 204
7:11–17 204
7:18–23 204
7:22 13, 14, 205
7:36–50 61
8:1 13, 13n33
8:22–25 61
8:26–39 57

8:40–56 57, 181
8:42 57
8:50 58
9:6 13, 13n33
9:22–27 190
9:35 57
9:43–45 190
9:51–19:27 186, 205
10:25–37 48
10:38–42 193, 194
11:1–4 254
11:13 63, 64
11:20 200
13:22–30 206
13:23–24 65
13:28–29 206
15:1–7 179
15:1–32 186
15:3–7 186
15:8–10 179, 186
15:11–32 164, 178–179, 186
16:16 13, 13n33
17:1–2 239
18:13 47
18:14 175
18:18–19 64
18:31–33 190
18:35–43 61
19:28–24:53 195
19:45–46 61
20:1 13, 13n33
20:9–19 200
20:13 201
20:14 201
22:1–24:53 186, 205
22:7–23 58
22:19 241n26
24:27 242, 247
24:46–47 31

John

1:1 20
1:1–3 58
1:1–18 56
1:14 70
1:19–34 56
1:19–4:43 66
1:29 56
1:32 56
2:13 68
2:13–22 61

2:21–22 197, 243n35
2:22 153, 197
3 65
3:16 29
3:24 66
4:43–54 206
6 58
6:4 68
6:25–59 254
6:40 31
6:48 65, 160
8:12 65, 160
8:58 58
10:7 65, 160
10:11 65, 160
10:30 58
11 193, 194
11–21 195
11:2 66
11:25 31, 65, 160
11:55 68
12:1 68
12:1–8 61
12:6 243n35
12:28–30 57
13:1–35 58
14:6 65, 160
15:1 65, 160
15:4 30
16:13–14 49
18–19 65
18:3–37 6
19:12–15 6
20:19 153, 197
20:28 96
20:30–31 31, 59, 62
20:31 29, 34
21:24–25 59, 62
21:25 70

Acts

1:12–14 153, 197
2:1–12 153, 197
2:14–40 248
2:20 22
9:20 40
11:26
13:5 40
13:14 40
14:1 40
20:35 62n22

Romans

1:1 4
1:2 5
1:3 5
1:4 5
1:5–6 5
2:16 11n28
11:33–36 149
14:17 17n41

1 Corinthians

9:21 251
10 247
11 254
11:1 161
11:17–34 235
15:1–11 5n6, 248
15:1–58 59
15:3 16n39
15:24 17n41

2 Corinthians

1:20 140
3:6 119
5:16 41, 83

Galatians

1:6–7 5
2:16 5
6:1 251

Philippians

4:7 149

Colossians

1:13 17n41
3:16 243
4:16 243

1 Thessalonians

1:5 5
2:2 5
2:4 5
2:8 5
2:9 5
2:11 17n41
3:2 5
5:22 243n38

2 Timothy

3:15 220n5
4:13 40
4:18 17n41

Hebrews

1:1–2 238
4:6 5
12:2 162

James

2:8–13 251

1 Peter

1:12 5
1:25 5
2:18–23 162
2:18–24 31
2:21 162
2:21–3:2 31
2:24 31, 162
3:1–6 162
3:15 70
3:18 16n39
4:17 5

Revelation

1:1 8n13
6:12 22
14:6 11n28
21 43

Pseudepigrapha and Apocrypha

Assumption of Moses

in toto 49n22

Bel and the Dragon

in toto 49n22

1 Clement

in toto 243n39
13.1–2 239
16.1–17 239n19
24.5 239n19
46.7–8 239

48.4 239n19
49.6 239n19

Gospel of the Ebionites

in toto 60n17

Gospel of Judas

in toto 239

Gospel of Peter

in toto 239

1 Enoch

in toto 49n22

Prayer of Azariah

in toto 49n22

Protoevangelium of James

in toto 239

Susanna

in toto 49n22, 114

Gospel of Thomas

in toto 186n2, 200, 239
65 201, 202
66 201n28

Other Jewish, Christian, and Classical Writings

Aquinas, Thomas

Summa Theologica

1 Q.1. art.10 124

Aristotle

Poetics

in toto 19n2, 172, 173

Athanasius

Life of Anthony

in toto 161n35

Augustine

City of God

in toto 79

Confessions

12 118, 124, 129

De Doctrina Christiana (On Christian Teaching)

1.35–40 158
1.36 156
1.36.41 141
4 118n9, 219

Harmony of the Four Gospels

in toto 53, 54, 59
1.3.5–6 71
1.4.7 71
1.5.8 71–72
1.7.9 71
3 58

Cyril of Alexandria

Homily on Luke 29

in toto 237–38n12

Homily on Luke 52

in toto 238n12

Didache

8.1 238n15
8.2 7n9, 238
11.3 7n9, 238
15.3–4 7n9, 238

Epiphanius

Against Heresies

30.13.7–8 60n17

Eusebius

Canons

in toto 53, 173

Commentary on Psalm 22

in toto 238

Demonstratio Evangelica

in toto 52–53, 59

Gospel Problems and Solutions

in toto 53n8

Kata Porphyriou

in toto 53

"Letter to Carpianus"

in toto 53

Irenaeus

Adv. Haer.

in toto 53
3.2.8 9n18
3.11.8 54n12, 71, 236

Jerome

Life of Malchus

in toto 161n35

Justin Martyr

First Apology

1.66 241n26
1.67 241
66.3 7n9
67.3 39–40

Origen

Commentary on John

1.3 237
1.4 237
1.5–12 237
1.6 237n11
1.7 237
1.10 237
1.14 237n11

Contra Celsus

in toto 53

Plato

Republic

in toto 19n2

Plutarch

Alexander

1.1 66–67

Pontius

Life and Passion of Cyprian

in toto 161n35

Porphyry

Contra Christianos

in toto 53

Seneca

Ad Lucilium

6.4 161n34

Suetonius

On the Life of the Caesars

in toto 29n31

Tatian

Diatessaron

in toto 52, 54, 59, 240

Author Index

Adam, A. K. M., 114n5, 120n14, 133n27
Ådna, J., 125n8
Aland, K., 52n2
Alexander, L., 8, 25, 26, 32n40, 32n42
Alexander, P., 29
Allison, D., Jr., 29, 30n35, 93n70, 113n3, 156n28, 161n32, 161n33, 161n34, 187n4, 190n8, 196n15, 246n47
Attridge, H., 238n14
Audi, R., 101n89, 102
Auerbach, E., 247n48
Aune, D., 40n4
Austin, J. L., 132

Balz, H., 5n5
Barbour, R. S., 17n41
Barth, K., 76, 82, 83, 84, 85, 91, 125n8
Bartholomew, C., 8n16, 38n1, 44n9, 80n20, 92, 95n73, 102n95, 115n6, 198n20, 199, 230n2, 252n56
Barton, J., 15n37, 22
Barton, S. C., 8n15, 15n37, 73, 88n52, 126n13, 200n26
Bauckham, R. J., 4n4, 22n6, 33n43, 46n15, 52n1, 59–60n16, 65n26, 65n27, 66, 93n70, 98, 99, 100, 101, 102, 104n97, 148, 151, 194n12, 194n13, 199n21, 232n4, 247n49
Beaton, R., 196n16
Billings, J. T., 91n66, 109n1
Bird, M. F., 194n12, 236n9
Blamely, K., 95n72
Bloch, M., 101
Bloesch, D., 149

Blomberg, C., 54n13, 60n17, 69n38
Blowers, P., 248n50
Blue, S., 129n19
Bock, D., 6n8, 93
Bockmuehl, M., 15n38, 73n49, 93n70, 138, 139n41, 148n9, 149n15, 193n11
Borg, M., 87
Bornkamm, G., 85
Bowden, J., 4n4, 26n19, 47n16, 61n20, 90n61, 241n25
Braaten, C. E., 82.30
Bradshaw, P., 241n24
Brown, J. K., 111n2, 136n34
Bruner, F. D., 255, 256
Bucer, M., 244n43
Bultmann, R., 41, 82, 83, 84, 85, 86, 88, 234
Burridge, R., 22n7, 23, 24, 25, 26, 27, 28, 29n32, 29n33, 30n37, 35, 70, 71n43, 235n7
Byrskog, S., 100

Cadbury, H. J., 249n52
Calvin, J., 68, 125, 244n43
Carson, D. A., 65, 139
Chakrabarti, A., 101n89
Chapell, B., 219n5, 220, 225
Charry, E., 79n16, 106
Childs, B., 14n34, 82n28, 86, 91, 125, 135, 194n12, 251n55
Coady, C. A. J., 100, 101
Collingswood, R. G., 101
Collins, A. Y., 4n3, 7, 22n7, 26, 27
Crawford, M., 58n15, 238n13, 254n57
Cross, F. L., 80n22

Crossan, J. D., 76, 77, 87, 88n52
Cullmann, O., 85, 86, 87, 97n79, 242

Daley, B. E., 90, 91, 123n1, 156
Davies, W. D., 246n47
Davis, E., 90n63, 123n1, 154n21, 156n27, 195n14, 197n18, 199n21
D'Elia, J., 32, 86n44, 86n45, 87n48
de Lubac, H., 124n5
Descartes, R., 79
Dickson, J. P., 6n7
Dilthey, W., 123n2
Dodd, C. H., 7n11, 104
Donaldson, J., 40n2
Donner, H., 125n8
Donovan, M. A., 242n31
Doriani, D., 156n29, 173n4, 216, 217, 218, 221, 222n11
Dostoevsky, F., 137n38
Dryden, J., 162n36
Dungan, D., 41n6, 245n44
Dunn, J. D. G., 93n70, 148n9

Eco, U., 18n1, 197n19
Edersheim, A., 28
Edwards, J. R., 7n10
Ehrman, B., 238n16
Evans, C. S., 76n8, 88, 106, 107, 115n6, 247n47

Farkasfalvy, D., 8
Farrar, F. W., 90n63, 123n1
Feinberg, P., 63
Ferrar, W. J., 53n8
Fokkelman, J. P., 179n5, 186n3
Ford, D., 85n43, 139n41
Fowl, S., 88n52, 124n6
Foxe, J., 161n35
Frame, J., 125, 126, 133, 134, 135n31
France, R. T., 4n3, 56n14, 117, 118
Frei, H., 92, 102, 103, 125, 147n8
Freytag, G., 172, 173
Funk, R., 77

Gabler, J., 135
Gadamer, H., 42n7, 113n4, 126, 128, 129n18, 129n19, 130, 134, 138
Gage, W. L., 81n26
Gaventa, B. R., 74n3, 146n2
Geisler, N. L., 63n23
Geldenhuys, N., 245
Gignilliat, M., 84n38
Gioia, D., 46

Goheen, M., 44n9, 198n20, 199
Goldingay, J., 98n81
Gould, E., 4n3
Green, J. B., 91n66, 92n67, 95n73, 124n6, 127n14, 137, 138n39, 138n40, 147n8, 219n5, 230n2
Greene, C., 92n67, 102n95
Greene-McCreight, K., 125n8
Greenman, J. P., 54n13
Guelich, R. A., 4n3

Hafemann, S. J., 125n8
Hagner, D. A., 15n38, 193n11
Hall, C. A., 90n64
Halliwell, D., 172n1
Harding, M., 239n17
Harrisville, R. A., 82n28, 89n58
Hart, T., 22n6, 46n15
Hartman, L., 243n36
Hawthorne, G. F., 133n26
Hays, R. B., 15n37, 15n38, 74, 75, 76, 77, 88, 89, 90n63, 93n70, 123n1, 146n2, 154n21, 156n27, 191, 195n14, 197n18, 199n21, 200n26, 201, 202
Heine, R., 237n11
Hengel, M., 4n4, 8n14, 9, 10, 16–17n40, 26n19, 27n28, 31n38, 33n44, 34, 47n16, 61n20, 73, 85n43, 90n61, 194n12, 241n25, 242, 243n32, 243n34, 243n36–38, 247n49
Henry, P., 82n27
Hill, C. E., 234n6, 239–40n21, 242n31, 243n39
Hill, E., 141n42
Hirsch, E. D., 123n3, 126n12, 129n19, 131
Hofius, O., 125n8
Holmes, M., 239n18
Hong, E. H., 138n38
Hong, H. V., 138n38
Hooker, M., 196n16
Hooper, W., 43n8, 97n76
Horbury, W., 5n7, 13n32
Howard, T. A., 78n12, 80n18, 80n19, 80n21, 80n23, 81n25
Hurtado, L., 240n23, 242n28

Iggers, G. G., 95n72
Isaacson, W., 32, 69

Jackson, M., 196n17
Jepp, E. J., 35n47
Johnson, K., 173n4, 221n8
Johnson, L. T., 88, 89, 93n70, 106n103

Kähler, M., 76, 82, 83, 85, 86
Käsemann, E., 77, 84, 85
Kealy, S., 52n5
Keener, C., 32n39, 67n33, 67n34, 93, 249
Keifert, P., 79n16
Kelsey, D., 92n67
Kierkegaard, S., x, 138n38
Kingsbury, J. D., 12n30
Klassen, N., 200
Knowles, M., 243n33, 243n37
Knox, J., 249n52
Köstenberger, A., 194n12
Kysar, R., 234, 235n7

Ladd, G. E., 32, 80n22, 82n31, 83n34, 85n42,
    86, 87, 90n61, 97n79
Lane, W. L., 4n3
Lang, B., 242
Larsen, T., 54n13
Laughery, G., 92n67
Leithart, P. J., 42n7, 91n66, 131n25
Lemcio, E. E., 38n1, 252n56
Lessing, G. E., 79, 83
Levenson, J. D., 94n71
Lewis, C. S., 43, 96–97n76, 114, 210
Lindbeck, G., 92n67
Loades, A., 103n96
Locke, J., 103
Lonergan, B., 87n49
Long, V. P., 98n80
Longman, T., III 98n80
Lowe, R., 125n8
Lull, T. F., 145n1
Luther, M., 39, 79n15, 144, 145, 160, 162
Luz, U., 113n4

MacDonald, D., 247n48
MacDonald, N., 84n38, 102, 103
MacEvan, E., 172n2
MacRae, G. W., 35n47
Mannheim, K., 80n23
Marcus, J., 4n3
Marsden, G., 32
Martin, R. P., 7n11, 133n26
Matilal, B. K., 101n89
Matson, J., 194n12
McCormack, B., 84n38
McDonald, L. M., 52n3, 233, 235n8, 240n22, 244
McDonough, S. M., 20n4, 226n12, 247n47
McKim, D. K., 244n43
McKnight, S., 6n8, 16n39, 78n12, 93, 148
Meier, J., 88

Meyer, B. F., 87n49
Mitchell, M., 54
Moller, K., 92n67, 102n95
Mosser, C., 61n21
Muller, R., 124, 244n43

Neilsen, C., 128n16, 129n18
Neusner, J., 29
Newman, C. C., 76n8, 76–77n11, 89n56
Niebuhr, B. G., 79n15
Niederwimmer, K., 238n14
Nobbs, A., 239n17
Nolland, J., 27, 28n29, 30n36, 118, 119n10, 190n8

O'Collins, G., 254n58
Oden, T. C., 90n64
O'Keefe, J. J., 91n65, 115n7, 198n21
Old, H. O., 242, 251
Osborne, G., 60n19, 68, 89n57, 129n17, 133n26
Osborne, K., 60n19
Osiander, A., 61

Packer, J. I., 220n7
Padgett, A., 79n16
Paget, J. C., 148n9
Pannenberg, W., 86
Pao, D. W., 15n38, 249n52
Parker, D., 235, 236n9
Parson, M. C., 249n52
Pasquarello, M., III, 219n5
Pearse, R., 53n8
Pellauer, D., 95n72
Pennington, J., 11n27, 20n4, 46n15, 58n15,
    72n48, 246–47n47
Perrin, N., 74n1
Petersen, W. L., 52n3, 240n22
Pevear, R., 137n38
Piper, J., 161n35
Placher, W., 146, 147
Plantinga, A., 80n20, 92n67, 102
Porter, S. E., 52n3, 233n5, 235n8
Powell, M. A., 32
Pratt, R., Jr., 129n17, 161n32
Pringle, W., 68n36
Provan, I., 92n67, 98n80

Rae, M., 75n7, 78n12, 78n14, 79n17, 82n29, 83,
    84n36, 84n37, 84n38, 84n39, 85n41, 85n43,
    88, 92n67, 96, 97n77, 101n89, 135n32, 148,
    149n13, 150
Rahlfs, A., 13n32
Ramsey, B., 119, 123n4

Ratzinger, J., 86
Renan. J., 81n26
Reno, R., 91n65, 115n7, 198n21
Riches, J., 191
Ricoeur, P., 92n67, 95n72, 101, 126, 128, 129, 138
Riddle, M. B., 53n11
Roberts, A., 40n2
Robertson, A. T., 52n2
Robinson, J. M., 85
Rowe, C. K., 15n35
Rue, L., 103n96
Ryken, L., 47, 48, 153, 170, 180n6, 180n7, 180n8

Sailhammer, J., 75n6
Salmond, S. D. F., 53n10, 69–70n39
Sawyer, J. F. A., 14n34
Schaff, P., 53n10, 53n11, 70n39
Schlatter, A., 86, 97n79
Schleiermacher, F., 82n28, 126
Schnabel, E. J., 148n11
Schneemelcher, W., 239n21
Schneider, G., 5n5
Schneiders, S. M., 126n13, 128n15, 129n20, 130, 131
Schreiner, T., 58n15, 254n57
Schweitzer, A., 83
Seitz, C., 154n21, 194n12
Sim, D., 191n9
Smith, D. M., 241n24, 241n25, 246
Smith, L. S., 79n15
Smith, M., 238–39n17, 239n20, 239n21, 240n22, 241n25, 242n31
Snodgrass, K., 15n38,
Spencer, S. R., 54n13
Spinoza, B., 79, 82n28
Stanton, G., 5–6n7, 7n9, 9n19, 9–10n22, 12n30, 15n38, 40n3, 40n4, 85n43, 139n41, 243n33
Steinmetz, D., 197n18, 199n21
Sternberg, M., 190n6
Stevenson, K. W., 254n58
Still, T., 245n44
Strauss, D. F., 80
Strauss, M., xin3, 35n48
Striver, D., 92n67
Sundberg, W., 82n28, 89n58

Talbert, C. H., 249
Tate, W. R., 111n2
Thiselton, A., 131n24, 132, 230n2

Thompson, M. M., 76n10
Thompson, M., 41n6
Tischendorf, C., 81n26
Todd, A. S., 242n29
Tolkien, J. R. R., 43, 46
Torrance, J. B., 242n29
Treier, D. J., 91n66, 109n1, 115n7, 125n7
Trigg, J., 239
Trobisch, D., 9n17, 9n20, 9n21, 10n25, 40n5, 235
Troeltsch, E., 81, 82, 83, 88, 94
Turner, M., 124n6, 127n14, 147n8
Twain, M., 116
Tyson, J. B., 249n52

Vanhoozer, K., 45, 120, 126, 132, 133, 134, 137n35
Vermes, G., 86
Vickers, B., 17n41
Vine, W. E., 139
Volokhonsky, L., 137n38
Voltaire, F. A., 79n15
von Ranke, L., 33, 79n15, 80, 94

Walton, S., 4n2, 67n32
Ward, T., 155
Watson, F., 86, 93n70, 97, 147n8, 149n15
Watts, R. E., 15n38
Webster, J., 84n38, 230n1
Wedderburn, A. J. M., 78n12
Wenham, D., 4n2, 17n41, 41n6, 67n32, 245n44
Wessel, W. W., 4n3
Westphal, M., 123n2, 126n12
White, H., 95n72
Wiarda, T., 45, 163, 188, 189, 190
Williams, D. M., 120n13
Williams, J., 190n6
Williams, R., 89, 90, 105
Willits, J., 148n10
Witherington, B., III 17n41
Wittgenstein, L., 132
Wolters, A., 44n9, 200n24
Wolterstorff, N., 102, 103n96, 126, 133
Wright, N. T., 15n38, 74, 75, 76, 77, 87, 88, 89, 93, 94, 97n79, 99, 106, 148n9, 222n11

Yarbrough, R. W., 82n28, 85n43, 104n97
Young, F., 17n41

Zacharias, H. D., 247n47
Zimmermann, J., 200